Printed in the United Kingdom at the University Press, The
Edinburgh Building, Cambridge CB2 2RU, United Kingdom
40 West 20th Street, New York, NY 10011–4211, USA
477 Williamstown Road, Port Melbourne, VIC 3207, Australia

© Cambridge University Press 2002

First Published 2002

Phototypeset in Baskerville by Wyvern 21 Ltd, Bristol
Great Britain at the University Press, Cambridge

ISSN 0261–1279

ISBN 0 521 81887 7

SUBSCRIPTIONS The subscription price (excluding VAT) of volume 21, which includes
postage plus electronic access to institutional subscribers only, is £70 (US $105 in USA and
Canada) for institutions, £40 (US $63 in USA and Canada) for individuals ordering direct
from the Press and certifying that the annual is for their personal use. An electronic only
price is available to institutional subscribers for £65 (US$100 in USA and Canada). Airmail
(orders to Cambridge only) £10.00 extra. Copies of the annual for subscribers in the USA
and Canada are sent by air to New York to arrive with minimum delay. Orders, which
must be accompanied by payment, may be sent to a book-seller, subscription agent or direct
to the publishers: Cambridge University Press, The Edinburgh Building, Shaftesbury Road,
Cambridge CB2 2RU. Payment may be made by any of the following methods: cheque
(payable to Cambridge University Press), UK postal order, bank draft, Post Office Giro
(account no. 571 6055 GB Bootle – advise CUP of payment), international money order,
UNESCO coupons, or any credit card bearing the Interbank symbol. EU subscribers (outside the UK) who are not registered for VAT should add VAT at their country's rate. VAT
registered subscribers should provide their VAT registration number. Japanese prices for
institutions (including ASP delivery) are available from Kinokuniya Company Ltd, P.O.
Box 55, Chitose, Tokyo. Orders from the USA and Canada should be sent to Cambridge
University Press, 40 West 20th Street, New York, NY 10011–4211, USA.

BACK VOLUMES Volumes 1–8 and 11–20 are available from the publisher at £62 ($102 in
USA and Canada).

NOTE Each volume of *Early Music History* is now published in the year in which it is subscribed. Volume 21 is therefore published in 2002. Readers should be aware, however, that
some earlier volumes have been subscribed in the year *after* the copyright and publication
date given on this imprints page. Thus volume 8, the volume received by 1989 subscribers,
is dated 1988 on the imprints page.

INTERNET ACCESS This journal is included in the Cambridge Journals Online service which
can be found at www.journals.cambridge.org. For further information on other Press titles
access http://www.cambridge.org.

EARLY MUSIC HISTORY 21

STUDIES IN MEDIEVAL
AND
EARLY MODERN MUSIC

Edited by
IAIN FENLON
Fellow of King's College, Cambridge

CAMBRIDGE
UNIVERSITY PRESS

CONTENTS

Page

ANNE-EMMANUELLE CEULEMANS (Université catholique de Louvain)
Instruments real and imaginary: Aaron's interpretation of
Isidore and an illustrated copy of the *Toscanello*   1

GABRIELA ILNITCHI (Eastman School of Music, University of Rochester)
Musica mundana, Aristotelian natural philosophy and
Ptolemaic astronomy   37

STEFANO LA VIA (Università degli Studi di Pavia)
Eros and *thanatos*: a Ficinian and Laurentian reading of
Verdelot's *Sì lieta e grata morte*   75

CHRISTIAN THOMAS LEITMEIR (Universität München)
Catholic music in the diocese of Augsburg *c*.1600: a
reconstructed tricinium anthology and its confessional
implications   117

ROBERT NOSOW (Cary, NC)
The debate on song in the Accademia Fiorentina   175

EMILIO ROS-FÁBREGAS (Universidad de Granada)
The Cardona and Fernández de Córdoba coats of arms
in the Chigi codex   223

REVIEWS
RICHARD FREEDMAN, *The Chansons of Orlando di Lasso and
their Protestant Listeners: Music, Piety, and Print in Sixteenth-
Century France*, and JEANICE BROOKS, *Courtly Song in
Late Sixteenth-Century France*
REBECCA WAGNER OETTINGER   259

ERIC CHAFE, *Analyzing Bach Cantatas*
JOHN BUTT   283

EDITORIAL BOARD

Early Music History (2002) Volume 21. © *Cambridge University Press*
DOI:10.1017/S0261127902002012 Printed in the United Kingdom

ANNE-EMMANUELLE CEULEMANS

INSTRUMENTS REAL AND IMAGINARY: AARON'S INTERPRETATION OF ISIDORE AND AN ILLUSTRATED COPY OF THE *TOSCANELLO*

Pietro Aaron (*c.*1480–*c.*1550) is the author of five music treatises. The first, *Libri tres de institutione harmonica* (Bologna, 1516), was composed in Italian and then translated into Latin by the humanist Giovanni Antonio Flaminio (1464–1536); the other four appeared in Italian, which made Aaron a pioneer in this regard.[1] The *Thoscanello de la musica*, the first of the vernacular treatises, proved very successful and was reissued three times in the course of the sixteenth century under the title *Toscanello in musica* (Venice, 1529, 1539, 1562). These reissues are very similar to each other, but are clearly distinct from the first edition, in particular by the addition of an appendix (*aggiunta*) on various questions concerning *musica ficta* and the modes of Gregorian chant.

As Aaron himself says, the *Toscanello* is an elementary handbook on singing (that is to say on notation) and composition, intended for those with an inadequate command of Latin:

QVesti sono precetti gli quali io non senza tollerabile ragione hò giudicati esser commodi & bastanti a quegli che di lettere latine mancano: per intrar nel lodatissimo collegio de gli musici: gli quali precetti con quello stile che mi hà concesso il mio debile & rozzo ingegno hò seruato: & da le questioni & disputationi troppo alte & oscure, mi sono astenuto: & de le cose pertinenti a la pratica si di cantare

I should like to thank here all those who have helped me in writing this article: Nicolas Meeùs, for his valuable information on matters organological; Didier Luciani, for telling me about the use of the shofar in Jewish tradition; Margaret Bent, for giving me the opportunity to present my research at All Souls College, Oxford (1 March 2001); Bonnie Blackburn and Leofranc Holford-Strevens, for their many helpful suggestions, and Leofranc Holford-Strevens for translating my article into English.

[1] *Thoscanello de la musica* (Venice, 1523); *Trattato della natura et cognitione di tutti gli tuoni di canto figurato* (Venice, 1525); supplement with no title or author's name (Venice, 1531); *Lucidario in musica* (Venice, 1545); *Compendiolo di molti dubbi* (Milan, after 1545).

come di comporre canti, niente hò lasciato che necessario mi sia paruto: con tal temperamento che (sel parer non minganna) nè la breuità partorisca oscurità, ne la lunghezza superfluità.[2]

These are (the) teachings that, not without tolerable reason, I have judged helpful and sufficient for those who are wanting in Latin letters to enter into the most laudable company of musicians; which teachings I have sustained with that style which my weak and rough intellect has permitted me. On the one hand, I have forborne too lofty and difficult questions and discussions, on the other I have left out nothing that I thought relevant of practical matters concerning both singing and composition, in such moderation that (if my opinion does not deceive me) neither brevity shall give birth to obscurity, nor length to superfluity.

The Bibliothèque Royale Albert Ier in Brussels possesses a copy of the 1529 *Toscanello* containing various annotations together with some remarkable drawings of instruments. This book, to be discussed in the following pages, belonged to the library of François-Joseph Fétis (1784–1871), musicologist and first director of the Conservatoire royal in Brussels.[3]

The first page of this *Toscanello* bears a handwritten name, in the same hand as the other annotations: Desiderio Ventura da Moro (Figure 1). In 1592 he published a collection of anonymous works for four (optionally five) voices in honour of St Francis. Amongst these compositions there is a little piece by Ventura himself, *Vergin ti vò pregare*, which shows that he had some musical talent.[4] Nothing else is known of him. Ventura clearly read the

Figure 1   Sigature of Desiderio Ventura da Moro

[2]   This text introduces the conclusion in all four editions of the *Toscanello*. All quotations follow the 1529 edition.

[3]   Fétis's collections were acquired upon his death by the Belgian state and are now held at the Bibliothèque Royale; cf. *Catalogue de la bibliothèque de F. J. Fétis acquise par l'État belge* (Bologna, 1877), p. v. The 1529 *Toscanello* is no. 5298 in the catalogue. An electronic facsimile will shortly appear on CD-ROM in the *Thesaurus musicarum Italicarum*, a series of electronic editions of Italian treatises directed by Frans Wiering of the University of Utrecht.

[4]   *Gioiello artificioso di musica, sopra la vita del glorioso, & serafico padre San Francesco, a quattro voci, con la quinta parte se piace, nuovamente composto, per un suo devoto religioso: et dal Sig. Desiderio Ventura da Morro di Iesi dato in luce. In Venetia, appresso Giacomo Vincenti. 1592.* Copy in Bologna, Civico Museo Bibliografico Musicale. Although the title page indicates that a fifth voice is optional, it is essential in Desiderio's composition. From the title we infer that Desiderio Ventura probably came from Morro d'Alba, a village not far from Iesi and Ancona. He had clearly read the *Toscanello* before publishing the *Gioiello*, for the preface of this work begins in the same way as that of Aaron's treatise.

Toscanello from one end to the other. At various places he added notes in a careful and legible hand, but with little originality of content. In general, they are visual markers (pointing hands, side notes) or paraphrases showing that he did his best to understand what Aaron was saying, but was not always in command of the subject. He took the trouble to correct the most trivial misprints,[5] but left untouched errors that make nonsense of the text.[6] In book 1, chapter 27, he commits an obvious mistake in identifying the sign C 31 (instead of C 32) as indicating imperfect major mode, perfect minor mode and imperfect tempus (Figure 2).[7]

From his annotations it may be deduced that apart from the *Toscanello* he knew at least three other music treatises. His drawings of instruments, in the margins of book 1, chapter 5, at first sight seem to have been inspired by the German theorist Sebastian Virdung's *Musica getutscht* (Basle, 1511), although this source is not explicitly cited. At book 1, chapter 34, Ventura da Moro refers to book 2, chapter 11 of Franchino Gaffurio's *Practica musicae* (Milan,

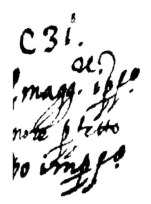

Figure 2   Ventura da Moro's misidentification of imperfect major mode, perfect minor mode and imperfect tempus by the sign C31

---

[5]   e.g. sig. B iii^v, second rest of the second pair in the second music example corrected; sig. D iii^r, misnumbering of book 1, ch. 30 corrected; sig. [E iv]^v, ch. 38, ll. 20 and 23 under heading, ¢ corrected to ф; sig. N iii^r, l. 11, 'pronunzi' changed to 'pronunzij'; *ibid.*, l. 14, 'Kzrie' corrected to 'Kyrie'; fol. O^v, l. 4, 'primieramnete' corrected to 'primieramente'.

[6]   Thus in book 1, ch. 11 (sig. C ii^v, l. 2), he did not correct 'tre longhe' to 'due longhe', even though it is an obvious mistake. Similarly, he did not try to emend the second music example in book 1, ch. 36, unintelligible though it is.

[7]   This note, caught in the binding, is incompletely visible on the microfilm. The full text runs: 'C3i/m[od]o magg[io]re i[m]p[er]f[ett]o/minore p[er]fetto/te[m]po imp[er]f[ett]o'.

3

1496) and to book 5, chapter 6 of the same author's *Angelicum opus* (Milan, 1508).[8] Aaron explains that under the signs C and ₵ the black maxima either undergoes sesquialteration or loses a quarter of its value. In the margin, against this assertion, stands the note reproduced in Figure 3. The legibility of this note is impaired by a correction. It seems originally to have run: 'Fra[n]chino nella Pr[actic]a et i[n] Angelicu[m] opus dice il [illegible word: probably 'medemo']' ('Franchino in the *Practica* and the *Angelicum opus* says [?]the same'). The last two words have been deleted and the text now reads: 'Fra[n]chino nella Pr[actic]a et i[n] Angelicu[m] opus dice la metà' ('. . . says half [its value]').

This annotation is interesting in that it reveals a reader's perplexity in the face of contradictory statements by Gaffurio and Aaron. The chapter of the *Toscanello* where the note occurs is entitled 'Cognitione de la massima, et longa di colore pieno'. At the end of this chapter, Aaron refers to what is commonly called *minor color*, in which blackened notes may give rise to a dotted rhythm and thus lose a quarter of their value. For his part Gaffurio states on the authority of his teacher Johannes Bonadies that imperfect blackened notes, when isolated or grouped in pairs, lose half their value and call forth a duple proportion, which is of course nonsense.[9] Ventura da Moro's note seems to show that he already

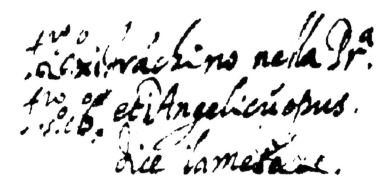

Figure 3   Ventura da Moro's reference to Gaffurio's *Practica musicae*
and *Angelicum opus*

---

[8]   Despite its Latin title, this is an Italian adaptation of the *Practica musicae*.
[9]   F. Gaffurius, *Practica musicae* (Milan, 1496; facs. repr. Farnborough, 1967), sig. [bb8]ʳ; trans. C. Miller (Musicological Studies and Documents, 20; American Institute of Musicology, 1968), p. 104.

knew Gaffurio's treatises when he read the *Toscanello* and cited them from memory. Later, he presumably checked the exact references, scribbled them in the margin, realized that he had made a mistake in the original note, and corrected it accordingly.

The drawings copied from Virdung's *Musica getutscht* are more surprising. Did Ventura da Moro own this treatise? Did he know German? Given that the *Musica getutscht* was the object of several translations and adaptations, these questions cannot be settled without a more detailed examination of his annotations.[10]

The first edition of the *Musica getutscht* was published (in two impressions) by Michael Furter at Basle in 1511; within a few years it was pirated by Johann Schoensperger at Augsburg. A French translation of the second part appeared at Antwerp in 1529.[11] This was based on a previous Flemish version, whose first edition is not preserved, but which was reissued in 1554 and in 1568.[12] These two translations contain only the second part of Virdung's treatise, dedicated to questions of notation and instrumental practice. They do not include the engravings reproduced by Ventura da Moro and will not be examined below. In 1536, Othmar Luscinius published at Strasbourg a Latin adaptation of *Musica getutscht*, entitled *Musurgia seu praxis musicae*.[13] This work borrows the original plates of the Basle edition of Virdung, though the text is quite different.[14] Finally, some of Virdung's illustrations reappear in Martin Agricola's *Musica instrumentalis Deudsch*.[15] However, these engravings are reversed in relation to the *Musica getutscht*, which is not the case with Ventura da Moro's drawings.

---

[10] For a detailed analysis of editions and translations of *Musica getutscht*, see E. M. Ripin, 'A Reevaluation of Virdung's *Musica getutscht*', *Journal of the American Musicological Society*, 29 (1976), pp. 189–223; G. Stradner, *Spielpraxis und Instrumentarium um 1500 dargestellt an Sebastian Virdungs Musica getutscht* (Forschungen zur älteren Musikgeschichte, 4; Vienna, 1983), pp. 8–40; B. Bullard, *Musica getutscht: A Treatise on Musical Instruments* (Cambridge, 1993), pp. 47–88.

[11] *Livre plaisant et très utile pour apprendre à faire et ordonner toutes tablatures hors le discant* (Antwerp, 1529).

[12] J. van Ghelen, *Dit is een seer schoon Boecxke om te leeren maken alderhande tabulatueren wten Discante* (Antwerp, 1554, repr. 1568). The French and Flemish translations are published in facsimile in *Livre plaisant, 1529, & Dit is een seer schoon boecxke, 1568*, introd. J. H. van der Meer (Early Music Theory in the Low Countries, 9; Amsterdam, 1973). As Bullard has shown, the Flemish translation is based directly on the German text, and in turn is the source of the French version (*op. cit.*, p. 56).

[13] It cannot be called a true translation, for Luscinius' text diverges noticeably from Virdung's.

[14] O. Luscinius, *Musurgia seu praxis musicae* (Strasbourg, 1536, repr. 1542).

[15] M. Agricola, *Musica instrumentalis Deudsch* ([Wittenberg], 1529).

Apart, therefore, from the two German editions of *Musica getutscht*, only Luscinius' Latin adaptation can have served as Ventura da Moro's source of inspiration, and further on we shall see that that indeed was the work he used. In the following pages, we shall first study chapter 5 of the *Toscanello* in order to place his drawings in their context; we shall then compare them with Aaron's, Virdung's and Luscinius' texts.

CHAPTER 5 OF *TOSCANELLO IN MUSICA*

Sources

Desiderio Ventura da Moro's drawings of instruments all stand in the margins of book 1, chapter 5 of the *Toscanello*, which is headed 'Cognitione di voci, et suoni, et varii istromenti'. This chapter essentially consists of a translation of Isidore of Seville's section 'De musica', though Aaron does not name his source.[16] When he departs from Isidore's text, he refers to various other authors (Pliny the Elder, Ovid, Julius Pollux, Martianus Capella), but nothing proves that he cites them at first hand.[17]

Who prepared the Italian version of Isidore's 'De musica' that Aaron used? It is well known that the theorist was weak in Latin, for he had had to call on Giovanni Antonio Flaminio to translate his *Libri tres de institutione harmonica*. Did Aaron, in drawing up chapter 5 of his *Toscanello*, use an existing translation and do no more than copy it out? Although this question cannot be answered with certainty, it is likelier that he was responsible for the translation

---

[16] 'De musica' takes up chs. 14–23 of book 3 of Isidore's *Etymologiae*, but in ch. 5 of the *Toscanello* Aaron does not use chs. 14–18 or 23. Fragments of ch. 16, however, appear in ch. 2 of the *Toscanello* ('Pythagora in fine fu diligente inquisitore, et messe insieme le consonanze de la musica, . . . tolta la pruoua da gli martegli de fabbri, et da lesstensioni de le chorde'; '. . . et crediamo esser la uerità quel che dice Moyse nel Genesi, che Tubal fu trouatore de la scienza musica, il qual fu de la stirpe di Cain nanzi il diluuio'). Isidore himself is cited by name at the end of ch. 1, some passages of which might equally be inspired by 'De musica'. The derivation of ch. 5 from Isidore was first recognised by Bonnie Blackburn ('A Lost Guide to Tinctoris's Teachings Recovered', *Early Music History*, 1 (1981), pp. 29–116, at p. 64 n. 80). For a translation of Isidore, 'De musica', see H. D. Goode and G. C. Drake (trans.), *Cassiodorus, Institutiones, Book II, Chapter V; Isidore of Seville, Etymologies, Book III, Chapters 15–23* (Colorado Springs, 1980), pp. 13–20, and O. Strunk, *Source Readings in Music History*, rev. L. Treitler (London and New York, 1998), pp. 149–55. Isidore's exposition in turn is based on various previous authors; cf. J. Fontaine, *Isidore de Séville et la culture classique dans l'Espagne wisigothique*, i (Paris, 1983), pp. 415–40.

[17] Since Aaron did not know Greek, this is especially true of the reference to Pollux.

himself, for although his text contains errors, it bears witness to a critical understanding of the strictly musical and organological content of his source.

A systematic comparison of the two texts shows numerous and by no means uninteresting differences between them.[18] Before we embark on this comparison, let it be said that the version of 'De musica' on which Aaron drew remains unidentified. Nevertheless, some of his 'mistranslations' may be imputed to it with certainty. For example, in paragraph 10 (cf. appendix), he translates 'vinno' ('lock of hair') by 'vino' ('wine')[19] and seems thereby to mistake the exact significance of 'vinnola' ('soft', not 'vinous' or 'drunk'). However, this error already appeared in an edition of 1493.[20]

A similar case occurs in paragraph 6, where Isidore describes the Hyperlydian mode as 'novissimus et acutissimus' ('the last and highest'). Aaron states that it is the first mode, probably on the basis of a variant in the same edition of 1493:

Est enim armoniae differentia & quantitas quae in vocis accentu vel tenore consistit: cuius genera in .xv. partibus musici diviserunt. ex quibus primus hyperlidius: novissimus et acutissimus hypodorius: omnium gravissimus.[21]

For it (tone) is the distinctive feature and quantifier of harmony, and consists in the accent or tenor of the voice. Musicians have divided its types in fifteen parts, of which the first is the Hyperlydian, the last and highest the Hypodorian, the lowest of all.

Faced with the contradictory qualifiers 'primus' on the one hand, and 'novissimus et acutissimus' on the other, Aaron contented himself with suppressing 'acutissimus'.

In paragraph 14, Isidore states that the word *tibicen* denotes the sound of the *tibia* and is derived from *tibia* and *cano* ('I sing, play an instrument'). Granted that this etymology is correct, the word refers to the player and not to the music played. In Aaron's text, this mistake is corrected, but that was already the case in some

---

[18] The texts of Isidore's 'De musica' and ch. 5 of the *Toscanello* are given in the appendix, divided into brief numbered paragraphs to which reference will be made in the following pages.

[19] One might suppose it was a misprint, but the spelling 'vino' reappears in all four editions of the *Toscanello*, while most errors of the first edition (1523) were corrected in the second of 1529.

[20] *Isidorus ethimologiarum Idem de summo bono*, per B. Locatellum mandato O. Scoti (Venice, 1493).

[21] The same variant is also found in a slightly earlier edition of the *Etymologiae* and *De summo bono*, published at Venice by Peter Löslein in 1483.

medieval sources.[22] In all probability, the version of Isidore used by Aaron also contained the correction.

Although we should thus avoid being too quick to accuse Aaron of not respecting Isidore, it is certain that his translation contains blunders and omissions. For example, in paragraph 3, the meaning of 'Nam proprium est ut litorei sonent scopuli' ('For the proper expression is that the rocks on the shore "resound"') escapes him when he writes: 'Il suono si domanda uoce, impero che questo é il proprio' ('Sound is called voice, for that is the correct term').[23]

The more or less fantastic etymologies that distinguish Isidore's great work are another stumbling block in Aaron's translation. Several of them are simply passed over in silence.[24] Others are taken over as they are or translated literally, with more or less fortunate results. For example, in paragraph 23, Isidore explains that *chorda* ('string') comes from *cor* ('heart'), because the vibration of the strings of the cithara resembles the beating of the heart in the chest. Aaron's translation is ambiguous: the Italian reader does not immediately understand that 'corde' is the ablative of Latin *cor*, since the same written form represents, in Italian, the plural of *corda* ('string'). Only the Latin spelling of 'chorde' ('strings') allows the two words to be distinguished.

In paragraph 3, Isidore associates *verberatus* and *verba*: 'Vox est aer spiritu verberatus, unde et verba sunt nuncupata'; 'voice is air beaten by breath, which is also why words (*verba*) are so called'.[25] The translation of 'verberatus' by 'percosso' ('Voce é aere percosso dal spirito, dalqual son chiamate uerba, cioé le parole') wipes out all resemblance to 'verba', which renders the phrase unintelligible.

Quite unexpectedly, in places Aaron attempts to correct Isidore's etymologies. Thus, in paragraph 25, Isidore derives *lyra*

---

[22] It appears for instance in the *Ars musica* of Johannes Aegidius de Zamora, a treatise written *c.*1300 that has nothing to do with Aaron's *Toscanello*. See Johannes Aegidius de Zamora, *Ars musica*, ed. M. Robert-Tissot (Corpus scriptorum de musica, 20; American Institute of Musicology, 1974), p. 112.

[23] Cf. too the translation of 'omnes qui voce *propria* canunt' (§2: 'all those who sing with their *own* voice') as 'tutti quegli gli quali cantano con la *prima* uoce' ('all those who sing with their *first* voice').

[24] Cf. §5: 'Euphonia est suavitas vocis. Haec et melos *a suavitate et melle* dicta'; §15: 'Calamus nomen est proprium arboris a calendo, id est fundendo voces vocatus'; §15 'Fistula autem dicta, quod vocem emittat. Nam φῶς Graece vox, στόλια missa appellatur.'

[25] This etymology, however, is condemned by Lactantius (*De opificio Dei* 15).

from Greek *lirin*, but there is no such word.[26] Even though he gives Isidore's etymology, Aaron summons up another, making *lyra* come from *lyrin*, which he translates 'cantare' ('to sing'). Unfortunately, this etymology is no better, for *lyrin* is no more Greek than *lirin*.

In some cases, Aaron's etymology is nearer the truth than Isidore's, as when he derives *tympano* from Greek *typto* (τύπτω, 'I strike'; cf. §27) where Isidore confuses *tympanum* (which denotes a drum) with *tympanium* (which in Pliny is a kind of flat pearl).[27] Likewise, in paragraph 29, he derives *sistro* from Greek *sio* (σείω, 'I shake'), whereas for Isidore the instrument's name comes from the goddess Isis. So far the origin of these corrections has not been identified, but it is possible that Aaron owes them to one or other humanist, perhaps Flaminio, rather than a written source.

The inadequate command of Latin and the bizarre etymologies are not the only cause of discrepancies between Isidore's text and Aaron's: the latter exhibits certain omissions that show Aaron to have approached his source with something of a critical spirit. Thus it is striking that he skips over Isidore's definitions of *diesis* and *tonus* (§5),[28] which are unintelligible and quite unlike those that Aaron himself gives later on:

Diesis est spatia quaedam et deductiones modulandi atque vergentes de uno in altero sono. Tonus est acuta enuntiatio vocis.

The diesis consists of certain intervals and passages in the melody, which descend from one sound to another. Tone is the high-pitched emission of a voice.

We shall return below to the critical judgement that Aaron displayed in translating Isidore.

Musical instruments

Following Isidore, at the start of chapter 5 of *Toscanello*, Aaron classifies instruments according to the 'nature of their sound', which may take three 'forms'. The first is harmonic and is represented by vocal music; the second is organic and is generated by the breath; the third is rhythmic and is produced by striking by the fingers. Isidore thus distinguishes between two categories of

---

[26] In Lindsay's edition (see appendix), this word is replaced by λnρεῖν, 'to talk nonsense'.
[27] *Historia naturalis* 9. 109.
[28] On these definitions, see Fontaine, *Isidore de Séville*, pp. 429–30; M. Titli, 'Le idee musicali di Isidoro di Siviglia tra *ars* e *peritia*', *Nuova rivista musicale italiana*, 34 (2000), pp. 181–97 at p. 194.

instruments: wind and percussion. To this latter category string instruments belong as well as what we should now call percussion instruments in the strict sense.

This joint grouping of string and percussion instruments may seem surprising in the light of current conventions, but it is not exceptional. Isidore has it from St Augustine.[29] At a later date, traces of it may be found in Michael Praetorius, who in part 1 of his *De organographia*[30] distinguishes ἔμπνευστα (wind instruments) and ἄπνευστα ('windless') instruments, further described as 'percussa' and 'klopffende Instrument'. Amongst these latter, he includes not only stringless (ἄχορδα) but also stringed instruments (ἔγχορδα).[31]

Having divided music into three categories, harmonic, organic and rhythmic, Aaron quotes in some detail Isidore's account of the first category, vocal music. For the other two categories, he cites a large number of instruments, whose invention he normally

---

[29] St Augustine, *De doctrina christiana* 2. 17. 20, §70, ed. and tr. R. P. H. Green (Oxford, 1995), pp. 88–9: 'Tres autem non propterea illa civitas locaverat quia in somnis eas viderat aut tot se cuiusquam illorum oculis demonstraverant, sed quia facile erat animadvertere omnem sonum, quae materies cantilenarum est, triformem esse natura. Aut enim voce editur, sicuti eorum est qui faucibus sine organo canunt, aut flatu, sicut tubarum et tibiarum, aut pulsu, sicut in citharis et tympanis et quibuslibet aliis quae percutiendo canora sunt' ('And the town had placed contracts for three not because they had seen them in a dream or because that number had appeared before the eyes of one of its citizens, but because it was a simple matter to observe that all sound, which is the essence of music, is naturally threefold. A sound is either produced by the voice, as by those who make music with their mouths, without a musical instrument, or by breath, as with trumpets and flutes [*sic*: strictly 'auloi'], or by percussion, as in the case of lyres, drums, or anything else that resonates when struck'); cf. *De ordine* 2. 14; *Enarratio in Psalmum CL* 8 (vv. 5–6).

[30] M. Praetorius, *Syntagma musicum*, ii: *De organographia* (Wolfenbüttel, 1619), p. 3; facs. ed. W. Gurlitt (Kassel, 1958).

[31] Aaron also mentions the more familiar subdivision into three categories, at the end of book 1, ch. 4. This goes back to Cassiodorus, *Institutiones* 2. 5, ed. R. A. B. Mynors, *Cassiodori Senatoris Institutiones* (Oxford, 1937) p. 144: 'Instrumentorum musicorum genera sunt tria: percussionalia – tensibilia – inflatilia. percussionalia sunt acitabula aenea et argentea, vel alia quae metallico rigore percussa reddunt cum suavitate tinnitum. tensibilia sunt cordarum fila sub arte religata, quae ammoto plectro percussa mulcient aurium delectabiliter sensum, in quibus sunt species cythar<ar>um diversarum. inflatilia sunt quae spiritu reflante completa in sonum vocis animantur, ut sunt tubae, calami, organa, pandoria et cetera huiuscemodi' ('There are three kinds of instruments, percussion, tension, and wind. Percussion instruments are brass and silver cymbals, or other instruments made of stiff metal that when struck give a sweetly ringing sound. Tension instruments consist of skilfully attached strings, which when struck with a plectrum delightfully soothe the ears; they include the various kinds of citharae. Wind instruments are those that when filled with blowing breath are quickened to the sound of voice, such as trumpets, panpipes, organs, *pandoria*, and other things of this kind').

relates to ancient mythology or the Bible. The majority of these instruments are also listed by Isidore and their order of presentation is the same: wind instruments (§§11–18) are followed by 'percussion' instruments (§§19–32), within which those with strings (§§20–6) precede percussion instruments proper (§§27–32). Nevertheless, the translation and interpretation of terms raise certain problems: very often, the instrument intended by Isidore is not the same as that envisaged by Aaron.

The brief glossary below lists all the instruments mentioned by Aaron in alphabetical order, with their Isidorian names in parentheses, and attempts to establish the meaning accorded them by each author.

ac(c)ettabuli (Is.: *acetabula, acitabula*; §19, 28): cf. cymbala

barbyti (Is.: *barbitae*; §21): cf. cithara

calamo (Is: *calamus*; §11, 15, 17). Amongst the aerophones, Isidore lists side by side the *calamus* and the *fistula*. In antiquity, *calamus*, a word of Greek origin (κάλαμος 'reed'), served to designate various wind instruments; the plural *calami* referred more specifically to panpipes.[32] *Fistula* is a Latin word with the general sense of 'pipe'. Curiously enough, Isidore equips the Greek word with an etymology from the supposed Latin verb *caleo* ('Calamus nomen est proprium arboris a calendo, id est fundendo voces vocatus'; '*calamus* is the name of a tree, so called from *caleo*, "I utter sounds"'), whereas for the Latin word he gives a Greek etymology ('Fistula autem dicta, quod vocem emittat. Nam φώς Graece vox, στόλια missa appellatur'; 'the fistula is so called because it emits a sound, for "sound" in Greek is φώς and "emitted" is στόλια'[33]). Clearly Aaron is not taken in by these far-fetched explanations, for which he substitutes his own descriptions, referring to Pliny and Ovid.[34] For Aaron, the *calamo* is a hollow reed used in the

---

[32] *The New Grove Dictionary of Music and Musicians*, 2nd edn (London and New York, 2001; hereafter *New Grove II*), s.v. 'calamus', iv, 817.

[33] Isidore has confused φώς 'light' with φωνή 'sound'; στόλια is Greek for 'scanty garments', but is derived from the same root as στέλλω, 'I send', in Latin *mitto*.

[34] The Elder Pliny states at *Historia naturalis*, 16. 164: 'Plura autem genera [sc. harundinum]. alia spissior densiorque geniculis, brevibus internodiis, alia rarior maioribus, tenuiorque et ipsa. calamus vero alius totus concavus, quem vocant syringian, utilissimus fistulis, quoniam nihil est ei cartilaginis atque carnis' ('There are several kinds [of reeds]. One is thicker and denser in its knots, with short distances between them, another of

'sampogne'. Strictly speaking, the Italian *zampogna* is a bagpipe,[35] but from the context Aaron appears to be thinking rather of the panpipe: he recalls the myth that Pan put together seven pipes of unequal length to make an instrument called *syrinx* in Greek and *fistula* in Latin. Here arises a fresh terminological confusion: whereas in Latin *fistula* is simply a pipe, Italian *fistola* is a panpipe and is no doubt the instrument Aaron had in mind when he wrote.[36]

campanello (§30): cf. tintinabulo

cantico (Is.: *canticum*; §24): cf. psalterio

choro (§18): Aaron describes the *choro* as a bagpipe with a blowpipe and a chanter, but no drone. This instrument is not mentioned by Isidore, for Aaron borrows his account of it from a later source, a letter to one Dardanus wrongly attributed to St Jerome. This work has a twofold source. In Hrabanus Maurus' *De universo* (844), the relevant matter forms the central part of the chapter 'De musica et partibus eius'. In a Munich manuscript dated to the tenth century, the text is presented for the first time as a letter. The first graphic representation of the Hieronymian instruments appears in a ninth-century Angers psalter.[37] Hanoch Avenary has shown

more open growth than the larger ones, and thinner. Another kind of reed is completely hollow; it is called *syringias*, and very useful for pipes, since it has no fibrous matter or flesh'). The myth of Pan and Syrinx is told in Ovid, *Metamorphoses* 1. 689–712.

[35] W. A. Cocks, A. C. Baines and R. D. Cannon, s.v. 'bagpipe', *New Grove II*, ii, 480.

[36] Cf. *New Grove Dictionary of Musical Instruments* (London and New York, 1984), s.v. 'fistola', i, 763. The *Grande dizionario della lingua italiana*, ed. S. Battaglia (Turin, 1961–), s.v. 'calamo⁴', ii, 513 cites a passage from the *Dialoghi d'amore* of Leone Ebreo (1460 × 1464–1521 × 1535) that very clearly describes the *fistula* as a panpipe: 'Ha in mano [il dio Pan] una verga e una fistula con sette calami' ('[the god Pan] holds in his hand a staff and a seven-reed pipe').

[37] R. Hammerstein, 'Instrumenta Hieronymi', *Archiv für Musikwissenschaft*, 16 (1959), pp. 117–34, at pp. 117–18 and Mary Remnant, s.v. 'chorus', *New Grove II*, v, 786–7. Hrabanus Maurus' text is as follows: 'Chorus quoque simplex pellis est cum duabus cicutis aereis, et per primam inspiratur: per secundam, vocem emittit' ('The chorus, too, is a simple skin with two brass pipes; it is blown by the first and gives out sound by the second': *De universo*, bk. 18, ch. 4, PL 111. 490 d). In the illustrations accompanying the letter to Dardanus, the 'chorus' looks more like a bladderpipe than a true bagpipe. The instrument is also listed by Virdung, though he turns it into a kind of trumpet (cf. below). The Hieronymian instruments are further studied by H. Avenary, 'Hieronymus' Epistel über die Musikinstrumente und ihre altöstlichen Quellen', *Anuario musical*, 16 (1961), pp. 56–80; C. Page, 'Biblical Instruments in Medieval Manuscript Illustration', *Early Music*, 5 (1977), pp. 299–309, repr. in *id.*, *Music and Instruments of the Middle Ages: Studies on Texts and Performance* (Variorum Collected Studies Series; Aldershot, 1997), no. I. Their representation in Virdung is discussed by Stradner, *Spielpraxis und Instrumentarium*, pp. 389–99.

that in the sources the letter to Dardanus is always presented together with fragments of Isidore's 'De musica'.[38] It is therefore possible that Aaron had access to a version of 'De musica' to which the letter was appended.

cithara, cithera (Is.: *cithara*; §1, 19–24). The Greek cithara is a string instrument that, like the lyre, is distinguished by its two arms, which extend as far as the soundbox and support a crossbar to which the strings are attached. However, it is not certain that Isidore's instrument is identical with the Greek cithara, for in §24 he describes the difference between the psaltery and the cithara as follows: '[Psalterium] est autem similitudo citharae barbaricae in modum Δ literae; sed psalterii et citharae haec differentia est, quod psalterium lignum illud concavum, unde sonus redditur, superius habet et deorsum feriuntur chordae, et desuper sonant. Cithara vero concavitatem ligni inferius habet' ('The psaltery resembles the barbarian cithara in the shape of the letter Δ; but the difference between the psaltery and the cithara is that in the psaltery the hollow wood from which the sound comes is on top, while the strings are below. In the cithara, on the other hand, the wooden concave part is below'). According to James McKinnon, this description implies that the cithara and the psaltery are harps, the cithara being held with the soundbox downwards and the psaltery with it upwards.[39]

Isidore alleges a twofold origin for the cithara: according to the Greeks, il was invented by Apollo, while the Jews attribute it to Tubal.[40] He derives the word from Greek κιθάρα (allegedly Doric for 'thorax') and lists various kinds of citharae: 'psalteria, lyrae, barbitae, phoenices et pectides, et quae dicuntur Indicae'. His enumeration combines instruments that modern organology would classify as lyres (*lyra, barbiton*) and as harps (*psalterium, pectis*). The identity of the *phoenices* and Indian citharae (*Indicae*) – tall enough to need two players – is uncertain. Finally, Isidore states that

---

[38] Avenary, 'Hieronymus' Epistel', p. 57.

[39] J. W. McKinnon, s.v. 'psaltery', *New Grove II*, xx, 521. Isidore's definition is taken from St Augustine, *In Psalmum LXXX Enarratio*, 5.

[40] The name Tubal is due to confusion between two individuals mentioned in Genesis, the half-brothers Jubal and Tubalcain (Gen. 4: 19–22). Jubal is the counterpart of Pan in Greek mythology; Tubalcain was a blacksmith. See C. Meyer, *Sebastian Virdung, Musica getutscht: les instruments et la pratique musicale en Allemagne au début du XVIᵉ siècle* (Paris, 1980), pp. 18–19, 92.

according to Vergil, ancient citharae had seven strings, said to have been invented by Mercury.

Overall, Aaron's translation of paragraphs 19–23 is faithful enough, even though it is hard to establish how he pictured the instruments that Isidore mentioned. For example, if the Greek βάρβιτος is a lyre, the same term, in the fifteenth and sixteenth centuries, denoted a variety of theorbo.[41] There is a significant difference between Isidore's and Aaron's texts. In paragraph 21, Isidore states that the ancients called the cithara *fidicula* or *fidex* because its strings are as much in harmony with each other as men who have mutual trust (*fides*). Aaron omits the passage, but takes it up a little further, in his description of the lyre (cf. below, s.v. lyra).

cymbali (Is.: *cymbala*; §28). In the plural, *cymbala* and *cymbali* refer, in both Isidore and Aaron, to cymbals, associated in Graeco-Roman Antiquity with orgiastic religious cults. Isidore describes them as kinds of *acitabula* ('Cymbala acitabula quaedam sunt, quae percussa invicem se tangunt et faciunt sonum'; 'cymbals are kinds of receptacles that, when clashed against each other, play each other and make a noise'). In Aaron's text there is a deviation: the two words are represented as synonyms ('Cymbali & accettabuli, sono alcuni istromenti gli quali percossi insieme, si toccano & fanno suono'). This interpretation is certainly not original with Aaron, being also found in other sources.[42]

cymbalo (Is.: *cymbalum*; §19, 29). Isidore exhibits *cymbalum* once in the singular, in a list of percussion instruments (§19), but does not explain it. Aaron translates it 'tamburo', but in §29 uses 'cymbalo' as a possible synonym of 'sistro' (q.v. below).[43]

---

[41] *Enciclopedia della musica*, ed. C. Sartori (Milan, 1964), s.v. 'barbitos', i, 184.

[42] Cf. Rome, Biblioteca Apostolica Vaticana, Barberini lat. 307, fols. 27^r–29^r: *The Theory of Music from the Carolingian Era up to 1400*, ii: *Italy*, ed. Pieter Fischer (Répertoire international des sources musicales, B III; Munich and Duisburg, 1968), p. 103. This text, dating from the end of the fourteenth century, is published under the title *Sententiae Isidori Episcopi ad Braulionem Episcopum de Musica* in M. Gerbert, *Scriptores ecclesiastici de musica*, i (Saint-Blaise, 1784; repr. Milan, 1931), p. 24. The same variant is presented by Vienna, Österreichische Nationalbibliothek, Cod. 67, fol. 29^r, published in W. Pass, 'Die Musikkapitel in der Isidor-Überlieferung der Österreichischen Nationalbibliothek Wien', in W. Pass and A. Rausch, *Mittelalterliche Musiktheorie in Zentraleuropa* (Tutzing, 1998), p. 117.

[43] This use of *cimbalo* seems to be normal in Italian (*Grande dizionario della lingua italiana*, s.v. 'cimbalo', iii, 144), even though Sartori's *Enciclopedia* does not mention it.

fide, fidicula (Is.: *fidex, fidicula*; §21, 25): cf. lyra

fistola (Is.: *fistula*; §11, 15): cf. calamo

lyra (Is.: *lyra*; §21, 25, 26). Isidore alludes to the mythological origin of the lyre, supposedly invented by Mercury. In his translation, Aaron does not include the part of the myth relating to Orpheus, probably because he has mentioned him in a previous chapter of the *Toscanello*.[44] Instead, he adds an explanation that in Isidore's text applies to the cithara. Isidore asserts that the cithara was called *fidicula* or *fidex* by the ancients (cf. s.v. cithara).[45] For Aaron these names apply to the lyre. This adaptation, made on his own account, is completely logical. First of all, *fidicula* and *fides* are regular terms for the lyre. Furthermore, the medieval term *fidula*, like *fidicula* derived from *fides*, means 'vielle'.[46] This same word is the origin of German *Fidel*, Italian *viella*, English *fiddle*, and numerous similar names in other European languages. Now in Aaron's day, the word *lira* could denote various bowed instruments of the vielle type (such as the lira da braccio), which explains Aaron's association of *lyra, fides* and *fidicula*.[47]

organo (Is.: *organum*; §11, 12, 31). According to Isidore, *organum* may refer in general to any musical instrument. He adds that among the Greeks, the bellows instrument has another name,[48] but in

---

[44] *Toscanello*, book 1, ch. 1, sig. A^v.

[45] There is no such word as *fidex: fidicula* is the diminutive of *fides* as *aedicula* is of *aedes*.

[46] *Enciclopedia della musica*, s.vv. 'fides', 'fidula', ii, 192; see too *Dictionary of Medieval Latin from British Sources*, ed. R. E. Latham and D. R. Howlett (Oxford, 1997), s.vv., v, 938–9.

[47] For the association, common in Aaron's time, between the ancient lyre and the modern lira see E. Winternitz, 'The Lira da Braccio', in *id.*, *Musical Instruments and their Symbolism in Western Art* (London, 1967), pp. 86–98, esp. pp. 89–90; *id.*, *Leonardo da Vinci as a Musician* (New Haven and London, 1982), pp. 25–38; L. C. Witten II, 'Apollo, Orpheus, and David: A Study of the Crucial Century in the Development of Bowed Strings in North Italy 1480–1580 as Seen in Graphic Evidence and Some Surviving Instruments', *Journal of the American Musical Instrument Society*, 1 (1975), pp. 5–55, esp. p. 9.

[48] This seems to be ὕδραυλις, which properly denotes the water organ, but may still have been used for the bellows organ; cf. Pollux 4. 70. Isidore's source for this passage is St Augustine, *Enarratio in Psalmum CL* 7 (v. 4), ed. E. Dekkers and J. Fraipont (Corpus Christianorum, series Latina, 40; Turnhout, 1956), 2195: 'Nam cum organum uocabulum graecum sit, ut dixi, generale omnibus musicis instrumentis; hoc cui folles adhibentur, alio Graeci nomine appellant. Vt autem organum dicatur, magis latina et ea uulgaris est consuetudo' ('For although "organ" is the generic Greek term, as I have said, for all musical instruments, this one, to which bellows are applied, the Greeks call by another name. Calling it "organ" is, rather, a Latin custom, and everyday usage at that'). On this passage see K. Tittel in A. von Pauly, G. Wissowa and W. Kroll (eds.), *Real-Encyclopädie der classischen Altertumswissenschaft*, s.v. 'Hydraulis', ix (Stuttgart, 1914), cols.

Latin it is usual to call it *organum*. This definition must have seemed inadequate to Aaron, who departs from Isidore's text and recognises in the organ only the bellows instrument used in churches.[49]

pandura (Is.: *pandorius, pandorium*; §11, 17). Isidore's description of this instrument clearly posed a problem for Aaron. Isidore includes the 'pandoria' in the list of wind instruments opening *Etymologies* 3. 21, which is borrowed from Cassiodorus' *Institutions*.[50] Further on, in paragraph 17, Isidore associates the 'pandorius' with the god Pan and describes that instrument as a panpipe.[51] Nevertheless, the Graeco-Roman *pandura* is not a wind instrument but a string instrument of the lute family.[52] It is quite hard to establish what Aaron understood by *pandura*.[53] Perhaps he had no very clear idea. In any case, it is interesting to note that he replaces Isidore's description with a reference to Julius Pollux, according to whom the *pandura* was a three-stringed instrument invented by the Assyrians.[54] Like Isidore, Aaron associates the *pandura* with Pan, but he does so on the authority of Martianus Capella,[55] which shows that in this passage Aaron does not trust Isidore.

69–70, who notes that the first possible (but ambiguous) instance of ὄργανον for 'bellows organ' in Greek is Theodoret, *De Providentia* 3 (PG 83. 589 a).

[49] The confused syntax whereby 'alquale' refers back to 'organo' as if it were the specific instrument and not the generic name apparently rests on a misinterpretation of Isidore's 'Hoc', which refers forward to 'cui', not back to 'Organum'.

[50] Cassiodorus, *Institutions* 2. 5, ed. Mynors, p. 144: 'inflatilia sunt quae spiritu reflante completa in sonum vocis animantur, ut sunt tubae, calami, organa, pandoria et cetera huiuscemodi' ('wind instruments are those that, filled with the blowing breath, are enlivened to the sound of their voice, such as trumpets, reed pipes, *organa, panduria*, and the others of this kind').

[51] The pandura is thus understood as the 'gift of Pan' (Πάν + δῶρον; cf. *Grande dizionario della lingua italiana*, s.v. 'pandorio', xii, 466).

[52] J. W. McKinnon, *New Grove II*, s.v. 'pandoura', xix, 30. Isidore's mistake was repeated by some Italian authors subsequent to Aaron: in particular, the *Grande dizionario della lingua italiana*, s.v. 'pandurio', xii, 466 adduces passages from Giambattista Martini (1706–84) and Niccolò Tommaseo (1802–74) in which the instrument is clearly identified with the panpipe.

[53] The *Grande dizionario della lingua italiana*, loc. cit., quotes a passage from Alessandro Citolini (*c*.1500–after 1565) in which the *panduro* is counted amongst other string instruments, but the context does not permit precise identification of the instrument concerned. The word *mandola*, derived from a conflation of *pandura* and *mano* (s.v. 'mandola', ix, 630), appears in Italian sources from the 1580s onwards denoting the ancestor of the mandolin (cf. J. Tyler, *New Grove II*, s.v. 'mandolin', xv, 737).

[54] Cf. Pollux, *Onomasticon* 4. 60.

[55] Cf. Martianus Capella, *De nuptiis Philologiae et Mercurii* 9. 906: 'uerum per medium quidam agrestes canorique semidei: quorum hircipedem pandura, Siluanum harundinis enodis fistula sibilatrix, rurestris Faunum tibia decuerunt' ('In the middle were some rustic and tuneful demigods, of whom Goat-Foot [Pan] was suited by his pandura, Silvanus by his

pettidi (Is.: *pectides*; §21): cf. cithara

phenici (Is.: *phoenices*; §21): cf. cithara

piva (§14): cf. tibia

psalterio (Is.: *psalterium*; cf. §19–21, 24). As stated above (s.v. cithara), the instrument described by Isidore is not a psaltery in the medieval sense of the term, but a triangular harp. Aaron omits this description, probably because it does not correspond to his conception of the instrument. In the list of string and percussion instruments in paragraph 19, he translates 'tympanum' by 'psalterii', which seems to show that for him the 'psalterio' is neither more nor less than the psaltery.[56] Following Isidore, Aaron registers *cantico* as a synonym for *psalterio*.

sambuca (Is.: *sambuca*; §16). Isidore mentions this amongst the wind instruments, but it is hard to determine what he is talking about. Properly, *sambuca* in Latin means a harp,[57] but it is unlikely that Isidore was thinking of a string instrument. He describes the *sambuca* as a 'symphonia', which may mean one of two things: a polyphonic instrument, or more specifically a double-skinned drum (cf. below, s.v.). The first interpretation seems preferable, given that according to Isidore the instrument is made of the same fragile wood as the *tibiae*. This leads one to suppose that Isidore considered the *sambuca* as a polyphonic wind instrument.[58] For Aaron, *sambuca* may have had another meaning: in Italian, *sambuca* encompasses various wind instruments (bagpipe, sackbut), but also string instruments (harp, hurdy-gurdy).[59]

sampogna (§15): cf. calamo

---

shrill pipe of knotless reed, Faunus by the countryman's aulos'); cited from L. Cristante, *Martiani Capellae* De Nuptiis Philologiae et Mercurii Liber IX, *traduzione e commento* (Padua, 1987), pp. 114–16.

[56] In Italian, *timpano* means 'kettledrum', but may also denote the dulcimer or psaltery (cf. D. Kettlewell, *New Grove II*, s.v. 'dulcimer', vii, 678–9).

[57] J. W. McKinnon, *ibid.*, s.v. 'sambuca', xxii, 205.

[58] R. Hammerstein observes that the description of the *sambuca* is sandwiched between two descriptions of panpipes, but does not make the inference that Isidore's *sambuca* too is a panpipe ('Instrumenta Hieronymi', p. 129).

[59] *Enciclopedia della musica*, s.v. 'sambuca', iv, 103; *Grande dizionario della lingua italiana*, xvii, 483 (curiously, this dictionary does not point out that the *sambuca* may be a hurdy-gurdy); F. Baines, E. A. Bowles and R. A. Green, *New Grove II*, s.v. 'hurdy-gurdy', xi, 878.

sistro (Is.: *sistrum*; §19, 29). The instrument described by Isidore is the Egyptian sistrum, a kind of U-shaped rattle equipped with a handle. Isidore states that the instrument is generally played by women, because it had a female inventor, the goddess Isis. Although Aaron alludes briefly to the instrument's Egyptian origin, his description of it is quite unlike Isidore's. In Italian, *sistro* denotes the ancestor of the triangle, a metal rod bent back on itself in the shape of a triangle, around which are mounted metal roundels that clash when the instrument is shaken.[60] This is the instrument that Aaron describes (though he does not mention its triangular shape); he notes that according to some the *sistro* is none other than the *cymbalo* used by Florentine girls in their dances.

symphonia (Is.: *symphonia*; §16, 27, 31, 32). In Isidore, *symphonia* may have one of two meanings: either the consonance of low and high pitches produced by the voice or a musical instrument,[61] or an instrument capable of producing such a consonance. The latter sense allows Isidore to apply the name *symphonia* to instruments as unlike as the *sambuca* (cf. s.v.) and a double-skinned drum (§32).[62] Aaron repeats Isidore's description of this drum faithfully enough,[63] but precedes it with a passage not found in Isidore (§31), in which he explains that, contrary to what some Latin authors assert, the *symphonia* is not a type of organ but a choral song in praise of God. This passage seems to be based on St Jerome's letter 21, to Pope Damasus.[64]

---

[60] *Grande dizionario della lingua italiana*, s.v. 'sistro', xix, 103.

[61] Cf. §4: 'Symphonia est modulationis temperamentum ex gravi et acuto concordantibus sonis, sive in voce, sive in flatu, sive in pulsu' ('Consonance is a blending in music of high and low through concordant sounds, whether in the voice, on wind instruments, or through percussion').

[62] According to Sartori, *sinfonia* is also used for the hurdy-gurdy, the bagpipe and the clavichord (*Enciclopedia della musica*, iv, 226).

[63] Curiously enough, however, Aaron insists that the name *symphonia* for a drum with double skin is current in his age ('non dimeno *al tempo nostro* dal uolgo symphonia si domanda un legno cauo da tutte due le parti, con una pelle distesa'; 'nevertheless in our time *symphonia* is the popular name for a piece of wood hollow on both sides with a skin stretched over it').

[64] 'Male autem quidam de Latinis symphoniam putant esse genus organi, cum concors in dei laudem concentus ex hoc vocabulo significetur: "συμφωνία" quippe "consonantia" exprimitur in Latino' ('But some of the Latins wrongly suppose the *symphonia* to be a kind of instrument, though this word means singing together harmoniously in praise of God; for the Latin for συμφωνία is *consonantia*'): Jerome, *ep.* 21. 29, ed. I. Hilberg (CSEL 54, 2nd edn, Vienna, 1996), p. 231. St Jerome's target may have been a source for Isidore's reference to the *symphonia* as a polyphonic wind instrument.

syringa (§15): cf. calamo

tibia (Is.: *tibia*; §1, 14, 16). The ancient *tibia* is an instrument similar to the Greek aulos, consisting of a pair of pipes with reed
mouthpieces. In paragraph 14, Isidore notes the instrument's
Phrygian origin and states that it is so called from having at first
been made of stags' shinbones or fawns'[65] shanks. Aaron's translation of this paragraph is highly ambiguous. The first occurrence
of the word 'tibia' is rendered by 'piva' ('bagpipe'), referring to a
very different instrument from that discussed by Isidore; there
seems to be no other instance of this equation. At the end of the
passage, however, Aaron repeats Isidore's 'tibia', without revealing what he means by the word.

tintinabulo (Is.: *tintinabulum*; §30). Aaron is considerably more
explicit in his description than Isidore, who is content to explain
that the word originates in the sound produced by the instrument.
Aaron records that it was used to call people to the baths[66] and
resembles the 'campanella' or little bell that summons the faithful to church.

tromba (Is.: *tuba*; §1, 3, 8, 11, 13). The Roman *tuba* was a bronze or
copper instrument similar to a straight trumpet.[67] Logically, Aaron
translates the word as 'tromba'. Isidore, citing Vergil, notes the
instrument's Etruscan origin, and also the use of the 'tuba' (properly the shofar) amongst the Jews as described in Ps. 80 (81),
according to which the new moon should be marked by blowing
the shofar. However, this tradition was lost very early on in Jewish
history: only the New Year continued, uninterruptedly, to be so
celebrated.[68] It certainly appears that Isidore was not aware that
the monthly blowing of the shofar had been abandoned, for this

---

[65] *Hinnulus*, properly a hinny, is here used for *inuleus*, 'fawn', as in Cant. 2: 9, 17, where it
is coupled with *cervus*. Aaron, not recognising the word, substitutes the long-legged crane.

[66] See Martial, *Epigrammata* 14. 163.

[67] J. W. McKinnon, *New Grove II*, s.v. 'tuba (ii)', xxv, 861.

[68] Cf. *Encyclopaedia Judaica*, 16 vols. (Jerusalem, 1971–2), s.v. 'moon', xi, cols. 290–1; s.v. 'shofar', xiv, cols. 1442–7; whereas at Ps. 81: 4 the Hebrew text instructs the shofar to be
blown 'at the new moon, at the full moon', the Aramaic version prepared for the
Complutensian Polyglot specifies 'in the month of Tishri' (*birach tishri*): see *Targum de
Salmos, edición príncipe del ms. Villa-Amil n. 5 de Alfonso de Zamora*, ed. L. Díez Merino (Madrid,
1982), p. 141, with Alfonso de Zamora's Latin translation at p. 268: 'Clangite in mense
tysri bucina: in quo mense statutus est dies solenitatis nostre' ('Sound the horn in the
month of Tishri, in which month the day of our celebration has been established').

passage seems to be based on St Augustine.[69] All the same, it is interesting to note that Aaron translates this passage just as it stands. The suggestion has been made that Aaron was of Jewish origin.[70] To be sure, it seems likely that he had Jewish ancestors, but the fact that he reproduces this passage appears to show that he was ill informed about Jewish practices in his own day and therefore that his education had not been strongly marked by Judaism. On several occasions Aaron omits or correct passages of Isidore that do not suit him; that is the case with the definition of the diesis, organ and *pandura*. If the passage on the use of the shofar in Jewish tradition had struck him as wrong, he would probably have left it out.

tamburo (§19, 27, 31): cf. tympano

tympano (Is.: *tympanum*; §19, 27). Isidore speaks of the *tympanum* in two places: in paragraph 19, in the list of 'percussion' instruments (which also include string instruments) and in paragraph 27, where he describes it as a kind of single-skin drum. On the first occasion, Aaron translates the word as 'psalterio' (q.v.), but the second time, he takes over the name 'tympano', which he considers to be synonymous with *tamburo*.

DESIDERIO VENTURA DA MORO'S DRAWINGS OF INSTRUMENTS

As we have seen, chapter 5 of Aaron's *Toscanello* consists of a more or less corrected and modified paraphrase of an almost thousand-year-old treatise, Isidore's 'De musica'. It does not grant us an overview of the musical instruments used in Italy at the beginning of the sixteenth century. By contrast, Virdung's *Musica getutscht* is a work explicitly intended to describe the instruments and the

---

[69] '*Tuba canite in initio mensis tubae*. Praeceptum erat ut in initio mensis tuba caneretur; et hoc usque nunc Iudaei corporaliter faciunt, spiritaliter non faciunt' ('*Sound the trumpet at the beginning of the month of the trumpet*. The commandment had been given that the trumpet should be sounded at the beginning of the month; which the Jews do in the physical sense but not the spiritual'): Augustine, *Enarr. in Ps. LXXX* 6. 4, ed. E. Dekkers and J. Fraipont (CCSL 39; Turnhout, 1956), p. 1123.

[70] *A Correspondence of Renaissance Musicians*, ed. B. J. Blackburn, E. E. Lowinsky and C. A. Miller (Oxford, 1991), pp. 89–92.

instrumental music of his time, even if the engravings in it are not free of errors nor the text itself flawless.[71]

The instruments listed by Virdung have been the object of numerous studies and will not be examined in detail in what follows.[72] Of Desiderio Ventura da Moro's eighteen drawings of instruments in the margins of the Bibliothèque Royale *Toscanello*, sixteen were taken from Virdung's treatise, or rather, as we shall see, from the Latin adaptation by Othmar Luscinius. These drawings are sufficiently faithful to the original engravings to leave no doubt as to Ventura da Moro's source of inspiration, even though not all the details are reproduced. Figure 4 shows his drawing of

Figure 4   Organ drawn by Ventura da Moro at the beginning of *Toscanello* ch. 5 (left) and organ in Virdung's *Musica getutscht*, sig. Cᵛ (right)

---

[71]   Ripin, 'A Reevaluation', pp. 208 ff., in particular, is very critical of Virdung. Nevertheless Bullard shows that some of his criticisms are unjustified and result from misunderstanding of Virdung's text (*Musica getutscht*, pp. 15–17), and that the deficiencies we perceive in the engravings are due to the difference between our expectations of an illustrated treatise and a sixteenth-century reader's. Rather than specific instruments, these engravings represent concepts. Virdung's reader did not expect them to reproduce all the details of every instrument (*ibid.*, pp. 18–23).

[72]   See esp. Stradner, *Spielpraxis und Instrumentarium*, and Bullard, *Musica getutscht*.

the organ, which is also illustrated on sig. C^v of *Musica getutscht* and p. 18 of *Musurgia*. In the original engraving, the instrument has twenty-three pipes (6+11+6) and a keyboard of nearly three octaves.[73] This arrangement is not respected in Ventura da Moro's drawing, which shows only nineteen pipes and ignores the alternation of white and black keys on the keyboard.

Table 1 gives an inventory of the instruments drawn by Ventura da Moro with references to their location in Virdung and Luscinius. The table shows that the majority of these labels are similar in

Table 1   *List of instruments drawn by Desiderio Ventura da Moro*

Aaron, *Toscanello*	Labelled by Ventura da Moro	Virdung, *Musica getutscht*	Label	Luscinius, *Musurgia*	Label
sig. Bii	Organum/Organo	sig. C^v	Orgel	p. 18	Organum
sig. Bii	Tromba di Girollamo	sig. Dij	Tuba hieronimi	p. 31	Tuba Hieronymi
sig. Bii	—	sig. C	Clareta	p. 24	Clareta
sig. Bii	Pive	sig. Biiij^v	Sackpfeiff	p. 21	Sackpfeiff
sig. Bii^v	sampogna, ò Calamo				
sig. Bii^v	fistula Hieronimi	sig. Dij^v	Fistula Hieronimi	p. 32	Fistula Hieronimi
sig. Bii^v	chorus/choro	sig. D^v	Chorus	p. 31	Chorus
sig. Bii^v	Cijthara per la quale è intesa l'Arpa	sig. Bij^v	Harpffen	p. 12	Cythara
sig. Bii^v	Cijthara Hieronijmi	sig. Ciij	Cythara Jheronimi	p. 29	Cythara Hieronymi
sig. Bii^v	Psalterium Decachordum	sig. Ciiij	Psalterium decacordum	p. 30	Psalterium Decachordum
sig. B [iii]	Psalterio	sig. Bij^v	Psalterium	p. 12	Psalterium
sig. B [iii]	Lijra	sig. B^v	Lyra	p. 9	Lyra
sig. B [iii]	Timpanum Jheronimi	sig. Ciij^v	Tympanum Jheronimi	p. 30	Tympanum Jheronimi
sig. B [iii]	Cijmbalo de Hieronimo	sig. Diij	Zymbalum Jheronimi	p. 33	Cymbalum Hieronymi
sig. B [iii]	Sistro				
sig. B [iii]	Tintinabulo	sig. Cij	Zymeln und Glocken	p. 25	Cimbala
sig. B [iii]	Tamburo	sig. D	paücklin	p. 27	—
sig. B [iii]	Aliud Psalterium Decachordum	sig. Ciiij	Psalterium decacordum	p. 30	Psalterium Decachordum aliud

---

[73] However, the organ is engraved in reverse. Cf. E. Ripin, 'A Reevaluation', p. 217.

Virdung, Luscinius and Ventura da Moro. However, some interesting exceptions may be noted. Sometimes Ventura da Moro translates a Latin or German label into Italian ('tromba di Girollamo', 'pive', 'psalterio', 'tintinabulo', 'tamburo'). That of the trumpet ('clareta') is missing.

At two points Luscinius' labels are markedly different from Virdung's ('Harpffen' ~ 'Cythara'; 'Zymeln und Glocken' ~ 'Cimbala'). For the large and small bell, Ventura da Moro uses Aaron's 'tintinabulo', but for the harp it is noteworthy that he borrows Luscinius' word: 'Cijthara per la quale è intesa l'Arpa'. This suggests that it was indeed Luscinius' treatise, not Virdung's, that he had before him. The manner in which the harp is portrayed affords corroboration: in Virdung the instrument is resting on its side, whereas Luscinius shows it standing up, and so does Ventura da Moro.[74] The label 'Aliud Psalterium Decachordum' constitutes another clear reference to Luscinius.

Two instruments drawn by Ventura da Moro are not featured in Virdung and Luscinius (Figure 5). The first is labelled 'sampogna, ò Calamo' and represents a panpipe; the second is labelled 'sistro' and represents a kind of tambourine. In all probability these drawings are original and were not inspired by an external source. The 'sampogna' corresponds strictly to Aaron's description; the 'sistro' – which for Aaron is a proto-triangle and not a tambourine – differs somewhat from it, but the difference may be due to a mistake on Ventura da Moro's part.

The number of Hieronymian instruments that Ventura da Moro drew is particularly striking. The only such instrument mentioned by Aaron is the 'choro' (q.v. above). Ventura da Moro rounds

Figure 5   Original drawings by Ventura da Moro

---

[74] According to Stradner, the position of the harp in Virdung's treatise may be due to a layout problem or to aesthetic considerations: all the instruments portrayed on sig. B ij[v] have their strings drawn horizontally (*Spielpraxis und Instrumentarium*, p. 192).

out his survey by reproducing eight of the eleven Hieronymian instruments illustrated by Virdung and Luscinius ('Tromba di Girollamo', 'fistula Hieronimi', 'chorus/choro', 'Cijthara Hieronijmi', 'Psalterium Decachordum', 'Timpanum Jheronimi', 'Cijmbalo de Hieronimo', 'Aliud Psalterium Decachordum').[75] Reinhold Hammerstein has shown that these instruments are not purely fictive objects; they exhibit more or less clear resemblances to instruments whose existence is attested, though in the letter to Dardanus they have a purely allegorical significance.[76]

In Virdung's treatise, the Hieronymian instruments are discussed after the normal instruments, as curiosities that no one has ever really seen or heard, and requiring rather to be understood in a spiritual sense.[77] Virdung states that he himself knows them only thanks to the illustrations in an autograph manuscript compiled by his master Johannes von Soest.[78] In contrast it is not clear that Virdung knew the text of the letter to Dardanus, which would explain the quite rudimentary nature of his comments.[79] For the same reason, unlike Aaron, he does not describe the 'chorus' as a bagpipe (cf. above, s.v. 'choro'), but as instrument with a mouthpiece and a bifurcated pipe in the middle. His picture of it, reproduced by Ventura da Moro, confirms this description: the central bulge in the instrument is not an air pocket, but two separate pipes (Figure 6).

The space allotted by Luscinius to describing the Hieronymian instruments is even more restricted than in Virdung. Although he

Figure 6   Chorus drawn by Ventura da Moro

---

[75] The instruments he omits are Alia Cythara Hieronymi (i), Alia Cythara Hieronymi (ii), Organum Hieronymi.

[76] Hammerstein, 'Instrumenta Hieronymi'.

[77] Virdung, *Musica getutscht* (Basle, 1511), sigs. C ij^v–C iii^r. The same thing had already been said in the letter to Dardanus (Hammerstein, 'Instrumenta Hieronymi', p. 120).

[78] Virdung, *Musica getutscht*, sig. C ij^v. The composer and theorist Johannes von Soest (1448–1506) was the founder of the Heidelberg *Hofkapelle*: see S. Keyl, s.v. 'Soest, Johannes (Steinwert) von', *New Grove II*, xxiii, 618–19.

[79] Stradner, *Spielpraxis und Instrumentarium*, p. 391; Meyer, *Sebastian Virdung, Musica getutscht*, p. 97.

reproduces the full set of illustrations in *Musica getutscht*, Luscinius merely states that the Hieronymian instruments are no longer in use and that he includes them only to satisfy the curious.[80]

Whereas Virdung and Luscinius clearly distinguish the Hieronymian instruments from musical instruments in use in their own day, Ventura da Moro juxtaposes instruments of both kinds according to simple associations of names. He draws the 'tromba di Girollamo' next to Aaron's remarks on the 'tromba', the 'fistula Hieronymi' next to that on the 'fistula', and so on. He does not append any explanation to his drawings; one may wonder whether he really read Luscinius' treatise, a question destined to remain unanswered.

CONCLUSION

The preceding pages show how three musical treatises fared with their readers: Isidore of Seville's 'De musica' in the hands Pietro Aaron, Aaron's *Toscanello* and Luscinius' *Musurgia* in those of Desiderio Ventura da Moro. Aaron's reading of Isidore bears witness to the gaps in his humanistic education, but also to his critical sense. Aaron is not content to translate Isidore in servile fashion. Though he cannot be considered a specialist in organology and instrumental music, he took the trouble to correct certain errors and adapt the text in the light of his knowledge. He did not hesitate to cite other authors – ancient and medieval – to broaden his ideas and refine his descriptions.

Ventura da Moro is a very different reader. His annotations in the *Toscanello* in the Bibliothèque Royale Albert Ier show a thorough reading, but at school level. It is striking that it should be one of the least original chapters of the *Toscanello* – based on a text almost a thousand years old, incessantly rehashed all through the Middle Ages – that affords him the most explicit display of his musical knowledge. In that display Ventura da Moro finds the opportunity for a comparison with a treatise that at first seems very different, Luscinius' *Musurgia*. From this work, in turn, he too draws chiefly on one of the more conventional passages, that devoted to the strange Hieronymian instruments.

[80] Luscinius, *Musurgia*, p. 28.

The passage of the *Toscanello* cited at the start of this article shows that Aaron intended his treatise for a public ignorant of Latin but anxious to learn musical notation and composition. Does Ventura da Moro match this description? Not really: his annotations reveal that he is as much a humanist as a practitioner. They are in no way original, but they show us what musical knowledge and interests might be found in a man of high education in the sixteenth century.

Université catholique de Louvain

APPENDIX

Comparison of Passages in Isidore of Seville and Pietro Aaron

Isidore of Seville, *Etymologiae*, ed. W. M. Lindsay (Oxford, 1911)[1]

Pietro Aaron, *Toscanello in musica* (Venice, 1529), book I, chapter 5

[Lib. III, cap. 19. De triformi musicae divisione.]

1. [1] Ad omnem autem sonum, quae materies cantilenarum est, triformem constat esse naturam. Prima est harmonica, quae ex vocum cantibus constat. Secunda organica, quae ex flatu consistit. Tertia rhythmica, quae pulsu digitorum numeros recipit. [2] Nam aut voce editur sonus, sicut per fauces, aut flatu, sicut per tubam vel tibiam, aut pulsu, sicut per citharam, aut per quodlibet aliud, quod percutiendo canorum est.

Ad ogni suono ilquale é materia de le cantilene, é manifesto la natura essere triforme. La prima é harmonica, laquale é composta di canti de le uoci. La seconda organica, laqual consiste di fiato. La terza rhythmica, laqual riceue gli numeri ne la percussione de gli diti. Impero che da la uoce si manda il suono, come per le fauci, cioé per la bocca, ouer per fiato: come per la tromba & piua, ouer per impulso: come per cythara, ouer per qualche altra cosa laqual percotendola é sonora.

[Lib. III, cap. 20. De prima divisione musicae quae Harmonica dicitur.]

2. [1] Prima divisio Musicae, quae harmonica dicitur, id est, modulatio vocis, pertinet ad comoedos, tragoedos, vel choros, vel ad omnes qui voce propria canunt. Haec ex animo et corpore motum facit, et ex motu sonum, ex quo colligitur Musica, quae in homine vox appellatur.

Per tanto harmonica si appartiene a comedie, tragedie, ouer chori, ouero a tutti quegli gli quali cantano con la prima uoce.

3. [2] Vox est aer spiritu verberatus, unde et verba sunt nuncupata. Proprie autem vox hominum est, seu inrationabilium animantium. Nam in aliis abusive non proprie

Voce é aere percosso dal spirito, dalqual son chiamate uerba, cioé le parole: propriamente la uoce é de gli huomini, ouer di animali irrationali: non propriamente il suono

---

[1] Lindsay's section numbers are given in square brackets.

27

sonitum vocem vocari, ut 'vox tubae infremuit', (Verg. *Aen.* 3. 556):

Fractasque a litore voces.

Nam proprium est ut litorei sonent scopuli, et (Verg. *Aen.* 9. 503):

At tuba terribilem sonitum procul aere canoro.

Harmonica est modulatio vocis et concordantia plurimorum sonorum, vel coaptatio.

4. [3] Symphonia est modulationis temperamentum ex gravi et acuto concordantibus sonis, sive in voce, sive in flatu, sive in pulsu. Per hanc quippe voces acutiores gravioresque concordant, ita ut quisquis ab ea dissonuerit, sensum auditus offendat. Cuius contraria est diaphonia, id est voces discrepantes vel dissonae.

5. [4] Euphonia est suavitas vocis. Haec et melos a suavitate et melle dicta. [5] Diastema est vocis spatium ex duobus vel pluribus sonis aptatum. [6] Diesis est spatia quaedam et deductiones modulandi atque vergentes de uno in altero sono. [7] Tonus est acuta enuntiatio vocis.

6. Est enim harmoniae differentia et quantitas, quae in vocis accentu vel tenore consistit: cuius genera in quindecim partibus musici dividerunt, ex quibus hyperlydius novissimus et acutissimus, hypodorius omnium gravissimus.

7. [8] Cantus est inflexio vocis, nam sonus directus est; praecedit autem sonus cantum. [9] Arsis est vocis elevatio, hoc est initium. Thesis elevatio, hoc est initium. Thesis

si dimanda uoce, come in quel luoco la uoce de la tromba fece fremito: et altroue le uoci rotte nel lito. Il suono si domanda uoce, impero che questo é il proprio: come gli scogli del lito suonano. Harmonia é modulatione di uoci, ouer coattatione di piu suoni.

Symphonia é temperamento di modulatione di graue & acuto, di suoni concordanti, o ne la uoce, o nel fiato: per questa symphonia certamente la uoce piu acuta o piu graue si concordano per tal modo, che ciascuno ilquale si discorda da quella, offende il senso del auditore: de laqual è contraria la dyasphonia, cioè la uoce discrepante, et dissonante.

Euphonia è suauita di uoce: questa appresso altri autori si domanda melos. Diastema è spatio di uoce di dui ouer piu suoni:

impero che la differenza del harmonia è quantita laqual consiste ne lo accento, ouer tenore de la uoce. Le generationi de laquale gli musici hanno diuiso in quindici parti, de lequali il primo si domanda hyperlydio: lultimo si domanda hypodorio di tutti grauissimo.

Canto è inflessione di uoce, ma il suono è diretto, & il suono procede [sic] il canto. Arsis è eleuatione di uoce. Thesis è positione di uoce.

28

vocis positio, hoc est finis.

8. [10] Suaves voces sunt subtiles et spissae, clarae atque acutae. Perspicuae voces sunt, quae longius protrahuntur, ita ut omnem inpleant continuo locum, sicut clangor tubarum. [11] Subtiles voces sunt, quibus non est spiritus, qualis est infantium, vel mulierum, vel aegrotantium, sicut in nervis. Quae enim subtilissimae cordae sunt, subtiles ac tenues sonos emittunt.

9. [12] Pingues sunt voces, quando spiritus multus simul egreditur, sicut virorum. Acuta vox tenuis, alta, sicut in cordis videmus. Dura vox est, quae violenter emittit sonos, sicut tonitruum, sicut incudis sonos, quotiens in durum malleus percutitur ferrum. [13] Aspera vox est rauca, et quae dispergitur per minutos et indissimiles pulsus. Caeca vox est, quae, mox emissa fuerit, conticescit, atque suffocata nequaquam longius producitur, sicut est in fictilibus.

10. Vinnola est vox mollis atque flexibilis. Et vinnola dicta a vinno, hoc est cincinno molliter flexo. [14] Perfecta autem vox est alta, suavis et clara: alta, ut in sublime sufficiat; clara, ut aures adinpleat; suavis, ut animos audientium blandiat. Si ex his aliquid defuerit, vox perfecta non est.

[Lib. III, cap. 21. De secunda divisione, quae organica dicitur.]

Soaue uoci sono sottile, & spesse, chiare, & acute. Voci perspicue sono quelle, lequali piu da lunge sono tirate, per tal modo che incontinente empiono, come il suono de le trombe. Voci sottile sono quelle, ne lequali non é spirito, come sono le uoci de gli fanciugli, ouer donne, o infermi: ouer come ne le chorde lequali per essere sottilissime rendono uoce sottile & tenue.

Voci pingue & grasse, sono quelle quando molto spirito esce fuora: come è la uoce de glihuomini. Voce acuta [è] sottile & alta, come uediamo ne le chorde. Voce dura é quella la quale uiolentemente manda fuora gli suoni, come il suono de gli troni & de le ancugini: qualunque uolta che il martello percuote nel duro ferro. Voce aspera & rauca, é quella laquale si disparge per minuti, & dissimili polsi. Voce cieca, é quella la quale subito che é mandata fuora, saccheta & tace soffocata, & piu da lunge non si produce: come é manifesto ne gi uasi di terra cotta.

Voce uinnola [è] molle & flexibile, é detta uinnola a uino, cioè a cicinno: quasi il ricciuolo mollemente ritorto. Voce perfetta, alta suaue & chiara: alta accio che in soblime sia sofficiente: suaue accio che gli animi de gli audienti accarezzi: chiara accio che empia gli orechi. Se di queste alcun manchera, non sara detta perfetta uoce.

11. [1] Secunda est divisio organica in his, quae spiritu reflante conpleta in sonum vocis animantur, ut sunt tubae, calami, fistulae, organa, pandoria, et his similia instrumenta.

12. [2] Organum vocabulum est generale vasorum omnium musicorum. Hoc autem, cui folles adhibentur, alio Graeci nomine appellant. Vt autem organum dicatur, magis ea vulgaris est Graecorum [?Latinarum[2]] consuetudo.

13. [3] Tuba primum a Tyrrhenis inventa, de quibus Vergilius (*Aen.* 8. 526):

Tyrrhenusque tubae mugire per aethera clangor.

Adhibebatur autem non solum in proeliis, sed in omnibus festis diebus propter laudis vel gaudii claritatem. Vnde et in Psalterio dicitur (81: 4): 'Canite in initio mensis tuba, in die insignis sollemnitatis vestrae.' Praeceptum enim fuerat Iudaeis ut in initio novae lunae tuba clangerent, quod etiam et hucusque faciunt.

14. [4] Tibias excogitatas in Phrygia ferunt: has diu quidem funeribus tantum adhibitas, mox et sacris gentilium. Tibias autem appellatas putant, quod primum de cervinis tibiis cruribusque hinnulorum fierent, deinde per abusionem ita coeptas vocari etiam quae non de cruribus ossibusque essent. Hinc et tibicen, quasi tibiarum cantus.

La seconda diuisione organica é in quelle cose, lequali sono compite di spirito reflante in suono de le uoci, che sono animate: come trombe, calami, organi, & altri simili istromenti.

Organo é uocabolo generale di tutti gli uasi musici: alquale si pone gli mantici: constituito ne la santa madre chiesa, in honore de lo onnipotente Iddio: & de la sua madre gloriosa.

La tromba prima fu ritrouata da gli Tyrheni, cioé da gli Toscani come Virgilio dice. Il suono de la toscana tromba muggiaua per laere: si usaua non solo ne le battaglie, ma in tutti gli di festiui per la chiarezza de le laudi, & de la allegrezza: per cio nel psalterio si dice, Cantate nel principio del mese con la tromba nel di nobile de la uostra solennita: perche era comandato a gli Giudei che in principio de la luna nuoua sonassino con la tromba: laqual cosa fanno anchora fin qui.

Le piue furno ritrouate in Phrygia: queste longo tempo si usauano solamente ne le sepulture de gli morti: & incontinente se usorno ne gli sacrificii de gentili. Tibie sono state nominate, perche prima de le tibie cioé de gli ossi del stinco di cerui o di grue si faceuano: di poi abusiue cosi cominciorno ad essere chiamate, & anchora al presente benche non si facciano di quegli

---

[2] According to Fontaine, 'Graecorum' is an ancient error (*op. cit.*, p. 433 n. 3). See above, n. 48.

15. [5] Calamus nomen est proprium arboris a calendo, id est fundendo voces vocatus. Fistulam quidam putant a Mercurio inventam, alii a Fauno, quem Graeci vocant Pan. Nonnulli eam ab Idi pastore Agrigentino ex Sicilia. [6] Fistula autem dicta, quod vocem emittat. Nam φῶς Graece vox, στόλια missa appellatur.

16. [7] Sambuca in musicis species est symphoniarum. Est enim genus ligni fragilis, unde tibiae conponuntur.

17. [8] Pandorius ab inventore vocatus. De quo Vergilius (*Ecl.* 2. 32):

Pan primus calamos cera coniungere plures

instituit, Pan curat ovis oviumque magistros.

Fuit enim apud gentiles deus pastoralis, qui primus dispares calamos ad cantum aptavit, et studiosa arte conposuit.

18.

ossi, non dimeno resta il nome: & di qui é deriuato tibicen: cioè colui il quale suona la tibia.

Calamo é canna laqual ha gli spatii fra nodi minuti, lunghi & dritti: ilqual essendo tutto concauo: ne hauendo punto di charta, ne di carne, é utilissimo (come scriue Plinio) a le sampogne. Et percio uien detto in greco syringa: che fistola significa in latino. Fu la sampogna inuention di Pan, iddio de pastori: ilqual non potendo goder uiua lamata nympha Syringa, essendo quella (come canta Ouidio) mutata in canne, per hauerla pur in compagnia, sette calami dispari colla cera aggiunse: & syringa da la nympha cioé sampogna chiamolla.

Sambuca in musica è specie di symphonia: & è una generatione di legno fragile, delquale si compongono anchora le tibie.

Pandura secondo Giulio polluce, è istromento trichordo ritrouato da gli popoli di Assyria. Martiano capella nel libro di musica lattribuisce al dio Pan.

Choro secondo san Girolamo è istromento musico di semplice pelle, composto con due canne di ferro: per la prima de quali si manda il fiato dentro: per laltra esce fuora la uoce.

[Lib. III, cap. 22. De tertia divisione, quae rhythmica nuncupatur.]

19. [1] Tertia est divisio rhythmica, pertinens ad nervos et pulsum, cui dantur species cithararum diversarum, tympanum quoque, cymbalum, sistrum, acetabula aenea et argentea, vel alia quae metallico rigore percussa reddunt cum suavitate tinnitum et cetera huiuscemodi.

La terza chiamata rithmica é quella, laquale appartiene a gli nerui & polsi a laquale si danno le specie uarie, cioé cithare, psalterii, tamburo, sistro, acettabuli di rame, & di argento, ouero altri istromenti: gli quali con rigore metallico percossi rispondono con suauita.

20. [2] Citharae ac psalterii repertor Tubal, ut praedictum est, perhibetur. Iuxta opinionem autem Graecorum citharae usus repertus fuisse ab Apolline creditur. Forma citharae initio similis fuisse traditur pectori humano, quo uti vox a pectore, ita ex ipsa cantus ederetur, appellatamque eadem de causa. Nam pectus Dorica lingua κιθάρα vocari.

Tubal secondo gli Hebrei fu inuentore de la cithara & del psalterio: secondo la oppenione de gli Greci. Luso de la cithara fu ritrouato da Apolline: la forma della cithera da principio fu simile al petto humano: dal quale cosi come la uoce procede, cosi da quella procede il canto: & per questa cagione é stata domandata cithera: perche il petto secondo la lingua dorica, si domanda cithera.

21. [3] Paulatim autem plures eius species extiterunt, ut psalteria, lyrae, barbitae, phoenices et pectides, et quae dicuntur Indicae, et feriuntur a duobus simul. Item aliae atque aliae, et quadrata forma vel trigonali. [4] Chordarum etiam numerus multiplicatus, et conmutatum genus. Veteres autem citharam fidiculam vel fidicem nominaverunt, quia tam concinunt inter se chordae eius, quam bene conveniat inter quos fides sit.

Sono state piu specie di cithare: come psalterii, lyre, barbyti, phenici, & pettidi: & quelle, le quali sono dette indice, sono sonate insieme da dui. Anchora sono alcune altre di forma quadrata, o triangolare. Il numero de le chorde é moltiplicato: & la generatione è commutata.

22. Antiqua autem cithara septemchordis erat. Vnde et Vergilius (*Aen.* 6. 646):

Septem discrimina vocum.

[5] Discrimina autem ideo, quod

Lantica cithera era di chorde sette come Virgilio dice: sette differenze di uoci: & impero dice differenti, perche niuna chorda rende simile suono a la chorda uicina. Per tanto

nulla chorda vicinae chordae simi-
lem sonum reddat. Sed ideo septem
chordae, vel quia totam vocem
implent, vel quia septem motibus
sonat caelum.

23. [6] Chordas autem dictas a
corde, quia sicut pulsus est cordis
in pectore, ita pulsus chordae in
cithara. Has primus Mercurius
excogitavit, idemque prior in nervos sonum strinxit.

24. [7] Psalterium, quod vulgo canticum dicitur, a psallendo nomina-
tum, quod ad eius vocem chorus
consonando respondeat. Est autem
similitudo citharae barbaricae in
modum Δ literae; sed psalterii et
citharae haec differentia est, quod
psalterium lignum illud concavum,
unde sonus redditur, superius
habet et deorsum feriuntur chordae, et desuper sonant. Cithara
vero concavitatem ligni inferius
habet. Psalterium autem Hebraei
decachordon usi sunt propter
numerum Decalogi legis.

25. [8] Lyra dicta ἀπὸ τοῦ
ληρεῖν,[3] id est a varietate vocum,
quod diversos sonos efficiat.

26. Lyram primum a Mercurio
inventam fuisse dicunt, hoc modo.
Cum regrediens Nilus in suos mea-
tus varia in campis reliquisset ani-

dice sette chorde: ouer perche sette
chorde adempiono tutta la uoce:
ouero perche il cielo suona col
mouimento di sette pianeti.

Chorde sono dette à corde, perche
cosi come il polso del cuore è nel
petto: cosi il polso de la chorda é ne
la cithera. Mercurio fu il primo inuentore de le chorde: & fu il primo
che strinse il suono ne le chorde &
nerui.

Psalterio il quale dal uolgo si
domanda cantico: é nominato da
psallo, cioé canto: perche a la uoce
di quello il choro consonando
risponde.

La lyra si chiama secondo alcuni
apò tu lirin, cioé dalla uarieta de le
uoci: perche fa diuersi suoni: secondo altri è detta da lyrin, cioè
cantare. Gli latini la chiamano
fidicula, ouer fide, perche tanto
consuonano tra se le chorde di
quella, quanto ben si accordano gli
huomini: tra i quali è fede.

La lyra prima fu trouata da
Mercurio in questo modo.
Ritornando il Nilo dentro da le sue
riue, & hauendo lasciato uarii ani-

---

[3] For ληρεῖν see above, n. 26.

malia, relicta etiam testudo est. Quae cum putrefacta esset, et nervi eius remansissent extenti intra corium, percussa a Mercurio sonitum dedit; ad cuius speciem Mercurius lyram fecit et Orpheo tradidit, qui eius rei maxime erat studiosus. [9] Vnde existimatur eadem arte non feras tantum, sed et saxa atque silvas cantus modulatione adplicuisse. Hanc musici propter studii amorem et carminis laudem etiam inter sidera suarum fabularum conmentis conlocatam esse finxerunt.

27. Tympanum est pellis vel corium ligno ex una parte extentum. Est enim pars media symphoniae in similitudinem cribri. [10] Tympanum autem dictum quod medium est, unde et margaritum medium tympanum dicitur; et ipsud, ut symphonia, ad virgulam percutitur.

28. [11] Cymbala acitabula quaedam sunt, quae percussa invicem se tangunt et faciunt sonum. Dicta autem cymbala, quia cum ballematia simul percutiuntur; cum enim Graeci dicunt σύν, βαλά ballematia.

29. [12] Sistrum ab inventrice vocatum. Isis enim regina Aegyptiorum id genus invenisse probatur. Iuvenalis (13. 93):

> Isis et irato feriat mea lumina
> sistro.

Inde et hoc mulieres percutiunt, quia inventrix huius generis mulier. Vnde et apud Amazonas sistro ad bellum feminarum exercitus vocabatur.

30. [13] Tintinabulum de sono

---

mali ne gli campi, lascio anchora una testuggine, la quale essendo putrefatta & gli nerui suoi rimasti distesi tra il corio: percossa da Mercurio, dette il suono: a similitudine de laquale Mercurio fece la lyra: & dettela ad Orpheo.

Tympano, cioè il tamburo, è pelle ouer corio disteso & appiccato a legno: & è mezza parte di symphonia. Tympano é detto da typto, cioé percuoto: perche come symphonia si percuote con una bacchetta.

Cymbali & accettabuli, sono alcuni istromenti gli quali percossi insieme, si toccano & fanno suono. Sono detti cymbali, perche con balematia insieme si percuotono: cosi gli Greci dicono cymbali, ballematia.

Sistro è nominato da sio, cioè conmuouo: é sonaglio di rame, per una stretta lama del quale retorta a modo di cintura alcune girelle trapassate per mezo: ogni uolta che le braccia lo scrollano, rendono uno suono stridolo. Pensano alcuni che non sia diuerso dal cymbalo, che le fanciulle a Firenze usano ne gli loro balli. Era usitato ne gli sacrificii disis dea de gli Egittii.

Tintinabulo anchora é istromento

vocis nomen habet, sicut [et] plausus manuum, stridor valvarum.

31.

32. [14] Symphonia vulgo appellatur lignum cavum ex utraque parte pelle extenta, quam virgulis hinc et inde musici feriunt, fitque in ea ex concordia gravis et acuti suavissimus cantus.

di rame: col quale la gente a hora di lauare, era chiamata al bagno. Fu detto dal suono, che fa tin tin: onde tintinnire é uerbo che pertiene al suono di tutti gli metagli: & fa conto che era come la campanella che chiama il popolo alla chiesa.

Et perche parlando del tamburo hauem fatto mentione de la symphonia, quella non è sorte di organo, come alcuni latini malamente pensano: ma un choro che cantano insieme in laude diddio: & questo si significa per il uocabolo: perche symphonia si exprime in latino consonanza deriuata da syn: cioè insieme, & phoni uoce: non dimeno al tempo nostro dal uolgo symphonia si domanda un legno cauo da tutte due le parti, con una pelle distesa: la qual gli musici percuotono di qua & di la con le bacchette: & si fa in quella da la concordanza del graue, & de lo acuto suauissimo canto.

Early Music History (2002) *Volume 21.* © *Cambridge University Press*
DOI:10.1017/S0261127902002024 Printed in the United Kingdom

GABRIELA ILNITCHI

MUSICA MUNDANA, ARISTOTELIAN NATURAL PHILOSOPHY AND PTOLEMAIC ASTRONOMY

Emanating from a cosmos ordered according to Pythagorean and Neoplatonic principles, the Boethian *musica mundana* is the type of music that 'is discernible especially in those things which are observed in heaven itself or in the combination of elements or the diversity of seasons'.[1] At the core of this recurring medieval topos stands 'a fixed sequence of modulation [that] cannot be separated from this celestial revolution', one most often rendered in medieval writings as the 'music of the spheres' (*musica spherarum*).[2] In the Pythagorean and Neoplatonic cosmological traditions, long established by the time Boethius wrote his *De institutione musica*, the music of the spheres is just one possible manifestation of the concept of world harmony. It pertains to a universe in which musical and cosmic structures express the same mathematical ratios, each of the planets produces a distinctive sound in its revolution and the combination of these sounds themselves most often forms a well-defined musical scale. Although the Neoplatonic world harmony continued to function in medieval cosmology as the fundamental conceptual premise, the notion of the music of the spheres, despite its popularity among medieval writers, was generally treated neither at any significant length nor in an innovative

This article is an expanded version of papers read in 1998 at the annual meeting of the Medieval Academy of America held in Stanford, California, and at the International Medieval Congress in Leeds. I should like to thank Edward Roesner, Stanley Boorman, Robert Kendrick and the two anonymous readers for their valuable comments and suggestions. All translations are my own, unless noted otherwise.

[1] 'Et primum ea, quae est mundana, in his maxime perspicienda est, quae in ipso caelo vel compage elementorum vel temporum varietate visuntur.' Boethius, *De institutione musica libri quinque*, ed. G. Friedlein (Leipzig, 1867), I.2, p. 187.23–6. English translation in C. Bower, *Fundamentals of Music* (New Haven and London, 1989), p. 9.
[2] 'Unde non potest ab hac caelesti vertigine ratus ordo modulationis absistere.' *De institutione musica* I.2, p. 188.6–7; *Fundamentals*, p. 9.

fashion. Quite exceptional in this respect is the treatise that forms the subject of the present study, a text beginning *Desiderio tuo fili carissime gratuito condescenderem* and attributed to an anonymous bishop in the late thirteenth-century manuscript miscellany now in the Biblioteca Apostolica Vaticana (Barb. lat. 283, fols. 37^r–42^v) but probably coming from a Franciscan convent in Siena. This seldom considered work affords a remarkable and special insight into the ways in which old and new ideas converged, intermingled and coexisted in the dynamic and sometimes volatile cross-currents of medieval scholarship.

In his edition of the treatise, Joseph Smits van Waesberghe considered it to be the work of Adalbold, bishop of Utrecht between 1010 and 1026.[3] His attribution relied primarily upon what he perceived to be conceptual and stylistic similarities between the text of the treatise and other works that can be attributed to Adalbold with a much higher degree of certitude, and among which Adalbold's commentary on Boethius' *O qui perpetua* occupied a central position.[4] Given the extent to which matters of style can become a subject for debate, I suggest that, for the time being and for dating purposes alone, we should look elsewhere for somewhat firmer grounds.

Evidence of a music-theoretical nature, for example, supports a date for the composition of the Barberini treatise later than 1026, the year of Adalbold of Utrecht's death. The author of the text refers to a gamut of nineteen pitches that are in turn divided into eight *graves*, seven *acutae* and four *superacutae*; the terseness of his statement and the lack of any surrounding explicatory material suggests that he must have been under the assumption that such a gamut was familiar to his readers.[5] To my knowledge, a nine-

---

[3] *Adalboldi Episcopi Ultraiectensis Epistola cum tractatu de musica instrumentali humanaque ac mundana*, ed. J. Smits van Waesberghe (Divitiae Musicae Artis A.II; Buren, 1981). In his review of the edition, Roger Bragard provides useful French translations of numerous passages in the treatise and a good summary of its contents; he does not contest, however, Smits van Waesberghe's attribution, dating or analysis of the text; see R. Bragard, 'Joseph Smits van Waesberghe et les *Divitiae musicae artis*', *Revue belge de musicologie*, 41 (1987), pp. 9–16. No other studies are dedicated to this treatise.

[4] The most recent edition of this commentary on *O qui perpetua*, which accepts Adalbold's authorship, appears in *Serta mediaevalia: Textus varii saeculorum X–XIII in unum collecti*, ed. R. B. C. Huygens (Corpus Christianorum, Continuatio Mediaevalis 171; Turnhout, 2000), pp. 121–40.

[5] *Epistola cum tractatu*, p. 22.1.

teen-pitch gamut with such a division does not appear in any other music-theoretical work prior to Guido of Arezzo's *Micrologus*, composed after 1026, and does not enter the mainstream of music-theoretical discourse until the twelfth century.[6] In addition, the Barberini author does not obtain the pitches of the gamut by means of ratios alone. While the 'primary consonances' (diapason, diapente and diatessaron) emerge from the usual duple, sesquialtera and sesquitertia ratios alone, the 'secondary consonances' (the tonus, ditonus, semitonus and semiditonus) are expressed by a combination of integrals and fractions that are the mathematical equivalent of the standard Pythagorean ratios. For example, the ditone is calculated thus: 'let two strings of equal dimensions and material be stretched, one by an eight-pound, the other by a nine-pound weight: there results the tone. Let a third string be added and stretched by ten pounds and one eighth: thus there emerges another tone. Between the first and the third string, therefore, there is a ditone.'[7] The Barberini author's use of a mixed

---

[6] For the most recent discussion pertaining to the dating of Guido's *Micrologus* see *Guido d'Arezzo's Regulae rithmice, Prologus in Antiphonarium, and Epistola ad Michahelem: A Critical Text and Translation*, ed. Dolores Pesce (Musicological Studies, 73; Ottawa, 1999), p. 1. The *graves, acutae* and *superacutae* are the division of the gamut from Γ to *aa* as it appears in the *Dialogus in musica* (ed. Martin Gerbert in *Scriptores ecclesiastici de musica sacra* (Saint-Blaise, 1784), i, pp. 253b–254a and 265b); the divisions are maintained but the gamut was expanded by Guido in the *Micrologus* to *dd* (ed. J. Smits van Waesberghe (Corpus scriptorum de musica, 4; Rome, 1955), pp. 93–5); see K.-J. Sachs, 'Musikalische Elementarlehre', in *Rezeption des antiken Fachs im Mittelalter* (Geschichte der Musiktheorie, 3, ed. F. Zaminer; Darmstadt, 1990), pp. 143–4. The Barberini author further associates the nineteen-pitch gamut with the 'sescupla' ratio (6:1), where 6 is the first perfect number: '. . . quod pondus chordae primae per senarium multiplicatum facit pondus chordae postremae, cum senarius numerum perfectorum numerorum primus occurat'. *Epistola cum tractatu*, p. 20.24. A perfect number is one whose sum of factors is equal to it; 6 = 1 + 2 + 3. A search in the TML database indicates that such associations are rather rare and do not occur in other works until the thirteenth and fourteenth centuries, more specifically in the works of Johannes de Grocheio and Johannes de Muris, among others. The entire segment on the *musica instrumentalis* in the Barberini text rightly awaits an in-depth study.

[7] 'Exemplum: tendantur duae chordae aequales et similes, una octo libris, alia novem: proveniet tonus. Addatur tertia chorda, et tendatur decem libris et earum octava unius; sic proveniet iterum tonus. Igitur inter primam chordam et tertiam fiet ditonus.' *Epistola cum tractatu*, p. 18.11–12. The Barberini author also provides the equivalent in ratios; see p. 19.13–14. The whole first octave is expressed by the following series: 8 . 9 . 10⅛ . 10 . 12 . 13½ . 14¾₆. 16; to obtain the pitches in the second octave, just double the weight associated with each one of the first initial strings, for all intents and purposes, ad infinitum; the nineteenth string is represented by 48 and, therefore, the ratio between the first and the nineteenth pitch of the gamut is 6:1. It should be noted, however, that the arabic numerals do not appear in the main text, but as marginalia in a later hand; the text, nevertheless, explicates the numbers and fractions in words.

combination of integers and fractions as an alternative to the Pythagorean ratios is quite unusual, certainly for the beginning of the eleventh century. This procedure, however, seems to have had some currency in the early fourteenth century, at the time that Jacques of Liège wrote his *Speculum musicae*.[8]

The present essay will put forth evidence that pertains to the cosmological and philosophical foundations of the Barberini author's treatment of the Boethian *musica mundana* and suggests that the treatise originated not in the intellectual environment of the eleventh century but rather in that of the thirteenth. For the time being, the author remains a bishop: the attribution 'Anonymi Ep[iscop]i tractatus de Musica' appears in the manuscript, albeit in a later hand, and was probably prompted by one of the author's own remarks: 'summoned away from study and prevented by pastoral duties'.[9] For all intents and purposes, however, the bishop remains anonymous.

The treatise as a whole is concerned with the three Boethian categories of *musica*: *instrumentalis*, *humana* and *mundana*.[10] According to the bishop, the study of this threefold *musica* in its quadrivial context prepares us 'to comprehend the incomprehensible'; it is in itself an epistemological continuum, a journey that takes us from *musica instrumentalis* to *musica humana* – which teach us how to obtain agreeable (instrumental) sounds and concordant (vocal) pitches, respectively – and ultimately to *musica mundana*, which 'surpasses by far all [other] disciplines', is the 'glory of philosophers' and makes one 'familiar with, and cognisant of, the divine plan'.[11]

The present essay concerns primarily the section dealing with *musica mundana*. In this part of the treatise, the bishop discusses three topics that are by and large standard in the Neoplatonic literature on the subject: the production of sound by the moving

---

[8] *Speculum musicae*, ed. R. Bragard (Corpus scriptorum de musica, 3; Rome, 1961), ii, p. 144.

[9] *Epistola cum tractatu*, p. 13.12.

[10] Boethius, *De institutione musica* I.2, pp. 187–9.

[11] 'Musica vero docet secundum proportionem ponderum comprehendere incomprehensibilia. Sunt enim tres species musicae: mundana, humana, instrumentalis. Instrumentalis docet invenire sonos delectabiles; humana: voces concordes. Mundana musica longe supereminet omnibus scientiis. Haec enim est deliciosa scientia. Haec: philosophorum gloria. Haec facit familiarem et conscium divini consilii.' *Epistola cum tractatu*, p. 14.3–5.

celestial bodies, the methods for calculating the specific pitches produced by the planets in their revolution, and the cosmic and musical proportions of those sounds. His treatment of each topic is unusual, however. As we shall see, his text manifests a broad spectrum of philosophical dispositions that inform not a static but a thoroughly dynamic model of the harmony of the spheres that is quite exceptional in musical cosmology prior to the Renaissance. His firm adherence to a Neoplatonic sounding universe notwithstanding, the bishop is dependent on Aristotelian natural philosophy, and he weaves into his discussion notions stemming from Aristotle's *De anima, Physica* and *Meteorologica*. Furthermore, his interpretation of the Boethian *musica mundana* develops on cosmological grounds derived not from theories advocating a concentric universe, but instead from the Ptolemaic system of eccentrics and epicycles current in the thirteenth century. The author thus reconciles traditions that on the surface appear to be conceptually contradictory: the Neoplatonic notion of the harmony of the spheres, Aristotelian natural philosophy and Ptolemaic cosmological models.

I. THE NEOPLATONIC FRAMEWORK

Written in epistolary form and style, the beginning of the Barberini treatise provides some insight into the author's disposition towards the subject of celestial music. The general narrative is internally consistent overall, and some of the personal details it includes appear to ring true rather than being mere rhetorical devices. The bishop warns his addressee that embarking on an investigation into *musica mundana* is a difficult enterprise, and that in his particular case this difficulty arises from both objective and subjective factors. He maintains that knowledge of the subject is fragmentary, since none of the earlier philosophers undertook the task of writing a treatise entirely devoted to *musica mundana*. Some even confessed their lack of competence in the subject, and most quoted from each other's works.[12] Furthermore, in a passage heavy

---

[12] 'De dulcedine mundanae musicae libemus aliquid modicum, exempli causa tantummodo, quandoquidem de ea nihil perfectum habemus. De ea namque tractatum facere nullus adhuc philosophorum praesumpsit. Fatebantur enim se nescire; sed singuli passim per diversos tractatus quippiam modicum mutue coronati sunt'. *Ibid.,* p. 23.1.

with autobiographical overtones, the bishop accuses some of his contemporaries of having hindered a genuine dialogue on the subject. His specific targets would seem to be the radical empiricists of the day, those thinkers adhering to philosophical positions that condoned only the kind of knowledge grounded in sensory experience, and then only in so far as it pertained to the terrestrial realm:

> I lectured not upon *musica*, as you say, but upon that raw and formless material for music, which formerly, as it were a kind of theme for debate on [celestial] motions, I meant – for me and not the others – to condemn to silence. I did so lest I should appear to undertake with boasting arrogance that which seems altogether impossible to those who are less subtle in their considerations [and] who deem probable only that which their bleary sight can contemplate up close. They marvel, they even mock with laughing declamations (the notion) that anyone should venture to measure the course of the planets, the magnitude of the [celestial] orbs and their distances from earth. Since they doubt whether, with the keenness of a sharper intellect, one can investigate those things subject to the senses [i.e. the planetary measurements], with what stupid guffaws they will laugh at the inquiry into those that escape the senses, especially the celestial music, or at anyone willing to undertake it.[13]

Summoned away from his studies and prevented by his pastoral duties from completing what he had started,[14] it is only now, in his old age and at the request of his younger disciple, that he finds the opportunity to write down some of his thoughts on the heavenly music. The culmination of long musing on the subject, his enterprise accords with the non-empirical philosophical approach, for it aims to 'serve the common good of others, whose finer insight unravels that which holds the heavenly bodies together and, with a kind of divinely acute ability, measures the high heavens, and deems those things that are subject to the senses to be relatively unworthy of study'.[15]

---

[13] 'Praelegi itaque non musicam, ut dicis, sed rudem illam et informem musicae materiam, quam olim mihi non aliis quasi quoddam thema proposui de motibus disputandi silentio damnare, ne viderer aliquid ex iactantiae supercilio promittere, quod quibusdam minus subtiliter intuentibus, omnino videtur impossibile, qui hoc solum probabile iudicant, quod sua potest lippitudo com(m)inus intueri. Mirantur enim, immo subsan(n)ant, et ridiculose declamant, quempiam planetarum cursus orbesque quantitates et a terra distantias audere metiri. Si igitur ea quae sensui subiecta sunt, acutioris ingenii subtilitate perpendi posse diffidunt: quo stupore, quo cachinno de his quae sensus effugiunt et maxime de musicae caelestis inquisitione vel aliquem agere velle ridebunt?' *Ibid.*, p. 12.5–7.

[14] 'A studiis etenim evocatus et pastorali cura praeventus, ut nosti, quod inceperam complere non potui.' *Ibid.*, p. 13.12.

[15] 'Sed ne tamen illorum qui terrena tantum sapiunt, videar magis sales effugere quam communi aliorum utilitati deservire, quorum subtilior acies superum conexa penetrat et divinae quodam subtilitatis ingenio caeli metitur ardua et subiacentia sensui, quasi suo reputat indigna studio.' *Ibid.*, p. 12.8 (punctuation altered).

The bishop's general rhetoric may very well derive from a desire to heighten the significance of his own work, and some of his auto-biographical reminiscences may prove to be too generic to serve as evidence for a precise positioning of the treatise in the larger intellectual currents of the time. This cautionary note notwith-standing, there emerge from his remarks manifestations of two opposing contemporaneous epistemological stances, one relying exclusively upon sensory perception, the other minimising its relevance.[16] As far as the subject of *musica mundana* is concerned, they can be summarised as follows: (1) the impossibility of being experienced by the senses renders the notion of *musica mundana* preposterous and its investigation foolish; and (2) the sensory implications are immaterial, for the subtleties of *musica mundana* are conceptual and of a divine nature, and only an investigation into the cosmic order and its underlying principles can account for it.

The presence in one text of two contemporaneous philosophical camps of unlike mind regarding the music of the spheres suggests that the bishop wrote his treatise at a time when the uncondi-tional acceptance of the Neoplatonic notion of the music of the spheres had begun to wane. It was not until the emergence of new philosophical and scientific paradigms in the thirteenth and four-teenth centuries, however, that medieval scholars began to ques-tion this particular understanding of the Boethian *musica humana*. Even though the notion of world harmony remained unchallenged as a philosophical and theological concept, the gradual assimila-tion during the thirteenth century of Aristotelian natural philos-ophy and of Greco-Arabic astronomy into Latin cosmological models made it increasingly hard for the literal interpretation of the *musica spherarum* to maintain itself.

As is well known, the most authoritative challenge came with the introduction to the West of the Latin translation of Aristotle's *De caelo* sometime in the late twelfth century. *De caelo*, the only cosmological treatise Aristotle wrote, was a powerful influence in

---

[16] In general terms, the situation appears to be similar to the late twelfth-century con-troversy between *medici* and *astrologi* to which Hermann of Carinthia bears witness, the *medici* restricting their inquiries to qualitative and perceptible events, the *astrologi* attempting to explain the physical facts in reference to the whole cosmos. Summarised in Hermann of Carinthia, *De essentiis: A Critical Edition with Translation and Commentary*, ed. C. Burnett (Texte zur Geistgeschichte des Mittelalters, 15; Leiden, 1982), pp. 22–5.

cosmological thought well into the seventeenth century, as witnessed by the number of commentaries and questions that it elicited. It also became the most authoritative refutation of the Pythagorean and Neoplatonic claim that the planets produce actual sound in their movements. After a brief summary of the Pythagorean claim, Aristotle maintains that:

melodious and poetical as the [Pythagorean] theory is, it cannot be true on account of the facts. There is not only the absurdity of our hearing nothing, the grounds of which they try to remove, but also the fact that no effect other than sensitive is produced upon us. Excessive noises, we know, shatter the solid bodies even of inanimate things; the noise of thunder, for instance, splits rocks and the strongest of bodies. But if the moving bodies are so great, and the sound which penetrates to us is proportionate to their size, that sound must need reach us in an intensity many times that of thunder, and the force of its action must be immense. Indeed the reason why we do not hear and show in our bodies none of the effects of violent force is easily given: it is that there is no noise.[17]

The authority of Boethius and his Neoplatonic *musica mundana* and the authority of the soundless cosmos of the Philosopher were coming face to face, and from the thirteenth century onwards scholars had to chose sides, negotiate between two contradictory views, or find suitable (or at least acceptable) compromises. The consequences this fascinating encounter had on the development of speculative musical thought of the later Middle Ages in general and on the treatment of *musica mundana* in particular are yet to be adequately examined. In the most comprehensive study to date on the fortunes of the Boethian *musica mundana* in the Middle Ages and Renaissance, James Haar suggested that by the mid-thirteenth century the Philosopher's stance was already at the root of some radical views.[18] Vincent of Beauvais maintained in his *Speculum naturale* that *musica mundana* must be taken in a metaphorical sense lest it perpetuate dangerous astrological tendencies.[19] In *Opus ter-*

---

[17] Aristotle, *On the Heavens*, trans. J. L. Stocks, in *The Complete Works of Aristotle: The Revised Oxford Translation*, ed. J. Barnes (Princeton, 1984), II.9 (290^{b}30–291^{a}6), p. 479. All other references are taken from Barnes's edition unless otherwise noted.

[18] J. Haar, '*Musica mundana*: Variations on a Pythagorean Theme' (Ph.D. diss., Harvard University, 1960), pp. 299–313.

[19] 'The above opinion on the harmony of the heavens is to be rejected, lest that ancient error of superstition concerning the cult of the celestial stars . . . having not only life, sense and motion, but even something of divinity in them seem to have a place even among us' ('Ob hoc autem praecipue praedicta sententia de coelorum concentu respuitur, ne antiquus ille superstitionis error de cultu coelestium syderum, . . . tamquam non solum vitam et sensum ac motum, sed etiam numinis aliquid in se habentium, apud nos etiam locum habere videatur'). Vincent of Beauvais, *Speculum naturale* XV, xxxii, in

tium, Roger Bacon pointed out that the theory persisted among the unlearned, and that Boethius, who merely recounted it, did not approve of it; Bacon himself rejected it altogether and declared that 'nulla est musica mundana'.[20] Furthermore, a significant number of music treatises from the thirteenth and fourteenth centuries wholly or partially embraced the Aristotelian refutation, in spite of their traditional dependence on Boethius.[21]

The anonymous bishop positions himself strongly in the Neoplatonic camp. As we have seen, he wrote his treatise despite possible ridicule from radical empiricists, who rejected the music of the spheres based upon the lack of sensory experience, a type of argument very much indebted to the Aristotelian position on the subject. Moreover, the bishop openly embraces the Neoplatonic perspective by accepting its basic premises as true: the celestial spheres produce sound in their movement, and those sounds effect musical harmony.[22]

A committed Aristotelian would argue that the bishop, like other Neoplatonists, offers no systematic demonstration of the presence of sound in the cosmos, and that the only rationales that he provides stem from empirical analogies with the sublunar world. He claims that it is obvious that planets must produce sound in their movement, as long as much smaller bodies in the sublunar world, such as birds, arrows, stones and rods, produce sound while moving through the air. At first, the source of this statement seems to be Macrobius' commentary on *Somnium Scipionis*.[23] Like Macrobius, the bishop maintains that planets produce sound in their rapid orbital movement in a manner similar to that of a rod

Bibliotheca mundi seu venerabilis viri Vincentii Burgundi ex Ordine Praedicatorum, episcopi Bellovacensis, Speculum Quadruplex: naturale, doctrinale, morale, historiale (Douai, 1624), i, p. 1112, col. 2. English translation in Haar, '*Musica mundana*', p. 306.

[20] '... nulla est musica mundana, licet secundum opinionem antiquorum Pythagoricorum duravit haec opinio apud vulgum ... Et ideo, quia Boetius fecit mentionem de ea in sua Musica, hoc non est nisi secundum opinionem vulgi recitando.' Roger Bacon, *Opera quaedam hactenus inedita*, ed. J. S. Brewer (London, 1859; repr. London, 1965), i, *Opus tertium*, p. 230.

[21] Haar, '*Musica mundana*', pp. 309–13.

[22] 'It came to mind what the philosophers said that the celestial bodies render sound in their motion and, even more importantly, that they produce musical harmony. This sounds convincing ...'. ('Subiit namque, quod dixerunt philosophi, superiora corpora suis motibus sonum reddere et, quod maius est, musicam harmoniam efficere. Hoc mihi persuadet ...'). *Epistola cum tractatu*, p. 24.15.

[23] *Commentarii in Somnium Scipionis*, ed. J. Willis (Bibliotheca scriptorum Graecorum et Romanorum teubneriana; Leipzig, 1970), 2.4.2–5, pp. 107–8.

whisked through the air: the faster they move the higher the pitch and vice versa. The bishop omits, however, the other two modes of sound production to which Macrobius refers in the same passage, vibrating strings and air columns in pipes. Instead, he generates a set of variants of the 'whisked rod' example, bringing in birds, arrows and stones that move through the air.

Upon more careful examination, however, the bishop's examples more likely relate to later medieval accounts of the Aristotelian modes of sound production, particularly as they appear in commentaries on Aristotle's *De anima* II.8, than to the passage in Macrobius.[24] Aristotle's text is devoted to a whole range of issues pertaining to sound production as well as to perception. Sound is produced when two bodies strike each other or when one body strikes another with a sudden sharp blow and air is violently expelled from between them.[25] A modification of the standard Aristotelian model appears in Averroes' commentary on *De anima*, where he maintains that when air is struck by a whip it acts both as the struck body and the expelled air, an example that was subsequently adopted by several Latin commentators, Albertus Magnus among them.[26] In theory, this modified model can be extended to cover other kinds of objects as well, for regardless of the nature of the object that moves through the air, the whiplash effect remains the same. The bishop may have ultimately con-

---

[24] The best study to date on the impact of Aristotle's *De anima* on medieval concepts of sound is M. Wittman, *Vox atque sonus: Studien zur Rezeption der Aristotelische Schrift 'De Anima' und ihre Bedeutung für die Musiktheorie*, 2 vols. (Pfaffenweiler, 1987); the second volume contains an edition of twelve commentaries on *De anima* II.8 from the mid-thirteenth to the mid-sixteenth century. For the role that Aristotelian natural philosophy had in general on the development of music-theoretical discourse and on the notational procedures of the later Middle Ages, see Dorit Esther Tanay, *Noting Music, Making Culture: The Intellectual Context of Rhythmic Notation, 1250–1400* (Neuhausen–Stuttgart, 1999).

[25] '. . . sed oportet firmorum fieri percussionem ad invicem et ad aera. Hoc autem fit, cum permaneat percussus aer et non solvatur. Unde si velociter et fortiter percutiatur, sonat; oportet enim pertingere motum rapientis fracturam aeris . . .'. I follow here the Latin translation of James of Venice printed at the bottom of the page in *De anima*, ed. C. Stroick, in Albertus Magnus, *Opera omnia*, ed. B. Greyer, vol. 7, pt. 1 (Aschendorf, 1968), p. 125.

[26] '. . . accidit quod ea que sunt velocis motus faciunt in aere sonum licet non percutiunt aliud, ut motus corrigie in aere'. Averroes, *Commentarium magnum in Aristotelis De anima libros* II.9, ed. F. S. Crawford (Cambridge, Mass., 1953), p. 250. See also Albertus Magnus, *De anima*, 2.3.18, p. 125. A detailed discussion of Aristotelian modes of sound production and perception appears in C. Burnett, 'Sound and its Perception in the Middle Ages', in C. Burnett, M. Fend and P. Gouk (eds), *The Second Sense: Studies in Hearing and Musical Judgement from Antiquity to the Seventeenth Century* (London, 1991), pp. 43–69; both Averroes and Albertus Magnus are mentioned on p. 52.

ceived of birds, stones and arrows producing sound in their movement through the air for reasons that are as Aristotelian as those of Averroes's whip.

Therefore, even when considered separately, outside the larger context of the bishop's treatise these sublunar sounds are likely to reflect Aristotelian models of sound production. When taken in conjunction with information the bishop provides in another passage in the treatise, this likelihood increases significantly. The passage in question occurs in the section devoted to the *musica instrumentalis*. Here, the bishop states:

> It should be noted too that a less malleable metal produces a more powerful sound; tin is thus more sonorous than lead; silver and gold more so than tin; copper is the more sonorous of them, the red copper more so than the white; glass is more sonorous than copper. In the case of metals, the closer they are to average solidity, the more agreeably they sound. Glass also sounds sweeter than silver because it is more solid. Glass actually sounds sweeter than any metal because, although less malleable, it is more solid; it cannot be hit very strongly, for it would render an intolerably high pitch.[27]

The sonority of metals is directly proportional to their malleability: the 'harder' a metal is, the more sonorous and vice versa. The scale of potential sonority resulting from the bishop's remarks is that of lead–tin–silver–gold–copper. The sound itself, once produced, possesses a tone that is contingent upon the solidity of the metal as well. In this case, however, it is the median degree of malleability that conditions the most pleasing sound in metals, which is manifest most perfectly in silver. Nevertheless, glass surpasses all metals because it is most sonorous, more so than copper, and produces the sweetest sound, more so than silver.

The distinction the bishop draws between the sonority of a metal and the quality of the sound that metal produces parallels the Aristotelian concept as expressed in the first statement in *De anima* II.8: that sound exists either in potentiality or in actuality. According to Aristotle, sound in potentiality is the sonorous quality of an object prior to its being struck, and 'soft' materials such

---

[27] 'Etiam notandum quod metallum inflexibilius violentiorem facit sonum et ideo stagnum fortius sonat quam plumbum; argentum et aurum quam stagnum. Aes vero violentius omnibus; rubeum (aes) autem violentius albo. Vitrum vero fortius aere. In metallis vero quae magis accedunt ad mediocritatem fortitudinis, amicabiliorem sonum faciunt. Vitrum quoque dulcius sonat argento, quia solidius est. Item vitrum dulcius sonat omni metallo quia solidius est, licet sit inflexibilius; non enim grandem recipit percussionem; quodsi reciperet, sonum intolerabiliter acutum redderet.' *Epistola cum tractatu*, p. 16.14.

as wool or sponge are not sonorous, while solid materials such as bronze are sonorous. The latter category alone can produce an actual sound. Aristotle himself does not go into the tone qualities of the actual sounds, but the topic had some currency in Latin commentaries on *De anima*. Albertus Magnus, for example, maintains that gold, silver and copper are more sonorous than tin and lead; this remark in effect provides a scale similar to that of the bishop. The tone of the actual sounds ranges from the dullest to the sharpest, produced by lead and copper, respectively; implicitly, silver is in the middle position and, therefore, produces the most balanced tone. Moreover, in order to temper the sharpness of the sound produced by copper, one has to mix copper with tin when making bells or organs.[28]

The evidence just presented suggests that the theories of sound production underlying the bishop's treatment of *musica mundana* are contingent upon Aristotelian models current in the thirteenth century. His philosophical position thus becomes almost paradoxical: in referring to birds and rods, he introduces sublunar sounds that are produced in Aristotelian fashion in support of a thoroughly Neoplatonic notion of planetary sounds, which in turn the Aristotelians completely rejected. It is an intellectual strategy that the bishop adopts throughout his treatise and that consistently helps him elegantly to circumvent and rather conveniently to overlook any dialectical friction that might emerge between a Neoplatonic conceptual framework and Aristotelian rationales.

The question Neoplatonists most often asked was, why can human ears not hear the harmony of the cosmos if the planets indeed produce sound in their movement? To account for this human limitation, the bishop offers two justifications: (1) the sound is not audible on account of the great distances separating the planets from earth; and (2) the sound is not actually heard because it is so loud that it deafens human ears.[29] Both explanations are Neoplatonic in character, yet the examples he invokes in support for each justification are, once again, indicative of his

---

[28] Albertus Magnus, *De anima* 2.3.17, p. 124.

[29] The latter is the standard justification derived from Cicero's *Somnium Scipionis* and adopted by all medieval thinkers who upheld the actuality of a music of the spheres; cf. Macrobius, *Commentarii* 2.4.14, p. 109. Aristotle also mentions it in *De caelo* II.9 in the context of his refutation of celestial harmony.

general intellectual strategy. In other words, although his reasoning is slightly challenging and at times quite muddy, his propensity to employ supporting arguments imbued with Aristotelian rather than Neoplatonic imagery comes again to the fore. At this juncture, however, his arguments develop from somewhat ambiguous analogies between visual and auditory perceptions. I suspect that these analogies reflect a mixture of details pertaining to propagation of sound and light most probably picked up from writings on optics and sources dependent on Aristotle's treatment of sight in *De anima* II.7.

For example, the bishop maintains that 'we see the flying birds, but we do not hear them, for hearing is more sluggish than sight', very much in a vein similar to that expressed by Roger Bacon in his *Opus maius*: 'We note in the case of one at a distance striking with the hammer or a staff that we see the stroke delivered before we hear the sound produced.'[30] The bishop also asserts that, just as the ear is continuously enveloped by the sound of the celestial bodies, the eye is continuously enveloped by air; both dull the perceptive capacity of their respective organs.[31] Consequently, 'the eye can not see the sun's ray, which is air illuminated by the sun, unless it moves out of its direct path'.[32] When the enveloping medium changes, the eye behaves differently: submerged in water, although it still cannot see the water itself, it can see the objects

---

[30] '. . . sic enim procul aves volantes videmus, sed non audivimus, eo quod auditus hebetior est visu'. *Epistola cum tractatu*, p. 25.19. Cf. R. Bacon, *The 'Opus maius' of Roger Bacon*, ed. J. H. Bridges (London, 1900), ii, at v.i.ix.4, pp. 72–3; English translation in A. C. Crombie, *Robert Grosseteste and the Origins of Experimental Science, 1100–1700* (Oxford, 1962), p. 147. Crombie maintains that for Bacon, light was analogous to sound in that the multiplication of its species through a medium was a kind of pulse propagated from part to part similar to the propagation of sound (p. 146). For a similar position see also Grosseteste's analogy between the cause of repercussion in light and in sound that appears in his commentary on *Analytica Posteriora* and cited in Crombie, pp. 113–15.

[31] Cf. Aristotle, *De anima* (419^a25–34), p. 667.

[32] '. . . sed et radius solis, id est aer illuminatus a sole, non videtur, nisi oculus sit extra radium'. *Epistola cum tractatu*, p. 25.20. This passage vaguely relates to Roger Bacon's discussion of the species of light in *De multiplicatione specierum*, probably written in the early 1260s: 'for an eye situated in a corner of the house does not see the sun, but the ray entering through a hole or window or other aperture, whereas if it is exposed to the principal ray, it will see the sun' ('quoniam oculus in angulo domus non videt solem, sed radium cadentem per foramen vel fenestram vel aliam aperturam; quod si ponatur ad radium principalem, videbit solem'), in *Roger Bacon's Philosophy of Nature: A Critical Edition, with English Translation, Introduction and Notes, of 'De multiplicatione specierum' and 'De speculis comburentibus'*, ed. and trans. D.C. Lindberg (Oxford, 1983), II.2.127–9, pp. 102–5. For 'illuminatus a sole', see II.2.28–30, p. 96.

in the water and, by implication, possibly the sun's rays.[33] Analogously, the bishop maintains that, although we are incapable of hearing the continuous sound of the planets under normal atmospheric circumstances, when the medium that enfolds our ears changes either through having the ears covered with our palms or placed in water, or on account of curtailing internal liquid, we can indeed catch hold of the sun's path and, by implication, of the celestial sounds.[34] Ambiguous details and shaky argumentation notwithstanding, the notion at the core of the bishop's discussion is Aristotelian and dependent upon the reception of *De anima*: the phenomena pertaining to visual and sound perception are analogous.

II. THE MODEL OF THE COSMOS

I have argued so far that the philosophical premises at the core of our bishop's discussion are unquestionably Neoplatonic, and that some of his arguments draw upon examples borrowed from the Aristotelian natural philosophy current in the thirteenth century. In so far as the cosmological framework is concerned, however, there is clear evidence that the bishop worked out neither a Neoplatonic nor a strictly Aristotelian model, but instead one heavily indebted to Ptolemaic astronomy. Instrumental in bringing Ptolemy's system to the scientific fore and providing a fuller and more precise measurement for the planetary motions were the translations of a variety of Arabic astronomical works in the twelfth century and that of Ptolemy's *Almagest* by Gerard of Cremona around 1175. As such, although described by several authors of the late antique period – Calcidius among them – the

---

[33] *Epistola cum tractatu*, p. 25.21–2. Possibly this would happen through multiple refractions. The imagery and in part the vocabulary (but not the tight argumentation) are reminiscent of yet another passage from *De multiplicatione* where Bacon discusses principles of refraction in media of different transparency; see Bacon, *De multiplicatione* II.2.36–84, pp. 98–101.

[34] I suggest a possible yet tenuous connection between this passage and Avicenna's revision of Aristotle's second mode of sound production (see above) in his commentary on *De anima*: 'Sound therefore happens as a result of the disturbance of a soft and fluid body squeezed between two bodies resisting it' ('Ergo sonus accidit ex commotione mollis corporis impetuosi, constricti inter duo corpora contraria sibi resistentia'), in *Avicenna Latinus. Liber de anima*, ed. S. Van Riet, 2 vols (Leiden, 1968–72), p. 164.83–5. Aristotle himself suggests in *De anima* II.7 (419^{b}18) that water, though less efficient than air, is a possible medium for the propagation of sound.

Ptolemaic system of eccentrics and epicycles did not enter the mainstream of Latin astronomical thought until the thirteenth century. Furthermore, the bishop's model of the cosmos manifests Ptolemaic characteristics that during the thirteenth century were transmitted in such widely popular works as Sacrobosco's *Treatise on the Sphere* and the anonymous *Theorica planetarum*, two prime astronomical texts in the Faculty of Arts curriculum at Oxford and, by 1255, Paris.[35]

The bishop conceives of a nine-sphere cosmos. The ether extends from the circle of fixed stars (*aplanes*) to that of the moon; this cosmos moves uniformly from east to west under the impetus of the starless ninth sphere (*anastros*), which thus functions as the Aristotelian *primum mobile*.[36] As Smits van Waesberghe remarked, the term *aplanes* appears several times in Macrobius' commentary on *Somnium Scipionis* and a host of Carolingian and post-Carolingian treatises in reference to the sphere of the fixed stars; *anastros*, on the other hand, is found in Martianus Capella's *De nuptiis* and some of its Carolingian commentaries referring to the 'outermost circle'.[37] The specific association of *anastros* with the ninth sphere conceived as the *primum mobile* seems to be peculiar to the bishop, however, and the context in which it appears echoes Robertus Anglicus' commentary on Sacrobosco's *Sphere*.[38]

---

[35] The popularity of Sacrobosco is also witnessed by a significant number of commentaries on *De sphera* that come from the thirteenth as well as the fourteenth century. For the Latin text and an English translation of Sacrobosco's *De sphera* and of the commentaries on *De sphera* by Robertus Anglicus, Michael Scot and Cecco d'Ascoli, see L. Thorndike, *The 'Sphere of Sacrobosco' and its Commentators* (Chicago, 1949). The anonymous *Theorica planetarum* has not been edited, but an English translation by Olaf Pedersen appears in E. Grant (ed.), *A Source Book in Medieval Science* (Cambridge, Mass., 1974), pp. 451–65.

[36] 'Certum est, quoniam totus aether ab applano usque ad lunam rotatur impetu nonae sphaerae, quae dicitur anastron, ab oriente in occidente(m) uniformiter.' *Epistola cum tractatu*, p. 25.17. The passage from Adalbold's commentary on *O qui perpetua* that Smits van Waesberghe mentions at this point in his edition features a different cosmic model. It lacks both the ninth sphere and the unidirectional motion of the whole cosmos. Adalbold's sphere of fixed stars moves from east to west while the planets have their own movement from west to east; as such the *aplanes* slow down the movement of the planets: 'dum speram applanetis ab Oriente in Occidentem, planetarum autem orbes ab Occidente convertit in Orientem. Applanetis enim festinationem sic obrotatio planetarum retardando temperat.' *Serta mediaevalia*, ed. Huygens, p. 129.

[37] *Epistola cum tractatu*, pp. 60–1.

[38] '. . . while there are nine celestial orbs, in the first orb there is no star, in the next orb beneath it are those stars which . . . are called "fixed"' ('cum novem sint orbes celestes, in primo orbe non est aliqua stella, in alio orbe sub illo sunt ille stelle . . . que dicuntur fixe'; Robertus Anglicus, *Commentary on the Sphere* (c.1271), in *The Sphere of Sacrobosco*, ed. Thorndike, p. 201 (English) and p. 145 (Latin); 'by this movement all nine spheres

In addition to this astronomical nine-sphere cosmos, the bishop alludes to a 'highest heaven' where the souls of the blessed sing.[39] This is most likely a reference to the *caelum empyraeum*, which emerged as the ultimate heaven and the abode of the blessed in the twelfth century. Like some thirteenth-century thinkers, such as Thomas Aquinas, Campanus of Novara and Robert Grosseteste, the bishop deems the *empyraeum* to be beyond the reach of rational investigation and in the domain of faith alone: 'To which one must ascend through humility of faith and not through the enjoyment of reason or violence of demonstration.'[40]

are moved in uniform and continuous motion by the force of the first sphere' ('isto motu moventur omnes novem spere motu uniformi et continuo raptu prime'), *ibid.*, p. 207 (English) and p. 153 (Latin).

[39] '. . . to seek the highest heaven, where not the planets but the fixed stars sing, not the ones in error but the saints' ('altius caelum appetere, ubi canunt non planetae, sed applani, non errantes, sed sancti'). *Epistola cum tractatu*, p. 27.2. This passage builds upon the two meanings of the term *errans*, astronomical and theological: the planets (*stellae errantes*) and the ones in error are placed in opposition to the fixed stars (*aplanes*) and the saints. In his commentary on the *Somnium Scipionis*, Favonius presents a slightly similar notion: 'The first circle, that which is above all the others, is the circles of the aplanes; since a uniform and continuous movement never ceases to act upon it, it is the subject of no error' ('Nam primus ac summus est aplanes, qui, quia semper uno ac iugi continuatus agitur motu, nulli videtur errori esse subiectus'); *Disputatio de Somnio Scipionis*, ed. and trans. R.-E van Weddingen (Collection Latomus, 27; Brussels, 1957), p. 33.16–17.

[40] 'Ad quod per fidei humilitatem, non per rationis elationem aut demonstrationis violentiam est ascendendum.' *Epistola cum tractatu*, p. 27.2. Bartholomeus Anglicus (fl. *c*.1230): 'The empyrean heaven is the first and highest heaven, the place of angels, the region and dwelling place of blessed men' ('coelum empyroeum est primum et summum coelum, locus angelorum, regio et habitaculum hominum beatorum'); *De genuinis rerum coelestium, terrestrium et inferarum proprietatibus* (Frankfurt, 1601; facs., with title *De rerum proprietatibus*, Frankfurt, 1964), pp. 379–80. Thomas Aquinas: 'the empyrean heaven cannot be investigated by reason because we know about the heavens either by sight or by motion. The empyrean heaven, however, is subject to neither motion nor sight . . . but is held by authority' ('quod caelum empyreum ratione investigari non potest: quia quidquid de caelis cognoscimus hoc est per visum aut per motum. Caelum autem empyreum nec motui subjacet nec visui . . .; sed per autoritatem est habitum'). *Scriptum super libros Sententiarum Magistri Petri Lombardi Episcopi Parisiensis*, ed. R. P. Mandonnet (Paris, 1929), ii, p. 71. Translation in E. Grant, *Planets, Stars, and Orbs: The Medieval Cosmos 1200–1687* (Cambridge, 1996), p. 377. Campanus of Novara (*c*.1205–96): 'Whether there is anything, such as another sphere, beyond the convex surface of this [ninth] sphere, we cannot know by the compulsion of rational argument. However, we are informed by faith, and in agreement with the holy teachers of the church we reverently confess that beyond it is the empyrean heaven in which is the dwelling place of good spirits'. ('Extra autem huius orbis convexam superficiem utrum sit aliquid utpote alia spera necessitate rationis non cognoscimus. Fidei vero informatione sancti ecclesie doctoribus assentientes reverentur confitemur extra ipsam celum esse empireum in quo est bonorum spirituum mansio'). *Campanus of Novara and Medieval Planetary Theory: Theorica planetarum*, ed. and trans. F. S. Benjamin, Jr., and G. J. Toomer (Madison, 1971), p. 182. I have opted here for the English translation in Grant, *Planets, Stars, and Orbs*, p. 377.

Down below, in the astronomical realm, the impetus of the ninth sphere effects not only the motion of the planets but also that of the comets, or shooting stars, below, which, as in Aristotle's *Meteorologica*, inhabit the space between the region of the upper air and the moon.[41] In addition to being carried along in the constant east to west motion of the zodiac, the planets themselves exhibit other types of motion as well. Both restlessly and at inestimable speeds, they move by longitude (*ante et retro*), that is, around the zodiac; by latitude (*dextrorsum, sinistrorsum*), that is, between the tropics; and by altitude (*sursum, deorsum*), that is towards and away from the earth.[42] The longitudinal motion itself can be broken down into the direct motion (*progressio*), station (*statio*) and retrograde motion (*retrogradatio*) of a planet, and, like all the other planetary movements, it is continuous. The station represents the point common to the direct and retrograde motions. The bishop conceives of it as the analogue of the 'instant' in the continuum of time, an analogy of motion and time that is lifted almost verbatim from Aristotle's *Physica*.[43]

Before the Ptolemaic cosmological system established itself in the Western astronomical mainstream, the regularly periodic longitudinal motion of the planets was sometimes explained as being caused by the force of solar rays, while the variations in planetary altitude were believed to be contingent upon planetary absides.[44]

[41] '. . . moreover, [the movement of the ninth sphere] carries in its impetus the upper part of the region of the air, in which comets, that is shooting stars, move in the manner of the stars [i.e., from east to west]' ('immo etiam conrotatur eius impetu pars aeris superior, in qua cometae et stellae crinitae moventur ad modum stellarum'). *Epistola cum tractatu*, p. 25.17. Cf. Aristotle, *Meteorology* I.4–7.

[42] 'The planets themselves move in this ether both forwards and backwards, rightwards and leftwards, upwards and downwards, as restless as they are of unfathomable speed' ('In ipso autem aethere moventur superiora corpora ante et retro, dextrorsum, sinistrorsum, sursum, deorsum, tam irrequieta quam inaestimabili velocitate'). *Epistola cum tractatu*, p. 25.17. Rather than on physical orbs, the bishop's planets seem to move freely through a type of fluid heaven similar to that of Ptolemy's *Almagest*.

[43] 'Now, since time cannot exist and is unthinkable apart from the now, and the *now is a kind of middle-point, uniting as it does in itself both a beginning and an end, a beginning of future time and an end of past* time . . . but if time exists, it is evident that motion must too, time being a kind of affection of motion' ('Si igitur inpossibile est esse et intelligere tempus sine ipso nunc, *nunc autem est medietas quedam, et principium et finem habens simul, principium quidem futuri temporis, finem autem preteriti* . . . At vero si tempus, manifestum est quia necesse est esse et motum, si quidem tempus est passio quedam motus'). Latin text from *Physica. Translatio vetus*, ed. F. Bossier and J. Brams, in *Aristoteles Latinus* VII 1.2 (Leiden and New York, 1990), p. 281 (251^{b}20–8). Emphasis mine.

[44] According to Bruce Eastwood, the explanation that the direct and retrograde motions of the planets were determined by the Sun are based on Plinian astronomical theories;

53

The bishop offers no specific astronomical explanation for the longitudinal motions of the planets. This comes as no surprise, for in general his discourse lacks systematic explanations and develops in a rather axiomatic mode. More often than not, he seems to expect of the reader a familiarity with the philosophical and cosmological content of his arguments, no matter how sketchy his presentation of that content is. For that familiarity to function correctly, however, one must assume that the conceptual models behind his discourse are relatively consistent and widespread. It is, therefore, reasonable to conjecture that the astronomical circumstances behind all three types of planetary motion, including the longitudinal, develop from one and the same model of the cosmos. And the bishop is definitely more generous in providing details about that cosmic model when he discusses altitudinal planetary motion:

> . . . each of the six planets, the farther away it is from earth according to whatever circle, the more efficacious it is; not because it is further, I say, but because it is faster and indeed more sonorous. Only the moon, the lower it is on its epicycle, the more efficacious it is, because there it is faster and more sonorous. On the eccentric, the farther it is from earth, the more efficacious, the faster and more sonorous it is.[45]

He unambiguously states that altitudinal motion is contingent upon a system of eccentrics and epicycles. By implication, both the longitudinal and the latitudinal planetary movements mentioned by him earlier in the treatise should be contingent on the same system. Moreover, he gives a rather detailed account of the eccen-

see B. Eastwood, 'Plinian Astronomical Diagrams in the Early Middle Ages', in E. Grant and J. E. Murdoch (eds), *Mathematics and its Applications to Science and Natural Philosophy in the Middle Ages: Essays in Honour of Marshall Clagett* (Cambridge, 1987), p. 148. However, the explanation also appears in Macrobius' *Commentarii* 1.20.5; several centuries later, Bartholomaeus Anglicus continues to elaborate on the same theory; see *De rerum proprietatibus* (1964 edn, p. 399, cited in Grant, *Planets, Stars, and Orbs*, pp. 453–4).

[45] '. . . quilibet sex planetarum quanto remotior est a terra secundum quemcumque circulum, efficacior est; non quia remotior, inquam, sed quia velocior, immo quia sonorior. Sola luna, quanto inferior est in epiclyco, tanto efficacior est, quia illic velocior et sonorior. Nam in excentri, quanto elongatior est a terra, tanto efficacior, tanto velocior, tanto sonorior.' *Epistola cum tractatu*, p. 29.9. An eccentric circle is 'a circle whose center is not at the center of the world, . . . or a circle with a displaced cusp, or an outgoing center'. *Theorica planetarum*, trans. Pedersen, par. 1. An epicycle is 'a small circle on whose circumference is carried the body of the planet, and the center of the epicycle is always carried along the circumference of the deferent' ('circulus parvus per cuius circumferentiam defertur corpus planete, et centrum epicicli semper defertur in circumferentia deferentis'). Sacrobosco, *Sphere*, p. 141 (English), p. 114 (Latin). For a discussion of this passage in the context of the bishop's *musica mundana* see below, p. 62.

tric and epicyclical lunar motions. To my knowledge, eccentrics and epicycles came to explain the observed planetary motions to the level of detail witnessed in the Barberini text only in the early thirteenth century, and as a direct result of the gradual integration of Ptolemaic astronomical theories in writings by Sacrobosco, Bartholomeus Anglicus and Robertus Anglicus, and in the anonymous *Theorica planetarum*, among other texts.[46] The bishop's reliance upon precisely those theories in order to frame his account of the celestial production of sound emerges as the strongest piece of evidence thus far in support for a thirteenth-century dating of his treatise. It also helps bring about his remarkably original interpretation of the celestial sounds.

III. THE PLANETARY PITCHES

If planets make sound in their various celestial motions, any Neoplatonist would ask, what are the exact pitches that produce the harmony of the spheres? The often-favoured solutions feature a combination of planetary pitches or intervals that produce a well-defined musical scale, albeit one that could be configured in any of several possible ways. Instrumental in the transmission of these cosmic configurations, in addition to Boethius, were a number of other late antique or early medieval writers, such as Pliny, Hyginus, Censorinus, Favonius and Martianus Capella.[47] Boethius accounts for two possible scales in his *De institutione*, one adopted from Nicomachus and the other from Cicero's *Somnium Scipionis*. The other writers offer scalar versions that reflect three slightly different yet related traditions going back to an alleged Varronian prototype.[48] Although all of them, including Boethius, adopted

---

[46] See Sacrobosco, *Sphere*, pp. 113–14 (Latin), pp. 140–1 (English); Robertus Anglicus, *Commentary on the Sphere*, pp. 193–5 (Latin), pp. 242–3 (English); Bartholomaeus Anglicus, *De rerum proprietatibus*, pp. 398–9.

[47] Pliny, *Naturalis historiae*, ed. C. Mayhoff (Stuttgart, 1967–96), II.22, p. 154; Hyginus, *De astronomia*, ed. B. Bunte (Lepzig, 1875), pp. 117–18; Censorinus, *De die natali liber*, ed. N. Sallman (Leipzig, 1983), 13.2–6; Favonius, *Disputatio de Somnio Scipionis*, pp. 42–3; Martianus Capella, *De nuptiis Philologiae et Mercurii*, ed. J. Willis (Leipzig, 1983), II.169–99, pp. 49–54; Boethius, *De institutione musica* I.27, p. 219.

[48] As one possible actualisation of the music of the spheres, the concept of the cosmic musical scale seems to have been adopted in the Latin tradition by Varro and disseminated by Varronian followers; see P. Tannery, *Recherches sur l'histoire de l'astronomie ancienne* (Paris, 1893), p. 330.

what Macrobius identified as the 'Chaldean' order of planets, their cosmic scales vary in terms of their ambitus, planetary intervals and, in the case of the two versions in Boethius, direction.[49] Most important, only Boethius assigns a specific pitch to each planet, and does so in both the Nicomachean and Ciceronian versions. All other authors speak not of pitches as such but of intervals that occur between two successive planets. Each of their planetary scales develops not as a succession of pitches but of three possible intervals: the semitone, the tone and the semiditone (tone and a half). The sequences of pitches – the musical scales – that can be generated from the various combinations of these standard planetary intervals are somewhat difficult to position in the standard Greater or Lesser Perfect Systems (see Table 1, where the starting pitch [D] has been chosen for convenience).

Widely disseminated during the Middle Ages, most of these planetary musical scales considered the distance of a planet from the eighth sphere, the primary mover, to be the principal factor in determining the musical pitch the planet produces: since the moon is the farthest from the sphere, it is therefore the slowest and thus produces the lowest sound; Saturn is the closest, therefore the fastest and produces the highest pitch. Nicomachus' scale was exceptional in prescribing the reverse: the moon produces the highest pitch and Saturn the lowest. In Nicomachus' case, the velocity of the planet, while still directly proportional to its pitch, is deemed to be directly proportional to the planet's distance from the eighth sphere: because the moon, for example, is the farthest planet from the eighth sphere, it is also the fastest and, therefore, produces the highest pitch. Both of these sets of criteria were entertained during the Middle Ages, with a clear preference for the former. A complementary factor was occasionally brought into the discussions, though rarely, if ever, systematically explored: the

---

[49] According to Macrobius, the disagreement between the Platonic and the Ciceronian order of planets comes from them having adopted the 'Egyptian' and the 'Chaldean' orders, respectively; see Macrobius, *Commentarii in Somnium* I.19.1–2, p. 73. The 'Egyptian' order has the Sun in the second position, following the Moon (i.e., Earth, Moon, Sun, Venus, Mercury, Mars, Jupiter, Saturn, Fixed Stars); the 'Chaldean' order has the Sun in the middle position between Earth and the starry sphere (i.e., Earth, Moon, Venus, Mercury, Sun, Mars, Jupiter, Saturn, Fixed Stars). In addition, Venus and Mercury can exchange positions in both systems. For a list and a brief discussion of authors who subscribed to one or the other orders see Jacques Flamant, *Macrobe et le néo-platonisme latin, à la fin du IVe siècle* (Leiden, 1977), pp. 421–4.

Table 1 *Planetary scales*

Pliny	Martianus Capella	Favonius/Censorinus	Hyginus	Boethius (Cicero)	Boethius (Nicomachus)
[e] Fixed stars					
	[e♭] Fixed stars				
		[d] Fixed stars	[d] Fixed stars		d Moon
[c♯] Saturn		[c♯] Saturn			
[c] Jupiter	[c] Saturn	[c] Jupiter			c Venus
[b] Mars	[b] Jupiter	[b] Mars	[b] Saturn		
	[b♭] Mars				b♭ Mercury
[a] SUN	[a] SUN	[a] SUN	[a] Jupiter	a Fixed stars	a SUN
			[G♯] Mars		
			[G] SUN	G Saturn	G Mars
[F♯] Venus	[F♯] Venus	[F♯] Venus	[F♯] Venus		
[F] Mercury	[F] Mercury	[F] Mercury	[F] Mercury	F Jupiter	F Jupiter
[E] Moon	[E] Moon	[E] Moon	[E] Moon	E Mars	E Saturn
[D] Earth	[D] Earth	[D] Earth	[D] Earth	D SUN	
				C Venus	
				B Mercury	
				A Moon	

size of the planet. It was generally assumed that the larger the planet, the more powerful the sound.

The bishop's approach is not only extremely idiosyncratic but methodologically very intricate. The harmony of the spheres that results from his speculations does not conform to either the Boethian or to the more general Neoplatonic prototypes outlined above. Unlike Boethius, he assigns no specific pitches to each planet. Unlike the other Neoplatonic writers, he asserts that not one, not two, but all three planetary factors determine the cosmic harmony, and that they do so not individually but in combination. Because of this there emerge ratios among the various planetary pitches that become contingent upon compound ratios of the size of the planet, its distance from earth and its *motus*.[50] Furthermore, we shall see that while the size of the planet remains constant, the two other parameters become variable under the influence of the Ptolemaic system adopted by the bishop. Most of this information as well as the bishop's guidelines for calculating the musical intervals among the planets appears at the end of the treatise, almost like an afterthought, the *Corollarium* in the modern edition. I believe, however, that the so-called *Corollarium* represents more than just an afterthought. In the main body of the text, the bishop comments: 'For the sizes of the planets are known and so are the variation of their motions and their distances from earth. These

[50] The bishop seems to use the term *motus* in two ways. When used 'properly', it signifies the 'motion' of a planet: 'The term "proportion of the movements" is properly used for the proportion of the spaces that the things moved traverse in equal segments of time' ('Proportio motu(u)m proprie dicitur: proportio spatiorum, quae mota transcurrunt in aequis temporibus'). *Epistola cum tractatu*, p. 28.4. In the 'improper' sense, left here untranslated, it relates to the arc of the zodiac that a planet traverses in its revolution in a given time; he also makes sure to point out that it is not a proportion of the actual space that the planets traverse, but a proportion of the minutes of arc: 'The proportion of a planet's *motus* to its own or to that of another is called – albeit improperly – the proportion of the minutes (of arc) that one planet advances in a short time to the minutes that it or another advances in the same length of time, not the proportion of distance to distance. For the further a minute of arc is from earth, the more space it occupies, even if the eye judges otherwise' ('Proportio motus unius planetae ad motum eiusdem vel alterius dicitur – quamvis improprie – proportio minutorum, quae progreditur unus planeta in aliquantulo tempore ad minuta, quae ipse vel alius progreditur in tanto tempore; non proportio spatii ad spatium. Nam unum minutum quanto remotius a terra, tanto maius spatium occupat, licet visus aliter iudicet'). *Ibid.*, p. 28.8. Simply put, this latter use of *motus* expresses the concept of angular velocity and thus relates to the technical term *motus* that in astronomical works indicates the angular distance of a planet from the first point of Aries; see, for example, *Theorica planetarum*, par 3, 17 and 41.

things in place, to find the harmonies one can resort to the two diagrams written below and supported on this side and that by some axioms that my insomnia of tonight has brought together.'[51] The diagrams have not survived, but the *Corollarium* delivers the information in such a terse mode that it is hard to see it as representing anything other than the axioms of the insomniac bishop. He creates here a methodological blueprint that will eventually yield a mathematically derived set of formulae for calculating the ratios between the planetary pitches.

The axioms in his first main line of argument, tabulated in Table 2, are as follows:[52]

1. In general terms, the motion of a planet is directly proportional to its pitch; that is, the ratio between the higher and the lower pitch is same as that between the greater and the lesser motion.

2. In the case of two planets that are of unequal size but that manifest the same motion, the size of each planet is inversely proportional to its pitch – that is, the larger the size the lower the pitch, and vice versa.

3. When both motion and size are variable, when we are therefore dealing with two planets of different sizes and covering unequal arcs of the zodiac, there emerges a compound ratio of the greater to the lesser motion and the lesser to the greater size; the ratio of two pitches thus produced depends upon this compound ratio.

Table 2   *Axioms: planetary pitch (P), size (S) and motion (M)*

Constant	Variable	Ratio
size	motion	$P_1/P_2 = M_1/M_2$
motion	size	$P_1/P_2 = S_2/S_1$
—	motion and size	$P_1/P_2 = M_1/M_2 \cdot S_2/S_1$

[51] 'Si ergo motus superiorum corporum, ut persuadent philosophi, sine sono non est, mihi videtur ostendi posse: . . . Quantitates enim planetarum sciuntur et variationes motuum et elongationes a terra. Quibus positis, ad has harmonias inveniendas, duo subscripta faciunt theoremata, quibusdam velut axiomatibus, hinc (et) inde circumfulta, quae illius noctis mihi congessit insomnitas.' *Epistola cum tractatu*, p. 26.23–4.
[52] *Ibid.*, p. 28.2–4.

So far, the principles that the bishop has put forth can work perfectly well in the concentric system of planetary spheres, and are, therefore, unexceptional in the context of traditional Neoplatonic speculation on the music of the spheres. A drastic departure from the customary line of Neoplatonic reasoning occurs, however, once he introduces into the equation the parameter of planetary elongation – that is, the distance of the planet from earth. The entire picture changes significantly and there is a manifold increase in the complexities involved in the production of various pitches. This is due to the fact that for him the concept of elongation represents not only the distance to earth of each one of the planets at a single given time, but also the distance to earth of one and the same planet at two different moments in time.

The axioms in his second line of argument, tabulated in Table 3, are as follows:[53]

1. When all three parameters are considered, the greater the elongation, the greater the motion and the lesser the size are, the higher is the pitch.

2. In the case of one single planet, the ratio between the pitch that planet produces in one position and the pitch it produces in another position consists of the compound ratio among its two motions and two elongations.

3. In the case of two different planets, the ratio between the pitch of the superior planet and that of the inferior planet derives from the compound ratio of the greater motion to the lesser, of the greater elongation to the lesser and of the lesser size to the greater.

Table 3 *Axioms: Planetary pitch (P), size (S), motion (M) and elongation (E)*

general	$P_1/P_2 = M_1/M_2$
	$P_1/P_2 = S_2/S_1$
	$P_1/P_2 = E_1/E_2$
one planet	$P_1/P_2 = M_1/M_2 \cdot E_1/E_2$
two planets	$P_1/P_2 = M_1/M_2 \cdot E_1/E_2 \cdot S_2/S_1$

[53] *Ibid.*, p. 28.5–7.

In the second axiom, the bishop introduces a temporal parameter in order to accommodate a situation not encountered in
standard Neoplatonic speculations: that one single planet can actually produce different pitches at different moments in time. He
maintains that the ratio between two of these pitches becomes
dependent upon the compound ratios of that planet's motions and
elongations at the two moments in time. For such compound ratios
even to exist, however, the elongation and the motion of each
planet must vary during the planetary revolution.

The concentric orbits and uniform planetary speed espoused in
the standard Neoplatonic cosmology can neither generate nor
accommodate variations such as these. The Ptolemaic system of
eccentrics and epicycles, on the other hand, can account for both.
As shown in Figure 1, in this cosmic model the elongation of each
planet does indeed vary on account of either the eccentric or the
epicycle, or both. It does so within the limits established by the
combined eccentric and epicyclical apogees and their combined
perigees. Moreover, in the Ptolemaic system, the velocity of a
planet does indeed vary as well, for it is contingent upon the position of the planet on its epicycle. As the centre of the epicycle
moves eastward on the eccentric deferent, a planet at the apogee
of its epicycle is said to be quickest because the direction of its
motion is the same as that of its orbital rotation (i.e., clockwise);
a planet at the perigee of its epicycle is said to be slowest because
it moves in a direction opposite to that of its orbital rotation. In

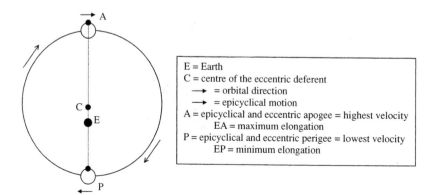

Figure 1   Planetary velocity and elongation

the case of the moon, however, the situation is reversed: because the rotation of its epicycle is in an anticlockwise direction, the moon at the apogee of its epicycle is said to be slowest and at the perigee, fastest.[54]

These parameters are only implied in the bishop's second axiom, but they are clearly explained several paragraphs later. He specifies here that the sounds the celestial bodies emit in their revolution are also contingent on the position of the planets on their respective epicycles: the higher a planet is on its epicycle, the faster and more sonorous it is (the opposite is true in the case of the moon).[55] The cosmic parameters, therefore, have a definite impact upon the pitches that the planets emit in their revolutions. On the one hand, both the elongation and the speed of a planet are each directly proportional with its pitch. On the other hand, when elongation and speed participate in a compound ratio, a given planet would emit the highest pitch at the combined apogees of both its eccentric deferent and its epicycle where it is the quickest; it would emit the lowest pitch at their combined perigees where the planet is the slowest. Larger orbital cycles notwithstanding, the situation can be mathematically formulated as follows: because both the elongation and the speed of a planet constantly change, the compound ratio of these two factors changes as well; consequently, the ratio of two pitches emitted by the same planet at two different moments in time is always different from 1.

The implications these details have on the kind of planetary music the bishop envisages are immense, for although he fully embraces the Neoplatonic doctrines in spirit, so to speak, he does not follow them to the letter. Standard Neoplatonism stipulates a never-changing planetary music, either by having each planet generate a continuous sound of invariable pitch or by assigning a fixed

---

[54] For the orbital direction on the eccentric see *Theorica planetarum* pars 11 (Moon), 32 (superior planets), 59 (Mercury) and 77 (Venus); see also Robertus Anglicus, *Commentary on the Sphere*, pp. 242–3. Although Robertus Anglicus mentions the speeds of the planets on their epicycles only in passing and in an astrological context elsewhere in the commentary, they appear in a more precise fashion in *Theorica planetarum* par. 15: 'When the moon is in the upper part of the circumference of the epicycle it moves from east to west and therefore has a slow motion. In the lower part the motion is in the opposite direction and therefore fast. The other planets behave in the opposite manner.'

[55] *Epistola cum tractatu*, p. 29.9. See above, n. 45.

interval between two successive planets. In the bishop's rendition of the planetary music, we can no longer conceive of a single constant pitch per planet. What he envisages, therefore, is that each planet emits a sound of varying pitch that rises and falls within a continuous field of pitches, and that the limits of this field are contingent upon the limits established by the planet's eccentric and epicyclical motion. Not until the early fifteenth century will another music theorist, in this case Giorgio Anselmi, assume that a single planet produces more than one pitch by reason of its epicyclical motion.[56]

Allowing for variable planetary distance and velocity – allowing, therefore, for planets to emit sounds of continuously varying pitch – negates the possibility of a single, fixed and continuously sounding celestial musical scale. Although the planetary alignment produces one particular scale at any given instant, at every other instant the changes in the orbital parameters will result in proportional changes in the pitch and, therefore, in the intervallic content of that scale. By adopting the dynamic Ptolemaic cosmological system, which causes each planet to emit a spectrum of pitches and together to generate a fluid type of celestial music, the bishop offers a reinterpretation of the Neoplatonic *musica mundana* that is, however, strikingly similar to that espoused by Hermann of Carinthia in his *De essentiis*. Hermann draws on notions found in Abu Ma'shar's *Introductorium*, a work that he had translated into Latin several years earlier.[57] Hermann's celestial

---

[56] Giorgio Anselmi, *De musica: dieta prima de celesti harmonia, dieta secunda de instrumentali harmonia, dieta tertia de cantabili harmonia*, ed. G. Massera ('Historiae Musicae Cultores' Biblioteca, 14; Florence, 1961), pp. 101–2. It is not the dynamic aspect, i.e. the multiplicity of sounds emitted by one single planet that is at issue here, but its relation to a specifically Ptolemaic system of eccentrics and epicycles. Several centuries earlier, commenting on Martianus' *De nuptiis*, Eriugena had described a dynamic music of the spheres as well; see, for example, B. Münxelhaus, 'Aspekte der Musica Disciplina bei Eriugena', in *Jean Scot Erigène et l'histoire de la philosophie. Colloque International du C.N.R.S.* (Paris, 1977), pp. 253–62. As I have shown elsewhere, Eriugena's dynamic music of the spheres was a direct outcome of the Plinian absidal cosmos he adopted (absides are circumterrestrial but not geocentric planetary circles, each *absis* having its own centre, path, length and motion); G. Ilnitchi, 'Celestial Harmony and Plinian Astronomy in the Eriugenian Commentaries on Martianus Capella's *De nuptiis*', paper read in 2000 at the Medieval and Renaissance Music Conference held in Oxford.

[57] Among the Arabic scholars, Abu Ma'shar Ja'far ben Muhammad ben 'Umar al-Balkhi, known in the Latin Middle Ages as Albumasar, was probably most influential. Heavily astrological and drawing on Aristotle's natural philosophy, his *Introductorium in astronomiam* was translated twice during the twelfth century: in 1133 by John of Seville and in 1140 by Hermann of Carinthia. In his controversial but stimulating book, Lemay argues

modulation consists of 'the sounds responding to the distance of the intervals, the single changes varying with harmonic modulation according to the ascent and descent of the planets';[58] the pitch, therefore, varies with the 'ascent and descent' of the planet, which is nothing else than the planet's movement on its eccentric and epicycle.[59] Hermann's account may be less specific, but his music of the spheres shares in common with that of our bishop both the cosmic framework and the ever-changing planetary sounds.

IV. THE ZODIAC AND CELESTIAL INFLUENCE

In his preoccupation with the methods through which mathematical ratios among the pitches are to be derived, the bishop provides little, if any, factual information regarding the pitches themselves. Although his reasoning process is not only cogent but also detailed and his mathematical formulas relatively easy to reconstruct, it is clear that, given the right astronomical tables, the reader may be expected to work out the types of ratios the bishop puts forth and to come up with concrete solutions on his own. After all, he claims that the sizes of the planets, their motions and their distances from earth are known, and, indeed, all this information was available in one form or another in the astronomical treatises of the day.[60] As far as I can tell, however, none

that many authors of the twelfth century came for the first time in contact with Aristotle's natural philosophy in Albumasar's *Introductorium*; see R. Lemay, *Abu Ma'shar and Latin Aristotelianism in the Twelfth Century: The Recovery of Aristotle's Natural Philosophy through Arabic Astrology* (Beirut, 1962). It is worth noting that, translated into Latin several decades earlier than Ptolemy's *Almagest*, Albumasar's *Introductorium* contains one of the earliest treatments of the Ptolemaic planetary motions according to the system of eccentrics and epicycles available in the Latin world; *ibid.*, p. 97.

[58] Hermann of Carinthia, *De essentiis* 68rG, and Burnett's commentary on pp. 292–4.

[59] *Ibid.* 68rE, and Burnett's commentary on pp. 291–2.

[60] In the *Almagest* Ptolemy establishes the absolute distances only for the sun and the moon, while in his *Hypotheses of the Planets* he calculates both the absolute distances for all the planets and the absolute size of their bodies. Although the *Hypotheses* was not available in Latin translation during the Middle Ages, its main concepts reached the Latin world through a host of Arabic sources in a manner that remains largely unknown; see Grant, *Planets, Stars, and Orbs*, p. 17. The first Latin writer to exploit the Ptolemaic technique for calculating the exact sizes and distances of the planets was Campanus of Novara in his *Theorica planetarum*, written most likely in the 1260s. For a more detailed discussion of these issues and of Campanus' dependence upon the Arabic tradition and especially Alfraganus, see *Campanus of Novara and Medieval Planetary Theory*, pp. 53–5. See also Robertus Anglicus' discussion based upon the data found in *Almagest* and elsewhere in his *Commentary on the Sphere*, pp. 194–5 (Latin) and p. 243 (English).

of the ratios he develops can be reduced to the traditional Neoplatonic ratios that express the musical consonances. In other words, there are no evident 2:1, 3:2 or 4:3 ratios that seem to emerge from these planetary relations and that would correspond to diapason, diapente or diatessaron and their compounds. Paradoxically, therefore, although his objective is to advance a systematic method of calculation of pitches that eventually develop among the planets in their celestial movement, he does not specify their nature in terms of common Pythagorean musical ratios. The bishop would thus seem to be inadvertently undermining the very foundations of *musica mundana*.

Explicit analogies between Pythagorean cosmic and musical ratios appear, however, at the onset of his discussion of *musica mundana*:

In the heavens there are four principal aspects: sextile, quartile, trine and opposition. The sextile consists of one-sixth of the path of the zodiac (*caelum*), that is 60°, compared with which the whole circle is six times as great; for example the weight (*pondus*) of the nineteenth string to that of the first. The quartile aspect occupies a fourth of the zodiac, that is 90°; it is in a 3:2 ratio to the 60° segment, which in music is called diapente. The trine aspect occupies a third of the zodiac, that is 120°; it is in a 4:3 ratio to the 90° segment, which in music is called diatessaron.

Thus, the ratio between the degrees of the trine aspect to those of the quartile produces the diatessaron, between the degrees of the quartile to those of the sextile aspect produces the diapente and between those of the trine and of the sextile aspect, the diapason. Similarly, the opposition makes the diapason to the quartile, the diapente to the trine, while the trine in ratio to the quartile is said to produce the diatessaron.[61]

What this passage reveals is that mathematical ratios characteristic of musical consonances do have a place in the bishop's model of the music of the spheres after all, but they occur not among the planets, as one would expect in standard Neoplatonic

[61] 'In caelo quattuor dicuntur esse aspectus principaliter: sextilis, quartus, trinus et oppositio. Sextilis: sextam partem caeli tenet, scilicet .LX. gradus, ad quos totus circulus sescuplus est, sicut et pondus ultimae undeviginti chordarum ad pondus primae. Quartus aspectus quartam partem caeli tenet, scilicet .XC. gradus, quorum proportio ad .LX. sesqualtera est, quae dicitur in musica diapente. Trinus aspectus tertiam partem caeli tenet, scilicet .CXX. gradus, quorum proportio ad .XC. gradus est sesquitertia, quae dicitur in musica diatessaron. Igitur gradus trini aspectus ad gradum quarti aspectus diatessaron faciunt; gradus quarti aspectus ad gradum sextilis aspectus diapente; gradus trini aspectus ad gradum sextilis diapason. Item oppositio ad quartum aspectum diapason facit, ad trinum diapente, et trinus ad quartum diatessaron facere dictus est.' *Epistola cum tractatu*, p. 23.2–7.

practice, but among the four aspects of the zodiac: the sextile, quartile, trine and opposition. The diagram in Figure 2 lays out the relationship between various segments on the circle of the zodiac, the ratios between the numerical degrees of the zodiacal *aspects*, and the musical consonances these ratios express. Not all possible zodiacal (or for that matter musical) ratios are accounted for. The bishop calculates only the ratios of 2:1, 3:2, 4:3 and 6:1 that correspond to the diapason, the diapente, the diatessaron and the interval of a *bisdiapason cum diapente*.

Treated as a proportional consonance with the ratio of 6:1, the latter interval of a nineteenth is very unusual in the general context of Pythagorean speculations.[62] Regardless, we have seen that the bishop seems to be particularly fond of it, and employs it not only in the context of *musica mundana* but also in his discussion of *musica instrumentalis* and *humana*. In the segment on *musica instrumentalis*, nineteen is the maximum number of strings that can enter proportional relationships 'because the weight (*pondus*) of the first string multiplied by six generates the weight of the hind-

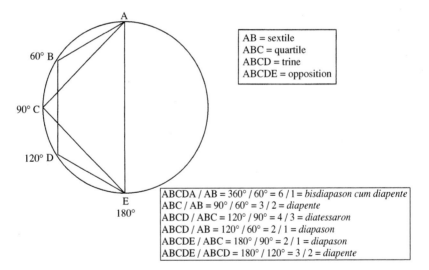

Figure 2   Planetary aspects and musical ratios

[62]   It does not appear, for example, in the table of intervals compiled by Klaus-Jürgen Sachs for his article 'Musikalische Elementarlehre', pp. 129–30.

most (highest?) string, since six is the first perfect number'. Together, these strings generate a nineteen-pitch gamut that the bishop maintains is characteristic of the *musica humana* as well. Here, the pitches are further arranged according to eight *graves*, seven *acutae* and four *superacutae*, which together form none other than the standard nineteen-pitch gamut as laid out by Guido of Arezzo in his *Micrologus*, chapter 2.[63] What is relevant to the present discussion is that the zodiacal *bisdiapason cum diapente* ratio of 6:1 in the context of *musica mundana* provides the mathematical and to some extent the ultimate cosmological endorsement for the gamut common to the other two Boethian types of *musica, instrumentalis* and *humana*.

The link between zodiacal aspects and musical consonances is extremely idiosyncratic, and no other medieval Latin treatise I have encountered features this association in an explicit manner. We do find it, however, in two Hellenistic works by Ptolemy: the *Tetrabiblos* and the *Harmonics*. Ptolemy provides the more detailed account of the relation between the zodiac and musical consonances in his *Harmonics*.[64] Knowledge of this treatise, however, entered the Latin world at the earliest towards the mid or late fourteenth century, and it is therefore very unlikely to have been the source for our treatise. On the other hand, the *Tetrabiblos* (or the *Quadripartitum*, as it was known during the Latin Middle Ages), where Ptolemy briefly yet specifically associates the zodiacal aspects with the consonant ratios 3:2 and 4:3,[65] was translated by Plato of Tivoli sometime around 1140, and soon after it became a standard text in the Latin West. If our treatise was composed in the thirteenth century, as its dependence upon Aristotelian natural philosophy and Ptolemaic astronomy suggests, Ptolemy's remarks in the *Tetrabiblos* may very well have provided the source of our author's zodiacal musical speculation.[66] Furthermore, the

---

[63] *Epistola cum tractatu*, p. 22.1. See above, n. 6.

[64] See T. J. Mathiesen, *Apollo's Lyre: Greek Music and Music Theory in Antiquity and the Middle Ages* (Lincoln, Nebr., and London, 1999), pp. 484–93.

[65] Ptolemy, *Tetrabiblos*, ed. and trans. F. E. Robbins (Loeb Classical Library, 435; Cambridge Mass., 1948), I.13, pp. 73–4.

[66] A similar relationship between planetary sounds and zodiacal aspects appears in Michael Scot, *Liber introductorius*, as mentioned in F. A. Gallo, "Astronomy and Music in the Middle Ages: The *Liber Introductorius* by Michael Scot', *Musica disciplina*, 27 (1973), pp. 5–9, at p. 8, n. 22.

similarities go even further, albeit in very general terms. Both writers position their remarks amidst accounts of the various positive and negative planetary influences on terrestrial things, and as such they make the proportions participate in the larger phenomenon of celestial causation. The bishop states:

In accordance with these aspects, the ray of the sun, refracted by the moon and reverberating in sublunar objects, has now one, now another effect: in the brain and the bone marrow, which concern physicians; in seas and shells and even in the varieties of wind, which concern seafarers; in herbs, arbours, infirmities and many other matters, which concern the unlearned and the common people.[67]

Although widely accepted during the Middle Ages, during the thirteenth century the medieval belief that celestial bodies have a controlling influence over the terrestrial region derived additional authority from Ptolemy's *Tetrabiblos*, as well as from Aristotle's *De caelo* and his writings on natural philosophy. They provided the intellectual basis for the notion that the incorruptible celestial substance excelled and, therefore, should influence the behaviour of corruptible bodies in the sublunar realm.[68] Further reinforcement came from a variety of Greek and Arabic works that became available in western Europe by the end of the twelfth century, among which probably the most influential was, once again, Abu Ma'shar's *Introductorium*. The bishop's remarks, however, are so terse and the information therein so meagre and of such general nature, that an attempt to determine whether they depend on a specific astrological tradition is bound to fail – with one possible exception: the 'doctrine of rays' as transmitted in al-Kindi's treatise, known in its late twelfth-century Latin

---

[67] 'Secundum hos aspectus radius solis, refractus in luna, et inferiora reverberans, alios et alios habet effectus; in cerebro et medullis, quod patet physicis; in mari et conchyliis, immo etiam in aeris varietatibus, quod patet marinariis; in herbis et arboribus et infirmitatibus, in rebus quampluribus, quod patet etiam idiotis et simplicibus.' *Epistola cum tractatu*, p. 24.11–12. While the general tone is similar to that in *Tetrabiblos* I.3, esp. pp. 25–30, and so is the order of the examples, the passage also echoes a segment from Abu Ma'shar's *Liber introductorii*: 'Nam et marinarii et illi qui volunt scire nubilum aspiciunt applicationem Lune ex eodem tempore ad hos dies et loca nota que nominavimus, sciuntque ex eis esse ventorum et nubilorum atque pluviarum et rorum . . .'; see *Liber introductorii maioris ad scientiam judiciorum astrorum*, ed. R. Lemay (Naples, 1995–6), pp. 132–3. See also Robertus Anglicus' comments on astrological medicine in his *Commentary on the Sphere*, pp. 228–9.

[68] For a discussion of the theories of celestial causation in the Middle Ages and beyond, see Grant, *Planets, Stars, and Orbs*, pp. 569–617, and J. North, 'Medieval Concepts of Celestial Influence: A Survey', in P. Curry (ed.), *Astrology, Science and Society: Historical Essays* (Woodbridge, 1987), pp. 5–17.

translation as *De radiis*.[69] I will concern myself here not with the whole complex of al-Kindi's astrological doctrines in *De radiis*, but only with those aspects that I believe to have found their way, directly or indirectly, into the bishop's assessment of the kind of relationship manifest between the planetary rays and celestial harmony.

Al-Kindi begins with the fundamental claim that 'the world of the elements and everything composed of them depends on the disposition of the stars'; the reason for this, he argues, is that the stars send their rays into the world.[70] The radiation varies with the nature of the star, its position in the *machina mundana* and the combination of rays from different stars, so that when the diverse rays coalesce into a single one, 'in every different place there is a different tenor of rays derived from the total harmony of the stars'.[71] If someone were granted a full understanding of the celestial harmony, he would also fully understand the elementary world and everything it contains, anywhere, anytime; for any thing in the elementary world is an effect of the whole celestial harmony.[72] The two notions that seem to have some bearing upon our discussion can be summarised as follows: the celestial harmony emerges as the ultimate cause of changes in the sublunar world through the agency of rays, and provides the ultimate knowledge. Similarly, the bishop maintains that the planets emit rays whose compound refraction fosters sublunar changes, and that knowledge of this very harmony will ultimately reveal the full extent of celestial causality.[73] His celestial harmony, although permeated

---

[69] The Latin text has been edited and briefly discussed by M.-Th. d'Alverny and F. Hudry, in 'Al-Kindi, *De radiis*', *Archives d'histoire doctrinale et littéraire du moyen âge*, 41 (1974), pp. 139–260. For a brief summary of its contents see L. Thorndike, *A History of Magic and Experimental Science*, i (New York, 1923), pp. 642–6, and the recent study by P. Travaglia, *Magic, Causality and Intentionality: The Doctrine of Rays in al-Kindi* (Florence, 1999), pp. 17–48.

[70] Al-Kindi, *De radiis*, p. 218.

[71] *Ibid.*, pp. 219–20.

[72] 'Si enim alicui datum esset totam condicionem celestis armonie comprehendere, mundum elementorum cum omnibus suis contentis in quocumque loco et quocumque tempore plene cognosceret . . . Omnis enim res, quam modica in mundo elementorum agens, totius celestis armonie est effectus.' *Ibid.*, p. 223. Al-Kindi argues also that through a knowledge of things in the elementary world it is possible to arrive at an understanding of the celestial harmony; in other words, one may come to know the effect by knowing its cause, or the cause by knowing its effect.

[73] 'Moreover, those very projections of rays, as said above, borrow their strength from music [i.e., the musical ratios in the zodiac]. Therefore, if philosophers establish that these

by al-Kindi's radiation, has a unequivocal musical component, however: the planets make sound, albeit it cannot be heard, and the compound refraction of their rays is contingent not only upon their eccentric and epicyclical motion but also upon the zodiacal aspects, which in turn relate to each other according to musical ratios.

One fundamental question comes to the fore. If the musical consonances pertain to planetary aspects that foster terrestrial changes, rather than to the Neoplatonic sounds that planets emit in their revolutions, how can one reconcile the notions of the music of the spheres and celestial causation, and integrate them in a harmonious conceptual whole? If there were such a relationship, it could not be simply explained by the influence of the heavens making itself felt in the sublunar world by means of conventional sound, for the harmony of the spheres cannot be heard and the ratios of the planetary aspects are by their very nature silent. I suspect that possible answers may emerge from considering the bishop's understanding of the term 'ray'. In the treatise, 'ray' appears in two contexts: in the passage, quoted above, in which he discusses celestial influences, and in the last paragraph of the treatise. Both times, as a primary vehicle for celestial influence on the terrestrial realm, the ray has a musical component.

From the thirteenth century onwards, the three agents of celestial causation most often identified and discussed by Latin scholars were motion (*motus*), light (*lumen*) and influence (*influentia*).[74] Not always, however, did writers clearly distinguish among these agents or their effects. Nor did they always consider the potency of celestial influence to be contingent upon the zodiacal aspects of the planets alone. Robertus Anglicus, for example, seems to combine light and influence into one type of ray, expressed as a single entity with a twofold action: 'a planet produces heat by the reflection of rays on the surface of the solid body and it also

---

musical projections of the rays, which are known as aspects, constitute the effects of the planets, far more the celestial harmony, once it has become known, fully will reveal the secret councils (of these effects)' ('Sed et ipsae proiectiones radiorum, ut supradictum est, vim suam mutuantur ex musica. Si igitur musicae proiectiones radiorum, quae dicuntur aspectus, effectus planetarum philosophis ostendunt, longe plenius harmonia caelestium, cum cognita fuerit, eorum arcana consilia revelabunt'). *Epistola cum tractatu*, p. 29.15.

[74] Discussed in some detail in Grant, *Planets, Stars, and Orbs*, pp. 586–615.

produces virtue by the same ray'.[75] He further argues that, in addition to being conditioned by the zodiacal aspects, the influences of motion and ray are intricately linked with the Ptolemaic astronomical system, for 'the moon and other planets have stronger dominion over inferior things when they are in their apogee than when they are in their perigee' because at the apogee they move faster, whereas the influence of the ray is stronger when the star is in the lower part (of the orbit) because then the ray is shorter.[76]

The ray, as celestial *influentia*, was most akin to light; yet *influentiae* were invisible and could penetrate solid opaque bodies, which light could not do. In his *De fluxu et refluxu maris*, written very likely between 1220 and 1230, Robert Grosseteste criticises and rejects the explanation of the tides offered by Alpetragius in *De motibus caelestibus*:[77] 'the other high and low tides take place when the moon is in the two quarters below the horizon, and its light cannot act on the sea. Since heavenly bodies can only act on lower bodies by their light, it is doubtful how the moon can be the cause of the motion of the sea'.[78] In the second half of the thirteenth century, however, Richard of Middleton argues that the same substantial forms of the celestial bodies that emit light rays radiate the influ-

---

[75] The whole passage reads: 'Also note that a star exerts influence in two ways, by motion and by ray. By motion it produces heat; by ray it produces heat and virtue. For it produces heat by the reflection of the rays on the surface of a solid body, and it also produces virtue by the same ray' ('Item nota quod stella influit dupliciter, per motum et per radium. Per motum influit calorem, per radium influit calorem et virtutem. Influit enim calorem per reflexionem radiorum ad superficiem corporis solidi. Influit etiam virtutem per eundem radium'). Robertus Anglicus, *Commentary on the Sphere*, p. 154 (Latin) and p. 209 (English).

[76] '. . . luna et alii planete habent dominium fortius super res inferiores quando sunt in auge sui circuli quam quando sunt in opposito sue augis . . . quia quando stella est in auge sui circuli, velocius movetur, et quanto velocius movetur, fortius influit in hec inferiora. Et forte, si loquamur de influentia que fit per radium, tunc fortior est influentia quando stella est in parte inferiori eo quod tunc radius est brevior.' *Ibid.*, p. 162 (Latin) and pp. 214–15 (English).

[77] That is al-Bitruji (fl. 1185), a Spanish Muslim scholar; his treatise was translated into Latin by Michael Scot in 1217 under the title *De motibus caelorum* and edited by F. J. Carmody, *De motibus caelorum: Critical Edition of the Latin Translation of Michael Scot* (Berkeley, 1952).

[78] R. Grosseteste, *On the Causes of the Tides*, in Grant, *Source Book*, p. 642; reprinted from R. C. Dales, 'The Text of Robert Grosseteste's *Questio de fluxu et refluxu maris* with an English Translation', *Isis*, 57 (1966), p. 461. Grosseteste's authorship has been hotly debated; see J. McEvoy, 'The Chronology of Robert Grosseteste's Writings on Nature and Natural Philosophy', *Speculum*, 58 (1983), pp. 629–30.

ence (*influentia*) as well, and that it is the *influentia* that causes the ocean tides.[79]

For Grosseteste, because light is the only causal agent and it cannot traverse the solid body of the earth, the action of the moon on the ocean tides is difficult to explain. For Richard of Middleton, the problem is non-existent, because to him it is not the light but the *influentia* of the moon that causes the tides. The bishop subscribes to this later interpretation of Alpetragius' theory. In the last paragraph of his treatise he states:

> Although the potency of rays is great, it is made far more powerful by *musica*. The planets do not operate less where [when?] they illuminate than where they do not illuminate. The moon rising at 90° longitude equally raises the ocean in India and in Britain, granted that it illuminates the former while it does not illuminate the latter. Sound can penetrate even the most solid objects; the ray [of light] cannot.[80]

Lunar rays cause the tides in Britain as those in India. Nevertheless, light cannot be the cause of the tides in Britain because it cannot penetrate solid objects. Since sound can penetrate solid objects (as long as they are porous, Aristotelians would argue), it is sound, therefore, that must be effecting the tides. Like Robertus Anglicus' rays, the bishop's rays seem to have a composite spectrum. He suggests that in addition to light there is some kind of sound that acts upon the terrestrial realm as a form of celestial *influentia*. The strength of these rays depends upon the musical ratios in the zodiac and, as mentioned above, understanding the general *modus operandi* of celestial causation is contingent upon understanding cosmic harmony, and vice versa.

There is reason to suspect that the anonymous author's views had a wider currency in thirteenth-century speculation on *musica mundana* than the survival of his treatise in one manuscript might imply. As mentioned earlier in this essay, around 1267, Roger

---

[79] 'Ad quintum dicendum quod corpora superiora non alterant ista inferiora per influentiam luminis tantum, sed etiam per motum et per influentia immissas a suis formis substantialibus cum radiis luminosis per quam influentiam causat luna mirabiles aestus oceani, hoc est fluxum eius et refluxum'. *Clarissimi theologi magistri Ricardi de Media Villa . . . Super quatuor libros Sententiarum Petri Lombardi questiones subtilissimae* (Brescia, 1591; facs., Frankfurt, 1963), p. 189, col. I.

[80] 'Verumtamen licet radiorum sit multa potentia, revera longe fortior est musica. Nam planetae non minus operantur, ubi radiant, quam ubi non radiant. Luna oriens existentibus in longitudine nonaginta graduum, et apud Indos et apud Brittanos, aequaliter extollit oceanum, licet illis radiet, istis non radiet. Sonus omnia solidissima penetrare potest; radius vero non potest.' *Epistola cum tractatu*, p. 29.12–13.

Bacon rejected the existence of *musica mundana* and maintained that Boethius only recounted an opinion of the unlearned. In the same passage from *Opus tertium*, Bacon reports that 'Other philosophers have said that *musica mundana* comes not from the sound of celestial bodies but from sound generated by the rays of those bodies, saying that [in the case of *musica mundana*] sound is generated ... from beams rarefying the air.'[81] He further argues that not all the rarefactions of the air can generate sound, but only those caused by percussion according to Aristotle; and since the ray does not percuss, but is generated by the potentiality of matter, celestial rays cannot generate sound. Bacon's relatively lengthy argumentation suggests that the 'sounding beam' theory he was rejecting had some advocates. However, as far as I know, these advocates have never been identified; the anonymous bishop may very well have been one of them.[82]

None of the bishop's statements can be traced to a specific source. His musings are very much informed by an internalised and sometimes imprecise awareness of a host of doctrines pertaining to Aristotelian production and propagation of sound, Ptolemaic astronomy and astrological speculations current about the mid-thirteenth century. In his treatise, rather than cancelling each other out, all these doctrines coalesce to form a relatively cogent conceptual system to support a notion of *musica mundana* that can be summarised as follows: (1) the continuous spectrum of pitches that each planet produces in its revolution depends upon

---

[81] 'Propter quod alii subtilius philosophantes dixerunt quod musica mundana non est ex sono coelestium corporum, sed ex sono generato ex radiis corporum illorum, dicentes sonum . . . generari . . . ex radiis rarefacientibus aerem.' R. Bacon, *Opus tertium*, p. 229.

[82] One other strong candidate is the anonymous author of the glosses on Boethius' *De institutione musica* found in Oxford, Bodleian Library, Ashmole 1524 and Milan, Biblioteca Ambrosiana Q.9.Sup., discussed in C. Panti's article 'Grosseteste's Theory of Sound', in F. Hentschel (ed.), *Musik — und die Geschichte der Philosophie und Naturwissenschaften im Mittelalter* (Leiden, 1998), pp. 14–16. As Panti points out, the glossator's theory of sound as incorporated light is similar to that espoused by Grosseteste and Albertus Magnus, among others. He applies this theory in order to solve the problem of how the music of the spheres is produced: the sound is produced by the light (*lux*) emitted by the celestial bodies; part of the *lux* that reaches us is visible, while the part that is incorporated in the most subtle air is perceived as sound; its composition is less dense than that of our hearing and, therefore, celestial sound is not audible to us ('Sed a corporibus celestibus continue lux diffunditur et penetrat partes huius aeris, et quod illius lucis absque incorporatione in subtili aeris venit ad nos visibile est; quod vero in aeris subtilissimo de illa luce incorporatur, et sic pervenit ad nos quantum est de natura sua audibile, est et sonus. Nobis tamen audibile non est, quia compositio nostri audibilis grossior est quam sit illius soni compositio'). *Ibid.*, p. 16.

compound ratios between the planetary sizes, elongations and motion at any given time; (2) in their course through the heavens planets reach certain 'zodiacal nodes', when their aspects form ratios analogous to those of musical consonances; (3) at these 'nodes', the pitches that the planets emit at that exact moment coalesce into 'sounding rays' of maximum strength and manifest themselves as *influentiae* upon the sublunar world. The bishop envisions a music of the spheres that cannot be heard but that nevertheless participates in the celestial influence on the sublunar world. He thus succeeds in neutralising one of the most powerful arguments that Aristotle offered in *De caelo*: that there is no noise in the heavens not only because we do not hear it, but also because 'no effect other than the sensitive is produced upon us' and we 'show in our bodies none of the effects of the violent force'.[83]

Eastman School of Music, University of Rochester

---

[83] Aristotle, *On the Heavens* II.9 (290^b30–291^a6), p. 479.

Early Music History (2002) Volume 21. © Cambridge University Press
DOI:10.1017/S0261127902002036 Printed in the United Kingdom

STEFANO LA VIA

EROS AND THANATOS: A FICINIAN AND LAURENTIAN READING OF VERDELOT'S SÌ LIETA E GRATA MORTE

The literary origins of the Italian sixteenth-century madrigal, as well as the presumed inexpressive nature of the so-called *prima pratica* as compared with the *seconda pratica*, perhaps represent two of the most abused commonplaces of modern musical historiography. Most scholars still believe that the linguistic, rhetorical and stylistic principles codified by Petrarchist humanists such as Pietro Bembo directly stimulated the birth of the new literary-musical genre.[1] Even more problematic is the attitude of those who extract the dichotomy *prima/seconda pratica* from its specific cultural context – the Artusi–Monteverdi controversy – and apply it to an extended historical period, largely covering the whole history of the madrigal itself.[2]

This essay partly summarises and partly develops a lecture I delivered in Italian at the University of Bologna (14 April 1999) as part of the cycle *Sei conferenze-lezioni su Medioevo e Rinascimento* organised by Giuseppina La Face Bianconi. More recently I presented a more concise version at the Medieval and Renaissance Music Conference (St Peter's College, Oxford, 20–2 August 2000), at the suggestion of Bonnie Blackburn. I should like to thank Professor La Face Bianconi and Dr Blackburn for giving me the opportunity to develop and present this work.

[1] See, above all, D. T. Mace, 'Pietro Bembo and the Literary Origins of the Italian Madrigal', *Musical Quarterly*, 55 (1969), pp. 65–86, whose theory has been accepted and variously developed by innumerable scholars. Among the exceptions, see J. Haar, 'The Early Madrigal: A Re-appraisal of its Sources and its Character', in I. Fenlon (ed.), *Music in Medieval and Early Modern Europe* (Cambridge, 1981), pp. 163–92, at pp. 175–9, and I. Fenlon and J. Haar, *The Italian Madrigal in the Early Sixteenth Century: Sources and Interpretations* (Cambridge, 1988), pp. 13, 15–46, at pp. 28–30; Haar and Fenlon pointed out, in particular, the wide cultural hiatus that separates the birth of the madrigal – a typically Florentine phenomenon – from Bembo's Petrarchism and its rather Venetian literary-musical developments; similar conclusions emerge also in S. La Via, '*Madrigale* e rapporto fra poesia e musica nella critica letteraria del Cinquecento', *Studi musicali*, 19 (1990), pp. 33–70. See also below, nn. 40–1.

[2] A first attempt to show the basic inconsistency of this musicological commonplace appears in S. La Via, 'Cipriano de Rore as Reader and as Read: A Literary-Musical Study of Madrigals from Rore's Later Collections (1557–1566)' (Ph.D. diss., Princeton

Neither of these views finds any solid foundation in the works of the first great madrigalist, Philippe Verdelot. A close look at his production shows not only a wide spectrum of literary interests but also a remarkable ability to give musical form to the structure as well as the content of a great variety of poems.[3] To realise this, and fully to appreciate Verdelot's mastery as a literary-musical exegete, it is essential not to undervalue the poems themselves, nor to base our musical analysis on superficial or even arbitrary textual readings.

A case in point is Verdelot's setting of the anonymous ballata-madrigal *Sì lieta e grata morte* (see Appendix 2 for an edition). Despite its sixteenth-century fame,[4] first revived in modern times by Alfred Einstein,[5] scholars have so far not essayed an interpretation of its textual and musical contents.[6] The only exception is

University, 1991), esp. Part I, and ch. 6, 'Cipriano between two *prattiche*? A Musicological Topos Revisited', pp. 14–125, at pp. 93–125.

[3] H. Colin Slim has already demonstrated this in a number of fundamental studies devoted to Verdelot, particularly in *A Gift of Madrigals and Motets* (Chicago and London, 1972), pp. 41–65, 81–104, 161–90. Cf. also D. L. Hersh [= D. Harrán], 'Verdelot and the Early Madrigal' (Ph.D. diss., University of California, Berkeley, 1963); and, more recently, H. C. Slim and S. La Via, 'Verdelot, Philippe', in *The New Grove Dictionary of Music and Musicians*, 2nd edn (London, 2001), xxvi, pp. 427–34.

[4] The earliest surviving sources of *Sì lieta e grata morte* are, respectively: the so-called 'Strozzi partbooks' (Florence, Conservatorio di Musica Luigi Cherubini, MS Basevi 2495, dated *c.*1530: madrigal no. 19); the 1533 and 1537 Venetian editions, by Scotto and Antico and by Scotto, of Verdelot's *Primo libro* for four voices (RISM 1533[2], isolated partbook in Paris, Bibliothèque Nationale de France, and RISM 1537[9], complete set in Bologna, Civico Museo Bibliografico Musicale, U308: madrigal no. 15); Adrian Willaert's *Intavolatura de li madrigali di Verdelotto da cantare et sonare nel lauto* (Venice: Ottaviano Scotto, 1536; RISM 1536[8], madrigal no. 15). Clear evidence of its growing success is the fact that in the first edition of *Di Verdelotto tutti li madrigali del primo, et del secondo libro a quatro voci* (Venice: Girolamo Scotto, 1540; RISM 1540[20]) *Sì lieta* is given pride of place as the opening piece of the whole collection; since then it has been reprinted – and variously rearranged – with almost no interruption up to Claudio Merulo's edition of *I madrigali del primo et del secondo libro a quatro voci nuovamente ristampati et da molti e importanti errori con ogni diligentia corretti* (Venice: Claudio da Correggio, 1566; RISM 1566[22]).

[5] A. Einstein, 'Claudio Merulo's Ausgabe der Madrigale des Verdelot', *Sammelbände der Internationalen Musik-Gesellschaft*, 8 (1906–7), pp. 220–54, 516, includes a still valuable edition of *Sì lieta e grata morte* (Anhang, pp. 249–54), based on RISM 1566[22], 1540[20] and 1556[27]. More recent editions of the madrigal have been made by Bernard Thomas and Jessie Ann Owens on the basis of different sources: see *Philippe Verdelot, 22 Madrigals for Four Voices or Instruments*, ed. B. Thomas (London, 1980), pp. 39–41 (*Sì liet'e grata morte*, based on 1537[9], 1536[8] and 1549[33] – the latter being a reprint of 1540[20]), and *Philippe Verdelot, Madrigals for Four and Five Voices*, ed. J. A. Owens (Sixteenth-Century Madrigal, 28–30; New York and London, 1989), vol. 30, pp. 81–5 (*Se lieta e grata morte*, based on 1537[9]).

[6] Even Hersh [Harrán], 'Verdelot and the Early Madrigal', pp. 90, 163, 175, 220, refers only sporadically to *Se lieta e grata morte* and only with regard to simple matters such as rhyme scheme, recurrence of initial rhythmic patterns and 'imitative motives', adoption of 'melodic word painting'.

a short statement by Bernard Thomas, as part of his introduction to the valuable CD anthology of *Italian Renaissance Madrigals* performed by the Hilliard Ensemble (EMI, 1992): after introducing Verdelot as 'probably the most expressive madrigal composer of his generation', Thomas describes his *Sì lieta* as 'one of the earlier pieces to exploit the death/orgasm metaphor that became so important later'.[7] An attentive reader of the anonymous text, however, will find no trace of such a sexual metaphor:

Sì lieta e grata morte	Such happy and welcome death
dagli occhi di madonna al cor mi viene	from my lady's eyes comes to my heart
che dolce m'è 'l morir, dolce le pene.	that sweet to me is dying, sweet the pain.
Perché qualhor la miro	For whenever I see her
volgers'in sì benigno e lieto giro,	turning in such kind and delightful motion,
subito per dolcezza il cor si more,	at once my heart dies of sweetness,
la lingua muta tace,	my tongue, mute, is silent,
ogni spirito giace	every spirit lies
attento per sentire	alert to perceive
un sì dolce morire.	such a sweet dying.
Ma tanto del morir gioisce 'l core	But so much does my heart rejoice in dying
che poi non sento noia,	that then I feel no discomfort;
anzi la morte si convert'in gioia.	rather, death turns into joy.
Dunque se la mia donna è di tal sorte	Thus, if my lady is of such a sort
che sentir fammi morte sì gradita,	as to make death so welcome to me,
che saria poi s'ella mi desse vita?	what would it be if she gave me life?

The opening tercet, the typical *ripresa* of a *ballata mezzana,* introduces the poem's main theme: it is the lady's gaze, her *occhi* – and no more than that – which conveys an oxymoronic feeling of sweet death to the poet's heart. The motif is then further developed in the two central *mutazioni*, where the poet describes the symptoms

---

[7] B. Thomas, introduction to the Hilliard Ensemble, *Italian Renaissance Madrigals* (recorded April 1991), London, EMI, 1992, pp. 2–4, at p. 2; here he seems to go far beyond what he had stated in the commentary to his Verdelot edition, p. 3: 'compared with the madrigals of Arcadelt, for instance, Verdelot's pieces have much greater emotional range. *Sì liet'e grata morte* is one of the more ambitious numbers, with great deal of internal contrast, and some word-painting on *morte* and *volgersi*; particularly effective is the way six bars of low, rather static writing prepare for the dramatic leap at bar 40.' In both comments (1980 edn, p. 7, and 1992 CD programme booklet, pp. 16–17), moreover, Thomas gives a quite free translation of lines 5 ('moving in her beatific course'), 6 ('my heart dies of happiness'), 8–9 ('every spirit sleeps / rapt to experience / [such a sweet death]') and 16 ('what would she be if she gave me life').

of his fulguration: just as *madonna* turns to look at him, his heart dies of sweetness (second tercet), he is struck dumb and all his inner spirits suddenly lie motionless so to perceive that sweet dying most intensely (central quatrain); a similar feeling of *voluptas dolendi* is eventually described in the second *mutazioni* (penultimate tercet) as a sort of emotional metamorphosis: so much does his heart enjoy 'death', that it literally turns it into joy. Finally the *volta*, the closing tercet, restores not only the A-rhyme (*morte/sorte*) but also the main key words of the opening tercet (*madonna/mia donna, sì grata morte/morte sì gradita*), this time to reach the crucial turning point of the poem: thus, if my lady's gaze has such effects on me as to make me enjoy death, then what would I feel if she 'gave me life'?

One wonders what kind of 'death' and 'life' the poet has in mind here. Is he just playing with words? or is he trying to tell us something deeper about love? Indeed, it would be impossible to answer such questions, that is, to understand *Sì lieta*, without considering the specific literary and philosophical tradition that lies behind the poem. This is a typically Florentine tradition, which directly connects the thirteenth-century *stilnovisti* – Guido Cavalcanti even more than Dante – to Lorenzo de' Medici's fifteenth-century *Canzoniere* and to its Platonic foundation, Marsilio Ficino's treatise on Love. (For the following discussion, see the quotations in Appendix 1, §§1–3.)

Cavalcanti's *Rime*, circulating widely in manuscript throughout the previous three centuries, were first published in Florence during the 1520s, and a good selection of them also appeared in Giunta's successful 1527 anthology of *Sonetti e canzoni di diversi antichi autori toscani*.[8] Two years later Giovan Giorgio Trissino, in his *Poetica*, would highly praise the 'sweetness and sharpness' of Guido's verses and variously quote them, side by side with those by Dante and Cino da Pistoia, as an alternative model to Petrarch's *Canzoniere*.[9] It is worth noting that Trissino, Bembo's main opponent, had also

---

[8] Cf. G. Cavalcanti, *Rime*, ed. M. Ciccuto, intro. M. Corti (Milan, 1996; 1st edn 1978), where a list of the primary manuscript and printed sources is given on pp. 48–9, including the reference to the *Sonetti e canzoni* (Florence: Eredi di Filippo Giunta, 1527).

[9] G. G. Trissino, *La poetica*, Divisions I–IV (Vicenza: T. Ianiculo, 1529). Trissino did not contest the authority of Petrarch but rather Bembo's and Sannazaro's exclusive use of Petrarch as a model: this is why he quotes Petrarch as often as Dante, Guido Cavalcanti, Cino da Pistoia and other great authors ('lj altri buoni autori') such as Boccaccio,

frequented the *Orti Oricellari* – the main centre of intellectual life in Florence between 1513 and 1522 – together with other key figures such as Machiavelli, Filippo and Lorenzo Strozzi, Francesco da Diacceto, Michelangelo and probably even Verdelot.[10] Already in this light, then, Verdelot's poetic choice may well be closely linked not only to a specific Florentine tradition, but also to an even more precise cultural context and literary trend, completely independent of Bembo's Petrarchism. Not so much in Petrarch's as in Guido's poetry, in fact, do we find almost entirely the imagery later to be revived by the author of *Sì lieta* (see Appendix 1, §1): the turn of madonna's eyes (Sonnet 4); the death which 'such a sweet gaze' conveys to the lover's heart, making him confuse pleasure with pain and rhyme *gioia* with *noia* (Sonnets 13, 15, 24, Ballata 32); and the almost theatrical animation of the inner spirits, to be taken as vital functions but also as allegorical projections of the poet's feelings (Sonnet 6, Ballatas 10, 34).[11]

Two centuries later, Guido became the privileged model for both

Guittone d'Arezzo, Francesco Sacchetti and even Lorenzo de' Medici (with particular reference to his ballata 'Donne belle io ho cercato': cf. Divisions II, IV, fols. 17^v, 67^v). As for Guido, after praising the peculiar 'dolceza et acume' of his style (Division I, fol. 5^v), Trissino quotes four of his most celebrated poems: the sonnet 'L'anima mia vilmente sbigottita' (ll. 1–4), the canzone 'Donna me prega' (ll. 21–4), the ballata 'Perch'io no spero di tornar giammai' (ll. 1–6, 1–16), and the isolated canzone stanza 'Se m'ha del tutto oblïato Merzede' (cf. Divisions III and IV, fols. 23^v, 24, 27^{r-v}, 32, 41, 45^v–46, 59, 59^v).

[10] On Bernardo Rucellai's gardens, the so-called *Orti Oricellari*, and on the complex events that led up to the conspiracy against Cardinal Giulio de' Medici, see esp. R. Von Albertini, *Das florentinische Staatsbewustsein im Übergang von der Republik zum Prinzipat* (Bern, 1955), translated into Italian as *Firenze dalla Repubblica al Principato: storia e coscienza politica* (Turin, 1970), pp. 67–85. Rucellai (d. 1514) had been a close friend of Lorenzo il Magnifico; Diacceto, one of the leading members of the Rucellai circle, had been Ficino's favourite disciple; moreover, Cardinal Giulio had always been on good terms with the Republican wing of the *Orti*, particularly with its leader Machiavelli, and in part even with other 'liberal' aristocrats such as Alessandro de' Pazzi or Battista della Palla, the real promoters of the conspiracy. On Verdelot's association with the Rucellai circle, and in particular with Machiavelli, see Slim, *A Gift*, pp. 53–61; Fenlon and Haar, *The Italian Madrigal*, pp. 37–45; Slim and La Via, 'Verdelot', pp. 427–8. On the key role played by the two Strozzi brothers in the early history of the madrigal, see F. A. D'Accone, 'Transitional Forms and Settings in an Early 16th-Century Florentine Manuscript', in L. Berman (ed.), *Words and Music: The Scholar's View. A Medley of Problems and Solutions Compiled in Honor of Tillman Merritt by Sundry Hands* (Cambridge, Mass., 1972), pp. 29–58, and R. J. Agee, 'Filippo Strozzi and the Early Madrigal', *Journal of the American Musicological Society*, 38 (1985), pp. 227–37. On Michelangelo's close relationships with both Lorenzo de' Medici and Cardinal Giulio, see below, n. 39.

[11] See the complete version of each of these poems (but see also Sonnets 5, 7, 16, 20, 22, 23, Canzone 9, 27, Canzone stanza 14, Ballatas 19, 26, 30, 31) in *Rime*, ed. Ciccuto; according to Maria Corti (*ibid.*, 'Introduzione', pp. 5–27), Guido's basically negative view,

Ficino's conception of contemplative love and Lorenzo de' Medici's poetry. Lorenzo's *Canzoniere*, in particular the sonnets included in his *Comento de' miei sonetti*, might be considered as a faithful reading of the Platonic doctrine already codified by his tutor in his treatise *Sopra lo amore* (see Appendix 1, §2: excerpts from Orations II, VI, VII).[12]

According to Ficino (Oration II, ch. 8),[13] he who falls in love 'dies' as his own thought abandons him and turns to the beloved, as his soul moves to the other's body. But if love is not requited, then the lover is said to be entirely dead, since he lives neither in himself nor in his beloved, and he has no hope to be resurrected; if love is requited, on the other hand, both lovers 'die' in order to be resurrected and 'live' one in the other. The 'double death' of the unrequited lover is then opposed to the requited lover's 'happy death' and double life: the latter is first resurrected in the beloved as he has the feeling of being requited, then comes back once again to life when he recognises himself in the beloved, and therefore he no longer doubts being loved.

Ficino's 'vital death' concerns the purely contemplative phase of the falling in love, and is the only experience capable of redeeming human beings, and of leading them to God (cf. also Oration VI, chs. 6, 8, 10).[14] Here too, as in Guido and Dante, the beloved's

his symptomatic paradox of falling in love as the loss of any rational faculty, reflects in particular Averroes's conception of love as the death of reason. The terms and images used in Petrarch's *Canzoniere* are quite different; see Francesco Petrarca, *Canzoniere (Rerum vulgarium fragmenta)*, ed. M. Santagata (Milan, 1996), for instance, in the Sonnets 2–3, 39, 61, 86–87, 94, 112, 131, 133, 141, 167, 171, 175, 183, or in the Ballatas 14, 59 and in the Canzone 73. Much closer to Guido, of course, is Dante, particularly in the first part of his *Vita nuova* (1283–90), ed. L. Magugliani (Milan, 1952), sections II–III, XIV, XVI, XIX, XXIV, XXVI.

12 First written in Latin with the title *Commentarium Marsilii Ficini florentini in Convivium Platonis de amore* (autograph MS in Biblioteca Apostolica Vaticana, Vat. lat. 7705, dated 1469; and Florence, Biblioteca Medicea-Laurenziana, Strozzi 98), the treatise was immediately translated into Italian by Ficino himself (*El libro dell'Amore*, Bibl. Medicea-Laurenziana, LXXVI, 73; and Florence, Biblioteca Nazionale Centrale, II.V.98), and printed posthumously as *Sopra lo Amore o ver' Convito di Platone* (Florence: Neri Dortelata, 1544). Its main sources are described in *Marsilio Ficino e il ritorno di Platone: mostra di manoscritti, stampe e documenti (Firenze, 17 maggio – 16 giugno 1984)*, ed. S. Gentile, S. Niccoli, P. Viti (Florence, 1984), pp. 60–1, 64–8, cat. nos. 46, 48–9, 50–2. I use the modern edition of M. Ficino, *Sopra lo amore, ovvero Convito di Platone*, ed. G. Rensi (Milan, 1998).

13 *Esortazione allo amore, e disputa de lo amore semplice, e dello scambievole* (Exhortation to love, and dispute on simple and mutual love): *ibid.*, pp. 40–4.

14 *Del modo dello innamorarsi* (On how to fall in love); *Come in tutte le anime sono due amori* (How two kinds of love live in every soul); *Quali doti abbino gli amanti dal padre dello amore* (Which gifts belong to the lovers of the father of love): *ibid.*, pp. 96–8, 102–3, 109–15.

eyes are seen as the concrete reflection of the divine rays, as a magical means of human salvation. Melancholic people, more than any others, need to experience contemplative love in order to survive (cf. Oration VI, ch. 9):[15] because of their extraordinary sensitivity, visual but also musical, and also by virtue of the restless activity of their inner vital spirits, they need constantly to experience beauty, by 'seeing' and 'listening to' it.

In this context (Oration VI, ch. 9,[16] but cf. also Oration VII, chs. 1 and 14)[17] the Greek poet Sappho, even more than the philosophers Socrates and Guido, stands out as Ficino's classical model of *amore malinconico*; this is hardly surprising, considering that Ficino's symptoms of falling in love are quite similar to those found in Sappho's famous fragment no. 31 (the only one that was certainly known at the time).[18] Here, in fact, one finds the earliest description of both the symptoms of amorous fulguration and the consequent Love/Death association later revived by the author of *Sì lieta e grata morte*, especially in the central quatrain:

---

[15] *Quali passioni sieno negli amanti per cagione della madre d'amore* (Which passions are in the lovers that are caused by the mother of love): *ibid.*, pp. 103–9.

[16] *Ibid.*, pp. 105–8.

[17] *Conclusione di tutte le cose dette, con la oppenione di Guido Cavalcanti filosofo* (Conclusions about everything that has been said, with the opinion of the philosopher Guido Cavalcanti); *Per quali gradi i furori divini innalzino l'anima* (By which degrees the divine furors raise the soul): *ibid.*, pp. 135–7, 155–7.

[18] The numbering of the fragment (31, not 2 as in other editions) is the one proposed in *Poetarum Lesbiorum Fragmenta*, ed. E. Lobel and D. L. Page (Oxford, 1955), and followed also in *Sappho et Alceus, Fragmenta*, ed. E. M. Voigt (Amsterdam, 1963). Fragment 31 was quoted as an instance of the sublime in Pseudo-Longinus' *De sublime* (1st c. BC), 10; its modern fame is also due to Catullus' quite free and incomplete Latin reworking, where even the final image of death is left out. Cf. P. Radiciotti, 'Introduzione', and F. Acerbo, 'Premessa', to the volume *Canti di Saffo* (Rome, 1992), pp. ix–xvi, xix–xxxvi; both Sappho's fragment and Catullus' version are edited and translated there on pp. 4–7. Even though Longinus' treatise would become widely known only from the second half of the sixteenth century (as I learn from Leofranc Holford-Strevens, pers. comm), it is still possible that a fine humanist such as Ficino had already had direct access to it and, therefore, to Sappho's Greek text as well. This would hardly be the case for Petrarch, whose double mention of Sappho (*Triumphus Cupidinis*, iv. 25–7, and *Triumphus Fame*, iia. 86–8) seems to rely instead on Horace (*Odes*, ii. 13, 24–5), not yet on Ovid (*Heroides*, xv. 99, discovered only during the fifteenth century); both Latin poets, together with Catullus, might even have inspired Raphael's famous melancholic portrait of Sappho (included in his *Parnassus*, Vatican, Stanza della Segnatura, 1509–11).

> . . . Oh, this is what makes my heart tremble,
> deep inside my breast:
> just as I look at you, for an instant,
> and suddenly I have no more voice,
> my tongue is broken,
> a sharp shudder of fire runs along my flesh,
> . . . I almost think I am dead.[19]

All these elements, in the end, come together in the later phase of Lorenzo's *Canzoniere* (see Appendix 1, §3a)[20] and in his final *Comento* (see Appendix 1, §3b);[21] in comparison, Bembo's later *Asolani* would indeed appear as a much more superficial and rigidly doctrinal vulgarization of Ficino's Platonic conception of love.[22] In Lorenzo's sonnets, just as in Ficino's inspired prose, madonna's 'murderous' gaze, its divine ray, pierces the poet's heart and causes him a 'sweet death', which is also the first step towards his erotic and mystical 'resurrection' (Sonnets 68, 92, 100, 108–9, quoted in Appendix 1, §3a).[23] And yet Lorenzo, himself dazzled by the divine ray of love, seems never to take this step: even in his last poems we find him suspended in 'a sweet existence, between death and life', his heart conforted by the same vital spirits that Guido and

---

[19] 'Τό μ' ἦ μὰν / καρδίαν ἐν στήθεσιν ἐπτόαισεν, / ὡς γάρ ἔς σ' ἴδω βρόχε' ὡς με φώναι- / σ' οὐδ' ἔν ἔτ' εἴκει, // ἀλλὰ κὰμ μὲν γλῶσσα ἔαγε, λέπτον / δ' αὔτικα χρῷ πῦρ ὑπαδεδρόμηκεν, // . . . τεθνάκην δ' ὀλίγω 'πιδεύης / φαίνομ' ἔμ' αὔτα.' My own translation of these two excerpts from fragment 31 (ll. 5–10, 15–16) is based partly on Acerbo's and Radiciotti's edition (quoted in n. 18), partly on that published in *Saffo, Alceo, Anacreonte, Liriche e frammenti*, ed. F. M. Pontani (Turin, 1965), pp. 18–19. I wish to thank Leofranc Holford-Strevens once again for kindly helping me improve both my understanding of the Greek text and my rendering of it in idiomatic English.

[20] Lorenzo de' Medici, *Canzoniere* (Florence, *c*.1464–83), ed. P. Orvieto (Milan, 1984, repr. 1996); on its various phases, and in particular its later anti-Petrarchist and Ficinian turning point, see P. Orvieto's splendid 'Introduzione', *ibid.*, pp. vii–xl.

[21] Lorenzo de' Medici, *Comento de' miei sonetti* (Florence, 1480–91), ed. T. Zanato (Florence, 1991).

[22] Cf. P. Bembo, *Gli Asolani* (Venice: Aldo Manuzio, 1505), modern edition in P. Bembo, *Prose della volgar lingua. Gli Asolani. Rime*, ed. C. Dionisotti (Turin, 1966), pp. 311–504: in particular Book I, entirely devoted to Perottino's unhappy love, chs. 12–16, pp. 337–44, and Gismondo's rather joyful replies in Book II, chs. 8–13, 22, pp. 393–408, 425–7; cf. also Bembo's *Rime* 3, 9–10, 57, 68, 79, 86, *Stanza* 45, and above all *Rime rifiutate*, Madrigal 9, 'È cosa natural fuggir da morte', originally included in Book I of the *Asolani* and later replaced with the Canzonetta 'Quand'io penso al martire'.

[23] Cf. Lorenzo de' Medici, *Canzoniere*, respectively 'Se in qualche loco aprico, dolce e bello', 'Quando morrà questa dolce inimica', 'Sì bella è la mia donna, e in sé raccoglie', 'Se talor gli occhi miei madonna mira' and 'Quando a me il lume de' begli occhi arriva'; but see also Sonnets 72–3, 75, 91, 95–6, 99, 105, 107.

Ficino had already described in detail (Sonnet 96, Canzone 117, quoted in Appendix 1, §3a).[24]

Lorenzo's phenomenological explanation, especially in his comment to Sonnet 11 (*Comento*, 11: 9–19, quoted in Appendix 1, §3b),[25] fits even more neatly the situation and vocabulary of *Sì lieta e grata morte*:

Se il mio *cuore* fortunato sospira quando è più presso alla *donna mia*, ne è cagione la *dolcezza* che lui *sente*, la quale è sì grande che tiene occupate tutte le forze e *spiriti vitali* e gli svia dal loro officio naturale alla *fruizione di quella dolcezza*. Se prima il *cuore* aveva bisogno di respirare e refriggerarsi, molto più ne ha bisogno sopravenendo tanti *spiriti*, e' quali di natura sono caldi. E di qui nasce il sospiro, e quinci si rinfresca il *cuore*; el quale, avendo già dimenticato se stesso, per sé *non si curava di morire, anzi* bramava *sì dolce e sì felice morte*.

(If my fortunate *heart* sighs when it is closer to *my lady*, this is due to the *sweetness* it *feels*, which is so great that it keeps all the strength and *vital spirits* busy, and diverts them from their natural office to the *fruition of that sweetness*. If earlier my *heart* needed to breathe and be refreshed, it needs that even more now with the sudden arrival of so many *spirits*, which are warm by nature. This gives birth to the sigh, and therefore refreshes the *heart*; which in turn, having forgotten about itself, *did not care about dying, and rather* longed for *such sweet and happy death*.)

Indeed, the similarities between Lorenzo's comment and Verdelot's anonymous poem are so striking that one might even think of a direct relationship between them: Lorenzo's specific terms may well have inspired, in particular, the very incipit of *Sì lieta*, its central quatrain and its penultimate tercet. Both poets, moreover, limit their experience to a one-way, ecstatic contemplation of the lady's eyes and of their divine beauty; their self-complacent 'sweet death' is not yet 'life' in the complete sense that Ficino had meant in his definition of reciprocal love. Their love, in fact, is still unrequited, suspended between death and life, confined in such a voluptuous and yet unresolved oxymoron. Hence the anonymous poet's final question: what would happen 'if my lady gave me life?': that is, if she returned not only my gaze but also my love? if she gave me the final proof that my love is entirely

---

[24] Cf. *ibid.*, 'Gli alti sospir' dell'amoroso petto' and 'Quando raggio di sole'; see also Sonnets 95, 109, 110.

[25] Lorenzo de' Medici, *Comento*, comment to Sonnet 11, 'Se il fortunato cor, quando è più presso', pp. 198–202. Cf. also *ibid.*: 'Proemio' 24–37, 60–2, 89–100 (with reference to Dante, Petrarch, as well as to Cavalcanti and his 'Donna mi prega'), pp. 136–8, 142–3; 'Nuovo Argumento' 19–26, pp. 173–4; comments to Sonnets 5, 9, 12, 22–3, 25–6, 30–5, 39–40, pp. 178–80, 191–5, 202–8, 251–62, 266–74, 285–311, 324–31.

requited? if she allowed me to accomplish my resurrection and final salvation?

We might wonder, at this point, whether Verdelot was able to catch the poem's subtle *concetti*, its literary and philosophic allusions, and even to give them musical expression. My impression is that he fulfilled both tasks: Ficino and Lorenzo – perhaps even Sappho and Guido behind them – have just given us the key to understanding not only the anonymous text but also Verdelot's profoundly expressive musical response to it.

Each compositional choice, indeed, contributes to the most effective musical representation of that Ficinian and Laurentian kind of *amore malinconico* which is at the heart of *Sì lieta e grata morte* (see my annotated edition of the madrigal, in Appendix 2, and Tables 1–2). The most obvious of such choices concern cleffing, ambitus and rhythm. The gloomy nature of Verdelot's reading, in fact, depends primarily on the dark colour of its compact texture and on its static declamation: that is, on its fairly low clef combination and ambitus, and on the homogeneous slowness of its pace, obtained through an almost exclusive adoption of white notation in the context of the so-called *misura comune* (the ¢ sign, denoting *alla breve* tactus).

What makes such *tardità* stand out most effectively, moreover, is the adoption of an almost pervasive homophonic writing; this is interrupted only in a few instances by brief imitative hints, usually at beginnings of lines and in connection with positive concepts of sweetness, pleasure and delight (see bars 10–15, 22–5, 40–1, 48–52, 61–6: 'che dolce . . .', 'volgersi in sì benigno e lieto giro', 'un sì dolce . . .', 'che poi non sente noia', 'che sentir fammi morte sì gradita, / che saria poi . . .'). Otherwise, particularly in the incipit and in the central symptomatic quatrain (bars 27–44), Verdelot seems to anticipate the 'choral recitative style' of Rore's and even Monteverdi's *seconda pratica* madrigals:[26] here too in fact – and this is not a unique case in Verdelot – we find the most clear and intel-

---

[26] Concerning the use of the so-called 'choral recitative style' in the madrigals of Monteverdi and some of his predecessors (Rore and Wert above all), see respectively A. Einstein, *The Italian Madrigal* (Princeton, 1949), i, pp. 417–18, ii, pp. 516, 724; D. Arnold, 'Seconda Pratica: A Background to Monteverdi's Madrigals', *Music & Letters*, 38 (1957), pp. 341–52, at pp. 345–6, 351; S. La Via, 'Origini del "recitativo corale" monteverdiano: gli ultimi madrigali di Cipriano de Rore', in *Monteverdi: recitativo in monodia e polifonia* (Rome, 1996), pp. 23–58.

ligible declamation of the poetic text, as well as the segmentation of the musical discourse in single phrases clearly marked by cadences (see Table 1 and the edition in Appendix 2).[27]

Even if each musical phrase usually corresponds to a single poetic line, the strongest cadential resolutions – followed by a simultaneous rest in all voices – are carefully adopted to mark the very incipit of the poem as well as the ending of its four main divisions and synctactic periods: that is, respectively, the ending of lines 3B (*ripresa* = period I), 10f (first *mutazioni* = period II), 13G (second *mutazioni* = period III) and 16H (*volta* = period IV). More or less weak and passing resolutions, on the other hand, never followed by a simultaneous rest, tend to be used within each block, particularly in the two central *mutazioni*, revealing Verdelot's attention to both metre and syntax. By virtue of their strategic position and of their clear perceptibility, however, cadences are also given a specific semantic function, which in turn appears to orient the tonal trend of the whole setting: their expressive function, in other words, is at work at both levels of micro- and macrostructure.

Table 1 sums up the madrigal's tonal-cadential plan, of which a synopsis is given in Figure 1: it shows, in the first place, the sharp preponderance of Phrygian and half-cadence types over the authentic model. My use of these terms is clarified in Appendix 3, which also offers a detailed definition and exemplification of each cadential type with reference to Verdelot's practice.[28] It will suffice here to recall that the negative, suspended, pathetic nature of both the Phrygian and half-cadence types is due mainly to the

---

[27] Many other madrigals by Verdelot exhibit a similarly homophonic writing, even with episodic adoption of choral recitative. Among them, particularly close to the typology and even to the expressive contents of *Sì lieta*, are *O dolce nocte* (Machiavelli, in the 'Newberry-Oscott Partbooks', *c*.1526–9, ed. Slim in *A Gift*), *Se mai provasti, donna, qual sia amore* (Bologna, Civico Museo Bibliografico Musicale Q21, *c*.1526, and RISM 1533², ed. Thomas, Owens), *Se voi porgesti una sol fiata* (1533², ed. Owens), *La bella man mi porse* (1533², ed. Owens), *Qual maraviglia, o donna* (1534¹⁶, ed. Owens), *Quando madonna Amor, lasso, m'invita* (1534¹⁶, ed. Owens), *Non è ver che pietade* (1537¹¹, ed. Owens). Cf. also Slim and La Via, 'Verdelot', p. 430.

[28] I have first defined and applied my analytical system in La Via, 'Cipriano de Rore as Reader and as Read', pp. 134–48 (theoretical principles), 152–398 (analyses and conclusions), completed under the supervision of Harold Powers; more recently I have further developed the same method in various essays, particularly in *Il lamento di Venere abbandonata: da Tiziano a Cipriano de Rore* (Lucca, 1994), and '"Natura delle cadenze" e "natura contraria delli modi": punti di convergenza fra teoria e prassi nel madrigale cinquecentesco', *Saggiatore musicale*, 4 (1997), pp. 5–51.

Table 1 *Formal outline and tonal plan of Verdelot's* Sì lieta e grata morte

			Cadences		
			Phrygian	Half-cadence (or Plagal imp.)	Authentic
Ripresa	**I**	1a	Sì lieta e grata morte	$g > A$	$d > A$	
		2B	dagli occhi di madonna al cor mi viene			
		3B	che dolce m'è 'l morir, dolce le pene.		$\rightarrow$ (ext.) $g > \mathbf{D}$	(x) $A^{>(d)}/g \rightarrow$
Mutazioni	**II**	4c	Perché qualhor la miro	$c > \mathbf{D}$		
		5C	volgers'in sì benigno e lieto giro,	(x) $c^6 > \mathbf{D}$		
		6D	subito per dolcezza il cor si more,			$A > \mathbf{d}^{\mathrm{unf}}$
		7e	la lingua muta tace,		$\rightarrow(g > \mathbf{d}) \rightarrow$	$A > \mathbf{d} \rightarrow$
		8e	ogni spirito giace		$\rightarrow d > A$	
		9f	attento per sentire			$\rightarrow A > \mathbf{d}^{\mathrm{unf}}/_{B\flat}$
		10f	un sì dolce morire.	$(g > A \rightarrow)$	$d > A$	
	III	11D	Ma tanto del morir gioisce 'l core	$((x)\ g^{>(a)}/\mathbf{d})$		
		12g	che poi non sento noia,	$((x)\ g^6 > [d^4]\ a$ $g^{>(a)}/_F$		
		13G	anzi la morte si convert'in gioia.	(x) $c^6 > \mathbf{D}$		
Volta	**IV**	14A	Dunque se la mia donna è di tal sorte	(x) $g^6 > A$		
		15H	che sentir fammi morte sì gradita,			(D > g)
		16H	che saria poi s'ella mi desse vita?	(x) $A > \mathbf{d} \rightarrow$	$\rightarrow$ (ext.) $g > \mathbf{D}$	

Key to Table 1

Poetic text

Numbers and letters in the left column designate respectively lines and rhymes; small and capital letters distinguish 7-syllable lines (such as 1a) from 11-syllable lines (such as 14A).

Vertical sonorities

Conventional letter-notation symbols designate single vertical sonorities or 'triads'; small and capital letters distinguish minor from major triads; for example: d = D minor triad; D = D major triad.

Small or capital letters, with no added symbols, designate 5/3 or 8/3 root-position triads; small letters with added superscript ^{unf} designate 8/8 unfilled triads (without a third); for example: d^{unf} = 8/8 unfilled triad rooted on D.

Added superscripts ^{6} and ^{4} designate respectively 6/3 and 6/4 triads (equivalent to 'first inversion' and 'second inversion'); for example: c^{6} = 6/3 C minor triad; d^{4} = 6/4 D minor triad.

d / D = primary tonal focus, or the pitch class of the lowest note in the sonority that ends the piece (*finalis* or *corda finale* in sixteenth-century modal terms).

a / A = secondary tonal focus (*confinalis* or *corda mezana* in sixteenth-century modal terms).

The linkage of one letter to the next through the symbol > denotes that one triad 'resolves' to the next, as in any type of cadence (see definitions and descriptions in Appendix 3):

g > A or c^{6} > **D** = Phrygian (abbr. Phry)
d > A or g > **D** = half-cadence (hc)
g > **d** = plagal imperfect (pla i.)
A > **D** or D > g = authentic (au)

The symbol (x) refers to the *sincopa* or suspension preceding the cadential resolution, as in: (x) c^{6} > **D** = 7–6 suspension (*sincopa di settima*) and Phrygian perfect 6–8 resolution.

Brackets and arrows denote the feeble, passing quality of a cadence, as in:

(D > g) = passing authentic cadence
A > d → (g > d) → = authentic resolution immediately followed by passing plagal imperfect cadence
((x) g^{6} > [d^{4}] a) = passing Phrygian cadence.

Evaded cadences (*fuggir la cadenza*) and cadential elisions are designated respectively as follows:

(x) A > $^{(d)}$/$_{B♭}$ = the expected authentic resolution onto d/D is evaded and diverted into g.

A > d^{unf}/$_{B♭}$ = the authentic resolution onto d, at the end of the poetic line, is 'elided' by the anticipated setting of the next line, with the effect of turning d into B♭.

→ (ext) = cadential extension with *protractio longae*.

Cadences

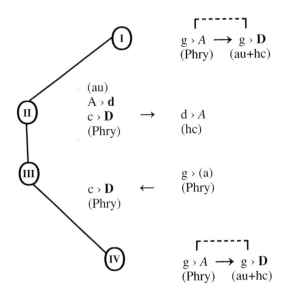

Figure 1

downward motion of their semitone resolution, which even leads to 'imperfection' in the case of the half-cadence; the more positive character of the authentic cadence, on the contrary, depends on its ascending and 'perfect' kind of resolution, which in this case is weakened, elided or even reversed.

The pathetic *gravità* of the Phrygian and half-cadence resolutions, onto A or D, which mark the first two sections of the madrigal (lines 1a, 3B, 10f, at *morte, pene, morire*, bars 4–5, 18–19, 42–4), is even increased, in sections III and IV, in association with more positive rhyme words such as *gioia* (line 13G, bars 54–5) and *vita* (line 16H, final two bars). At this level too, as in that of rhythm, Verdelot chooses to underscore the negative, painful member of the oxymoron to the detriment of its pleasant and joyful counterpart.

The same logic appears to inform, at the macro-structure level, the overall tonal-cadential plan of the piece, its coherence and symmetry as well as its inexorably negative trend. The expected positive resolution onto the main 'tonal focus' of the madrigal[29] –

---

[29] The useful term 'tonal focus' was first used by Karol Berger in a paper presented at the Symposium *Tonal Coherence in Pre-Tonal Polyphony* (Princeton, April 1987). Harold Powers later adopted the same term to designate 'either or both of two things: a cluster of dia-

its initial and final **D** sonority – not only is rare and feeble, but is repeatedly denied or reversed in various ways: (1) externally, by means of a specular overturn or 'cadential chasm' – from A > **D** to d > *A* (half-cadence) or g > *A* (Phrygian) – with pathetic emphasis on the alternative tonal focus *A*; (2) internally, by means of negative cadence models that either resolve directly onto **D** or transform the original authentic close A > **D** into the half-cadence g > **D**, as in the cadential extensions of the *ripresa* and *volta*.

The resulting symmetry of the whole tonal-cadential architecture (see the synopsis in Figure 1) faithfully mirrors not only the structure of the ballata-madrigal (the varied return of the opening tercet in the final *volta)* but also the parallel circularity of its concepts: the return of the 'welcome death' inspired by the gaze of 'my lady'. The final rhetorical turn towards 'life', being also a turn from reality to idealization, does not allow Verdelot to close the piece with a positive authentic cadence to **D** (see bars 65–73). The solemn extension with *protractio longae* and suspended half-cadence g > **D**, albeit conventional, gives definitive stress to the negative member of the oxymoron (i.e. of the *voluptas dolendi)*, in a way that renders almost mimetically the lover's unresolved suspension between death and life.

The overall coherence and homogeneity of Verdelot's setting, however, does not prevent him from giving some kind of relief also to the oxymoron itself, by means of a cleverly designed upward/downward oscillation of the melodic profile. At first, the ascending motion and its reversal correspond exactly to the 'sweet death' positive/negative sequence: see, for instance, in the incipit (opening five bars), the quasi-fauxbordon oscillation of the three compact upper parts against the bassus; particularly elegant, in the cantus, is the reversal of the stepwise diminished fourth ascent,

tonically adjacent pitch classes of the order of three to six, within which one or two predominate; a tonal center around which pitches and pitch relationships cluster or seem to be dominated. In medieval/Renaissance theoretical terms, tonal focus would be either a diatonic species of the fourth or fifth, or a degree in a Guidonian hexachord. Tonal focus is meant for concrete analysis of pieces or parts of pieces, and is hence likely to be a matter of judgement in any particular instance': H. S. Powers, 'Monteverdi's Model for a Multimodal Madrigal', in F. Della Seta and F. Piperno (eds), *In Cantu et in Sermone: For Nino Pirrotta on his 80th Birthday* (Florence, 1989), pp. 185–219, at pp. 185–6, n. 5. Cf. also S. La Via, 'Monteverdi esegeta: rilettura di *Cruda Amarilli / O Mirtillo'*, in M. Caraci Vela and R. Tibaldi (eds), *Intorno a Monteverdi* (Lucca, 1999), pp. 77–99, at p. 86, n. 16.

from $C\sharp_3$ up to F_3 (at *Sì lieta e grata*),[30] into descent of a diminished fifth, from G_3 down to $C\sharp_3$ (melisma at *morte*). A similar up-and-down fluctuation comes back even at the 'metamorphic' line 13G, when the order of the two opposing units is inverted (bars 52–5, *anzi la morte* vs. *si convert'in gioia*): once again, not only in the cantus but in all three upper voices, evoking the quasi-fauxbourdon oscillation of the incipit. In the simplest possible way, then, Verdelot is showing here the interchangeability of the two oxymoronic units, or, in other words, that process of mutual penetration that distinguishes an oxymoron from a real antithesis.

Also at this level, however, it is the element of *gravità* and melancholic pathos that in the end prevails over that of sweet *piacevolezza*:[31] the final segment of each melodic phrase (especially in the cantus) is always descending, and its stepwise motion tends to outline harsh intervals such as the diminished fourth and fifth, or pathetic figures such as the Phrygian tetrachord. A direct consequence of such a prevalently descending tendency is the gradual lowering and restriction of the overall ambitus, what any sixteenth-century theorist would consider as a generic symptom of a plagally oriented kind of 'modality'.

Sì lieta e grata morte, however, poses some serious problems of modal attribution, especially with reference to the eight-mode system, the only one Verdelot could possibly have been familiar with (see Table 2). We find neither this madrigal, nor its unusual tonal type – *cantus mollis*, low clefs (C2–C4–C4–F4), final D – in any modally ordered collection of the time.[32] Perhaps a traditional the-

---

30 Here, as well as in Appendix 3, subscript numbers are attached to capital letters to designate pitch level: with reference to the Guidonian hexachordal system, G_1 corresponds to Gamma *ut*, C_2 to C *fa ut*, C_3 to c *sol fa ut*, and C_4 to cc *sol fa*.

31 The stylistic dichotomy *gravità/piacevolezza* (or *dolcezza*), traditionally one of the landmarks of Bembo's Petrarchism (cf. P. Bembo, *Prose della volgar lingua* (Venice: Tacuino, 1525), in Bembo, *Prose*, ed. Dionisotti, pp. 146 ff.), was already quite familiar to Lorenzo de' Medici, who applied it not only to Petrarch but also, and above all, to Guido Cavalcanti: 'Chi negherà nel Petrarca trovarsi uno stile grave, lepido e dolce, e queste cose amorose con tanta gravità e venustà trattate . . .?'; 'E Guido Cavalcanti, di chi di sopra facemmo menzione ['Proemio' 61, p. 142], non si può dire quanto commodamente abbi insieme coniunto la gravità e la dolcezza, come mostra la canzone sopra detta ['Donna me prega'] e alcuni sonetti e ballate sue dolcissime': Lorenzo de' Medici, *Comento*, ed. Zanato, 'Proemio' 95, 99, pp. 147, 148; later on, *ibid.*, 'Nuovo Argomento' 31, p. 175, Lorenzo uses similar terms to describe the beauty of his beloved lady : 'Era la sua bellezza, come abbiamo detto, mirabile: . . . l'aspetto suo grave e non superbo, dolce e piacevole'.

32 Cf. H. S. Powers, 'Tonal Types and Modal Categories in Renaissance Polyphony', *Journal of the American Musicological Society*, 34 (1981), pp. 428–70.

Table 2   *Tonal type and possible modal representation in Verdelot's*
Sì lieta e grata morte

(1) tonal type: ♭ = *cantus mollis*, or B♭ system
C2 = 'low' clef combination (cantus: C2, altus: C4, tenor: C4, bassus: F4)
D = pitch class of the lowest note in the last sonority

(2) ambitus of each voice, species of 8ve/5th/4th, cadences:

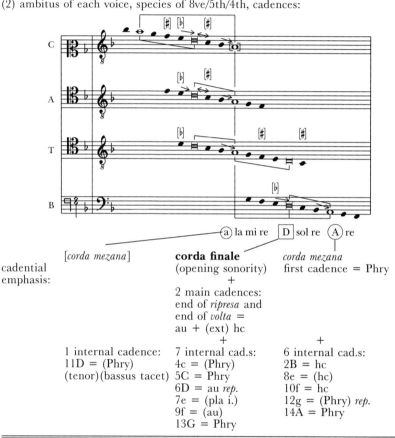

	(a) la mi re	D sol re	(A) re
	[*corda mezana*]	**corda finale**	*corda mezana*
cadential emphasis:		(opening sonority)	first cadence = Phry
		+	
		2 main cadences: end of *ripresa* and end of *volta* = au + (ext) hc	
		+	+
	1 internal cadence: 11D = (Phry) (tenor)(bassus tacet)	7 internal cad.s: 4c = (Phry) 5C = Phry 6D = au *rep.* 7e = (pla i.) 9f = (au) 13G = Phry	6 internal cad.s: 2B = hc 8e = (hc) 10f = hc 12g = (Phry) *rep.* 14A = Phry

Key to Table 2

Downward and upward arrows between notes indicate semitone tendency only in relation to the two main pitch classes of the piece (**D** and *A*), corresponding to the modal *finalis* (Zarlino's *corda finale)* and *confinalis* (Zarlino's *corda mezana*).

Accidentals within square brackets indicate occasional alteration of diatonic pitches (usually at cadence points).

au = authentic cadence   Phry = Phrygian cadence
hc = half-cadence   (ext) = cadential extension
pla i. = plagal imperfect cadence   *rep.* = repeat

orist such as the Florentine Pietro Aaron would have ascribed it to the first mode,[33] whose positive and joyful ethos,[34] however, hardly fits the unquestionably grave and melancholic character of Verdelot's madrigal. From the rather retrospective viewpoint of dodecachordal theorists such as Gioseffo Zarlino, on the other hand, the tonal type of *Sì lieta* might be seen as an *ante litteram* representation of the Hypoaeolian mode 10, transposed a fifth lower by B flat, perhaps with an inner Hypophrygian (even more than Hypodorian) commixture.[35] The particularly close connection between the two plagal modes 10 and 4, according to Zarlino himself, is due basically to their common species of fourth (D–C–B♭–A), besides, naturally, their descending *modo di procedere* and low ambitus; for these reasons, he also attributes to them exactly the same melancholic and plaintive 'nature', particularly suitable to *materie amorose*.[36]

Here our exegetic circle might find its final closure. Zarlino's modal terms, even though hypothetical and retrospective,[37] would fit perfectly the essence of Verdelot's reading, and would give

---

[33] Cf. P. Aaron, *Trattato della natura et cognitione di tutti gli tuoni di canto figurato non da altrui più scritti* (Venice, 1525), chs. 1–3, and in particular ch. 4, 'Dichiaratione del primo et secondo tuono', unnumbered folio. According to Aaron, 'any song whose Tenor ends on D sol re' – including those 'with the *B molle*', since this does not affect the species of fifth – 'will undoubtedly be ascribed to either the first or the second mode'. In the case of *Sì lieta*, Aaron's first mode (rather than the second) seems to fit quite well the octave species in the tenor (with the regular fifth below the 'transformed' fourth, and not vice versa) as well as its whole *processus*. For a discussion of Aaron's terms, cf. H. S. Powers, 'Is Mode Real? Pietro Aron, the Octenary System, and Polyphony', *Basler Jahrbuch für historische Musikpraxis*, 16 (1992), pp. 9–52, at p. 28 *et passim*.

[34] Cf. Aaron, *Trattato*, ch. 25, 'Della natura et operatione di tutti gli tuoni', unnumbered folios, where the first mode is associated with affections of 'happiness, joy and hilarity' (*letitia, gaudio et hillarità d'animo*).

[35] G. Zarlino, *Le istitutioni harmoniche* (Venice: F. dei Franceschi, 1558), part IV, chs. 5–29, pp. 301–5, and esp. ch. 19, 'Del secondo modo', ch. 21, 'Del quarto modo', and ch. 27, 'Del decimo modo', pp. 322–3, 324, 332. On Zarlino's humanistic interpretation of Glareanus' dodecachordal system, and on his rather modern conception of 'transposition' (as opposed to Aaron's 'transformation'), *modo di procedere*, modal species, relationship between tenor and the other voices, and *natura contraria* of authentic and plagal modes, see La Via, 'Natura delle cadenze', pp. 14–22, 42–50.

[36] On mode 10 and its structural as well as affective connection with modes 2 and 4 – also with reference to Verdelot's four-voice motet *Gabriel archangelus locutus est Zachariae* (1532[10]) – cf. Zarlino, *Istitutioni*, p. 332; on the similarly grave, melancholic and plaintive nature of these three plagal modes, see also pp. 322–4.

[37] It must be stressed here that Zarlino's reference to Verdelot, just quoted above in n. 36, is not at all exceptional: indeed, in the whole *Istitutioni harmoniche* Verdelot's madrigals and motets stand out among Zarlino's main practical models, second only to Willaert's *Musica nova*.

further confirmation to everything that has emerged from my analysis. At every level, indeed – from rhythm, melody and texture to cadential and tonal strategy – Verdelot's music appears to be aimed at the most melancholic, at times even funereal, representation of the anonymous poet's fatal experience of amorous fulguration, and, behind that, of a specifically Florentine, Platonically oriented conception of *amore contemplativo*. Without going beyond the limits of a working hypothesis, one might even see in early madrigals such as *Sì lieta e grata morte* the particular reflection of a wider cultural phenomenon: the Florentine political and artistic revival, during the 1520s, of the cult of Lorenzo il Magnifico, whose main promoter was Cardinal Giulio de' Medici (since 1523 Pope Clement VII), Verdelot's own patron,[38] who commissioned his early madrigals as well as Michelangelo's Biblioteca Laurenziana and Medici chapel in San Lorenzo.[39]

---

[38] R. Sherr, 'Verdelot in Florence, Coppini in Rome, and the Singer "La Fiore"', *Journal of the American Musicological Society*, 37 (1984), pp. 402–11, at pp. 402–4, 409, has uncovered and published a letter from Niccolò de Pictis which documents Verdelot's entrance into the service of Cardinal Giulio de' Medici in May 1521; see also N. Pirrotta, 'Rom', in *MGG*, xi, p. 706; Slim, *A Gift*, pp. 53–62, and Slim and La Via, 'Verdelot', pp. 427–8. See also above, n. 10, and below, nn. 39 and 40. Authoritative scholars such as Haar and Fenlon, however, tend to exclude the possibility that the Medici family, and in particular Cardinal Giulio, might have played a primary role in the Florentine patronage of the early madrigal, also on the ground of Verdelot's association with Machiavelli and the *Orti Oricellari*, and of his supposed opposition to the Medici family: see Haar, 'The Early Madrigal', p. 164, and I. Fenlon, 'Context and Chronology of the Early Florentine Madrigal', in M. Muraro (ed.), *La letteratura, la rappresentazione, la musica al tempo e nei luoghi di Giorgione* (Rome, 1987), pp. 281–93, at pp. 283–5.

[39] The Florentine renewal of the Golden Age of Lorenzo il Magnifico started during the papacy of Giovanni de' Medici, Leo X (1513–21); it is in this period (1519) that Michelangelo began to work on his decorative sculptures of the Medici chapel, encouraged in particular by Cardinal Giulio, who, as Pope Clement VII (1523–34), would later commission Michelangelo's Biblioteca Laurenziana (1524–7, 1533–4); both works represent a tribute to the Medici dynasty as a whole, but also a retrospective celebration of Lorenzo as politician, patron of the arts and man of letters. In the same years, various retrospective homages were addressed to Lorenzo by different persons, such as the biographer Niccolò Valori (*Vita Laurentii Medicis*, dedicated to Leo X in 1518), the Republican Machiavelli (*Istorie fiorentine*, commissioned by the Medici in 1518), the aristocrat Alessandro de' Pazzi (*Discorso*, 1522, written at the explicit request of Cardinal Giulio), the literary critic Trissino (*La poetica*, 1529; see above, n. 9), the painter Pontormo and the artists who decorated Lorenzo's villa at Poggio a Caiano after the Medici restoration in 1512. See, in particular, Von Albertini, *Firenze dalla Repubblica al Principato*, pp. 69–70, 78–83; C. de Tolnay, *Michelangelo*, iii: *The Medici Chapel* (Princeton, 1970, 1st edn 1948), pp. 7–13, 26, 33–5, 63–75; J. S. Ackerman, *The Architecture of Michelangelo* (Harmondsworth, 1970, 1st edn 1961), pp. 97–122, at pp. 98–104; H. Hibbard, *Michelangelo* (New York, 1974), pp. 177–219; J. Cox-Rearick, *Dynasty and Destiny in Medicean Art: Pontormo, Leo X, and the Two Cosimos* (Princeton, 1984), Parts I–III, pp. 15–227.

Even outside such a hypothesis,[40] both Verdelot's poetic choice and his sensitive musical response suggest once again that the traditional Petrarchan- and Bembist-oriented view of the literary origins of the sixteenth-century madrigal should be further re-examined, widened and also reconciled with its primarily Florentine roots.[41] The profound expressivity of Verdelot's music also seriously challenges the even more schematic *prima/seconda pratica* opposition: here, as elsewhere, the composer is clearly interested in mirroring and highlighting not only the formal surface of his chosen poetry but also its inner meanings, up to the point of offering us a key to their clarification and deep understanding. Even though he is not as yet interested in the musical dramatization of poetic contrasts and antitheses, some of his solutions – including his tonal, cadential and melodic strategies – clearly anticipate those that Cipriano de Rore, the supposed 'founder' of the *seconda pratica*, will restore and bring to perfection in his later masterpieces.[42]

Università degli Studi di Pavia

[40] A hypothesis in line with the recent conclusions reached by F. A. D'Accone, 'Lorenzo il Magnifico e la musica', in *La musica a Firenze al tempo di Lorenzo il Magnifico, Congresso internazionale di studi (Firenze, 15–17 giugno 1992)*, ed. P. Gargiulo (Florence, 1993), pp. 219–48, at pp. 246–8. Here D'Accone stresses the key role played by Lorenzo in promoting transalpine polyphony in late fifteenth-century Florence, and even in laying the groundwork for the imminent birth of the madrigal; he identifies in particular the Fleming Heinrich Isaac, Lorenzo's favourite composer (a stable member of the Medici court from 1484 to 1496 and still in Florence between 1512 and 1517) as the true predecessor of early madrigalists such as Bernardo Pisano, Francesco Layolle and Philippe Verdelot.

[41] In this broader sense my Ficinian and Laurentian reading of Verdelot further substantiates the historical view of the Florentine origins of the Italian sixteenth-century madrigal already proposed by several American and British scholars in the 1970s and 1980s. Besides the essays by Haar (1981), Fenlon and Haar (1988), D'Accone (1972), Agee (1985) and Fenlon (1987) cited in nn. 1, 10 and 38, see also F. A. D'Accone, 'Bernardo Pisano and the Early Madrigal', in *Internationale Gesellschaft für Musikwissenschaft: Report of the Tenth Congress* (Ljubljana, 1967), ed. D. Cvetko (Kassel, 1970), pp. 96–106, and J. Haar, 'Madrigals from the Last Florentine Republic', in S. Bertelli and G. Ramakus (eds), *Essays Presented to Myron P. Gilmore* (Florence, 1978), ii, pp. 383–403.

[42] From this angle, Verdelot's *Sì lieta e grata morte* is a forerunner in particular of Rore's sombre setting of Della Casa's sonnet 'O sonno, o della queta, humida, ombrosa', analysed in La Via, 'Natura delle cadenze'.

APPENDIX 1

Some Antecedents and Possible Literary Sources of *Sì lieta e grata morte*

1. Guido Cavalcanti, *Rime*

4. 5:	quando li *occhi gira*
9. 4:	mostrando per lo viso agli *occhi morte*
13. 1:	Voi che per li *occhi* mi passaste 'l *core*
15. 11–12:	. . . ritornerebbe in allegrezza e 'n *gioia*.
	Ma sì è al *cor dolente* tanta *noia* . . .
24. 9–14:	Ma quando sento che *sì dolce* sguardo
	dentro degli *occhi* mi passò al *core*
	e posevi uno spirito di *gioia*,
	di farne a lei mercé, di ciò non tardo:
	così pregata foss'ella d'Amore
	ch'un poco di pietà no i fosse *noia*!
32. 1–4:	Quando di *morte* mi conven trar *vita*
	e di pesanza *gioia*,
	come di tanta *noia*
	lo spirito d'amor d'amar m'invita?
6. 1–4:	Deh, *spiriti miei*, quando mi vedete
	con tanta pena, come non mandate
	fuor della mente parole adornate
	di pianto, dolorose e sbigottite?
10. 13–16:	Questa pesanza ch'è *nel cor* discesa
	ha certi *spirite'* già consumati,
	i quali eran venuti per difesa
	del *cor dolente* che gli avea chiamati.
34. 18–21:	Pieno d'angoscia, in loco di paura,
	lo spirito del cor dolente giace
	per la Fortuna che di me non cura,
	c'ha volta *Morte* dove assai mi spiace.

2. Marsilio Ficino, *Sopra lo Amore*

II. 8: Platone . . . disse: quello amatore è un animo nel proprio corpo morto, e nel corpo d'altri vivo . . .

Platone chiama l'amore amaro, e non senza cagione, perché qualunque ama, muore amando . . .

Muore amando qualunque ama: perché il suo pensiero dimenticando sé, nella persona amata si rivolge. . . .

Due sono le spezie d'amore, l'uno è semplice, l'altro è reciproco.

L'amore semplice è dove l'amatore non ama l'amato. Quivi in tutto l'amatore è morto, perché non vive in sé . . . e non vive nell'amato, essendo da lui sprezzato. . . .

Adunque in nessun luogo vive chi ama altrui e non è da altrui amato; e però interamente è morto il non amato amante; e mai non resuscita . . .

Ma dove lo amato nell'amor risponde, l'amatore almen che sia nell'amato vive. Qui cosa maravigliosa avviene, quando duoi insieme si amano: costui in colui e colui in costui vive. . . .

Una solamente è la morte nell'amore reciproco; le resurrezioni sono due: perché chi ama muore una volta in sé, quando si lascia; risuscita subito nell'amato quando l'amato lo riceve con ardente pensiero; risuscita ancora quando egli nell'amato finalmente si riconosce, e non dubita sé esser amato. O felice morte alla quale seguono due vite!

VI. 6: coloro che sono nati sotto una medesima stella sono in tal modo disposti che la immagine del più bello di loro, entrando per gli occhi nell'animo di quell'altro, interamente si confà con una certa immagine, formata dal principio di essa generazione, così nel velame celestiale dell'Anima, come nel seno dell'anima. . . .

Tre cose senza dubbio sono in noi: Anima, Spirito e Corpo. L'Anima e il Corpo sono di natura molto diversa, e congiungonsi insieme per mezzo dello Spirito, il quale è un certo vapore sottilissimo e lucidissimo, generato per il caldo del cuore dalla più sottil parte del sangue.

VI. 8: ogni amore comincia dal vedere . . .

lo amore del contemplativo si chiama 'divino', dello attivo 'umano', del voluttuoso 'bestiale'.

VI. 9: per lungo amore gli uomini pallidi e magri divengono . . .

La intenzione dello amante tutta si rivolta nella assidua cogitazione della persona amata . . . dove l'assidua intenzione dell'animo ci trasporta, quivi volano ancora gli spiriti . . .

Questi spiriti si generano nel caldo del cuore, dalla sottilissima parte del sangue. . . .

Inverso questa [persona amata] sono tirati ancora gli spiriti, e volando quivi continuamente si consumano . . . Di qui il corpo si secca e impallidisce: di qui gli amanti divengono malinconici. . . .

I collerici e i melanconici seguitano molto i diletti del canto e della forma, come unico rimedio e conforto di loro complessione molestissima, e però sono a le lusinghe di Amore inclinati: come Socrate il quale fu giudicato da Aristotele di complessione malinconica. E costui fu dato allo Amore più che uomo alcuno, secondo che egli medesimo confessava. Il medesimo possiamo giudicare di Saffo poetessa, la quale dipinge se stessa melanconica e innamorata. . . .

Chi negherà lo Amore essere ignudo? perché nessuno lo può celare: con ciò sia che molti segni scuoprino gli innamorati: cioè il guardare simile al toro e fiso, il parlare interrotto, il colore del viso or giallo, or rosso, gli spessi sospiri, il gittare in qua e in là le membra, i continui rammarichi . . .

VI.10: il raggio della Bellezza che è copia e padre dell'Amore ha questa forza, che e' si riflette quivi onde ei venne, e riflettendosi tira seco lo amante. Certamente questo raggio disceso prima da Dio e poi passando nello Angelo, e nell'Anima, . . . e dall'Anima nel corpo preparato a ricevere tal raggio facilmente passando, da esso corpo formoso traluce fuora, massime per gli occhi, come per transparenti finestre: e subito vola per aria, e penetrando gli occhi dell'uomo che bada, ferisce l'Anima, accende lo appetito. . . .

Questo medesimo avviene alle volte agli Amanti e agli Amati . . .

VII.1: Guido filosofo . . . seguitò lo Amore socratico in parole e in costumi.

Costui con gli suoi versi brevemente conchiuse ciò che da voi di Amore è detto. . . .

Guido Cavalcanti filosofo tutte queste cose artificiosamente chiuse nelli suoi versi. . . .

Imperocché quando ne' suoi versi dice: *sole e raggio*, per il Sole intende la luce di Dio, per il raggio la forma de' corpi.

VII.14: Quattro adunque sono le spezie del divino furore: il primo è il furore poetico, il secondo il misteriale cioè sacerdotale, il terzo la divinazione, il quarto è lo affetto dello amore. . . .

Orfeo da tutti questi furori fu occupato, . . . Ma dal furore amatorio spezialmente sopra gli altri furono rapiti Saffo, Anacreonte e Socrate.

3. Lorenzo de Medici

(a) *Canzoniere*:

68. 9–14:
> Né sa più il tristo core omai che farsi:
> o fuggir ne' begli occhi alla sua morte
> o ver lontan da quei morir ognora.
> Dice fra sé : 'Se un tempo in quelli occhi arsi,
> *dolce era il mio morir, lieta mia sorte*:
> onde meglio è che ne' belli occhi mora.'

92. 12–14:
> Risponde sorridendo Amore allora:

'*dolce è mia morte*, . . .
e sempre vive Amore'.

96. 1, 4, 5–8, 12–14: Gli alti sospir dell'amoroso petto . . .
caldi ancor nel mio cor hanno ricetto.
Gli narran le parole che ha lor detto
Amore, in dolci e tacite favelle;
tutti gli spirti allor per udir quelle
correndo, resta *il core* oppresso e stretto. . . .
Là *vita e morte*, onde partì, par faccia:
così uno spirito in due alterna e move
un dolce viver ch'è fra morte e vita.

100. 9–11: Oh bella morte e, oh, dolor süavi!
Oh pensier' che portate ne' sospiri,
ad altri ignota, al cor tanta dolcezza!

108. 1, 4–5, 12–14: Se talor gli occhi miei madonna mira . . .
però sovente *i suoi begli occhi gira*
verso li miei . . .
Giunto al mio cor, che in lei vie più s'accende,
la pigra speme e lunga pietà caccia:
così vede i miei spirti allor contenti.

109. 1, 9–14: Quando a me il lume de' begli occhi arriva . . .
Li spirti incontro a quel dolce splendore
da me fuggendo lieti vanno, in cui
(e loro il sanno) Amor gli uccide e strugge.
Se la mia vista resta o se pur fugge,
che morta in me allor vive in altrui,
dubbio amoroso solva il gentil core.

117. 18–26: Venne per gli occhi pria
nel petto tenebroso
degli occhi vaghi il bel raggio amoroso,
e destò ciascun spirto che dormiva,
sparti pel petto, sanza cure ozioso.
Ma tosto che sen giva
in mezzo al cor la bella luce viva,
gli spirti, accesi del bel lume adorno,
corsono al core intorno.

(b) *Comento de' miei sonetti*:
Nuovo Argumento 25: Veramente quando la natura gli creò, non fece solamente due *occhi*, ma *il vero luogo dove stessi Amore e insieme la Morte*, o vero vita e 'nfelicità degli uomini che fiso gli riguardassino.

5. 4–7 ff.: E però se mi trovavo alla presenza di lei, el viso suo, veramente angelico, pareva al cuore dolce e altero: dolce perché così veramente era, altero gliele faceva parere el dubbio . . . della poca pietà. . . . Di questo suo timore nasceva in lui l'affanno, e però li *spiriti vitali*, correndo per soccorrere al *cuore*, lasciavano la faccia mia senza colore, pallida e smorta.

11. 9–19: Se 'l mio *cuore* fortunato . . . sospira in quel tempo quando è più presso alla donna mia, . . . ne è cagione la *dolcezza* che lui sente, la quale è sì grande che tiene occupate tutte le forze e *spiriti vitali* e gli svia dal loro officio naturale alla *fruizione di quella dolcezza*. . . . se prima il cuore aveva bisogno di respirare e refriggerarsi, molto più ne ha bisogno sopravenendo tanti spiriti, e quali di natura sono caldi. . . . E di qui nasce il sospiro, e quinci si rinfresca il *cuore*; el quale, avendo già dimenticato se stesso, *per sé non si curava di morire, anzi* bramava *sì dolce e sì felice morte*.

40. 19: Godevomi adunque non solamente quella presente bellezza, ma ancora la speranza di molto più *dolce morte*, la quale . . . con grandissimo desiderio aspettavo, perché quanto maggiore erano le offese, cioè el desiderio di tanta bellezza, più dolce si faceva la morte. E però la speranza di questa morte mi empieva il cuore di tanta dolcezza, che il cuore già se ne nutriva e viveva: intendendo questa morte nella forma che abbiamo detto morire li amanti, quando tutti nella cosa amata si trasformano . . . E però questa morte non solamente è dolce, ma è quella dolcezza che puote avere l'umana concupiscienzia, e per questo da me come unico remedio alla salute mia era con grandissima dolcezza e desiderio aspettata come vero fine di tutti i miei desiderii.

Stefano La Via

APPENDIX 2

Annotated Edition of Verdelot's *Sì lieta e grata morte*

Preliminary notes

The present edition of *Sì lieta e grata morte*, far from being a critical edition in the strict sense, is based primarily but not exclusively on the earliest complete surviving printed source of Verdelot's madrigal: *Il primo libro de' madrigali di Verdelotto, novamente stampato, et con somma diligentia corretto* (Venice: Ottaviano Scotto, 1537) (RISM 1537[9]; Bologna, Civico Museo Bibliografico Musicale, U308). Of both the first edition – issued in 1533 by the Scotto family and Andrea Antico (RISM 1533[2]) – and an otherwise lost second edition [1535–6], only a single bass partbook survives (respectively in Paris, Bibliothèque Nationale de France, Thibault collection, and in Florence, Biblioteca Nazionale Centrale): see Fenlon and Haar, *The Italian Madrigal*, pp. 296–9.

Not surprisingly, this source presents a few mistakes in the poetic text, and almost no accidentals. Both the correction of such mistakes and the addition of editorial accidentals reflect musical, exegetic and analytical considerations which have often found confirmation in other relevant sources: in particular, the earlier but incomplete Florentine manuscript known as the 'Strozzi partbooks' (Florence, Conservatorio di Musica Luigi Cherubini, MS Basevi 2495: Cantus, Tenor, Bassus, *c.*1530; see Fenlon and Haar, pp. 159–61); and Adrian Willaert's *Intavolatura de li madrigali di Verdelotto* (Scotto 1536 = RISM 1536[8]). Later sources have also been consulted such as Scotto's and Gardano's respective editions of *Di Verdelotto tutti li madrigali del primo et del secondo libro a quatro voci* (Scotto 1540, 1549 = RISM 1540[20], 1549[33]; Gardano 1556 = RISM 1556[27]), and Claudio Merulo's final edition of *I madrigali del primo et secondo libro di Verdelot a quattro voci* (RISM 1566[22]).

Significant variants in the poetic text:

1a: *Sì lieta e grata morte*
    Sì lieta (Strozzi *c.*1530; 1536[8]; 1537[9] Tenor; later sources) vs.
    Se lieta (1536[8] Index title; 1537[9] Cantus, Altus, Bassus)

3B: *che dolce m'è 'l morir, dolce le pene*
    dolc'et le pene (Strozzi *c.*1530) vs.
    dolce le pene (1536[8], 1537[9], later sources)

6D: *subito per dolcezza il cor si more*
    dolceza . . . muore (Strozzi *c.*1530) vs.
    dolcezza . . . more (1536[8], 1537[9], later sources)

14A: *Dunque se la mia donna è di tal sorte*
  Dunque (Strozzi *c.*1530; later sources) vs.
  <u>*Donque*</u> (1536[8]; 1537[9])

16H: *che saria poi s'ella mi desse vita*
  che saria poi <u>se la</u> mi des<u>si</u> vita (Strozzi *c.*1530)
  che saria poi se<u> </u>la mi desse vita (1536[8])
  che s<u>e</u>ria poi s'ella mi desse vita (1537[9] Tenor)
  che saria poi <u>si la me</u> desse vita (1537[9] Cantus, Altus, Bassus)
  che saria poi s'ella mi desse vita (later sources)

The musical text given in the two earliest vocal sources of *Sì lieta* (Strozzi *c.*1530 and 1537[9]) is almost identical: I have found only one mistake in the Strozzi tenor partbook (bar 27, at 'sub<u>ito</u>', A, B♭, <u>B♭</u>); but I have also accepted the rhythmic solution given in the manuscript bass partbook, at bar 63: 'morte' = ♩. ♪ instead of ♩♩ in all the other sources (including 1537[9]).

Original accidentals in 1537[9] are indicated above the stave with the symbol *; the symbol † at bar 62 in the bassus (E♭ at 'sentir') refers to the only accidental found in the Strozzi partbooks.

Given their high quantity, accidentals found in other sources have also been inserted within the musical text without brackets. Almost all of them correspond to the accidentals already included by Willaert (1536[8]) and Merulo (1566[22]), listed below:

Cantus:	2	5	11	14	15	20–1	24	26–7	37	39	54	61	68
1536[8]	C♯	C♯					F♯		C♯	C♯	E♭	C♯	
1566[22]	C♯	C♯	C♯	C♯	C♯-B-C♯	F♯	F♯	F♯	C♯	C♯		C♯	C♯

Altus:	5	8	9–10	12	16	24	25	29	32	44	55	61	69
1536[8]	C♯	E♭	C♯	F♯	F♯	E♭	B	C♯	C♯	C♯	F♯	C♯	
1566[22]	C♯	E♭	C♯	F♯	F♯	E♭	B	C♯-B-C♯	C♯-B-C♯	C♯	F♯	C♯	F♯

Tenor:	2	12	14	19	23	25–6	38	59	64–5	73
1536[8]	F♯	C♯	C♯	F♯	F♯	E♭	F♯	C♯	F♯	F♯
1566[22]			C♯	F♯	F♯	E♭	F♯		F♯	F♯

Bassus:	8	24	26	36	54	62	67	71
1536[8]	E♭	E♭ B	E♭	C♯	E♭*	E♭		F♯
1566[22]	E♭	E♭ B	E♭	C♯	E♭	E♭	C♯	F♯

* 1536[8], bar 54: in the fourth line of the tablature (representing the C-string in the lute) number 5 (= F) should be read as number 3 (= E♭).

Entirely new accidentals (not found in any of the sixteenth-century sources here consulted) have been inserted only in three cases, at bars 13 (cantus, 'mo-[rir]', F$\sharp$) and 22 (cantus, 'mi-[ro]', E$\flat$; altus, '[mi-]ro', F$\sharp$); they are indicated above the stave with the symbol +.

I have kept the original notation (including the ¢ sign, denoting *alla breve* tactus), with *Mensurstrich* and no bars between staves, in order to render more faithfully its basically 'white', slow-paced character, and to make visible more clearly single note values (without ligatures) as well as rhythmic-melodic figures.

Literary and musical annotations are intended to help the reader follow my analysis. Numbers and letters above the stave (such as 1a, 2B, etc.) signal the beginning of each line in the poetic text (see also the Key to Table 1); vertical lines mark the corresponding caesuras between musical phrases. Letter-notation symbols beneath the stave designate the corresponding sonorities, harmonic progressions and cadences (see also Table 1 and related Key). Cadence resolutions are also highlighted within the musical text by means of arrows (half-tone resolution) and hyphens (step motion or skip in the accompanying voice/s).

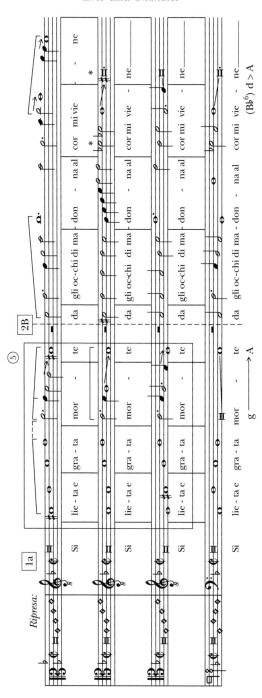

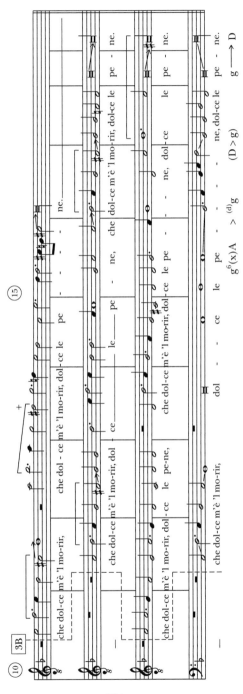

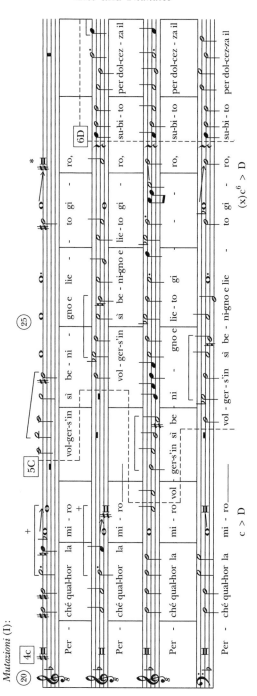

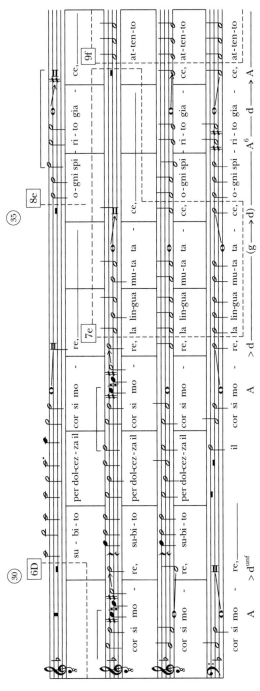

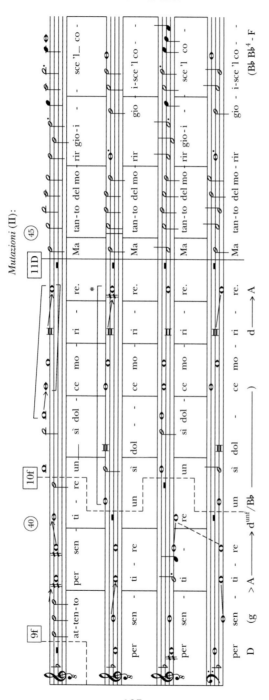

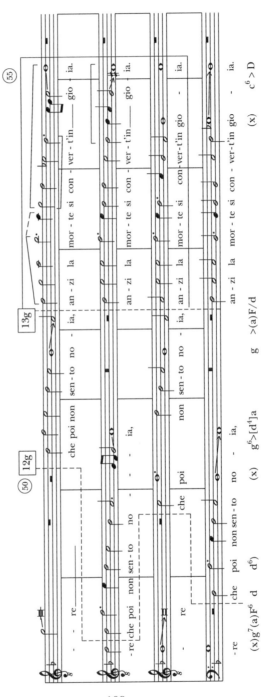

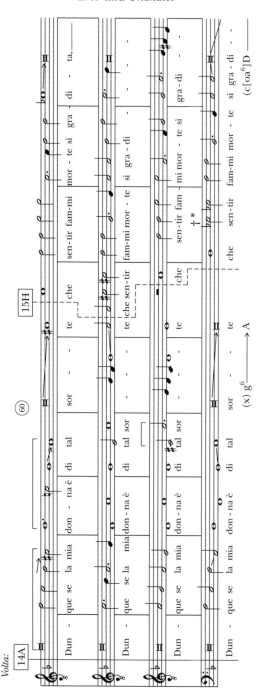

109

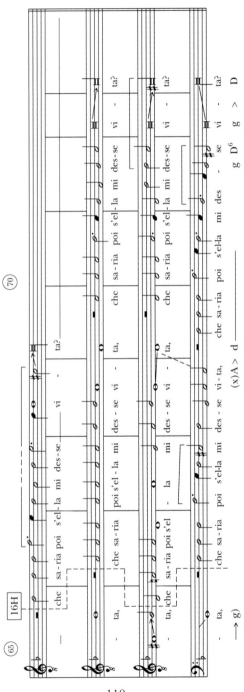

APPENDIX 3

Verdelot's Use of Cadences in *Sì lieta e grata morte:* Definitions and Examples

I. Authentic Cadence

Equivalent to the modern 'authentic' cadence – but still alien to its tonal and harmonic function V > I – it does not even correspond necessarily to a 'perfect' cadence in the strictly sixteenth-century, Zarlinian sense. What makes a cadence authentic, in fact, is not so much the perfect resolution of the structural voices – into an octave or unison – as two additional factors, which contribute to its positive, syntactic, strongly assertive character:

- The upward motion of the half-step resolution, which can be represented with the symbols 7 > 1 (denoting not yet 'leading-note > tonic' in the modern sense but rather an ascending semitone resolution into the pitch class corresponding to the root of the final triad).
- The fact that the ascending semitone, usually placed in one of the upper voices (as the final part of the so-called *clausula cantizans*) is accompanied in the lowest sounding voice either by the upward skip of a fourth or by the downward skip of a fifth (5–1, *clausula basizans*); a third structural voice – usually in one of the middle voices (but sometimes also in the cantus), never in the lowest voice as in the 'perfect' Zarlinian model – may also accompany the same resolution by downward step (2–1, *clausula tenorizans*).

In the case of *Sì lieta* (cf. Appendix 2 and Table 1), quite significantly, Verdelot adopts only six cadences of this kind (out of 20), and even tends to deprive them of their usual dynamic character and syntactic function. Not only is their occurrence always internal (first setting of both the repeated lines 3B and 16H; lines 6D, 9f, 15H), but their passing resolution is also variously weakened, elided, evaded or even reversed, and never followed by a simultaneous rest in all voices. Moreover, the cadential suspension typical of Zarlino's *cadenza diminuita* (7th–6th, 2nd–3rd or 4th–3rd, usually produced by syncopation in the *clausula cantizans*), is here used only twice (lines 3B and 16H) and in association with two of the weakest cadential caesuras of the whole madrigal (bars 15–16, 68–9): in both cases, in fact, the authentic cadence is first 'announced' by the syncopation in the upper voice and then turned more or less dramatically into a half-cadence; in the former, extreme case (3B, 'pene'), the cadence is first prepared in the most emphatic way (by extended melismatic syncopation in the cantus) and then immediately evaded before the cadential extension (see my detailed description below). All the remaining cadences belong to the 'simple' type (Zarlino's unsuspended *cadenza*

111

semplice), either perfectly homorhythmic (line 9f) or lightly decorated (lines 6D, 15H).

The presence of all three structural *clausulae* characterises only the first, three-voice authentic cadence (line 6D, 'il cor si more', bar 29: A > d^{unf}) as well as its amplified repetition (bars 32–3: A > d, with use of all four voices): notice the stable permanence, from one phrase to the next, of the *cantizans* and *basizans* in the altus and bassus pair, while the *tenorizans*, first sung by the tenor, is eventually taken up by the cantus and repeated an octave above. This is actually the only instance, albeit repeated, of a full authentic close in the whole madrigal. Only in one other case (line 15H, 'gradita', bars 64–5: D > g) do we find both the *cantizans* and the *basizans* resolutions typical of the authentic type (with no *tenorizans*), but they are compressed in the two lower voices, and there is no real break between the ending of line 15H ('gradita') and the beginning of line 16H ('che saria'), due to the anticipated entry of cantus and tenor.

In two similar but still weak instances (line 9f, 'sentire', bars 39–40; line 16H, 'vita', bars 68–9), the whole harmonic effect is that of an authentic cadence A > d, even though, at a strictly melodic level, the *clausula basizans* is missing (as in a more commonly Zarlinian kind of 'perfect cadence'): the bassus anticipates its pause, without completing (at least immediately) its expected upward skip of a fourth (A$_1$–[D$_2$]), and yet this is implicitly accomplished – and made clearly audible – by the tenor, with its typical downward step motion, E$_2$–D$_2$. The feeble character of both these cadences also depends on various other factors:

- bars 39–40: not only does the simultaneous 'evaporation' of altus and bassus cause the resolution of the remaining cantus/tenor pair into a quite empty d-sonority (8/8, with no third and fifth), but the anticipated beginning of the next phrase (line 10f, 'Un sì [dolce]', altus/bassus), has the effect of turning immediately that unfilled d-sonority into a major triad rooted on B flat, causing also the 'elision' of the cadence itself: in other words, the very ending of line 9f (empty d, '[senti-]re') coincides with the beginning of line 10f (B flat, 'un sì [dolce]');
- bars 68–9/ 70–3: the authentic resolution of all voices (confirmed even by the delayed skip of a fourth in the bassus, at the reprise of 'saria') is here comparatively much stronger; and yet the conventional *protractio longae* in the cantus, with cadential extension carried out by the three lower voices, leads inevitably to the inner dissolution of the authentic cadence itself and to its definitive transformation into 'half-cadence' (see my definition below): from A > d to g > D.

An even more dramatic kind of extension, to be sure, is already used to seal the opening *ripresa* section (line 3B, 'che dolce m'è 'l morir, dolce le pene', bars 15–16/16–19): the *clausula cantizans*, in the cantus, is here resolutely 'evaded' by all the other voices, as in a typical *fuggir la cadenza* (represented with the symbols $A^{> (d)}/g$); not only is the expected d-sonority immediately avoided and replaced by a G minor triad, but this seems to be asserted by means of a clear authentic cadence (D > g, at 'morir' in the altus, and at '[pe-]ne' in the bassus, bars 16–17) which is in turn reversed into a half-cadence, g > D, identical to the one in the final close.

II. Half-cadence, Plagal Imperfect, Phrygian

These three cadential types, albeit different from one another, are equally characterised by the downward motion of the half-step resolution, which also contributes to their variously negative, suspended, pathetic nature.

Over two-thirds of the cadences used in Verdelot's *Sì lieta* belong to this category (14 out of 20): eight to the Phrygian type, five to the half-cadence type and one to its plagal imperfect variant. Their specific placement in the whole architectural plan of the madrigal, moreover, is always strategic and structurally relevant: three of the four sections of the madrigal (I, II, IV: the framing *ripresa* and *volta* as well as the first *mutazioni*) invariably start with a Phrygian cadence and end with a half-cadence, while the remaining section III (second *mutazioni*) includes Phrygian cadences only. The fact that only the latter type (in five out of eight cases) is further emphasised by cadential suspension – the half and plagal cadences being either 'simple' or lightly decorated – further confirms the special importance given by Verdelot to the pathetic cadence par excellence.

1. Half-cadence

In a half-cadence (equivalent to the homonymous modern type but alien to its I > V harmonic function) the descending semitone – 4 > 3 if referred to the final root-position triad – is in one of the upper voices and is accompanied in the lowest sounding voice either by the downward skip of of a fourth or the upward skip of a fifth. Due to the 'imperfect' resolution of its structural voices, the half-cadence turns out to be the reversed form of the authentic type; if seen from this angle – and thus if referred not to the final but to the starting triad of the cadence – the function of its downward half-step resolution may also be read as 1 > 7 and considered a reversed *clausula cantizans;* the same kind of structural reversal applies to the *basizans* (1–5) and to the optional *tenorizans* (1–2).

Such a structural reversal, or 'cadential chasm', characterises all the half-cadences of *Sì lieta*, in particular both the extremely grave and suspended half-cadence extensions adopted by Verdelot to close respectively the opening *ripresa* (bars 15–19) and the final *volta* (bars 69–73). In both instances, in fact, an identical half-cadence g > D (with reversed *cantizans* and *basizans* resolutions compressed in the two lower voices) not only weakens and transforms the main suspended authentic cadence A > d (which in the first case is even evaded) but reverses a rather passing but similarly authentic resolution D > g, occurring respectively within the extension itself (bars 16–17, altus/bassus, 'pene'/'morir') and before the extension, at the end of the previous line (bars 64–5, tenor/bassus, 'gradita').

If the three remaining half-cadences (lines 2B, 8e, 10f; 'mi viene', 'giace', 'morire'; bars 8–9, 36–7, 42–4) sound even more pathetic and gloomy, this depends also on the downward motion of the *clausula basizans*, and on the consequent parallel descent of all (or almost all) voices. The same, quite slow-paced half-cadence d > A is here repeated with just a few variants: both the structural *clausulae* are always given at the same pitch-level (D_2–A_1 in the bassus, D_3 > $C\sharp_3$ either in altus or cantus), as well as the rather neutral *altizans* (variously ending into A_2 either in tenor or altus, evaporated in the case of line 8f); what changes is merely the placement of the additional semitone common to the plagal and half-cadence types (F_3 > E_3, cantus: lines 2B and 10f vs. F_2 > E_2, tenor: line 8e). Notice, in the first and third instances (lines 2B and 10f), how the same closing formula of a descending diminished fifth ($B\flat_3$ > A_3–G_3–F_3 > E_3 in the Cantus) is carefully applied to quite different words, concepts and – therefore – note values: a fluent melismatic gesture at 'viene' (bars 8–9), whose initial Phrygian flavour ($B\flat_3$ > A_3) is underscored by the ascending step resolution in the tenor (G_2–A_2); a syllabic, rather slow and heavy series of four semibreves and a breve at 'dolce morire' (bars 41–4), with static repeat of A_2 in the tenor ('[mo] rire').

2. Plagal imperfect cadence

What I call a plagal imperfect cadence (to be distinguished from a 'plagal perfect' cadence) differs from a half-cadence in the more feeble quality of its resolution and the minor quality of both its starting and ending root-position triads: the downward half-step motion (6 > 5), in fact, does not lead from octave or unison to an imperfect consonance (as in a half-cadence), but rather connects an imperfect consonance (usually a third or tenth) to a fifth.

In *Sì lieta* the plagal imperfect cadence occurs only once, and just in passing, to underscore the lover's symptomatic loss of speech (line 7e, 'la lingua muta tace', bars 33–5). Quite significantly, this is the only line in the whole madrigal that is not declaimed by the cantus; compressed below its prolonged D_3 (at '[mo-]re', the final syllable of the previous line), the static choral recitative of the three lower voices (with repeated d minor triad at 'la lingua muta') is only temporarily marked by the most feeble and 'silent' cadence in the whole setting (at 'tace'): the downward half-step resolution in the altus does nothing but repeat for the last time, with augmented values, the same $Bb_2 > A_2$ gesture that has already been obsessively reiterated at the words 'lingua muta'; the descending semi-tone in the altus is accompanied by the upward skip of a fifth in the bas-sus, $G_1–D_2$, while the tenor steps down from G_2 to $F\sharp_2$ (not to $F\sharp_2$ as in a half-cadence), and the cantus literally *tacet* (i.e. interrupts its upper D_3 pedal point, at the strong beat of bar 35).

Notice the close similarity between the whole setting of line 7e and both the cadential extensions that close the opening and the final sec-tions of the madrigal (lines 3B, 16H, bars 15–19, 68–73): what makes the difference is the very adoption of plagal instead of half-cadence resolu-tion, in the context of a fairly static 'choral recitative' writing; all this is clearly dictated not only by syntactic and rhetorical needs but also, and above all, by precise expressive purposes on Verdelot's part.

3. Phrygian cadence

In a Phrygian cadence, the descending semitone (*clausula tenorizans*, $2 > 1$ if referred to the final triad) is usually in the lowest voice, sometimes also in one of the upper voices, and is always accompanied by upward-step motion in the other structural voice (*clausula cantizans*), with conse-quent 'perfect' resolution. If considered as a sort of variant of the half-cadence (and similarly related to its authentic model), the function of its downward half-step resolution may also be read as $6 > 5$ (without losing its identity as *clausula tenorizans*).

Its primary role in *Sì lieta* goes beyond the simple numerical data (8 cadences out of 20 are Phrygian) and is evident at every single level. Each section of the madrigal invariably starts with a Phrygian cadence, and section III (the second *mutazioni*) includes only cadences of this type. Its constant recurrence contributes decisively to the melancholic, self-com-placent, *voluptas dolendi* tone of the whole setting.

Last but not least, this is the only cadential model that even plays a consistent metric and prosodic function: its almost identical repetition further underscores the consonance between both the 4c/5C rhyming cou-plets ('miro' / 'giro' = $c > D / c^6 > D$, bars 22, 26–7) and the quite dis-tant but still rhyming 1a/14A lines ('morte' / 'sorte' = $g > A / g^6 > A$, bars 4–5, 60–1). In both cases the progression from seven-syllable to eleven-syllable line – i.e., in Bembo's terms, from 'piacevolezza' to 'gra-vità' – corresponds to the progression from a relatively pleasant and light to a rather grave and solemn form of Phrygian cadence: the *tenorizans* downward half-step resolution is placed at first in one of the upper parts (respectively altus at 'morte', and cantus at 'miro': bars 4–5, 22), later in the bassus (at 'sorte' and 'giro', bars 60–1, 26–7); moreover, the *cantizans* upward-step motion, at first plainly stated in the bassus as in a 'simple' kind of cadence (at 'morte' and 'miro', bars 4–5, 22), is later reinforced by means of cadential suspension and placed in one of the inner voices (respectively altus at 'sorte', and tenor at 'giro', bars 60–1, 26–7). In the case of lines 1a/14A, the metric/prosodic and rhetoric/semantic functions are indissolubly related, as the return of the same Phrygian cadence onto A signals quite clearly the return not only of the opening rhyme but also of the main terms of the poetic discourse, first introduced in the incipit.

Three of the four remaining Phrygian cadences, all included in the second *mutazioni* section (lines 11D, 12g, 13G, 'core', 'noia', 'gioia': bars 47–8, 49–50/51–2, 54–5), are characterised by the suspension and perfect resolution of the two structural voices, even though this is accomplished in a progressively stronger fashion. In each case, as in the most classical and fully resolving kind of Phrygian cadence, the syncopated *clausula cantizans* (either in cantus or altus) is placed above the *clausula tenorizans* (either in tenor or bassus). But in the first two instances the 'staggering' of the two vocal pairs (cantus/tenor vs. altus/bassus) has the effect of variously obscuring, weakening and eliding the two-voiced resolution (bars 47–8, 49–50); the resulting gradual 'evaporation' culminates at the end of line 12g ('non sento noia', bars 50–2), where the cantus and tenor voices are left alone, and their expected Phrygian resolution is even evaded (the tenor descends from G_2 to F_2 instead of rising to A_2). In the last case, on the contrary (bars 54–5, 'in gioia'), both the full texture and the homophonic writing are resumed, and all voices participate in the strongest Phrygian cadence in the whole madrigal: $c^6 > D$, almost identical with the previous one at 'lieto giro' (bars 26–7), and similarly meant to underscore by contrast the melancholic nature of that 'joy'; its new strength – justified by obvious syntactic reasons – depends also on the placement of the two structural *clausulae* in the outer voices as well as on the fact that its full resolution is clearly marked by a simultaneous rest of a semibreve in all voices.

Early Music History (2002) Volume 21. © Cambridge University Press
DOI:10.1017/S0261127902002048 Printed in the United Kingdom

CHRISTIAN THOMAS LEITMEIR

CATHOLIC MUSIC IN THE DIOCESE OF AUGSBURG c.1600: A RECONSTRUCTED TRICINIUM ANTHOLOGY AND ITS CONFESSIONAL IMPLICATIONS

After decades of suffering and agony, Catholicism in Augsburg entered a phase of gradual recovery around 1550. The first half of the sixteenth century was characterised by the rapid expansion of the Reformation and the marginalisation of the Catholics in the town. At the zenith of Protestant predominance, the Lutherans even managed to force the entire Catholic clergy into exile from 1537 to 1547 and for a few months in 1552.[1] The episcopate of Cardinal Otto Truchsess von Waldburg (1543–73), however, marked a turning point for Catholics in Augsburg. The Peace of Augsburg (1555) conceded political parity to the Catholic minority in town. Due to Otto von Waldburg's zealous activities, his severely decimated flock even managed to grow again slowly over the years. Combining

Earlier versions of this essay were read at the Jahrestagung der Gesellschaft für Bayerische Musikgeschichte at Donauwörth in May 2001 and at the Medieval and Renaissance Conference at Spoleto in July 2001. For valuable help and critical suggestions at various stages I am particularly indebted to Margaret Bent, Bonnie Blackburn, Fred Büttner, Barbara Eichner, Marie Louise Göllner, Severine Grassin, Wayne Heisler, Robert Kendrick, Franz Körndle, Noel O'Regan, Klaus Pietschmann, Jane Roper and Bernhold Schmid. I should also like to express my gratitude to various librarians and archivists at the British Library, the Museo Civico Bibliografico Musicale in Bologna, the Bayerische Staatsbibliothek, the Staats- und Stadtbibliothek Augsburg, the Studienbibliothek Dillingen and the Bayerisches Hauptstaatsarchiv Ausgburg. Without the assistance of these institutions my reconstruction of the *Triodia sacra* would not have been possible. An edition of the unica in this anthology is given in the appendix of my article 'Bernhard Klingensteins *Triodia Sacra* (1605): Ein rekonstruierter Sammeldruck als Schlüsselquelle für das Musikleben der Spätrenaissance in Süddeutschland', *Musik in Bayern* (2002).

[1] H. Immenkötter, 'Kirche zwischen Reformation und Parität', in G. Gottlieb et al. (eds), *Geschichte der Stadt Augsburg: 2000 Jahre von der Römerzeit bis zur Gegenwart* (2nd edn, Stuttgart, 1985), pp. 391–412, at pp. 392–400.

diplomatic slyness with fervent commitment, the prince-bishop took efficient measures not only to push forwards the consolidation of Catholicism in the free imperial city of Augsburg and his diocese, but also to display this revival before the envious eyes of his enemies on the Protestant side. This double strategy can best be seen in the following three examples. First, von Waldburg founded a Catholic university at Dillingen in 1549. Owing to notorious conflicts with the city council of the free imperial city of Augsburg, in 1486 the residence of the prince-bishops of Augsburg was transferred to Dillingen (Figure 1).[2] The violence of anti-Catholic sentiments in Augsburg later even necessitated the provisional transfer of the episcopal seat to Dillingen, a peaceful town in episcopal territory (*Hochstift Augsburg*) that was at a safe distance of some 50 kms from Augsburg. The foundation of a seminary with an attached university at Dillingen answered the prince-bishop's desire to establish a higher standard of education for prospective priests of his diocese. It is notable that Otto von Waldburg, one of the most ardent advocates of the Catholic reformation, was among the pioneers to realise this project, later to become a major concern of the Council of Trent. In the initial years the seminary was run by Dominicans of great learning, such as the renowned Spanish theologian Pedro de Soto.[3] In 1564, however, Otto von Waldburg delegated the direction of the university to the *Societas Jesu*. It was under the supervision of the Jesuits, efficient propagators of Catholic renewal, that the university of Dillingen soon flourished as the leading centre of counter-reformatory education in southern Germany (see Figure 2).[4] The

[2] R. Kießling, 'Augsburg zwischen Mittelalter und Neuzeit', in Gottlieb et al. (eds), *Geschichte der Stadt Augsburg*, pp. 241–51, at p. 241.

[3] Pedro de Soto gained a great reputation among contemporaries as the author of a celebrated series of prayers for the Council of Trent. Set to music by Waldburg's *maestro di cappella* Jacobus de Kerle, the *Preces speciales* received enormous attention among the fathers of the council. Within the diocese, they became so popular that the official printer of the University of Dillingen, Sebald Mayer, reissued de Soto's prayers, with the words slightly altered to accommodate the more general needs of the Catholic community in Germany: the *Preces pro Salubri Generalis Concilii Continuatione & Conclusione* (1551) thereby became *Preces speciales pro Salute Populi Christiani* (1558).

[4] For general information on the history of the University of Dillingen, see especially the following publications: T. Specht, *Geschichte der ehemaligen Universität Dillingen (1549–1804) und der mit ihr verbundenen Lehr- und Erziehunganstalten* (Freiburg im Breisgau, 1902; repr. Aalen, 1987); A. Layer, 'Die Residenz- und Universitätsstadt Dillingen in der Musikgeschichte', *Jahrbuch des Historischen Vereins Dillingen*, 80 (1978), pp. 197–204; R. Kießling (ed.), *Die Universität Dillingen und ihre Nachfolger: Stationen und Geschichte einer Hochschule in Schwaben* (Dillingen, 1999).

Figure 1   Etching of Dillingen by Matthaeus Merian, *Topographia Suevia* (1643) reproduced from Kießling (ed.), *Die Universität Dillingen*

Figure 2 The University of Dillingen, viewed from the south. Etching by Wolfgang Kilian, 1627, reproduced from Kießling (ed.), *Die Universität Dillingen*

international fame of *Collegium Dilinganum* was expressed by the flattering nickname 'the Swabian Rome'.[5]

Another important initiative launched by von Waldburg concerned the printing market. The rise of the Reformation had taught that printers played a considerable part in the successful dissemination of Luther's doctrines and anti-papist polemics. Cardinal von Waldburg had learnt this lesson and consequently devoted his energy to the establishment of devoutly Catholic printing houses in his diocese. This strategy worked much more smoothly in Otto's residence town of Dillingen than in the aggressive confessional climate of Augsburg. In 1549 von Waldburg persuaded Sebald Mayer from Ingolstadt to open a printing press at the new University of Dillingen.[6] Although seemingly a sign of economic property, the high number of publications issued in the 1550s involved financial risks and obligations that nearly ruined Mayer's press. In order to save it from imminent bankrupcty, Otto bought the press from Mayer in 1560 and eventually bequeathed it to the Jesuits, in 1568.[7] Sebald Mayer, his son Johann and Johann's wife Barbara were employed by the university. Issuing altogether some 1,200 books until Barbara's death in 1619,[8] the Mayer press became a stronghold of Catholic printing in southern Germany, which actively promoted counter-reformatory writings. These two initiatives, the foundation of a Catholic university and the setting-up of a loyal printing market, concerned the propagation of Catholic reform on an intellectual and visual level.

The third innovation was the foundation of a music chapel at the cathedral of Augsburg in 1561. Through the activities of the music chapel the renaissance of Catholicism in Augsburg also found an audible expression. Facilitated by an endowment made in the will of the canon Jakob Heinrichmann,[9] the establishment

[5] H. Immenkötter, 'Universität im "schwäbischen Rom" – ein Zentrum katholischer Konfessionalisierung', in Kießling (ed.), *Die Universität Dillingen und ihre Nachfolger*, pp. 43–77.

[6] H.-J. Künast, 'Die Akademische Druckerei der Universität Dillingen', *ibid.*, pp. 595–626, at p. 600.

[7] O. Bucher, 'Sebald Mayer, der erste Dillinger Buchdrucker 1550–1576', *Jahrbuch des Historischen Vereins Dillingen*, 54 (1952–3), pp. 125–30.

[8] This approximate number is extrapolated from Künast's table in 'Sebald Mayer', p. 598.

[9] H. Fischer and T. Wohnhaas, 'Miscellanea zur Augsburger Dommusik', in F. Brusniak and H. Leuchtmann (eds), *Quaestiones in musica: Festschrift für Franz Krautwurst zum 65. Geburtstag* (Tutzing, 1989), pp. 123–45, at pp. 127–8.

of a cantorate at the cathedral met von Waldburg's passion for polyphonic music. Already at the Council of Trent, Cardinal von Waldburg ranked among the most fervent opponents of a ban on polyphony in the liturgy. He sought to achieve his purpose by commissioning two elaborate works from the director of his private chapel, Jacobus de Kerle, that were to comply with the recent ideas about reform in an exemplary manner. The *Preces speciales* and in particular de Kerle's *Sex Misse* (both Venice: Gardano, 1562) had a great impact on the fathers at Trent and enjoyed a broad dissemination after the Council.[10] Even if von Waldburg's diplomatic missions as papal ambassador of the Holy Roman Empire (*Protector Germaniae*) prevented him from frequent visits to Augsburg, the music chapel at the cathedral was never short of support from the bishop. Thus it soon achieved a high reputation that spread far beyond the city walls and at the same time filled the Protestant citizens of Augsburg with envy. The fame of the chapel, however, only reached its apex after von Waldburg's death. Under the direction of Bernhard Klingenstein (1545–1614) the musical standards were raised to a degree that gloriously heralded the restored power of Catholicism in town.

BUSINESS PARTNERS

The three factors characteristic for the Catholic revival in late sixteenth-century Augsburg just delineated form the context for the music print to which this essay is devoted. This source, called *Triodia sacra*, contains a collection of sacred music for three voices by various composers and was edited by Bernhard Klingenstein, *Kapellmeister* at the cathedral of Augsburg.[11] The anthology was published in 1605 by Adam Meltzer, who owned a printing press at Dillingen. The reasons why Klingenstein preferred Meltzer to the big publishers in Munich or Nuremberg are manifold. The

---

[10] These aspects are discussed extensively in chapter 4 of my thesis on the sacred music of Jacobus de Kerle within the context of sixteenth-century confessionalisation: 'Zwischen Kirche und Kunst: Eine Fallstudie zur "katholischen" Musik der Spätrenaissance am Beispiel der Werke von Jacobus de Kerle' (in preparation).

[11] A concise summary of Klingenstein's biography, which takes into account all previous scholarship on the composer, is given in M. Schmidmüller, 'Die Augsburger Domkapellmeister seit dem Tridentinum bis zur Säkularisation', *Jahrbuch des Vereins für Augsburger Bistumsgeschichte*, 23 (1989), pp. 69–107, at pp. 75–8.

close connection between Augsburg and Dillingen, residence town of the bishops of Augsburg and home of the diocesan university, might have influenced Klingenstein's choice in the first place. It was only natural that a canon of Augsburg Cathedral who intended to bring out a book would turn first to a printer either at Augsburg or at Dillingen. At the time of publication of Klingenstein's *Triodia sacra*, however, the Augsburg alternative did not appear very promising, since the only Catholic printer in town, Mang, had opened his press only in 1601 and still lacked professional experience in music printing.[12] As far as the Dillingen option was concerned, Meltzer was the most attractive candidate. Although not the official printer at the Jesuit university, Adam Meltzer had passed his apprenticeship with Johann Mayer and worked subsequently at the university press until he set up his own business in 1603. In complementary contrast to his colleague Johann Mayer, Meltzer specialised in music printing.[13] He seems to have mastered the specific techniques of typesetting music very quickly, for in the two years before the publication of Klingenstein's *Triodia sacra* he had already brought out a number of music prints. The majority of these publications featured works of Jacob Reiner, *Kapellmeister* at the monastery of Weingarten (*Liber motettarum*, 1603; *Sacrarum missarum sex vocum . . . liber primus*, 1604; *Missae tres cum litaniis de SS. Sanguine Christi . . . Liber primus*, 1604; *Canticum gloriosiss. Vir. Dei genetri. Mariae*, 1605). Moreover, Meltzer published the first volume of Christian Erbach's series of proper settings for the liturgical year, *Modorum sacrorum tripertitorum* (1604), and the *Fasciculus cantionum ecclesiasticarum* by Michael Tonsor (1605).[14] This impressive output clearly marks the work of an experienced printer who had soon surpassed the stage of a novice. Klingenstein thus did not a take a risk in asking Meltzer to print his *Triodia sacra* in 1605. In addition, Klingenstein even had first-hand testimony of

---

[12] T. Wohnhaas, 'Notizen zu Druck und Verlag katholischer Kirchenmusik in Augsburg', *Jahrbuch des Vereins für Augsburger Bistumsgeschichte*, 31 (1997), pp. 152–64, at p. 155.

[13] On Meltzer's activity as a printer in Dillingen see O. Bucher, 'Adam Meltzer (1603–1610) und Gregor Hänlin (1610–1617) als Musikaliendrucker in Dillingen', *Gutenberg Jahrbuch* 1956, pp. 216–26, at pp. 216–21. Out of the entire output of fifty-five publications issued by the Meltzer press (continued after Meltzer's death by Gregor Hänlin) an overwhelming majority of prints (44) contained polyphonic music. See J. Focht, 'Die Musik im Umkreis der Jesuiten-Universität', in Kießling (ed.), *Die Universität Dillingen und ihre Nachfolger*, pp. 533–78, at p. 549.

[14] Bucher, 'Adam Meltzer . . . als Musikaliendrucker in Dillingen', pp. 217–18.

Meltzer's reliability, since one year earlier Meltzer had printed Klingenstein's other anthology, the *Rosetum Marianum*, containing thirty five-part settings of different stanzas from the popular Marian hymn 'Maria zart'.[15] Apart from these general considerations, the very contents of the *Triodia sacra* also recommended publication by Meltzer. As will be shown below, Klingenstein's anthology was designed for use at the Jesuit university of Dillingen. Therefore it was convenient to have it printed within easy reach, ideally in town. And since the official university printer, Mayer, did not have the equipment or the specialist knowledge to undertake this enterprise, Adam Meltzer was the favourite candidate. In the light of his specialisation and his previous job at the university, the Jesuits often sought Meltzer's help in difficult printing matters, and he in turn remained a loyal partner of the university until his death in 1609.

These circumstances explain why Klingenstein's choice fell on the Meltzer press when he was seeking the ideal printer for his *Triodia sacra*. Yet there was also a third party that was to have a share in this business, namely the Jesuit administration of Dillingen University. It remains an open question whether Klingenstein received a commission from the Jesuits at Dillingen or whether the cooperation followed his own initiative. Nevertheless, it is beyond doubt that the *Triodia sacra* were intended for use by the students of the University of Dillingen. While Klingenstein's dedication (see Appendix 1, including an English translation)[16] singles out two brothers who were registered as students in Dillingen, it also is addressed to students in general, 'thinking that these [tricinia] would serve at the same time for all musical youth'. Moreover, as Klingenstein states, his anthology was compiled in order to provide exemplary sacred compositions for students at an affordable price. This agenda must have met the warm approbation of the Jesuit authorities who were in charge of the University of Dillingen. For after initial reservations concerning polyphonic music, the Jesuits had soon learnt to value and use music as a particularly powerful instrument for the

---

[15] For a critical edition of this collection see B. Klingenstein, *Rosetum Marianum*, ed. W. E. Hettrick (Recent Researches in the Music of the Renaissance, 24–5; Madison, Wis., 1977).

[16] I should like to express warm thanks to Leofranc Holford-Strevens for his learned translations of these texts.

propagation of Catholicism.[17] Music not only played an important role in academic life in general, it also formed an integral part of the curriculum, outstanding in its 'multimediality'.[18] The musical activities included, for example, the participation at Mass and the Divine Office, the singing of sacred music (both monophonic and polyphonic) in class, the use of vernacular songs for catechism instruction[19] and the performance of musical numbers in Jesuit dramas.[20]

As a consequence, both *Kapellmeister* Klingenstein and the university hoped to profit from their cooperation. From Klingenstein's perspective, the conditions could hardly have been more promising: the fact that the *Triodia sacra* were published directly at the university warranted a prosperous marketing potential, at least on a regional scale. In addition, subsidies from the Jesuits might have contributed to keep the selling price low and open up an even broader market. Klingenstein highlights that his anthology on the whole appeals to an almost universal range of prospective buyers: 'For some lack the money to purchase large volumes containing a great number of polyphonic compositions; others lack a larger choir of musicians, others again lack both. These odelets are on sale for a few pence, and can be sung by more or fewer singers'). As the anthology contained only compositions for three voices, the music could be performed flexibly by singers of varying number (starting with a minimum of three) and talent. Klingenstein underscored the latter on the title page, announcing that his anthology would satisfy the requirements of beginners as well as of advanced singers ('tam ad tironum, quam peritiorum usum'; see

---

[17] T. Culley, SJ, *Jesuits and Music*, i: *A Study of the Musicians Connected with the German College in Rome during the 17th Century and of their Activities in Northern Euorpe* (Sources and Studies for the History of the Jesuits, 2; Rome and St. Louis, 1970), pp. 15–22.

[18] Focht, 'Die Musik im Umkreis der Jesuiten-Universität', pp. 541–2. R. Haub, 'Jesuitisch geprägter Schulalltag', in *Das Kurfürst-Maximilian-Gymnasium zu Burghausen: Vom Kolleg der Societas Jesu zur Königlich Bayerischen Studien-Anstalt*, ed. D. Grypa and W. Gutfleisch (Würzburg, 1997), pp. 41–51, at p. 43.

[19] B. Duhr, *Geschichte der Jesuiten in den Ländern deutscher Zunge in der ersten Hälfte des XVI. Jahrhunderts*, i (Freiburg im Breisgau, 1913), pp. 455–60.

[20] The latter aspect was recently explored in an illuminating series of essays by Franz Körndle, '*Ad te perenne gaudium*: Lassos Musik zum *Vltimum Judicium*', *Die Musikforschung*, 53 (2000), pp. 68–70; '*Apocalipsis cum figuris*: Orlando di Lasso und das Theater der Jesuiten', *Einsichten*, 17 (2000/1), pp. 48–50; 'Herodes und der Antichrist auf der Kollegienbühne: Orlando di Lasso in Regensburg und das Theater der Jesuiten', *mälzels magazin*, 4 (2001), pp. 4–8.

Appendix 1). But in addition to these nearly optimal marketing conditions, the *Triodia sacra* offered Klingenstein a welcome opportunity to present his chapel at Augsburg Cathedral at its best: as will be demonstrated below, he primarily drew upon compositions that were exclusively documented in the music manuscripts of his chapel, lost since the secularisation.[21] This enabled him to kill two birds with one stone. On the one hand, the anthology offered an opportunity to exhibit exclusive gems from the repertory of his chapel. On the other hand, he allowed the public only a glimpse of his treasures, since he did not include more than the three-voice portions of originally larger works or cycles.[22]

The Jesuits in turn received from their business partner a collection of sacred music that could readily be integrated into the everyday curriculum, in other words a 'school book' for music-making in class. Despite the loss of any correspondence between Klingenstein and the rector of the university at Dillingen, it can be presumed that the Jesuits did not hesitate to dictate the standards that the material supplied ought to meet. Accordingly, they were certain to obtain from Klingenstein an anthology tailor-made for their educational purposes at the college. Beyond the immediate teaching context, however, Klingenstein's *Triodia sacra* had even more to offer. Propagators of the Catholic faith as fervent and ruthless as the Jesuits could not have failed to see the promising propects of making this anthology an instrument for their

---

[21] According to Adolf Sandberger (*Bemerkungen zur Biographie Hans Leo Hasslers und seiner Brüder, sowie zur Musikgeschichte der Städte Nürnberg und Augsburg im 16. und zu Anfang des 17. Jahrhunderts* (Denkmäler der Tonkunst in Bayern, 5, pt. 2; Leipzig, 1904, p. lix, n. 6), the repertory of the chapel is documented only until the end of the eighteenth century. Therefore it is likely to have been sold during the course of the large-scale expropriation of ecclesiastical property in the early nineteenth century. Unfortunately, despite the combined efforts of musicologists, it has not been possible to trace more than a few scattered volumes, the majority of which are now kept at the Bischöfliche Zentralbibliothek at Regensburg. In February 2002, however, I discovered evidence at the British Library that at least a number of music prints from the cathedral repertory are still extant; see below, n. 24.

[22] From the designation 'partim ex lectis auctoribus selecti, partim recens conditi' (partly selected from choice authors, partly newly composed) on the title page, the second phrase does not adequately describe the character of the items selected by Klingenstein. The collection does not contain a single work that had not been taken over from previous music prints and at the same was published complete. It does not seem a reasonable motivation for a composer to write only a three-part section, such as a verse of a sequence, for a tricinium anthology, when the rest of the composition would be of no use for this publication. Therefore it is likely that Klingenstein on principle selected three-part portions from existing musical works.

counter-reformatory mission, the rebuilding of the Catholic church in the spirit of Trent. An anthology of 'Catholic' church music, musically distinguished and consistent with Catholic orthodoxy, could be turned into a very subtle weapon in their anti-Protestant propaganda, a weapon that could persuasively strengthen the Catholic position and attack the Protestants on the musical as well as the denominational battle line. What is more, through their cooperation with Klingenstein the Jesuit authorities reserved the possibility of intervention or censorship in case Klingenstein's selection was considered to follow their party line insufficiently.

OBSTACLES: INCOMPLETENESS AND REMOTENESS

The institutional and propagandistic frame in which Klingenstein's anthology is located exposes a rich context, clearly suggesting that the *Triodia sacra* are more than a peripheral source for late Renaissance music and music-making in Catholic southern Germany. As a consequence, a thorough analysis of its content and context provides valuable insights into a broad range of issues, including late sixteenth-century aesthetics and ecclesiastical politics connected with music. It is unfortunate that previous scholarship has ignored such a potentially valuable and far-reaching source. This situation, strange at first sight, is due to two circumstances, both of which have hindered study of the *Triodia sacra* up to the present day. First, the *Triodia sacra* have not been transmitted in a complete copy; from the entire edition of 1605 only a single partbook has survived, the *Inferior Vox*.[23] And secondly, since 1862 this partbook has been housed at the British Library,[24] which

[23] The weak transmission of the *Triodia sacra* edition does not necessarily imply that it was not a success on the contemporary music market. Taking into account that Klingenstein's anthology was made for use, the fact that only one partbook has survived suggests the contrary: the available copies must have been used frequently. Therefore it is likely that wear and tear is more responsible for the dramatic loss of exemplars than their (alleged) poor appeal to prospective buyers.

[24] During research visits to the British Library I discovered that the British Museum acquired large amounts of Continental music prints, particularly in the 1860s (revealed by acquisition stamps in the respective books). An examination of the invoices of that period indicated that the majority of books were bought at an auction of Usher & Co. at Berlin in 1861. In a number of cases it has been possible to trace the provenance of individual copies, specified by *ex libris* entries. These findings clearly suggest that most prints acquired by the British Museum were originally ecclesiastical property, sold or stolen during the secularisation, with provenance mainly from Augsburg and Bavarian Swabia. It is unfortunate that this repertory, which belongs to the world's finest collec-

somewhat surprisingly happened to be beyond the range of German musicologists studying the regional history of their own country. This was certainly true for the period between the two world wars, when Alfons Singer prepared his thesis on the life and works of Bernhard Klingenstein, submitted in 1921 and still the only extended study on this subject. Under the constraints of the immediate post-war period Singer could provide little more than the indication that Klingenstein's *Triodia sacra* existed: 'The fact that the only copy is kept at the British Museum at London made its inspection impossible. At present an enquiry there would have been hopeless.'[25] Yet one cannot help wondering why subsequent scholarship has remained ignorant of this source, even though the British Library had undoubtedly become 'accessible' again for scholars from the Continent. To mention only the most recent examples, the *Triodia sacra* are not even mentioned in Josef Focht's historical survey of music at the University of Dillingen, published in 1999 in the *Festschrift* celebrating the 450th anniversary of its foundation.[26] Neither does Alexander Fisher's thesis on confessional music in Counter-Reformation Augsburg contain more than a passing reference to this source.[27] In this sense, the following discussion of Klingenstein's anthology, complemented by a (partial) reconstruction of its contents, explores an undiscovered but important spot at the margins of musicological scholarship. What is more, the reconstruction of the *Triodia sacra* marks the first step to overcoming the major obstacles caused by the incomplete source material. An analysis of the (reconstructed) content and the elucidation of its context will thus provide a reasonable factual ground for conclusions and speculations ranging from regional

---

tion of sixteenth- and seventeenth-century music prints from Germany, has not received the attention it deserves.

[25] A. Singer, *Leben und Werke des Augsburger Domkapellmeisters Bernhardus Klingenstein 1545–1614* (Ph.D. diss., Munich 1921 (typescript)), p. 97: 'Von dem Werk hat sich nur ein einziges Stimmbuch erhalten, und war die "vox inferior". Da sich dieselbe im Britschen Museum in London befindet, war eine Einsichtnahme unmöglich; eine diesbezügliche Anfrage dortselbst wäre zurzeit aussichtslos gewesen.'

[26] Focht, 'Die Musik im Umkreis der Jesuiten-Universität'.

[27] A. J. Fisher, 'Music in Counter-Reformation Augsburg: Musicians, Rituals and Repertoire in a Religiously Divided City' (Ph.D. diss., Harvard University, 2001), pp. 226–7. Fisher's vague knowledge of the contents of the *Triodia sacra* seems to have come from scattered remarks in the secondary literature. Unfortunately, this did not prevent him from making unwarranted assumptions about the musical compositions of the anthology and the strategy behind their collection.

music history and general questions of aesthetics to the history of the Counter-Reformation. It is necessary to anchor an examination like the following, which to a considerable extent involves speculative assumptions, in firm evidence. Therefore my analysis will take as starting point the editor's preface, the only part of Klingenstein's *Triodia sacra* that can justly be assumed to have been transmitted identically in the lost partbooks of the two upper voices.

THE PREFACE

In his preface, Bernhard Klingenstein dedicated his anthology of forty-four sacred compositions to two young patricians: the brothers Johann Wolfgang and Johann Egolph von Leonrod, who studied at the University of Dillingen from 1598 and 1599 respectively to 1607.[28] Since the Leonrod brothers were pursuing their studies at Dillingen when the *Triodia sacra* were published, it becomes apparent that Klingenstein used a *pars pro toto* dedication in order to designate the larger circle of recipients for whom the anthology was intended, that is, the students of the Jesuit university of Dillingen. Besides the two young men, the prologue mentions Georg Resch (1576–1643), who acted as the youths' educator ('studiorum . . . vestrum moderator') during their academic education at Dillingen and accompanied them during their subsequent studies at the universities of Orléans, Siena and Perugia. Resch's biography, intertwined from early on with the Jesuits of southern Germany, reveals paradigmatically the prospects for promotion that the Jesuit network offered to talented young men regardless of their birth. With its help, the son of a poor fisherman in Dillingen managed to pursue an astonishing career after his studies at the Jesuit universities of his home town and Munich, the

---

[28] For biographical details on the Leonrod brothers and Resch I am greatly indebted to Paul B. Rupp, director of the university library at Augsburg and administrator of the database of biographies of Bavarian Swabians, an enormously valuable research tool for local and regional historians. After having studied at Dillingen, Orléans, Siena and Perugia until 1610, the ways of the Leonrod brothers had parted by 1620. From that year Johann Wilhelm is recorded as 'Herr von Münsterhausen and Tennenlohe', while his brother Johann Egolph held the position of a bursar of Eichstätt and Burgau ('eichstättischer Pfleger and burgauischer Kämmerer'). Johann Egolph is also known to have married into the Hundt von Lauterbach family.

apex of which was marked by his promotion to assistant bishop of the diocese of Eichstätt.[29]

Klingenstein's prolegomena, however, provide even more explicit clues that clearly suggest that the *Triodia sacra* are closely tied to the Jesuit context. To mention only the most striking examples, the *Hexastichon*, preceding the dedicatory address (see Appendix 1), alludes to the pedagogical motto of the Jesuits, 'Non multa sed multum', indirectly expressed in the final phrase: 'Ex multis semper non nisi pauca placent':

> Let others concert with thirty different voices
> And add lyres and trumpets to them,
> But do not you despise these 'Triodia', though contained in only
> three partbooks.
> They may attract less praise, but exhibit no less art.
> Sweeter than three hundred crows sings a single nightingale;
> Out of many things only a few ever provide real pleasure.

It might be significant that Klingenstein's comparison between the sweet melodies of the nightingale and the raucous cawing of a murder of crows is paralleled in a contemporary Jesuit school drama from Fulda: this play, called *Dialogus musicae*, theatrically stages a singing contest between nightingales and cuckoos, including drastic caricatures of other 'uncultured' animals.[30] Thus, this analogy suggests that Klingenstein drew upon a metaphor that was popular to some extent in Jesuit circles of the period.

Klingenstein's dedicatory address begins with a political pleading: 'He is wasting his time, most noble youths, who in these days thinks of removing the art of singing from the state.' He could hardly have expounded his position more clearly: quite bluntly, any plans to abolish music are described as vain. And although he refers explicitly only to the state ('è Repub.'), his criticism surely reminded his contemporaries of recent events in the history of the Catholic Church – above all the debates about banning polyphonic

---

[29] Born in 1576, Georg Resch was registered as student in Dillingen from 1585 and continued his secondary education at the Jesuit grammar school in Munich in 1596. After obtaining the degree of Master of Philosophy in 1599 he was ordained at the cathedral of Augsburg in 1602. After two years as priest in the parishes of Meining (near Starnberg, from 1603 to 1604) and Unterbrunn (1604–5) he became educator of the Leonrod brothers. After this interval, he took up his priestly duties again in 1610 and was promoted to assistant bishop of the diocese of Eichstätt in 1611. He died in 1643.

[30] I am grateful to Franz Körndle for drawing my attention to this play, a manuscript copy of which is housed at the Hessische Landesbibliothek Fulda, 4° C 13, fols. 150ʳ–155ʳ.

music from the liturgy at the Council of Trent and the legend that Palestrina saved church music through the impression his *Missa Papae Marcelli* made on the church fathers at the Council.[31] It is striking that the myth was established only a short time after the publication of Klingenstein's *Triodia sacra* by another person closely associated with the Jesuits. Agostino Agazzari, *maestro di cappella* of the Jesuit Collegium Germanicum and the Seminario Romano in Rome, was the first person to bring this seminal myth into the world, reported in the preface of his thorough-bass treatise of 1607.[32] It can hardly be a coincidence that the danger of a ban on sacred polyphony is conjured up almost simultaneously with a time when these problems had long been settled. In addition to their temporal vicinity, these references show up in the publications of musicians who held positions at Jesuit colleges: Agazzari at Rome and Klingenstein as music director at the Jesuit college of St Salvator in Augsburg.[33] While this fact alone does not permit any firm conclusions, it is too striking to be left unremarked. Thus, notwithstanding the risk of overinterpretation, I should like to add at least some hypothetical annotations. Attempting a plausible explanation of this peculiar coincidence, it could be argued that Agazzari was not making up the Palestrina myth entirely on his own, but that he was referring to something circulating orally in Jesuit circles around 1600. This interpretation is supported by Pierre Galliard and Michael Heinemann, who emphasised the Jesuit background of this myth from a different angle.[34] Without

---

[31] On this issue see the following seminal studies: O. Ursprung, ch. 2, 'Die tridentinische Reform der Kirchenmusik', in his edition of Jacobus de Kerle, *Preces speciales* (Denkmäler der Tonkunst in Bayern, 26; Augsburg, 1926), pp. xlii–lix; K. Weinmann, *Das Konzil von Trient und die Kirchenmusik* (Leipzig, 1919); E. Weber, *Le Concile de Trente et la musique: de la réforme à la Contre-Réforme* (Musique-Musicologie, 12; Paris, 1982); K. G. Fellerer, 'Das Konzil von Trient und die Kirchenmusik', in *Geschichte der katholischen Kirchenmusik*, ii: *Vom Tridentinum bis zu Gegenwart*, ed. Fellerer (Kassel, 1976), pp. 7–9.

[32] A. Agazzari, *Del sonare sopra 'l basso con tutti li stromenti* (Siena, 1607; repr. Bologna, 1969), p. 11.

[33] Singer, *Bernhardus Klingenstein*, p. 29, and T. Kroyer, 'Gregor Aichingers Leben und Werke. Mit neuen Beiträgen zur Musikgeschichte Ingolstadts und Augsburgs', introduction to Gregor Aichinger, *Ausgewählte Werke* (Denkmäler der Tonkunst in Bayern, 10, pt. 1; Leipzig, 1909), p. l. I have not been able to find any firm evidence to support Kroyer's and Singer's assertion that Klingenstein was in charge of the choir at St. Salvator. See also Fischer, 'Music in Counter-Reformation Augsburg', p. 225.

[34] This presumption is already expressed in P. Galliard, 'Histoire de la légende palestrinienne', *Revue de musicologie*, 57 (1971), pp. 11–22, at pp. 11–12, and M. Heinemann, *Giovanni Pierluigi da Palestrina und seine Zeit* (Laaber, 1994), pp. 63–4. See also F. Körndle, 'Was wusste Hoffmann? Neues zur altbekannten Geschichte von der Rettung der Kirchenmusik auf dem Konzil von Trient', *Kirchenmusikalisches Jahrbuch*, 83 (1999), 68–90, at pp. 68–9.

doubt, the propagation of Palestrina as the saviour of sacred polyphony fits neatly in the Jesuit agenda of establishing Rome as the model for Catholic christendom. For Palestrina was the first distinguished composer of the papal chapel who was not only not a foreigner from beyond the Alps, but even a 'native' Roman, born in the immediate surroundings of this capital.[35] The perspective of the contemporary Jesuits might thus help to explain why the story of the imminent ban of polyphony was revived even when this threat had long been overcome. From this perspective, the perpetuation of the legend that sacred polyphony was once in danger of abolishment could act as a constant reminder for composers not to leave the orthodox line, manifested in declarations of the Council. Otherwise, the ban might still be enacted.[36] This reading, although hypothetical, is in accord with virulent tendencies characteristic of the Jesuits of the period: their propagation of Rome as model for Catholic christendom, their zeal for organising all aspects of life in the spirit of Catholic orthodoxy and their notorious battle against heresy and its roots. Although the reservations and even the hostility of the Jesuits at the time of Ignatius of Loyola was soon superseded by a far more tolerant, even friendly attitude, these legends might act as a moralistic admonition to constant vigilance.[37]

One might read Klingenstein's attempts to defend music against its (supposedly) imminent abolishment as unrealistic and, at worst, hysterical. The emphatic character of his pleading, however, demands that it be taken seriously. The background sketched above is capable of explaining what made Klingenstein write so passionate a justification of sacred music. True, at first his argument does not go beyond the common praise of music, supported by the testimony of classical authorities, ranging from the Ancient Greek writers Plutarch and Athenaeus to the early medieval theologian and philosopher Cassiodorus. But then he departs from the level of rhetorical commonplaces, and his pleading culminates in the contention that only a person who is insane and inhuman

---

[35] See Heinemann, *Palestrina*, p. 63.

[36] It is often overlooked that the abolition of elaborate church polyphony, expressed in the decree *Docta Sanctorum* by Pope John XXII around 1324, was a legal precedent that had not been withdrawn by the time of the Council of Trent (and even up to the twentieth century!). See Körndle, 'Was wusste Hoffmann?', pp. 69–74.

[37] Culley, *Jesuits and Music*, i, pp. 15–17.

could reproach music: 'I omit to praise that which no one unless devoid of healthy and human feeling has disparaged.' Yet, harsh as this polemical statement appears, it is immediately moderated in the further course of his argument. For Klingenstein leaves no doubt that the music he advocates is of a purity and excellence that would never have justified a ban. Moreover, he is eager to declare that the selection of sacred polyphony provided in his anthology does not contain anything impure or reproachable, but is above such criticism. According to the rhetorics of this genre, Klingenstein describes his choice in more metaphorical terms ('I deemed it appropriate to . . . sing you these tricinia, selected not from the Marsyases but from the very Phoebuses, that is the most outstanding masters of singing').

THE COMPOSERS

But who were those composers Klingenstein elevated to Apollonian heights, far beyond the reach of ecclesiastical reproaches? Do the individual pieces gathered in the *Triodia sacra* really meet the high demands that Klingenstein claimed? And if they do, what are the common traits they share? Owing to the incomplete source material of this print these questions can only partially be solved. In order not to leave all of them unanswered, however, I have tried to reconstruct the two missing partbooks by way of tracking down parallel transmissions of the respective pieces.[38] The result of this enterprise is presented synoptically in Table 1, while Table 2 specifies in detail the sources (prints and manuscripts) containing concordances to *Triodia sacra* compositions.

The composers on which Klingenstein drew for his selection of *tricinia* can be divided into four different groups:

[38] A major obstacle to this enterprise is that many items of Klingenstein's anthology are middle sections taken from larger compositions. Thus in many cases it it was not sufficient to check the incipit entries in library catalogues. In addition, it proved necessary to consult the original sources. Due to these constraints, the table is provisional as far as the unica are concerned. Nevertheless, it should be reasonably reliable, since it covers at least all printed works of the relevant composers. With regard to potential concordances in music manuscripts, the catalogues of all major European libraries have been consulted. Potential concordances in manuscripts were consulted in many libraries in southern Germany and northern Italy. This geographic limitation is justified by the fact that most of the composers represented in Klingenstein's anthology were active in these regions.

Table 1 *Reconstruction of the contents of* Triodia sacra *(1605)*

Bold type indicates unica. Italics designate the caption in the original source. *MA* = *Missale secundum ritum Augustensis ecclesie* (Dillingen, 1555).

No.	Composer	Text incipit	Caption genre (source)	Clef combination
1	Bernhard Klingenstein	**Reple tuorum**	*De Sancto Spiritu* (antiphon for first Vespers)	? ? c3
2	Bernhard Klingenstein	**Crucifixus**	mass section	? ? c3
3	Bernhard Klingenstein	**Caesaris tu fasces**	*De Sancto Laurentio* (sequence versicle, *MA* 311)	? ? c4
4	Bernhard Klingenstein	**Crucifixus**	mass section	? ? c4
5	Bernhard Klingenstein	**Benedictus**	mass section	? ? c4
6	Orlandus Lassus	Crucifixus	mass section (*Missa super Congratulamini mihi*)	g2 c2 c3
7	Antonio Mortaro	Decantabat populus	motet	c1 c1 f4
8	Philipp de Monte	Christe eleyson	mass section (*Missa Inclina cor meum*)	g2 c2 c3
9	Jacob Regnart	**Benedictus**	mass section	? ? c4
10	Tiburtio Massaino	**Crucifixus**	mass section	? ? f3
11	Jacobus Peetrinus	Mane nobiscum domine	Latin canzonetta	g2 c1 c3
12	Jacobus Peetrinus	Iam quod quaesivi	Latin canzonetta	g2 c1 c4
13	Jacobus de Kerle	**Illuxit dies**	*De Resurrectione* (sequence versicle, *MA* 119)	? ? c4
14	Jacobus de Kerle	**Et tremens**	*De Ascensione* (sequence versicle, *MA* 137)	? ? c3
15	Gregor Aichinger	Augusta civitas Dei	motet (prima pars)	? ? c3
16	Jacob Reiner	Domine exaudi	motet section	g2 c2 c3
17	Christian Erbach	**Benedictus**	mass section	? ? f4
18	Christian Erbach	**Crucifixus**	mass section	? ? c3
19	Conrad Stuber	**Laudate pueri**	psalm setting (Ps. 112: 1, 3, 5/6, 8, doxology)	? ? c2/c3/c4

20	Johannes Eccart	Crucifixus	mass section (*Missa Mon cœur se recommande*)	g2 c2 c3
21	Orlandus Lassus	Crucifixus	mass section (*Missa super Le Berger et la Bergere*)	g2 c2 c3
22	Antonio Mortaro	Sicut mater consolatur	motet	c1 c1 f4
23	Bernhard Klingenstein	**Te libri virgo**	*De Asumptione BMV* (sequence versicle, MA 311)	? ? f4
24	Bernhard Klingenstein	**De cœlo Patris vox**	proper setting or sequence versicle	? ? ? f4
25	Johannes Lockenburg	**Crucifixus**	mass section	? ? c3
26	Lambert de Sayve	**Crucifixus**	mass section	? ? c3
27	Jacobus Gallus (Handl)	Benedictus	mass section (*Missa super Elisabeth Zachariae*)	g2 c2 c3
28	Johannes a Fossa	**Cum iam renovatus**	*De S. Michaële* (sequence versicle, MA 332)	? ? f3
29	Jacobus de Kerle	**Quem laudat sol**	*De SS. Trinitate* (sequence versicle, MA 187)	? ? f4
30	Philipp Zindelin	**Crucifixus**	mass section	? ? f4
31	Clemens non Papa	Et resurrexit	mass section (*Missa J'ay veu le cerf*)	c1 c1 c3
32	Orlandus Lassus	Sicut locutus est	Magnificat section (*Magnificat Octavi toni Benedicta es*)	c1 c1 c4
33	Gregor Aichinger	Sicut locutus est	Magnificat section	g2 g2 c3
34	Bernhard Klingenstein	**Fecit potentiam**	Magnificat section	? ? c3
35	Jacob Regnart	**Quia fecit**	Magnificat section	? ? c4
36	Philipp de Monte	Esurientes	Magnificat section (*Magnificat Octavi Toni*)	c1 c3 c4
37	Giuglio Gigli da Imola	**Sicut locutus est**	Magnificat section	? ? c4
38	Giovanni Palestrina	**Monstra te esse**	hymn section (*Ave Maris stella*)	? ? c3
39	Christian Erbach	**Sicut locutus est**	Magnificat section	? ? c4
40	Conrad Stuber	**Fecit potentiam**	Magnificat section	? ? c3
41	Bernhard Klingenstein	**Fecit potentiam**	Magnificat section	? ? f4

Table 2 *Concordances for compositions in the* Triodia sacra

No.	Composition and concordances	Modern edition
6	Orlando di Lasso, Crucifixus from *Missa super Congratulamini mihi Praestantissimorum divinæ musices auctores missae decem* (Leuven: Phalèse & Bellère, 1570)	*SWNR* 7
7	Antonio Mortaro, *Decantabat populus Israel Sacrae cantiones tribus vocibus concinendae* (Milan: Tini & Besozzi, 1598 and subsequent editions), no. 9	
8	Philippe de Monte, Christe from *Missa Inclina cor meum* Brussels, Conservatoire de Musique, mus. ms. 27089	*Missa Inclina cor meum*, ed. C. van den Borren (Düsseldorf, 1930)
11	Jacobus Peetrinus, *Mane nobiscum, Domine Il I° Libro del Iubilo di San Bernardo con alcune canzonette spirituali* (Rome: s.n., 1588)	Appendix 2
12	Jacobus Peetrinus, *Iam quod quæsivi Il I° Libro del Iubilo di San Bernardo con alcune canzonette spirituali* (Rome: s.n., 1588)	Appendix 2
15	Gregor Aichinger, *Augusta civitas Dei Divinarum laudum ex floridis R. D. Iacobi Pontanis . . . Pars prima* (Dillingen: Meltzer, 1609), no. 8 no complete version transmitted	
16	Jacob Reiner, *Domine exaudi Cantionum piarum . . . tribus vocibus* (Munich: Berg, 1586)	Appendix 2
20	Johannes Eccard, Crucifixus from *Missa Mon cœur se recommande* Augsburg, Staats- und Stadtsbibl., MS Tonk Schl 17, no. 4; Munich, Bayerische Staatsbibl., Mus. ms. 57	*SWNR* 11
21	Orlando di Lasso, Crucifixus from *Missa super Le Berger et la Bergere Quinque Missæ . . .* (Venice: Gardano, 1570)	*SWNR* 3
22	Antonio Mortaro, *Sicut Mater Sacrae cantiones tribus vocibus concinendæ* (Milan: Tini & Besozzi, 1598 and subsequent editions), no. 6	
27	Jacobus Gallus, Benedictus from *Missa super Elisabeth Zachariæ* Augsburg, Staats- und Stadtsbibl., MS Tonk Schl 18, no. 8	DTÖ 117
31	Clemens non Papa, Et resurrexit from *Missa J'ay veu le cerf*	CMM 4/vi

Table 2 *Continued*

No.	Composition and concordances	Modern edition
32	Orlando di Lasso, Sicut locutus est from *Magnificat Octavi Toni Benedicta es* *Liber primus cantiones sacrae Magnificat* . . . (Munich: Henricus, 1602)	*SWNR* 15
33	Gregor Aichinger, Sicut locutus est *Vespertinum Virginis Canticum sive Magnificat quinis vocibus varie modulatur* (Augsburg: Custos (apud Praetorium), 1603), and subsequent editions	Appendix 2
36	Philippe de Monte, Esurientes from *Magnificat Octavi Toni* Augsburg, Staats- und Stadtsbibl., MS Tonk Schl 20	*VIII Magnificat*, ed. Georg van Doorslaer (Düsseldorf, 1930)

CMM = Corpus Mensurabilis Musicae
DTÖ = Denkmäler der Tonkunst in Österreich
SWNR = Orlando di Lasso, *Sämtliche Werke. Neue Reihe*

1. Musicians active at Augsburg or with connections to either the cathedral of Augsburg or the Fugger family

By far outnumbering the rest, the first group consists of musicians from Augsburg or with close connections to the musical life there. As might have been expected, the editor, Klingenstein, is at the head of this group. The choirmaster himself contributed about a fifth of the works presented in the *Triodia sacra*. Three compositions are by Jacobus de Kerle (*c.*1531–91), who resided in Dillingen in 1563 as *Kapellmeister* of Cardinal Otto of Waldburg's private chapel, dissolved later that year. But his patron and constant supporter re-employed him, as soon as an adequate position became vacant at Augsburg Cathedral. From 1568 to 1575 he served there as cathedral organist. Otto Ursprung, author of a comprehensive monograph on de Kerle, relates the story that de Kerle left Augsburg full of resentment at Klingenstein. After the death of the *Kapellmeister* Anton Span in 1574 de Kerle applied for his position, hoping the chapter would remunerate his loyalty over many years to Otto of Waldburg and the chapter with this promotion. Yet the chapter passed him over and hired the musically inexperienced Bernhard Klingenstein. Despite this obvious disadvantage, the chapter favoured Klingenstein: in contrast to the foreigner de Kerle he was an inside candidate who had studied at the cathedral school and continuously served at the cathedral chapel from the 1550s.[39] This turn of events aroused de Kerle's anger.[40] And not unjustly so, because Klingenstein had yet to receive a thorough training in composition. For this purpose the chapter engaged Jean de Cleve, the retired *Kapellmeister* of Archduke Karl of Habsburg at Graz, who taught Klingenstein from 1578 to 1582.[41] I shall return to this point below.

Gregor Aichinger (1564–1628), Christian Erbach (*c*.1568–1635) and the cornettist Philipp Zindelin (*c*.1570–1622) held positions both in households of the Fugger family and the cathedral. Although Aichinger was not employed at the cathedral chapel, the long-serving organist of SS Ulrich and Afra nevertheless was associated with the cathedral chapter since he held prebends there. After positions as organist to the church of St Moritz as successor of Hans Leo Hassler from 1602 to 1614, Christian Erbach served first as assistant, then as main organist at the cathedral of Augsburg. In this role Erbach is presumably depicted in Figure 3, which shows the cathedral chapel during the council of the diocese in 1610. The elderly man directing the choirboys can with some certainty be identified as Bernhard Klingenstein himself, then aged 75. Beyond that, the musicians in the painting cannot be assigned to individual members of the chapel.

An interesting case is the Protestant Johannes Eccard (1553–1611), who was to be celebrated later as the main representative of the 'Berlin Protestantism' style of composition.[42] In this light, the appearance of his Crucifixus setting in Klingenstein's anthology is puzzling. A possible reason why it was nevertheless included (perhaps even against denominational reservations of the Jesuits) might have been that the respective mass had already been composed in 1578. At that time Eccard was studying with Lasso in Munich and serving in the household of

[39] Singer, *Bernhardus Klingenstein*, pp. 23–6.
[40] Ursprung, *Jacobus de Kerle*, pp. 90–1.
[41] Singer, *Bernhardus Klingenstein*, pp. 26, 29. Although seemingly curious, the decision to hire a musically inexperienced member of the chapel as choirmaster was characteristic for the cathedral chapter at Augsburg: Klingenstein's successors Aichmiller and Merz also received their appointment prior to the beginning of thorough compositional training. See Kroyer, 'Gregors Aichingers Leben und Werke', p. l, n. 1.
[42] C. Böcker, *Johannes Eccard: Leben und Werk* (Berliner musikwissenschaftliche Arbeiten, 17; Munich and Salzburg, 1980), *passim*.

Figure 3 The cathedral chapel of Augsburg at Mass during the
Council of the Diocese in 1610
Painting by Thomas Maurer in the Choir Sacristy of Augsburg Cathedral, repro-
duced from Denis A. Chevalley (ed.), *Der Dom zu Augsburg* (Munich, 1995), Pl. 250.
Photo by Eberhard Lantz

Jacob Fugger in Augsburg. It was only one year after the composition of the parody mass *Mon cœur se recommande* that Eccard
entered the Protestant sphere, receiving an appointment as *Vice-
Kapellmeister* at the Court of the Margrave of Brandenburg-
Ansbach. The two Latin canzonette of Jacobus Peetrinus
(*c*.1553–*c*.1593) were available in at least two printed editions, but
possibly Klingenstein's attention was drawn to this composer by
his connection with the Fugger family, as Peetrinus' patron in
Rome was the Count of Montfort, nephew of Jacob Fugger.
Moreover, these works are settings of spiritual texts by St Bernard
of Clairvaux, whose writings were in vogue among the Catholics
of the early seventeenth century.[43]

2. Musicians from the Munich court chapel

The second group encompasses musicians of the Munich court
chapel. In the 1560s Cardinal Otto of Waldburg had established
a frequent musical exchange between the cathedral chapel of
Augsburg and the musicians of the nearby residence of the Dukes
of Bavaria.[44] Therefore it is not surprising that Klingenstein drew
heavily on works by his colleagues from Munich. Orlando di Lasso
(*c*.1530–94), one of the most distinguished composers of this
period, is represented with three three-voice sections from liturgical compositions. Notably, Lasso's parody Magnificat on Josquin's
Benedicta es, the source for no. 32 of Klingenstein's anthology, is
recorded at Augsburg in a choirbook manuscript as early as 1583,
preceding the first printed edition by nearly twenty years. This
choirbook belonged to the Benedictine monastery of SS Ulrich and
Afra in Augsburg, the other flourishing centre of Catholic
polyphony in the city besides the cathedral.[45] Owing to the loss of
all the musical sources of the cathedral and the lack of any contemporary inventories we do not know whether Klingenstein's

---

[43] Fisher, 'Music in Counter-Reformation Augsburg', pp. 292, 299–300. The fashion for
polyphonic settings of texts by St Bernard also found vivid expression in the diocese of
Augsburg. Aichinger published his *Odaria lectissima ex melitiss. D. Bernardi Iubilo* in 1601
(printed by Custos); Erbach's *Mele sive cantiones sacræ* (Augsburg: Schultes, 1603) were
also based on texts by St Bernard. In addition, Adam Meltzer issued the *Rhythmus, et
Suavissima D. Bernardi Oda, vulgo iubilus dicta* by Johannes Feldmayer in 1607, and his wife
Sabrina the *Parvulus flosculus, ex melitissimo D. Bernardi Iubilo delibatus* by Christian Keifferer
from Weissenau in 1610.

[44] Ursprung, *Jacobus de Kerle*, pp. 11–15.

[45] *Ibid.*, pp. 85–6.

chapel also possessed a copy of this work. Yet this is not improbable, since the two institutions were in close contact.[46]

Moreover, Klingenstein drew upon an otherwise unknown sequence versicle of Johannes de Fossa (*c.*1540–1603), *Vice-Kapellmeister* under Lasso and upon Lasso's death in 1594 *Kapellmeister* of the Munich court chapel. Further compositions by musicians from this institution were written by the organist Johannes Lockenburg (*c.*1530–*c.*1591) and the instrumentalist Giuglio Gigli da Imola (fl. 1600). A subcategory is formed by pupils of Lasso. Besides Johannes Eccard, already mentioned above, Klingenstein's choice fell on Jacob Reiner (before 1560–1606), who had studied with Lasso in the 1570s. Later on he was to become choirmaster at the abbey of Weingarten. In addition, it is striking that Reiner extensively published at the Meltzer press during the early seventeenth century (see above). Possibly Klingenstein had learnt to value this master through these prints, because he had already asked Reiner to contribute to his *Rosetum Marianum* collection of 1603.

3. Musicians from Habsburg courts

The third group of musicians represented in Klingenstein's *Triodia sacra* consists of composers from Habsburg courts and the Imperial Court in particular. Jacob Regnart (*c.*1540–99) served the house of Habsburg nearly all his life and several members of this dynasty throughout his career. Philippe de Monte (1521–1603) filled the position of the choirmaster at the Imperial Chapel of Rudolph II, while Lambert de Sayve (*c.*1549–1614) served as director of the choir in the chapel of Rudolph's brother, the Archduke Matthias of Habsburg, which was to become the Imperial Chapel upon Matthias's succession in 1612. Jacobus de Kerle was appointed court chaplain at Rudolph's court in 1582, a post he held until his death. Although not a member of the Imperial Chapel, Jacobus Gallus (1550–91) established close connections with this institution during his time as cantor at the church of St Jan in Prague.

Among the musicians included in this category, Tiburtio Massaino (*c.*1550–1609) is the one most loosely associated with the

[46] It should be noted that another early manuscript copy of this mass, dating from 1582, belonged to the church and college of St Michael in Munich, the splendid base of the Jesuits in the city centre.

Habsburg family. The Italian composer served as a singer and chaplain in the court chapel of Archduke Ferdinand II at Innsbruck in 1589–90. Therafter he was employed by Wolf Dietrich of Reithenau, Archbishop of Salzburg. After little more than one year, however, Massaino was banned from Salzburg for delicate reasons: the Augustinian canon was convicted for homosexual conduct. He then took refuge in Prague, where he became acquainted with members of the Imperial Chapel, particularly with Philippe de Monte. He stayed in Prague, and over the course of time his ill reputation was cleared. Later he returned to his native country, where he managed to start a second career, eventually receiving an appointment as choirmaster at the cathedral of Piacenza.

4. Other backgrounds

The fourth and last group includes the figures who do not fall clearly into a specific category: Conrad Stuber (*c*.1550–*c*.1605) belongs to the composers who had previously contributed compositions to Klingenstein's other editorial project, the *Rosetum Marianum*.[47] Conrad Stuber might have become an attractive candidate for both prints because he was *Kapellmeister* at the court of Eithelfriedrich IV in Hechingen, one of the most ardent Counter-Reformers in southern Germany. For this reason, the Jesuits were doubtlessly pleased with Klingenstein's decision to include a composition by Stuber, if this choice was not guided by their recommendation.

Music prints seem to have been the source of the works of Clemens non Papa (*c*.1510–*c*.1555) and Antonio Mortaro (fl. 1587–1610) that Klingenstein included in his *Triodia sacra*. In

---

[47] It is curious that, although the *Triodia sacra* was envisaged not more than one year after the publication of the *Rosetum Marianum*, the composers represented in the two collections show surprisingly little overlap. Of the thirty-three composers who contributed polyphonic settings of stanzas of *Maria zart*, only nine are also in the *Triodia sacra*, i.e., Gregor Aichinger, Christian Erbach, Johannes a Fossa, Bernhard Klingenstein, Jacob Regnart, Jacob Reiner, Lambert de Sayve, Conrad Stuber and Philipp Zindelin. This striking difference, however, is due to the different nature of the two projects: all settings of the *Rosetum Marianum* were commissioned by Klingenstein particularly for this anthology, while for the *Triodia sacra* he drew on pre-existing material, the repertoire of his chapel at Augsburg Cathedral. Accordingly, the former collection contains exclusively works by contemporary composers, while a considerable amount of tricinia in the latter anthology are by masters who had died many years before its publication in 1605 (e.g., Clemens non Papa, Lassus, Palestrina, de Monte, de Kerle). For a more detailed account of the *Rosetum Marianum* see Singer, *Bernhardus Klingenstein*, pp. 51–96, and the modern edition by W. E. Hettrick (including the accurately researched and updated introduction).

Clemens's case, this assumption is supported by the appearance of his mass movement in the same mass print as Lasso's *Missa super Congratulamini mihi*, from which Klingenstein chose the Crucifixus section. The two motets of Antonio Mortaro (nos. 7 and 22) were first published in his popular motet print *Sacrae cantiones* in 1598. This volume not only enjoyed several new editions, but received broad dissemination, particularly in the south German and Habsburg lands.[48]

Last but not least, Giovanni Pierluigi da Palestrina (1525–94) constitutes a curious case. Oddly enough, the *Triodia sacra* do not contain any works from the Roman school, which had become the celebrated model of Catholic polyphony, nor compositions written by members of the *Societas Jesu*. But it is even more surprising that somebody like Palestrina, although generally considered the most prominent composer in the Catholic area, is remarkably underrepresented with only one work. To increase the perplexity, this composition (a movement of an *Ave maris stella* setting) is not transmitted in any source apart from Klingenstein's *Triodia sacra* (see Figure 4). As a consequence, Palestrina scholarship has not taken this work into account. Ultimately, the unique transmission of this piece, completely atypical for compositions by Palestrina, casts reasonable doubt on its attribution. The final section of this article will present a possible explanation for this puzzling fact.

TRICINIA: SACRED AND PROFANE, CATHOLIC AND PROTESTANT

So far I have scrutinised the *Triodia sacra* from different perspectives, proceeding from general matters to more specific ones like Klingenstein's preface and the composers represented in his anthology. The next step takes an even narrower focus: the investigation of the compositions considered worthy to be included in the publication. Glancing through Table 1, one cannot fail to note the overwhelming predominance of liturgical compositions among

---

[48] It is noteworthy that the 1598 printed edition of Mortaro's *Sacrae cantiones* includes a partbook that gives the compositions in full score, though without texts ('Partitio Sacrarum Cantionum'). This volume is now kept at the Civico Museo Bibliografico Musicale in Bologna. I am very grateful to Barbara Ventura, librarian at this institution, for assistance.

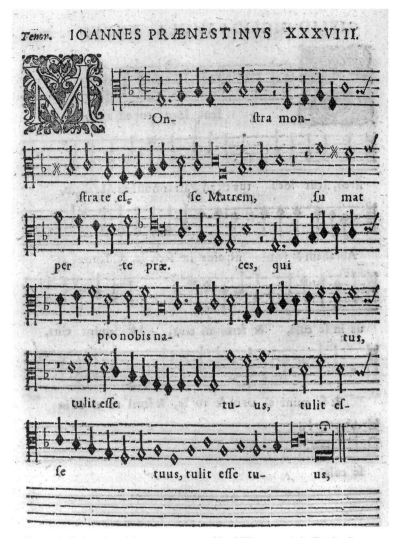

Figure 4 Palestrina, *Monstra te esse*, no. 38 of Klingenstein's *Triodia Sacra*.
Reproduced with permission of the British Library

the total content of the *Triodia sacra*: masses (16), Magnificats (9), sequences (6), psalms (1), other propers (1 or 2) and hymn settings (1). By contrast, motets (4) and madrigals or canzonette (2), which usually prevail in prints addressed to a broad public, only play a marginal role in Klingenstein's selection.

A comparison of the *Triodia sacra* with other *tricinia* anthologies of the period helps to explain this striking imbalance.[49] Table 3 provides a survey of tricinia publications between 1570 and 1610. From this list it becomes clear that the market for tricinia was dominated by secular compositions. The majority of these prints were issued in Italy or southern Germany and the German publications often reprinted pieces from Italian repertory, adapted to the German market by translations of the original texts, attesting to the popularity that three-voice *canzonette* enjoyed among a broad public in both countries. It is difficult to imagine that the Jesuits were not dissatisfied, given the enormous dissemination of these secular compositions. Moreover, due to their convivial and often even frivolous character, these *canzonette* must have appeared to them as the epitome of the 'lascivum et impurum' condemned by the Council of Trent. The combination of orthodoxy, pragmatism and utilitarianism, characteristic for the Jesuit approach, might thus have created a strategy such as the following: given the popularity of three-voice compositions, the Jesuits intended to propagate an emphatically sacred counterpart to these secular collections. This plan rests on the premise that the public demand responded more to the three-voice texture, with its more flexible performing conditions, than to the actual content of the respective collections. But even if public taste was not as indifferent as expected (clearly a reasonable alternative!), the active use of a sacred collection of tricinia at the university itself would at least help to turn its own students away from the dangerous temptations arising through contamination with the profane repertory.

As usual, the Jesuits' battle was fought simultaneously against secular temptations in general, and their Protestant enemies in particular. The anthologies of sacred polyphony (shown in bold in Table 3), demonstrate a clear geographic division: the Italian market is dominated by vernacular *canzonette spirituali*, while in Germany three-voice settings with Latin or German texts prevail. It cannot be overemphasised that nearly all of the latter were printed by Protestants (chiefly in Nuremberg and Erfurt). In

---

[49] J. E. Lindberg, 'Origins and Development of the Sixteenth-Century Tricinium' (Ph.D. diss., University of Cincinnati, 1988) provides an excellent and comprehensive analysis of tricinium publications in the sixteenth century, particularly of the first three quarters of the century. Read against the material Lindberg presents, the unusual nature of Klingenstein's anthology, with its emphasis on liturgical compositions, is striking.

Table 3 *Printed anthologies of polyphony for three voices, 1570–1615*

Note: This list provides a provisional survey of anthologies containing exclusively settings for three voices, based primarily on RISM B I: *Recueils imprimés XVIe–XVIIe siècles* (Munich, 1960). Music publications by individuals are included in so far as they are mentioned in Bruce Bellingham's article 'Tricinium' in *NG II* or in J. E. Lindberg, 'Origins and Development of the Sixteenth Century Tricinium' (Ph.D. diss., University of Cincinnati, 1989). Instrumental music is not included. Full details are given only for sacred collections; secular collections are cited by short title. Publications containing sacred music exclusively are listed in bold type.

Prior to the specified period the following anthologies deserve to be mentioned:

1559 Wolfgang Figulus, **Tricinia sacra ad voces pueriles** (Nuremberg, 1559)

1567[2] **Tricinia sacra** (Nuremberg: Gerlach, 1567): Clemens non Papa, Debuissons, Galli, Heylanus (3), O. di Lasso (2), Loys, de Novo portu (2), Prenner (5), Regnart (4), Vaet (3), anon. (6)

1572[6] *Il primo libro delle justiniane a tre voci* (Venice: Scotto, 1572; = 1578[19], 1586[13])

1573 Christian Hollander, *Triciniorum . . . fasciculus* (Munich: Berg, 1573)

1574 Jean de Castro, **Triciniorum sacrorum . . . liber I** (Leuven: Phalèse & Bellère, 1574)

1574[3] **La Fleur de chansons a trois parties** (Leuven: Phalèse, and Antwerp: Bellère, 1574)

1575[14] *Il secondo libro delle giustiniane a tre voci* (Venice: Scotto, 1575)

1583[3] **Il primo libro delle laude spirituali a tre voci.** *Stampata ad instanza delli Reverendi Padri delle Congregatione dello Oratorio* (*Rome*: Gardano, 1583 = 1585[9]): anon. (30)

1584 Jacob Regnart, *Tricinia, kurtzweilige teutsche Lieder zu dreyen stimmen* (*Nuremberg*: Gerlach, 1584; = Munich: Berg, 1590)

1584[10] *Il secondo libro delle canzoni a tre voci* (Venice: Vincenzi & Amadino, 1583)

1585[7] **Canzonette spirituali de diversi a tre voci. Libro primo** (Rome: Gardano, 1585; = 1588[5]), 3 vols.: Dragoni, Giovanelli (2), Marenzio (2), Nanino, Quagliati (16), anon. (3)

1585[8] **Madrigali spirituali a tre voci di Lelio Bertani et di Costanzo Antegnati** (Brescia: Sabbio, 1585): Antegnati (9), Bertani (10)

1586[12] *Il gaudio primo libro de madrigali . . . a tre voci* (Venice: Scotto, 1586)

1587[6] *Fiori musicali de diversi auttori a tre voci* (Venice: Vincenzi, 1587; = 1590[18])

1587[7] *Canzonette a tre voci* (Venice: Amadino, 1587; = 1594[9]?)

1588[12] **Teutsche Psalmen: geistliche Psalmen, mit dreyen Stimmen, welche nit allain lieblich zu singen, sonder auch auff aller hand Art Instrumenten zugebrauchen** (Munich: Berg, 1588): O. di Lasso (25), R. de Lasso (25)

1588[19] *Giardinetto de madrigali et canzonette a tre voci . . . Libro primo* (Venice: Amadino, 1588)

1588[20] *Fiori musicali di diversi auttori a tre voci. Libro secondo* (Venice: Vincenzi, 1588; = 1598[10])

Table 3 *Continued*

1588[25]   *Canzonette a tre voci, di Giuliano Paratico.* Libro secondo (Brescia: Marchetti, 1588)

1588[26]   *Canzonette di Paolo Quagliati a tre voci . . . Libro secondo* (Rome: Gardano, 1588)

1588[30]   *Dodekatonon musicum triciniorum . . . Neue auserlesene Tricinia . . . in den Druck verfertiget von Henningo Dedekindo . . .* (Erfurt: Baumann, 1588)

1589[10]   *Canzonette a tre voci . . . Libro primo* (Venice: Amadino, 1589)

1591[13]   **Canzonette spirituali a 3 voci composti da diversi ecc. musici** (Rome: [Verovio], 1591; = 1599[7]): Anerio, Giovanelli, Griffi, Ingegneri, de Macque (3), Marenzio, del Mel (10), Nanino, Pacelli (2), Santini

1592   Jean de Castro, **Triciniorum sacrorum, quae moteta vocant . . . liber unus** (Antwerp: Phalèse & Bellère, 1592)

1592[5]   **Il devoto pianto della gloriosa Vergine, et altre canzonette spirituali à 3 voci, composte novamente da diversi eccellenti musici** (Rome: [Verovio], 1592): Anerio, Giovanelli (2), Griffi, di Macque, del Mel, Nanino (3), Pacelli (2), Santini (2)

1592[20]   *Il terzo libro delle fiammelle amorose . . . A tre voci* (Venice: Amadino, 1592; = 1596[15]?)

1594   S. F. Fritzius, **Etliche deutsche geistliche Tricinia** (Nuremberg, 1594 (lost), only mentioned in *NG II*)

1594[10]   *Di Ippolito Baccusi . . . il primo libro de madrigali a tre voci* (Venice: Amadino, 1594)

1594[15]   *Il primo libro delle canzonette a tre voci* (Venice: Amadino, 1594)

1597[16]   *Madrigali a tre voci . . . Libro primo* (Venice: Gardano, 1597; = 1551[10], 1555[28], 1561[11], 1569[22], 1569[23])

1597[21]   *Canzonette à tre voci* (Venice: Gardano, 1597; = 1597[22], 1606[13])

1598   Gregor Aichinger, **Tricinia Mariana, quibus antiphonae, hymni, Magnificat, litaniae, et variae laudes ex officio Beatiss. Virginis suavissimis modulis decantantur** (Innsbruck: Agricola, 1598; = RISM 1609[2] Dillingen: Meltzer 1609, including an additional motet by Reiner)

1599[11]   *Canzonette a tre voci* (Venice: Vincenti, 1599)

1599[14]   *Il quarto libro delle canzonette a 3 voci* (Milan: Tini & Besozzi, 1599)

1600[12]   *Il secondo libro delle canzonette a tre voci* (Venice: Amadino, 1600)

1600[17]   *Canzonette leggiadre a tre voci* (Milan: Tini & Besozzi, 1600)

1601   Gregor Aichinger, **Divinæ laudes ex floridis Iacobi Pontani potissimum decerptae, modisque musicis ad voces ternas factae** (Augsburg: Custos (apud Praetorium), 1602; repr. Dillingen: Meltzer, 1609)

1601[8]   *Canzonette alla romana . . . a tre voci* (Venice: Gardano, 1601)

1603   Gregor Aichinger, **Ghirlanda. Di Canzonette spirituali a tre voci** (Augsburg: Praetorius, 1603, [2]1603, [3]1604)[a]

1603   Stephanus Calvisius, **Tricinia. Auserlesene Teutsche Lieder, der meisten theil aus des Königlichen Propheten Davids Psalterio gezogen, neben etlichen anderen geistlichen und anmütigen Politischen Texten** (Leipzig: Apel, 1603)

1603[7]   *Canzonette a tre voci . . . Libro secondo* (Venice: Vincenti, 1603; = 1604[14])

1603[12]   *Canzonette a tre voci . . . Libro primo* (Venice: Vincenti, 1603; = 1604[18], 1607[23])

Table 3 *Continued*

1604 Karl Hagius, *Neue deutsche Tricinien* (Frankfurt am Main: Richter, 1604)
1604[13] *Fiori musicali a tre voci* (Antwerp: Phalèse, 1604)
1605[1] **Triodia sacra, sive modi musici ternis vocibus tam ad tironum, quam peritiorum usum facti . . . Liber I** (Dillingen: Meltzer, 1605)
1605[3] **Sacrarum melodiarum tribus vocibus compositarum, ab Josepho Hoelzlin Cive augustano & musico** (Nuremberg: Wagemann, 1605): Jer. Hölzlin, Jos. Hölzlin (17), Jeep
1605[10] *Canzonette a tre voci . . . Libro quinto* (Siena: Ghini, *c*.1605)
1605[11] *Le Vergini d'Ippolito Baccusi. Madrigali a tre voci libro secondo* (Venice: Amadino, 1605)
1605[12] *I nuovi fioretti a tre voci* (Venice: Amadino, 1605; =1607[17])
1606[8] *Leggiadre nimphe a tre voci* (Venice: Gardano & fratelli, 1606)
1606[13] *Canzonette, mit dreyen Stimmen . . . mit teutschen Texten beleget* (Nuremberg: Kauffmann, 1606; cf. 1597[21], 1597[22])
1607[11] **Canzonette spirituali a tre voci, di Marcantonio Tornioli senese . . . Libro primo** (Venice: Gardano & fratelli, 1607): Cenui, Tornioli (20)
1607[14] *Canzonette alla romana* (Antwerp: Phalèse, 1607)
1607[25] *Johann-Jacobi Gastoldi und anderer Autorn Tricinia . . . mit teutschen weltlichen Texten* (Nuremberg: Kauffmann, 1607)
1608[4] **Lodi, et canzonette spirituali. Raccolte da diversi autori: & ordinate secondo le varie maniere de' versi. Aggiuntevi à ciascuna maniera le loro arie nuove di musica à tre voci assai dilettevoli** (Naples: Longo, 1608): anon. (all)
1608[22] *Newe teutsche Canzonetten mit dreyen Stimmen . . . mit unser Sprach . . . unterlegt* (Frankfurt: Richter, 1608)
1609[2] **Tricina Mariana, quibus Antiphonæ, Hymni, Magnificat, Litaniæ, et variæ laudes ex officio Beatissi. Virginis suavissimis modulis decantantur, in usum tum sodalium, tum aliorum cultorum et amantium matris Dei, &c. auctore R. D. Gregorio Aichinger** (Dillingen: Meltzer, 1609): Aichinger (18), Reiner
1609[2] *Canzonette et arie a tre voci . . . Libro primo* (Venice: Raverii, 1609)
1609[25] *Scherzi musicali a tre voci di Claudio Monteverde* (Venice: Amadino, 1609)
1610 Johannes Jeep, *Schöne ausserlesene liebliche Tricinia, . . . mit lustigen Teutschen Texten ersetzet* (Nuremberg: Wagenmann, 1610)
1610[7] Antonio Mortaro, **Sacræ cantiones tribus vocibus concinendæ. Una cum basso ad organum** (Venice: Amadino, 1610)
1611 Michael Prætorius, Bicinia und Tricinia (Hamburg and Wolfenbüttel: Hering, 1611)

During the specified period the following bicinia collections were published (cf. RISM B I): 1579[7], 1584[9a], 1586[6], 1590[19], 1591[19], 1591[27] (*Bicinia sacra*, Nuremberg: Gerlach, 1591), 1594[13], 1598[13], 1607[7], 1607[18], 1609[4] (+ B.c.), 1609[19].

---

[a] The subsequent editions are described in Ernst Fritz Schmid (rev. Bettina Schwemmer), 'Aichinger, Gregor', *MGG*[2], *Personenteil*, i, col. 267.

addition, it appears that even if printers from Catholic cities did publish tricinia collections, they were primarily directed to Protestant buyers. The most prominent example of this phenomenon is certainly the *Teutsche Psalmen: geistliche Psalmen* (Munich: Berg, 1588) by Orlando di Lasso and his son Rudolf, which present the psalms in a German translation and not according to the Vulgate.

Viewed in this context, it becomes evident that the Jesuits of Dillingen played a key role in establishing an emphatically Catholic type of tricinia in Germany, defined in opposition to its secular and Protestant counterparts. It is remarkable that Klingenstein's *Triodia sacra* acted as the prototype for the constitution of this new (and consciously pioneering) paradigm. On the German market, the *Triodia sacra* was only preceded by two other collections of sacred polyphony for three voices, both of which display an equally Catholic repertory: the *Tricinia Mariana* (Innsbruck, 1598) and the *Divinae laudes* (Augsburg, 1601), each containing original compositions for three voices by Gregor Aichinger. It is surely more than a coincidence that Klingenstein's only precursor was a Catholic priest and musician who was not only active at Augsburg, but had also cultivated a warm relation with the Jesuits from his academic studies at their universities. It was the Meltzer press at Dillingen that bore the fruit of these ties. During the first decade of the seventeenth century, Aichinger published both extensively and (almost) exclusively at Dillingen. Many of his music prints enjoyed several editions. Others, originally published elsewhere, were reprinted. Quite significantly, the second editions of the above-mentioned prints *Divinae laudes* and *Tricinia Mariana* (with an additional motet by Reiner) belong to the latter category, both reissued at Dillingen in 1609. This fact provides yet another piece of circumstantial evidence for the assumption that the Jesuits of Dillingen were among the first actively to instrumentalise the popularity of tricinium collections for the propagation of a pure Catholic repertory. And this agenda suggests a plausible answer to the question why Klingenstein's *Triodia sacra* shows so striking a predominance of liturgical compositions.[50] A

---

[50] Given the admirable richness of Fisher's thesis on 'Music in Counter-Reformation Augsburg', it is unfortunate that he fails to recognise the liturgical impulse of Catholic sacred music composed after the Council of Trent. In his determination to ascribe a dis-

complementary explanation, however, can be given by adapting the editor's perspective: Klingenstein, in search of appropriate three-voice compositions for his anthology, obviously drew on the repertory of his own chapel. As this was an ecclesiastical chapel, it is not surprising that its choirbooks contained primarily liturgical polyphony.

THE COMPOSITIONS

The homogeneity of genre found in the *Triodia sacra* is paralleled by a similar homogeneity of compositional style. In the majority of cases, the latter is characterised by an imitative fabric in which the single voices are merged in smooth and – despite the three-voice texture – sonorous harmonies. Good examples are the Benedictus from the *Missa super Elisabeth Zachariae* by Jacob Handl, presented in Example 1, and Aichinger's Sicut locutus est from the *Magnificat super Liquide perl'amor*, to be found in Appendix 2.[51] Next in importance are passages in simple counterpoint, which, although occurring less often, are fairly common.[52] Reiner's motet *Domine exaudi*, no. 16 in Klingenstein (see Appendix 2), gives a paradigmatic impression of this musical fabric. It is noteworthy that even if some works unambiguously show tendencies towards a madrigalesque setting of the text (as would not be surprising in the case of Lasso and his followers), the text-expressive devices never exceed the boundaries of well-balanced structural clarity. The maximum degree of tone-painting found in the *Triodia sacra* can be seen paradigmatically in Peetrino's Latin canzonetta *Mane*

tinctly Catholic character exclusively to patently Marian, eucharistic or other characteristically devotional compositions, Fisher plays down the relevance of liturgical music for Catholic music of the Counter-Reformation. Judging from this slightly distorted and narrow perspective, he disregards the markedly Catholic profile of Klingenstein's *Triodia sacra*, stating: 'The texts of the pieces selected by Klingenstein seem to have no overt religious significance, consisting mainly of individual movements from the Mass and Magnificat' (p. 227).

[51] Appendix 2 to this essay provides an edition of (reconstructed) tricinia not available in a modern edition.

[52] It is notable that chordal writing is also typical for the majority of musical numbers in Jesuit dramas of the period. In particular, the polyphonic choruses written by Christian Erbach for the drama *Didymus* (1613) come very close stylistically to the *contrapunctus simplex* compositions in Klingenstein's *Triodia sacra*. For a partial edition of one of Erbach's two choruses, contained in Staats- und Stadtbibliothek Augsburg, 8° H 1840, see Fisher, 'Music in Counter-Reformation Augsburg', pp. 103–4.

Example 1 Jacobus Gallus (Handl), Benedictus
from the *Missa super Elisabeth Zachariae*

nobiscum, Domine, based on a poem by St Bernard of Clairvaux (no.
11; see Appendix 2). Peetrino responded to the few words inviting
a musical interpretation in a simple but nonetheless striking way.
The word 'pulsa' is illustrated quite blatantly by a rhythmical
'knocking' of two semiminims, alternating between the voices or
voice pairs – a madrigalism that is both economical and efficient
(bars 10–12). Neatly integrated in the straightforward musical fabric, which ranges from decorated simple counterpoint to pseudo-
imitations (e.g., bars 1–2), is the interpretation of 'illustra' (bars
7–8). The musical figure, a melisma in short note values, is
achieved by embellishing the fundamental melodic progressions

with auxiliary or passing notes. A more sophisticated form of tone-painting characterises the musical rendition of the word 'reple' (bars 17–24). The text of the last verse, formulating the prayer 'Fill the world with sweetness', appears twice. Upon its repetition the rhythmic tempo, dominated by minims and semiminims, shifts to a higher level. Then, from bar 21, minims and semibreves prevail. The technique of slowing down in the closing passage, straightforward and inconspicuous as it seems, expresses the text quite subtly: as the fabric thickens at the repetition of the prayer, it suggestively signals that the Lord had already heard the prayer and indeed 'filled' the world – even if not exactly in the sense wished.[53]

It has to be emphasised that the level of text expression apparent in Peetrino's settings already represents an extreme, by far exceeding the average degree of tone-painting in the *Triodia sacra*. As far as the partial reconstruction of its tricina permits so general a conclusion, it can be said that in all compositions the rules of counterpoint are strictly observed. The fabric is always correct, smooth and at times even dry. Bold harmonic progressions and other exuberant means of text expression, which the church might disapprove, are entirely absent.

These stylistic features certainly matched the Jesuits' insistence on genuine and pure church music that was to eschew any 'lascivious' sensationalism or musical extravagance. From a modern perspective, these compositions might thus be disregarded as aesthetically irrelevant, if not boring. On the other hand, it is precisely these aspects which represent a more general stream of sacred music around 1600, regardless of denomination, the emergence of what was to be called the *stylus ecclesiasticus*.

In addition to the homogeneity of style and genre, the distribution of voice registers is also fairly uniform. As can be gathered from the clef combinations shown in Table 1, two upper voices (g2, c1 or c2) are supported by a bass in lower register, which is more flexible with regard to cleffing (from c3 to f4). This design is definitely tailor-made for the pedagogic context to which

---

[53] Needless to say, Peetrino's text-expressive devices do not work when the second stanza is sung to the same music. Hence it becomes clear that his composition is mainly concerned with the text of the first stanza – the usual procedure in settings of polystrophic texts.

Klingenstein's anthology belongs. At Jesuit universities or grammar schools of the period, tricinia were performed with the students singing the upper voices, accompanied by an educator or teacher from the staff, who took over the bassus part and conducted the ensemble.

In every aspect discussed so far, Klingenstein emerges as an editor who took great care to avoid any offences against the Church's norms. It is therefore all the more surprising that his *Triodia sacra* also included a few parody compositions on *secular* models (see Table 4), a technique vehemently condemned by Church authorities in the context of the Council of Trent.[54] It is true that the use of secular models for liturgical compositions received a more tolerant assessment as time proceeded. Nevertheless, one has to wonder whether and why the Jesuit heads of the university did not object to the fact that an official publication of the university was 'contaminated' with material that, although tacitly tolerated, was far from being officially approved by the Catholic Church. The reasons for this curious phenomenon are manifold. First and foremost, the musical excellence of a composition as a whole may have been the decisive criterion when offences occurred in either occasional details or exterior circumstances such as the use of a frivolous model – an important, though often underrated, factor.[55] In this regard, the generally orthodox musical style of all pieces in the anthology more than compensated for individual offences. Furthermore, a milder judgement might seem to be appropriate if the trespassing composer was commonly held in great esteem and respected as an authority. Consequently, amidst the 'impure' pieces among the *Triodia sacra*, at least the mass sections by Lasso and Clemens might have been excused. Lasso and Clemens had, after all, the reputation of nearly 'classical' authorities.

[54] Weber, *Le Concile de Trente et la musique*, pp. 86–90; Weinmann, *Das Konzil von Trient und die Kirchenmusik*, pp. 49–56; Palestrina, *Pope Marcellus Mass*, ed. L. Lockwood (New York, 1975), p. 12. A well-balanced account from a more recent perspective is given in F. Körndle, 'Das musikalische Ordinarium Missæ nach 1400', in *Messe und Motette*, ed. H. Leuchtmann and S. Mauser (Handbuch der musikalischen Gattungen, 9; Laaber, 1998), pp. 154–88, esp. p. 175.

[55] This aspect will be more extensively explored and elaborated in my thesis. David Crook justly speculates that from the perspective of sixteenth-century musicians, the holiness of a sacred or liturgical text might have transformed the originally secular model into a 'sacred gift'. See D. Crook, *Orlando di Lasso's Imitation Magnificats for Counter-Reformation Munich* (Princeton, 1994), pp. 80–2.

Table 4 *Parody compositions in the* Triodia sacra *and their models*

Parody Compositions on Secular Models

Clemens non Papa, *Missa J'ay veu le cerf*	Pierre de Manchicourt, *J'ay veu le cerf.* French drinking song, text by an anonymous author. Source: Manchicourt, *Le neuviesme livre des chansons à quatre parties* (Antwerp: Susato, 1545)
Johannes Eccard, *Missa mon cœur se recommande*	Orlando di Lasso, *Mon cœur se recommande à vous.* Chanson, text by Marot. Source: *Quatorsieme livre de chansons à quatre & cinq parties, d'Orlande de Lassus & autres autheurs* (Paris: Roy & Ballard, 1567; RISM 1567[8] = 1571[1] = 1575[8])
Orlando di Lasso, *Missa Super Le Berger et la Bergere*	Nicolas Gombert, *Le bergier et la bergiere.* Chanson, text by an anonymous author. Source: *Le cinquiesme livre contenant trente et deux chansons . . . composées par maistre Nicolas Gombert et aultres excellens autheurs* (Antwerp: Susato, 1544; = RISM 1544[13])

Parody Compositions on Sacred Models

Jacobus Gallus, *Missa super Elisabeth Zachariæ*	Jacobus Gallus, De S. Ioanne Baptista. *Elisabeth Zachariæ.* Motet on a liturgical text. Source: Gallus, *Quartus tomus musici operis* (Prague: Nigrinus, 1590)
Orlando di Lasso, *Missa Super Congratulamini mihi*	Orlando di Lasso, *Congratulamini mihi omnes.* Motet. Source: Lasso, *Sacræ cantiones . . . quinque et sex vocum* (Venice: Gardano, 1566; = 1569e = 1578e = 1578g = 1599a)
Orlando di Lasso, *Magnificat Octavi Toni Benedicta es*	Josquin Desprez, *Benedicta es.* Motet. Earliest printed source: *Liber selectarum Cantionum* (Augsburg: Grimm & Wyrsung, 1520; = RISM 1520[4]) and many subsequent editions
Philippe de Monte, *Missa Inclina cor meum*	Philippe de Monte, *Inclina cor meum.* Motet. Source: de Monte, *Liber II. Sacrarum Cantionum cum quinque vocibus* (Venice: Scotto, 1573)

Yet it is also imaginable that Klingenstein did not want to arouse the Jesuits' suspicion unnecessarily and therefore hid the pieces endangered by Jesuit censorship amongst the unproblematic compositions, which made up the majority of his collection.[56] This would have been easy to achieve, because in the *Triodia sacra* only the author and text incipit are specified and *not* the larger works from which those sections were taken. In addition, the passages for few voices in masses and Magnificat cycles were normally only loosely, if at all, connected with the model. This custom might thus have supported Klingenstein's 'window-dressing' tactics, a strategy which might justly be termed 'Jesuitical'. For the same reason that the connection with the offensive model was hardly recognisable to non-connoisseurs, it might ultimately have found even the Jesuits' approval.[57]

Nonetheless, these particular items in Klingenstein's anthology break significantly with those compositional conventions. Clemens non Papa's Et resurrexit (Example 2) is perhaps the most striking example, as the allusion to Manchicourt's drinking song *J'ay veu le cerf* could hardly have escaped recognition. The unambiguous quotation of the incipit of this chanson becomes even the more 'dangerous' when one takes into account that students have always tended to be familiar with the repertory of songs featuring a bawdy text. As a consequence, it is likely that aesthetic appreciation acted as the decisive criterion for the Jesuits' approval, provided that they recognised the problematic pieces as such in the first place.

---

[56] In that case one would have to pose the question whether Klingenstein simply wanted to eschew justifying his choice or whether he included the 'impure' material for subversive reasons. Unfortunately, there is no evidence for either alternative.

[57] In a forthcoming study on 'An Instance of Early Modern Music Censorship', David Crook discusses a source (Munich, Bayerische Staatsbibliothek, Clm 9237, pp. 31–5) that provides illuminating insights into musical censorship among the German Jesuits in late Renaissance. This late sixteenth-century document was written by Ferdinand Alber, rector of the Jesuit College in Munich in the 1580s and from 1591 Provincial of the south German province of the *Societas Jesu*. Alber sets out a number of criteria for the evaluation of musical compositions and includes a list of permitted and prohibited songs. Among the pieces listed in the category *Cantiones quo ad textum et notas prohibitæ* (songs prohibited on account of their text and music), Alber explicitly bans all parody masses on secular models. That Jesuit censors scrutinised not only the texts but also the music is indicated in Alber's §3, which obliges the Superior to consider all structural features ('ædificationis omnis ratio') in the examination of any composition that aroused suspicion. I am greatly indebted to David Crook for generously sharing the texts of his paper with me.

Example 2a   Clemens non Papa, Et resurrexit
from the *Missa J'ay veu le cerf* (mm. 1–8)
after the *Opera omnia*, ed. K. Ph. Bernet Kempers, vi, p. 122

Example 2b   Pierre de Manchicourt, *J'ay veu le cerf*, mm. 1–9
after the *Opera omnia*, ed. K. Ph. Bernet Kempers, vi, p. 140

156

PROPOSITIONS AND CONCLUSIONS

The final part of this essay is dedicated to questions and puzzles that so far have remained unanswered. The first issue to be addressed is the allegation that Klingenstein's anthology primarily draws upon the repertory of the cathedral chapel in Augsburg, a premise on which some of the previous conclusions rested. At first sight, there is no hard evidence to prove this hypothesis. As stated above, nearly all the musical sources from this chapel have been lost since the early nineteenth century and no contemporary inventory has survived. There is, however, considerable circumstantial evidence that points to this conclusion. First, out of the entire contents of the *Triodia sacra* twenty-eight pieces, more than half of its content, are not transmitted in any other source. Second, it is striking that all of these unica are liturgical compositions. And third, the composers of these works are known either to have held positions at Augsburg themselves or at least to have established contact with Klingenstein (for instance, as contributors to his *Rosetum Marianum* of 1604). Summing up these indications, it can justly be assumed that these compositions were written exclusively for the music chapel at Augsburg Cathedral and perhaps even commissioned by this institution. An examination of the chapter minutes (*Domrezeßbücher*), which contain account and administrative information, helped to produce more corroborating evidence for this supposition. Despite considerable gaps within the collection of account books for the period in question, it was possible to discover a number of payment records involving composers represented in the *Triodia sacra* with unica (their names are highlighted in bold in Table 5).[58] In 1577 Johannes Eccard received 5 Taler for the composition of a mass, which, though not specified, may have been his *Missa Mon cœur se recommande*, the source of Klingenstein's item no. 20. Smaller amounts of money were given to Conrad Stuber for the dedication of compositions in 1586, possible candidates for the psalm and Magnificat sections in the *Triodia sacra*. And in 1587 Jacobus de Kerle was compensated with

---

[58] This examination partly draws upon previous studies of chapter minutes by Kroyer, 'Gregor Aichingers Leben und Werke', p. lix, and Singer, *Bernhardus Klingenstein*, pp. 30–1. As the entries concerning musical affairs have not been published so far, they are listed in Table 5, which covers the period from 1560 to 1605.

Table 5 *Payments for compositions in the chapter minutes of Augsburg Cathedral (1560–1605)*

Between 1560 and 1610 the following *Domzessionalien* (chapter minutes) are missing: 1562, 1571, 1579, 1582, 1583, 1588, 1590, 1593, 1594, 1596, 1597, 1598, 1605, 1607. The shelfmark of the minutes books is given in parentheses after each year. The shelfmark numbers refer to the following collection at the Bayerisches Hauptstaatsarchiv Augsburg: Hochstift Augsburg, Neuburger Abgabe, Akten. The names of composers in Klingenstein's anthology are given in bold type.

1576 (5509)
17 February 1576
Jo: Friderich Missa
Joachim Friederichs meinem G. Herrn dedicirteß Missa, soll dem Capellmaister zugeställt, und beÿ Ime Capellmeister ob diß ein neüe Composition erkhundiget, auch wo dem allßo Er Friederich demwegen verehrt werde.

1577 (5510)
27 February 1577
Dedicatio Missæ.
Johannj Eckhart. Fuggerischem Componisten. so Meinem H. Herrn, ein Missam offerirt, sollen 5. Thaller verehrt werden.

1578 (5511)
15 January 1578
Meßgesang Munus.
Dem welschen Componisten sollen meinen G: Herrn offerirter Messordnung halber 10 fl. verert werden.

1580 (5512)
23 September 1580
Jo: Lottero 4 fl.
Johannes Lotterus H. dht zur Inspruglich Capellsinger meinem gnedigen Herrn offerierten Compositiones Missa halber 4 fl. zu vereren.

1581 (5513)
1 February 1581
Blasius Tribauer Missæ dedicatio.
Blasius Tribauer Musicus offerirt meinem gnedigen Herrn ein Missen quinque vocum, weill solliche Composition von dem Capellmeister geriembt, soll Er Musicus mit 4 fl. verert werden.

1586 (5516)
21 July 1586
Conrado Stubero presbitero offerirter gesang halber. wellche Herrn Capellmeister zugestält sollenwerden .1. fl. zugäben/
[Further entries with regard to Stuber are mentioned in Singer, *Bernhardus Klingenstein*, p. 30. The entries below the dates 21 June and 16 September 1586, however, do not contain any information on Stuber, nor do any other entries within the same account book.]

Table 5 *Continued*

24 October 1586
Johann Vischer von Großenaurach seinem offerierten gesang halber Commune
responsum zugeben

1587 (5517)
25 March 1587
de Kerlin Vererung
Dem Herrn Kerli offerirter Cancionum halber mitt 15 fl. zu verehren

9 September 1587
Orlando
Dem orlando zu München. Isst meinem gnädigen Herrn offerirter Vererung
Cancional halber mit 25 fl. zu verehren befolchen.

1589 (5518)
29 März 1589
Jo: Galli a Stain Canicones [*sic*]
Joannis Galli a Stain meinen gnedigen Herrn offerirte canciones. sollen dem
Herren Capellmeister zugestölt werden und uf dabei befindung seines fleis und
discretion, Er mitt 4 fl. verert. Wie auch sunsten Zur Weiteren befürderung
seine qualitates obseruirt werden.

23 June 1589
Orlando Erung
Dem Orlando di Lasso zu Minchen sollen Meiner gnedigen Herrn offerierten
Exemplars seiner Neulich im Truckh gegertigter Mössen halber 10 fl. verert
werden.

30 June 1589
Cancional Erung
Gedeon Leben von Littich so hievor vmb dem . . . [pale, illegible] gesungen,
Soll meinem gnedigen Herrn dedicirten geschriebenem Cancionals halber .15.
fl. verehrt werden.

7 July 1589
Gedeon Leban von Littich sollen uff sein bitt umb mehrere ergözlichkeitt,
Meinem gnedigen Herrn hievor dedicirten Cancionals halber noch 4 fl.
gegeben werden

4. Oktober
offerirt Cancional
Heinrich Leutgebs fl. Württembergischen Ingrosisten vnd musici, Meinem
gnedigen Herrn offerirt Eucharisticum canticum Beatæ Virginis Mariæ, soll
dem Herrn Capellmeister uns darin Zuversehen ob der Text nitt corrumpiert
vnd wie es mit der Composition beschaffen seÿ zugestölt. sich dabei befolchen
werden, wie Er die sachen befinden werde, Meinem günstigen Herrn
Thumbscholaster bericht zu gäben vnd sonderlichen auch was solliches zu
schreiben werdt sein möchten, Man auch darnach gögen Ime Leutgeben eine
Verehrung zu erhalten habe

Table 5 *Continued*

25. Oktober
[pale, illegible] Musicus vererung.
Heinrich Leutgeben fürstlichen Württembergischen Ingroßisten und Musici
seiner offerirten Compositionum halber 5 fl. zu göben

1592 (5520)
15. Oktober
Musici Erteilung
Martinus Langgeredern, und Nicolaus Zengen Componisten sollen Ire meinem
gnedigen Herrn offerierte gesang wiederumb gegöben und 1:fl pro viatico
mittgeteilt werden.

---

15 Gulden for the dedication of polyphonic music (*offerirter cantionum halber*).[59]

Supported by this testimony, it is nearly certain that the repertory of the Augsburg Cathedral chapel formed the primary
resource for Klingenstein's *Triodia sacra*. In turn, this relationship
provides valuable indirect clues for a hypothetical reconstruction
of this repertory, previously hindered by the enormous loss of
source material. On a specific level, these clues allow one to make
reasonable assumptions about individual pieces, like the potential
identification of works mentioned in the account books. Taking a
broader perspective, however, the *Triodia sacra* even shed light on
the agenda of Klingenstein's activities as *Kapellmeister* of Augsburg
Cathedral, hitherto uncovered. The predominance of compositions
for the proper among the unica in his anthology suggests that
Klingenstein started on the creation of a (new) polyphonic proper
cycle for the liturgical year. This liturgical impulse represents a
characteristic tendency of post-Tridentine Catholic church music
that was also shared by Klingenstein's colleagues at the
Benedictine monastery of SS Ulrich and Afra in Augsburg and at
the Munich court chapel. Despite the similarity of intent, the focus
of activity at these institutions is clearly different from that of
Klingenstein and his chapel. The updating efforts at SS Ulrich and

---

[59] Through records at institutions outside Augsburg other unica of the *Triodia sacra* can be
documented. Bernhard Klingenstein, for instance, received payments for 'songs and
masses' from Duke Wilhelm V of Bavaria in 1582; see W. Boetticher, *Orlando di Lasso
und seine Zeit. 1532–1594* (Kassel, 1958), pp. 536–7.). Together with the *Triodia sacra* items
nos. 2, 4, 5 this is the only evidence for Klingenstein's activity as a composer of masses.

Afra and at the Munich court chapel were primarily concerned with a new hymn cycle for Vespers.[60] At these (and supposedly many other) institutions innovations were necessitated by the introduction of the revised Roman breviary, the *Breviarium Romanum, ex decreto Sacrosancti Concilii Tridentini restitutum, Pii V Pont. Max. jussu editum* (1568), which the papal bull *Quod a nobis* declared compulsory for all Catholics.[61] There is no evidence that Klingenstein made similar efforts to adapt the Vesper hymns to the Romanised standard. By contrast, the *Triodia sacra* compositions document that Klingenstein's efforts were particularly devoted to an entirely different repertory that was both pre-Tridentine and regional: sequences. Apart from mass and Magnificat settings, Klingenstein's anthology contains principally polyphonic versicles of sequences for the solemnities of Easter, Ascension, Holy Trinity (de Kerle: nos. 13, 14, 29), Pentecost, Assumption, St Laurence (Klingenstein: nos. 1, 2, 23) and St Michael (Fossa: no. 28). Klingenstein's project of creating a new sequence cycle appears puzzling not so much because of its extremely conservative outlook. More crucially, it seems at striking odds with the radical curtailment of this repertory by the church authorities at Trent. For this reason one wonders why the Jesuits, who eagerly propagated the Romanisation of the Catholic Church, would have approved of the presentation of pre-Tridentine sequence versicles in Klingenstein's anthology.

To some extent, these puzzles can be explained by reference to the peculiar historical circumstances of liturgical reform in the diocese of Augsburg. Originating in the Carolingian era, the Augsburg rite was officially exempt from the Tridentine reform of the liturgy, which permitted the continuation of any rite that had been in use for more than 200 years.[62] Consequently, Otto von

---

[60] D. Zager, 'Liturgical Rite and Musical Repertory: The Polyphonic Hymn Cycle of Lasso in Munich and Augsburg', in I. Bossuyt et al. (eds), *Orlandus Lassus and his Time* (Peer, 1995), pp. 215–31; and id., 'Post-Tridentine Liturgical Change and Functional Music: Lasso's Cycle of Polyphonic Latin Hymns', in P. Bergquist (ed.), *Orlando di Lassso Studies* (Cambridge, 1999), pp. 41–63. A study of Lasso's involvement in the updating of the hymn repertory can also be found in Franz Körndle's *Habilitationsschrift* on the Munich court chapel in the sixteenth century (forthcoming).

[61] P. Batiffol, *History of the Roman Breviary*, trans. Atwell M. Y. Baylay (London, 1912), pp. 191–200.

[62] F. A. Hoeynck, *Geschichte der kirchlichen Lithurgie des Bisthums Augsburg. Mit Beilagen: Monumenta liturgicæ Augustanæ* (Augsburg, 1889), pp. 36–8.

Waldburg acted in accord with the Council when he published a revised version of the *Missale secundum ritum Augustensis ecclesie* in 1555, printed by Sebald Mayer at Dillingen. As indicated in Table 1, the sequence versicles included in the *Triodia sacra* all refer to this source. Considerable confusion, however, arose when Bishop Otto von Gemmingen, following his Counter-Reformatory desire to Romanise his diocese, introduced the Roman rite in 1597 notwithstanding the legal exemption.[63] Yet the Catholic clergy in general and the cathedral chapter in particular successfully opposed this reform. Their resistance was so obstinate that Otto von Gemmingen conceded the publication of a supplement to the Roman missal, which contained the traditional proper texts for a number of regional feasts. This supplement, the *Proprium Augustanum*, was issued twice in 1597 and in 1605.[64] It was only at the diocesan synod in 1610 that Bishop Heinrich von Knoeringen managed to re-enforce the Roman rite for the entire bishopric. This strong conservatism, which had hindered the effective intro-duction of the Roman rite prior to 1610, explains why Klingen-stein's sequence project could have been envisaged on orthodox grounds.

The historical context furthermore suggests that he planned his polyphonic sequence cycle in the 1580s, when his contributor Jacobus de Kerle was still alive. Since de Kerle, who composed sequences for a number of major solemnities, died in 1591, the project must have reached at least an advanced stage by then, if it had not already been completed. In this case the sequence cycle initiated by Klingenstein considerably preceded the first attempts at Romanising the Augsburg rites, undertaken by Otto von Gemmingen in 1597. Correspondingly, the respective polyphonic sequences, not included in the Roman rite, could easily be jus-tified even from the perspective of 1605. This reason, if any, might have won the Jesuits' approval of the sequence versicles in Klingenstein's *Triodia sacra*, although they generally advocated the abolition of the Augsburg rite. The sequence portions presented in this anthology furthermore suggest that Klingenstein asked composers like Johannes de Fossa and Jacobus de Kerle to con-tribute to the choirmaster's own production of sequences, which

[63] *Ibid.*, pp. 38–40.
[64] *Ibid.*, pp. 303–5.

certainly formed the basis of this enterprise. It is worthwhile mentioning that de Kerle's participation in this project is at odds with
the traditional view of his personal relationship with Klingenstein.
As mentioned earlier, Otto Ursprung believed that de Kerle bore
a notorious grudge against Klingenstein, his more successful com-
petitor in the application for the position of *Kapellmeister* at
Augsburg Cathedral.[65] Yet in the light of the discoveries made
above, it becomes obvious that de Kerle's resentment must have
been short-lived, for otherwise he would not have continued to col-
laborate with his former rival Klingenstein.[66]

The fact that Klingenstein turned to the repertory of his chapel
in search of pieces for an anthology also sheds light on the mys-
terious *Monstra te esse* by Palestrina, exclusively transmitted in the
Triodia sacra. It is true that the unique transmission of this piece
contradicts the usual source situation of Palestrina's works, which
are either broadly disseminated in printed editions or documented
in the manuscripts of the papal chapel.[67] One might therefore
be inclined to regard Klingenstein's attribution of this piece
to Palestrina as spurious. Yet a closer examination reveals
that Palestrina's authorship is not as questionable as it might
first appear. Through Cardinal Otto von Waldburg, bishop of
Augsburg, the chapels of Augsburg and the Vatican had established intensive contacts from the early 1560s. Frequently resid-
ing at Rome, Otto von Waldburg was not only a fervent opponent
of the abolition of polyphonic music from the liturgy at the
Council, but also an active patron of musicians in Rome.[68] To
mention only one example, in 1561 he launched an exchange of
compositions by Lasso and Palestrina between Rome and Munich[69]
– a diplomatic mission said to have had some impact on the
Council's decrees on music.[70] Keeping this background in mind, it

---

[65] See above, n. 40.

[66] According to the entries of the chapter minutes, de Kerle is documented as having contributed to the repertory of Klingenstein's chapel until at least 1587 (see Table 5).

[67] A striking exception are Palestrina's compositions written at request of Guglielmo
Gonzaga for the chapel of St Barbara in Mantua. The respective repertory was only discovered after the Second World War in the library of the Milanese conservatory. See K.
Jeppesen, 'The Recently Discovered Mantova Masses of Palestrina', *Acta musicologica*, 22
(1950), pp. 36–47.

[68] F. Zoepfl, *Kardinal Otto Truchseß von Waldburg* (Lebensbilder aus dem Bayerischen
Schwaben, 4; Munich, 1955), pp. 25–32.

[69] This fact was first noted by Ursprung, *Jacobus de Kerle*, pp. 12–13.

[70] Weinmann, *Das Konzil von Trient und die Kirchenmusik*, pp. 35–7.

is reasonable that Palestrina might have dedicated an exclusive copy of an *Ave maris stella* setting to his patron von Waldburg. This assumption appears even more plausible in the light of von Waldburg's appointment as titular bishop of Preneste, Palestrina's home town, in 1570.[71] This position would surely have intensified the contact between von Waldburg and Palestrina. Accordingly, it could very well account for the fact that Palestrina's composition became an exclusive part of the musical repertory at the cathedral of Augsburg. Owing to the loss of this repertory by the early nineteenth century, no other source than Klingenstein's hitherto unstudied *Triodia sacra* bears witness to this composition. This is admittedly only a speculation. But together with the preceding considerations it argues persuasively for the profit that is to be drawn from the study of fragmentary and neglected musical sources. As the present study has shown, fragments are capable of providing valuable missing links in our fragmented and incomplete understanding of music history.

Universität München

[71] *Ibid.*, p. 34.

APPENDIX 1

The Title Page, Epigram and Preface of the *Triodia sacra*

The title page, epigram and preface are transcribed from the unique copy of the *Inferior Vox* partbook in the British Library, shelfmark C.255.a.

fol. 1ʳ:

TRIODIA SACRA

SIVE MODI
MVSICI TERNIS VO-
CIBUS TAM AD TIRONVM,
QVAM PERITIORVM VSVM FACTI,
ET PARTIM EX LECTIS AVCTORIBVS
delecti, partim recens conditi.
Liber I.
A
BERNARDO KLINGENSTEIN
Cathedralis Ecclesiæ Augustanæ Musices
præfecto.

VOX INFERIOR
DILINGÆ
In officina Typographica ADAMI
MELTZER.
M. D. CV.

fol. 1ᵛ:

HEXASTICHON
Ter deno certent alij discrimine vocum,
Atque fides addant vocibus atque tubas.
Tu ne temne tribus contenta triodia cartis
Forte minus laudis: non minus artis habent.
Dulcius una canit coruis philomela trecentis
Ex multis semper non nisi pauca placent.

fol. 2ʳ: NOBILISSIMIS ET ORNATISSIMIS ADOLESCENTIBVS *IOANNI GVILIELMO*, ET *IOANNI EGOLPHO* A LEONROD IN Truegenhouen Münsterhausen & Dischingen, à Christo S.

FRustra est, nobilissimi adolescentes, qui hodie canendi artificium è Repub. tollere cogitat: nec minus actum agit qui idem ciuibus laudare &

165

Christian Thomas Leitmeir

suadere studet, hic enim soli facem inferre & rem commendare instituit iam omnibus retro sæculis vsu perpetuo omniumque ferè gentium auctoritate tantopere commendatam & firmatam, vti nemo infirmare amplius aut eleuare possit; ille ipsa extinguere sidera nec quicquam conatur. Mitto ergò ex Plutarchis, Athenæis, Cassiodoris, & his æuo maioribus minoribusque illam celebrare disciplinam, quæ nunquam in obscuro iacuit, aut incelebris fuit. Mitto laudare quam nemo, nisi sano & humano simul sensu destitutus vituperauit. Vos ergo, maioresque vestros, adolescentes præstantissimi, tanto humaniores, adeoque magis homines arbitror, colo & veneror, quanto maiori humanitatis studio huius elegantissimæ artis cultores complectimini. Quod [fol. 2ᵛ] ego, quamvis in hoc amplissimo præstantissimorum Musicorum concessu & senatu, pedarius & postremissimus, coram sæpius & Dilingæ, & in ditionibus vestris sum expertus, quando & clarissimi nobilissimique parentes & aui vestri, atque cum his R. & doctis: vir D. Georgius Reschius studiorum vestrorum moderator, & vos ipsi officiosissimé liberalissimeque accepistis, perindeque obseruastis, ac si nouus aliquis Orpheus ab inferis extitisset. Qua ego vestra in me beneuolentia inuitatus, meis putaui partibus conuenire, vti Gratias Gratijs reponerem, vobisque hæc triodia non ex Marsyis, sed Phœbis ipsis, hoc est præstantissimis canendi magistris delibata multorum exemplo canerem, illisque nonnunquam etsi impari symphonia accinerem, quæ ex quadraginta, inscriptis singulorum nominibus facilè animaduertetis, ratus hæc vniuersæ simul iuuentuti Musicæ seruitura. Alijs enim æs deest magna plurimorum concentuum volumina coemendi; alijs chorus Musicorum plenior, alijs vtrumque. Hæc odaria & paucis assibus comparantur, & à pluribus paucioribusque decantari possunt. Valete adolescentes ornatissimi, & liberales artes, artiumque excultores, vti facitis, colite, memoriamque nominis vestri virtute vestra æternitati consecrate. Augustæ Vindel. ferijs D. Vdalrici Vrbis patroni. M.D.CV.

Nob. & dig. vestræ studiosissimus
Bernhardus Klingenstein

To the most noble and accomplished youths Johann Wilhelm and Johann Egolph von Leonrod in Trügenhoven, Münsterhausen and Dischingen, salvation from Christ.

He is wasting his time, most noble youths, who in these days thinks of removing the art of singing from the state; no less is he doing what has already been done who strives to praise and urge it upon the citizens, since he sets about carrying a torch into sunlight and commending a thing already so much commended and established in all ages past by perpetual use and the authority of well-nigh all peoples that no one can any more weaken or slight it; he tries in vain to put out the very stars. I therefore omit to praise, out of the Plutarchs, Athenaeuses, Cassiodoruses and their predecessors and successors, that discipline which has never lain in darkness or gone unpraised. I omit to praise that which no one unless devoid of healthy and human feeling has disparaged. You, therefore, and your elders, most outstanding youths, I consider the more civilised, and therefore more human, respect and revere them, the more you embrace with greater love of civilisation those who pursue this most elegant art. Which I, though in this most honourable gathering and senate of outstanding musicians the last among backbenchers, quite often experienced publicly both at Dillingen and in your domains, when only your most renowned and most noble fathers and grandfathers, and with them the reverend and most learned man Dr Georg Resch, the director of your studies, and you yourselves received me most kindly and generously, and looked after me as if a new Orpheus had risen from the dead. Encouraged by this your good will towards me, I deemed it appropriate to my place that I should return favour for favour, and following the example of many sing you these tricinia, selected not from the Marsyases but from the very Phoebuses, that is the most outstanding masters of singing, and at times sing in harmony, albeit unequal, with them, which from the forty, with the names of the individuals attached, you will easily observe, thinking that these would serve at the same time for all musical youth. For some lack the money to purchase large volumes containing a great number of polyphonic compositions; others lack a larger choir of musicians, others again lack both. These odelets are on sale for a few pence, and can be sung by more or fewer singers. Farewell, most accomplished young men, and, as you are doing, cultivate the liberal arts and those who cultivate those arts, and consecrate to eternity the memory of your name by your virtue. Augsburg, on the feast of St Ulrich, patron of the city [4 July], 1605.

> He who is most zealous for your nobility and dignity
> Bernard Klingenstein

APPENDIX 2

Edition of Reconstructed Compositions from the *Triodia sacra*

This appendix presents a reconstructed edition of four compositions not yet available in a modern edition.

Jacobus Peetrinus, *Mane nobiscum, Domine* (no. 11)

> Quando cor nostrum visitas,
> Tunc lucet ei veritas,
> Mundi vilescit vanitas
> Et intus fervet caritas.

Source: *Di Iacobo Peetrino il primo libro del Iubilo di S. Bernardo con alcune canzonette spiri-tuali scritte & intagliate a tre et quattro voci* (Rome, 1588), p. 4

Jacobus Peetrinus, *Iam quod quaesivi* (no. 12)

Iesus, cum sic diligitur,
Hic amor non extinguitur.
Non tepescit nec moritur,
Plus crescit at accenditur.

Source: *Di Iacobo Peetrino il primo libro del Iubilo di S. Bernardo*, p. 18

Christian Thomas Leitmeir

Jacob Reiner, *Domine, exaudi* (no. 16)

170

Source: *Cantionum piarum . . . tribus vocibus* (Munich: Berg, 1586), no. 5: 'Quintus Psalmus'

Christian Thomas Leitmeir

Gregor Aichinger, *Sicut locutus est* (no. 33)

Source: *Magnificat Liquide perl'amor*, in *Vespertinum Virginis Canticum sive Magnificat quinis vocibus varie modulatur* (Augsburg: Custos (apud Praetorium), 1603), Cantus, p. 16; Quintus, p. 16, [Altus], p. ?; *Inferior Vox* taken from *Triodia sacra*.

Early Music History (2002) Volume 21. © *Cambridge University Press*
DOI:10.1017/S026112790200205X Printed in the United Kingdom

ROBERT NOSOW

THE DEBATE ON SONG IN THE ACCADEMIA FIORENTINA

For James Haar on his 70th Birthday

The sixteenth century in Italy was a time when academies of all kinds flourished as venues, and often as arbiters, of literature and high culture. A casual look at the academies might give the impression that they were mostly social in nature, that they functioned as a pastime for bored aristocrats and ambitious *letterati*. As originally constituted, the Accademia degli Umidi, founded 1 November 1540, indeed fitted this description, but with one difference characteristic of Florentine society – it was organised by twelve men of various social classes with a common interest in poetry and language.[1] The academy expanded considerably under the patronage of Duke Cosimo I de' Medici and on 25 March 1541 was reconstituted as the Accademia Fiorentina. Its avowed purpose was to promote the Tuscan language as an instrument of literature and knowledge, in an age when mastery of Latin was required of any educated man. In advancing the cause of

Research on the Accademia Fiorentina was undertaken in 1993–4 at Villa I Tatti, the Harvard University Center for Italian Renaissance Studies in Florence. Funding was provided through the generosity of the National Endowment for the Humanities, the Francesco E. De Dombrowski Bequest and the Robert Lehman Endowment Fund. I am most grateful to the late Nino Pirrotta for his advice on the early stages of research, and to Tim Carter and James Haar, who provided expert commentary on the typescript. I also wish to thank the staffs of the Sala di Manoscritti della Biblioteca Nazionale Centrale di Firenze and the Biblioteca Riccardiana for their manifold and kind assistance.

[1] The initial members were Giovanni Mazzuoli, Cynthio d'Amelia Romano, Niccolò Martelli, Filippo Salvetti, Simon della Volta, Pier Fabbrini, Bartolomeo Benci, Gismondo Martelli, Michelangelo Vivaldi, Antonfrancesco Grazzini, Baccio Baccelli and Paolo de Gei, known as Pylucca Scultore. See A. De Gaetano, *Giambattista Gelli and the Florentine Academy: The Rebellion against Latin* (Florence, 1976), p. 101, citing Florence, Biblioteca Marucelliana, MS B III 52, fol. 1ʳ. All three volumes of the original *Atti* survive in the Biblioteca Marucelliana: MSS B III 52, B III 54, B III 53, in chronological order. Many other documents from the Accademia Fiorentina have been lost, but were recorded or cited in the eighteenth century.

vernacular literature, the Accademia Fiorentina, like other academies of the time, greatly extended the programme of Italian humanism, making available the fruits of humanist thought and enquiry to a larger public.

In the presentation of poetry, the Accademia inherited a set of practices that were in process of change. The performance of poetry to music *all'improvviso* followed a long-standing and powerful cultural tradition on the Italian peninsula, one that was fostered especially in humanist and courtly circles. Yet by 1540, the polyphonic madrigal had become the dominant secular genre of the age, one that owed much of its early development to Florence and Rome. The madrigal of the 1540s, influenced by the poetics of Pietro Bembo, strongly reflected the nuances and rhetoric of the poetic text.[2] As a result, it claimed intellectual legitimacy as a powerful new medium for Italian poetry.

In 1543, a furious debate broke out in the Accademia Fiorentina, bringing two competing visions of Italian song into sharp definition: one based on oral conception in the performance of accompanied song, the other based on musical composition and the notation of mensural polyphony. At the centre of the debate stands the figure of Alfonso de' Pazzi, an aristocratic satirist, academician and defender of the improvised tradition. In literary history, Alfonso de' Pazzi has all but been forgotten, and none of the satires or letters to be discussed has ever been cited in the musicological literature.[3] The controversy took place in terms of both cultural values and musical practices. The debate on song in the Accademia Fiorentina illuminates, in microcosm, the relationship between music and poetry at a crucial point of expansion in Italian humanist culture.

---

[2] On the influence of Bembo, see D. Mace, 'Pietro Bembo and the Origins of the Italian Madrigal', *Musical Quarterly*, 55 (1969), pp. 65–86; J. Haar, 'The Early Madrigal: A Reappraisal of its Sources and Character', in I. Fenlon (ed.), *Music in Medieval and Early Modern Europe: Patronage, Sources, and Texts* (Cambridge, 1981), pp. 175–7; J. M. Miller, 'Word-Sound and Musical Texture in the Mid-Sixteenth-Century Venetian Madrigal' (Ph.D. diss., University of North Carolina at Chapel Hill, 1991); M. Feldman, *City Culture and the Madrigal at Venice* (Berkeley and Los Angeles, 1995), ch. 5, pp. 123–55.

[3] The only biography is G. Pedrotti, *Alfonso de' Pazzi, accademico e poeta* (Pescia, 1902), which says nothing concerning Alfonso's musicianship. G. Manacorda, *Benedetto Varchi: l'uomo, il poeta, il critico* (Pisa, 1903), pp. 46–9, offers a brief account of the poetry as well.

THE PERFORMANCE OF POETRY

The original statutes of the academy refer to the writing of 'o Epitaffj o madrigali o sonetti o altra qualsivoglia composizione', and the production of poetry became a major preoccupation of the Accademia Fiorentina.[4] New poems were undoubtedly presented at the regular Thursday evening banquets, especially the satirical verse known as *cicalate* (literally, 'prattlings'). Private lectures, which usually took a work by Petrarch or Dante as their starting point, were delivered as well. Public lectures were presented on Sundays, the first in Italy open to the general public, and attracted large crowds.[5]

Flexibility of presentation may well have been characteristic of poetic performance at this period, as attested by a chapter of Antonfrancesco Doni's *I marmi*, published in Venice in 1552.[6] Doni, a wandering writer and printer of Florentine birth, was elected among the *statuarij* or official recorders of the Accademia Fiorentina on 11 February 1546, and shortly after was named secretary.[7] He is the probable compiler of a manuscript of ten madrigals dedicated to Duke Cosimo I de' Medici.[8] In 1546–8, while still in Florence, Doni also printed a small number of books officially connected with the Accademia, under licence from Cosimo I.[9] The chapter in *I marmi* is introduced with the comment that in Florence 'it was customary on occasion to sing *all'improvviso* to the lira rhymes of every sort, so that it seemed they were raining down from that cupola'.[10] The five interlocutors, including Giovanni

---

[4] M. Maylender, *Storia delle accademie d'Italia*, 3 vols. (Bologna, 1926–30), iii, p. 364.
[5] De Gaetano, *Giambattista Gelli*, pp. 109–12; S. Salvini, *Fasti consolari dell'Accademia Fiorentina* (Florence, 1717), p. 2; E. Cochrane, *Florence in the Forgotten Centuries, 1527–1800* (Chicago and London, 1973), p. 68. I am indebted to Russell E. Murray, Jr., for providing a photocopy of Salvini's work.
[6] A. F. Doni, *I marmi*, 2 vols., ed. E. Chiòboli (Bari, 1928), i, pp. 105–28.
[7] Florence, Biblioteca Marucelliana, MS B III 52, fols. 34^v–35^v. According to Salvini, *Fasti consolari*, p. 63, Doni was the first Secretary of the Accademia Fiorentina.
[8] J. Haar, 'A Gift of Madrigals to Cosimo I: The Ms. Florence, Bibl. Naz. Centrale, Magl. XIX, 130', in *The Science and Art of Renaissance Music*, ed. P. Corneilson (Princeton, 1998), pp. 300–22, originally published in *Rivista italiana di musicologia*, 1 (1966), pp. 198–224.
[9] On Doni's recruitment as a printer and his rapid displacement by Lorenzo Torrentino, see Cochrane, *Florence in the Forgotten Centuries*, p. 69.
[10] Doni, *I marmi*, i, p. 108: 'so certo che a questi Marmi si soleva talvolta cantare all'improvviso su la lira, e d'ogni sorte rime, che pareva che le piovessin giù da quella cupola'. The cupola is the Brunelleschi dome of the cathedral of Santa Maria del Fiore.

Mazzuoli and Niccolò Martelli, two founders of the Accademia, have come together for just this purpose. They present a series of five eight-line *stanze*, two sonnets, two *capitoli* in terza rima, a *canzone*, two sestinas, a pastoral *ballata* and two madrigals.

The evening begins with the words 'Retune that lira' ('Ritempera cotesta lira'), a probable reference to the lira da braccio.[11] Despite the quicksilver nature of the conversation, specific performance details emerge for four of the poems. Varlungo, a shoemaker, begins with the first comic *stanza*, then Nuto, a fisherman, and Visino, a stationer, join in, stringing improvised verses together.[12] The exercise takes on aspects of a literary game. At one point Nuto sings 'The lira's out of tune, tum, tum, tum, and tinted'.[13] Afterwards, Mazzuoli comments 'That string afforded me the great pleasure of breaking, because I didn't like your tune, and your rhymes even less.'[14] Martelli reads a Venetian sonnet, and since he later asserts 'I don't want to sing, because I am not a musician', a declaimed rendition is likely.[15] For the lyrical *canzone*, written by the *improvvisatore* and violist Maestro Iacopo de' Servi, Mazzuoli asks for a rendition 'In the bowed style' ('In modo d'archetti').[16] As the group is breaking up, the last madrigal is given by Visino, one of his own composition. He rushes off before anyone can render criticism, but Mazzuoli exclaims, 'How, in his bizzare musical composition, he would make water and fire combat in notes, and then make those two contraries unite! I wish Adriano [Willaert], Cipriano [di Rore] and [Vincenzo] Ruffo had sprinkled me; oh, what beautiful music would he hear!'[17] Despite Mazzuoli's outburst, the Florentines never do sing from parts. Visino performs

---

[11] *Ibid.*, i, p. 109. On the lira da braccio, see the discussion below.

[12] As documented in Salvini, *Fasti consolari*, 39, the real Niccolò Martelli created improvised *stanze*, subsequently recorded in a manuscript, *Giardino di Prato*, dated 1534. In a letter to Girolamo Amelonghi, dated 20 April 1546, Martelli mentions 'VISINO Setaiuolo che tien Cancellaria à tutti gli Accademici & altri amici suoi'. See Niccolò Martelli, *Il primo libro delle lettere* (Florence, 1546), fols. 88ᵛ–89ʳ.

[13] Doni, *I marmi*, i, p. 111: '(Lira scordata, um, um, um, e tinta).' The word *tinta* may refer to the common practice of colouring the strings.

[14] *Ibid.*, i, p. 111: 'Quella corda m'ha fatto il gran piacere a rompersi, perché non mi piaceva questo tuo suono e manco le rime.'

[15] *Ibid.*, pp. 112, 115: 'Non vo' canti, ché io non son musico.'

[16] *Ibid.*, p. 115.

[17] *Ibid.*, p. 126: 'Come vi si farebbe sopra il bizzarro componimento di musica e far con le note combatter quell'acqua e quell fuoco, e poi unire quei due contrarii! Adriano, Cipriano, e il Ruffo vorrei che me spolverizzassino. O che bella musica s'udirebbe egli!'

the madrigal by himself, from written music ('con le note'); the lute would have been the instrument of choice to accompany such a performance.

Doni's *Dialogo della musica* of 1544, which he published in Venice just before returning to Florence, offers the contrasting portrait of a literary academy in northern Italy, and sheds particular light on the musical practices of such gatherings: the first part is set in Piacenza, the second (by implication) in Venice.[18] Unlike the Florentine gathering, most of the activity revolves around the performance of madrigals from parts, which Doni includes in the publication. During the second day's entertainment, which consists both of informal *ragionamento* and the singing of madrigals, one of the company, Ottavio Landi, sings several *ottave rime* by Madonna Virginia Salvi, a 'bella donna virtuosa'.[19] He accompanies himself on the *viuola* (vihuela da mano or possibly viola da gamba); unlike the madrigals that preceded them, the stanzas are published without music. At the end of the same day, the lady of the company, Selvaggia, turns to Landi, saying 'Ottavio, take up your lira, and I will commence; and later we will say farewell.' Then follows the singing, no doubt *ex tempore*, of four sonnets in praise of one Madonna Isabetta Guasca, with instrumental accompaniment on the lira da braccio. Once again, the sonnets appear without music.[20]

The music for singing sonnets *all'improvviso*, as portrayed in the *Dialogo della musica*, most likely consisted of standard *arie di cantare* such as those printed in Venice decades before by Ottaviano de' Petrucci.[21] Gioseffo Zarlino testifies to the continued use of *arie* in

---

[18] See J. Haar, 'Notes on the *Dialogo della Musica* of Antonfrancesco Doni', in *The Science and Art of Renaissance Music*, pp. 271–99, originally published in *Music & Letters*, 47 (1966), pp. 198–224.

[19] A. F. Doni, *Dialogo della musica*, ed. G. F. Malipiero and V. Fagotto (Vienna and Milan, 1965), pp. 209–11. The musical performance is followed by a discussion of contemporary women poets.

[20] *Ibid.*, pp. 315–17: 'Ottavio, pigliate la lira, che io incomincio; e poi diremo a Dio.'

[21] *Arie* appear in RISM 1505³, fol. 14ʳ, 'Modo di cantar sonetti' (textless) and RISM 1505⁶, fol. 9ʳ, 'Per sonetti. Più volte me son messo'. Other works in RISM 1505⁵ are labelled 'Sonetto' and provided with partial text, at fols. 15ᵛ, 16ʳ and 18ᵛ. See the detailed study by F. Brancacci, 'Il sonetto nei libri di frottole di O. Petrucci (1504–14)', *Nuova rivista musicale italiana*, 25 (1991), pp. 177–215; 26 (1992), pp. 441–68. A Neapolitan collection from mid-century is *Aeri racolti insieme con altri bellissimi aggionti di diversi, dove si cantano Sonetti, Stanze e Terze Rime*, ed. R. Rodio (Naples, 1577); discussed and inventoried in H. M. Brown, 'The Geography of Florentine Monody', *Early Music*, 9 (1981), pp. 147–68.

Venice at mid-century, referring to 'a certain *modo* or, as we say, *aria di cantare*; since those are the *modi di cantare* on which we now sing the sonnets and *canzoni* of Petrarch, or the *rime* of Ariosto'.[22] They could be performed by solo voice with one of several instruments. Benedetto Varchi, in his lecture 'Delle parti della poesia', read before the Accademia Fiorentina in 1553, cites the lira, lute and gravicembolo under the category of *Citaristica*, or the music of string instruments, which also comprehends the category of *Lirica*, or lyric music.[23]

A keyboard manuscript of the later sixteenth century, now housed in the Biblioteca Nazionale Centrale di Firenze, preserves both an 'Aria di Sonetti' (Example 1) and two versions, closely related to each other, of 'La 3ᵃ rima'. The textless 'Aria di Sonetti' may have been intended for a singer to accompany herself at the harpsichord, doubling the top line. Similar settings of textless *arie* appear in lute manuscripts of the period.[24] The texture is crudely homophonic, the harmony reminiscent of the *passamezzo antico*. If sung to a sonnet text, the setting is entirely syllabic, except for ornamental flourishes on the beat before a cadence, correspond-

[22] G. Zarlino, *Le istitutioni harmoniche* (Venice, 1558; facs. New York, [1965]), pt. 3, ch. 79, p. 289: 'un certo Modo, overo Aria, che lo vogliamo dire, di cantare; si come sono quelli modi di cantare, sopra i quali cantiamo al presente li Sonetti, o Canzoni del Petrarca, overamele le Rime dell'Ariosto'. On the *aria*, see J. Haar, 'The "Madrigale Arioso": A Mid-Century Development in the Cinquecento Madrigal', in *The Science and Art of Renaissance Music*, pp. 222–38, originally published in *Studi musicali*, 12 (1983), pp. 203–19; id., *Essays on Italian Poetry and Music in the Renaissance, 1350–1600* (Berkeley and Los Angeles, 1986), pp. 44–6, 84–9, 169–70; J. W. Hill, *Roman Monody, Cantata, and Opera from the Circles around Cardinal Montalto*, 2 vols. (Oxford, 1997), i, pp. 57–66.

[23] B. Varchi, 'Delle parti della poesia', in *Opere*, 2 vols., ed. G. B. Busini (Trieste, 1859), ii, pp. 698–9. The specificity of the term 'lira' can be seen from the full passage, which compares ancient and modern instruments: 'Il suono è di due maniere, perché si fa o mediante le corde, o mediante il fiato o spirito umano, come anticamente nelle tibie e nelle fistole o vero zampogne, ed oggi nei flauti, pifferi, tromboni, cornette ed altri stromenti somiglianti; e questa sorte di musica, la quale si chiama dai Greci Auletica, è manco nobile di quell'altra maniera, che si fa mediante le corde, come anticamente nelle cetere, onde si chiamava Citaristica, sotto la quale si comprendeva ancora la Lirica; ed oggi si vede nelle lire, nei liuti, nei gravicemboli e in tutti gli altri strumenti così fatti.'

[24] V. Coelho, 'Raffaello Cavalcanti's Lute Book (1590) and the Ideal of Singing and Playing', in *Le concert des voix et des instruments à la Renaissance: actes du XXXIVᵉ Colloque international d'études humanistes, Tours, Centre d'études supérieures de la Renaissance, 1–11 juillet 1991*, ed. J.-M. Vaccaro (Paris, 1995), pp. 423–42. In Magliabechi XIX, 115 the two works called 'La 3ᵃ rima' appear on fols. 1ᵛ and 6ʳ. The music provides four phrases, of which the first two are rhythmically parallel, each setting one line of text. The third phrase is harmonically parallel to the first, to accommodate the poetic rhyme (*aba*). The fourth, more florid phrase probably constitutes an instrumental *ripresa*, played between stanzas, as Coelho suggests, pp. 438–40.

Example 1 Anonymous, *Aria di Sonetti*, Florence, Biblioteca Nazionale Centrale, MS Magl. XIX, 115, fol. 15ʳ

ing to the strong, penultimate syllable of Italian verse. Given the length of the flourishes, underscored by dashes in the manuscript, the chord would be drawn out as long as necessary to accommodate all the notes. The four phrases of the 'Aria di Sonetti' cadence in the bass on D, B♭, G and G, corresponding to the four lines of the quatrains. The first three phrases could be repeated for the two tercets, with the most elaborate ornamentation reserved for the third, rather than fourth, cadence, since that would represent the close of the poem. While commitment to paper in effect freezes the *aria* in place, a skilled musician would vary melody, ornamentation and harmony in accordance with the content and structure of the poem.

The lira da braccio (often referred to only as the *lira*) was played specifically to accompany lyric song *all'improvviso*; only two pieces of music written for it have ever been recovered.[25] It appears in

[25] H. M. Brown and S. S. Jones, 'Lira da braccio', in *The New Grove Dictionary of Music and Musicians*, 2nd edn. On Pesaro, Biblioteca Oliveriana, MS 1144, which contains the two works for the instrument, see the manuscript facsimiles and discussion in S. S. Jones, *The Lira da Braccio* (Bloomington, Ind., 1995), pp. 98–9, 108–14.

numerous Cinquecento paintings, such as Dosso Dossi's 'Apollo and Daphne' of the 1520s (Figure 1). The lira da braccio was considered the equivalent of the classical lyre, and its characteristic flared peg box may have been symbolic of the sun, associated, like

Figure 1   Dosso Dossi, *Apollo and Daphne*. Rome, Galleria Borghese.
Photo courtesy of Scala Istituto Fotografico, Florence

poetry and music, with the god Apollo.[26] Its venerable lineage may be judged by its employment for the *stanze* of Angelo Poliziano's *Orfeo*, staged probably at Mantua in 1480.[27] Dossi's allegory emphasises the quality of divine inspiration, with bow lifted high towards the skies. Antonfrancesco Grazzini, in an epitaph on Giovanni Mazzuoli, specifically mentions the lira da braccio in its classical associations, so clearly portrayed in 'Apollo and Daphne'. He writes of the Muses:[28]

> E come amor le spira,
> Cantando il bel concetto in su la lira,
> Lodar tutti i suoi gesti all'improvviso,
> E di poi se ne andaro in paradiso.

> And how love inspires them,
> Singing the fine conceit upon the lira,
> To praise all his [Mazzuoli's] deeds *all'improvviso*,
> And thus they betake themselves to paradise.

As for the lute, its versatility as a contrapuntal instrument allowed it to accompany both improvised song and solo madrigals. Howard Mayer Brown writes that we have 'every reason to believe that sixteenth-century musicians arranged virtually every sort of madrigal for solo voice and lute'.[29] In 1536 Adrian Willaert published a volume of madrigals by Verdelot for lute and solo voice, but without the vocal part.[30] Manuscripts with madrigals for lute and voice are also found in the Bibliothèque Nationale in Paris and the Biblioteca della Società Filarmonica of Verona.[31] The

---

[26] R. Brandolini, *On Music and Poetry (De musica et poetica, 1513)*, ed. and trans. Ann Moyer (Tempe, 2001), pp. 28–9, writes of the *Lyra* that 'Apollo himself may be allowed to use it – Apollo who, as the poets imagine, loved Daphne the daughter of Peneus, and at times lamented with his lyre his own love and the girl's cruelty; it may be allowed, then, to imitate diligently that greatest god of poets' ('liceat usurpare et Apollinem ipsum, quem poetae fingunt Daphnem Penei filiam adamasse atque interdum lyra et suos amores et puellae saevitiam deplorasse, liceat, inquam, praecipuum poetarum numen studiosissime imitari').

[27] On *La fabula d'Orfeo*, see N. Pirrotta and E. Povoledo, *Music and Theatre from Poliziano to Monteverdi*, trans. K. Eales (Cambridge, 1982), pp. 3–25.

[28] A. F. Grazzini, *Rime burlesche, edite ed inedite*, ed. C. Verzone (Florence, 1882), pp. 149–52; 'Al Magnifico M. Giovanni Cavalcanti nella morte del Padre Stradino' (ll. 88–92).

[29] H. M. Brown, 'Bossinensis, Willaert and Verdelot: Pitch and the Conventions of Transcribing Music for Lute and Voice in Italy in the Early Sixteenth Century', *Revue de musicologie*, 75 (1989), pp. 25–46, at p. 29 n. 13.

[30] *Intavolatura de li madrigali di Verdelotto da cantare et sonare nel lauto, intavolati per Messer Adriano [Willaert]* (Venice: Ottaviano Scotto, 1536). See the discussion in Brown, 'Bossinensis, Willaert and Verdelot', pp. 28–32.

[31] Paris, Bibliothèque Nationale de France, Res. Vmd. MS 27; Verona, Biblioteca della Società Filarmonica de Verona, MS 223.

latter manuscript contains separate sections for soprano, tenor and bass, each inscribed with a vocal staff and a lute intabulation, with the poetic text placed in between. It includes the succinct comment, 'He who knows not how to play and sing, should not trouble his head over this book.'[32] Full transcriptions of madrigals for lute may have been sung as solo songs as well, with the instrument doubling the soloist's melodic line. Composers, of course, set not only original madrigal verse, but sonnets, *ottave rime* and Petrarchan *canzoni*. Since settings of Petrarch were standard fare, three- or four-voice intabulations were appropriate for use and reuse by poet-singers, such as Visino, with their own poems.

At the same time, the madrigal could also incorporate elements of the unwritten tradition. Two of Francesco Corteccia's madrigals from the *Libro Secondo de Madriali a quatro voci* of 1547, *Io dico et diss' et dirò* and *S'io potessi voler*, are built upon tunes that may have been used by *improvvisatori* to sing *ottave rime*, the eight-line stanzas of Italian epic poetry.[33] *Io dico et diss' et dirò* (Example 2) sets a stanza from Ariosto's *Orlando furioso*.[34] The *aria* remains in the soprano, sung four times, each time setting two lines of poetic text. Around it the other voices move in free, vigorous counterpoint. A five-voice, cyclic setting by Jacob Arcadelt of Petrarch's *canzone Chiare fresche e dolci acque*, published in 1555, likewise contains an *aria* in the soprano, which is varied in the same manner a singer would employ in a series of stanzas.[35] According to James Haar, such embedded melodies became common in the mid-sixteenth century.[36] Another madrigal by Francesco Corteccia, *Liet' et beati spirti*, from the *Libro Primo de Madriali a quatro voci* of 1547, sets a sonnet text in such a way that the two quatrains and two tercets each end with extensive musical rhyme, a schematic

---

[32] 'Chi non sa sonare e cantare non s'impazza in questo libro', inscribed on the first rear guard leaf, verso, of the first fascicle (Soprano); cited in F. Rossi, 'Manoscritto di opere italiane per liuto', *Il Fronimo*, 9 (1981), pp. 28–37, at p. 29. Rossi, pp. 28–30, provides a description and inventory of the three surviving sections of the manuscript: Soprano, Tenore and Basso (the Alto book is missing).

[33] *S'io potessi voler* is published in F. Corteccia, *The Second Book of Madrigals for Four Voices*, ed. F. A. D'Accone (Music of the Florentine Renaissance, 9; Neuhausen–Stuttgart, 1981), pp. 104–5.

[34] A. Einstein, 'Ancora sull'aria di Ruggiero', *Rivista musicale italiana*, 41 (1937), pp. 167–9.

[35] Haar, 'The *Madrigale Arioso*', pp. 225–6.

[36] Haar, *Italian Poetry and Music*, p. 99. Haar, p. 90, comments that 'Our failure to recognize this practice is one of the many things separating our rather abstract knowledge of Renaissance music from the multiple resonance it actually had.'

Example 2   Francesco Corteccia, *Io dico et diss' et dirò*, bars 1–11, from *The Second Book of Madrigals for Four Voices*, ed. D'Accone, p. 86

pattern that could be adopted to other texts.[37] The tercets, in fact, rhyme *cde ecd*, so that textual and musical rhyme do not correspond, as they would in the pattern *cde cde*.[38] These works might represent the sort of music favoured by academicians such as Benedetto Varchi: a more contrapuntally refined version of the improvisatory style, but conceived and performed with musical notation.

THE PASQUINATA OF 15[44]

The prime evidence for the debate on song in the Accademia Fiorentina, and its most extended document, takes the form of an open letter signed 'Pasquino Patritio Romano' (Document 1). Hundreds of anonymous poetic satires and letters of the age were attributed to this mythical personage. The practice began in Rome early in the sixteenth century, when satirical verses began to be posted on an ancient statue popularly called 'Pasquino', hence the term *Pasquinata*. The letter, with a probable date of 30 September 1544, survives in a single, elegant, seventeenth-century copy.[39] It begins:

Reverend and Magnificent Musicians with the Notes

So that you may be aware of how much I regret that rare and perfect things are subjected to the censure of every foolish judgement (such as is your own), I have not wanted to fail to write you the present, so that for those who will read it, it may be the paragon of truth, to you the signature of shame, and to me only the satisfaction of refuting with reason the great number of you who, beyond all good custom and manners, lacerate the most noble Maestro Alfonso de' Pazzi, Governor of the Staff of the Sicilia, and foremost creator of that harmony that makes you go mad with anger, green with envy, and expire of jealousy: to whom all the praises, all the dignities, and all the honours are more befitting than to that idiot Josquin, to that ignorant [castrated lamb] Gombert, or to that ill-bred sheep in a green field [Verdelot,] held by you in such esteem and veneration;

---

[37] Edited in F. Corteccia, *The First Book of Madrigals for Four Voices*, ed. F. A. D'Accone (Music of the Florentine Renaissance, 8; Neuhausen–Stuttgart, 1981), pp. 28–31.

[38] The disparity between musical and textual rhyme suggests that Corteccia's madrigal was originally composed to a different sonnet, one with a different rhyme scheme. The text, by Corteccia's fellow academician Giambattista Gelli, dates from 1541, on a political subject; see De Gaetano, *Giambattista Gelli*, 37.

[39] The manuscript is a miscellany in which the *Pasquinata* comprises a single fascicle, physically distinct from the surrounding material. The date is written as 'MDxiiij', with the first two letters ligated. The most likely explanation for the error is that the seventeenth-century copyist inadvertently omitted the letter 'l' after the 'x', so that it should have read 'MDxliiij.'

since from the fountain of his rare talent is poured the perfection of sweet music without notes, in which so many elevated and generous spirits have toiled in vain, without ever having been able to penetrate so far as his continuous fancy has pierced.

The document is unprecedented in that it combines a spirited attack on the practice of written polyphony with a simultaneous defence of the unwritten tradition of Italian song. The letter launches a broadside against the entire polyphonic tradition, whose representatives it names as Josquin, Gombert and Verdelot. Josquin is chosen as the figure of near-mythic stature to whose standard every composer of the age is compared. Gombert is invoked as a pre-eminent living composer of Latin polyphony and Verdelot is the musician most closely identified with the early madrigal in Florence. Josquin and Verdelot are French in origin, if not in culture, while Gombert figures as a Flemish master at the court of Emperor Charles V. Against these musicians the author counterpoises one Alfonso de' Pazzi, master of 'la perfetione della dolce Musica senza Note'.

In addressing the letter to 'Reverendi, et Magnifici Signori Musici con le Note' the anonymous author decries above all the quality of *writtenness* in polyphonic music. He makes his argument primarily against the artificiality of polyphony. Artificiality inheres in the act of writing, which interposes itself between composer and musician, between musician and audience. The discussion plays on one of the broad fault lines of the Mannerist period of the mid-sixteenth century, the distinction between natural and artificial in works of art and literature.[40] Improvised music is not calculated, but relies on the immediate fancy (*ghiribizzo*) and skill of the singer, who is also its creator:

Nor do you consider how rare are those things of nature that yield to art. Therefore, music with the notes being an artificial thing, and discovered in this world by that philosopher, thanks to those drunken blacksmiths, it will have to yield to the natural one invented by God in the other [world], which without notes, without lines and without rests moves the sky in such order; and just as this is ruled in the air, being a celestial thing, so this Alfonsale is ruled with the air [*aria*] of his counterpoint and miraculous judgement.

---

[40] J. Shearman, *Mannerism: Style and Civilisation* (Harmondsworth, 1967), pp. 37–38, 98–100. Shearman, pp. 21, 140, 151, enumerates other qualities of mannerism that might apply to the madrigal: 'complexity', 'density of motif' and 'the exaggerated pursuit of variety'.

The letter turns the tale of Pythagoras and the blacksmiths on its head. It also employs the double meaning of the word *aria* – as a physical body and as melody – to connect the music of the spheres with the singer's *aria* or characteristic melodic line and manner of performance. The singer creates his *aria* directly from experience and imagination, hence the song is ruled by him in the same way that the heavens are governed by cosmic harmony. To judge from the *Pasquinata*, counterpoint itself does not arouse animosity, only its manner of production. The lack of ability to create in song, or in counterpoint, upon the moment becomes a serious drawback for any singer 'con le note', who is lost without the piece of paper or parchment before his eyes or fixed in his memory.

In the same vein, the letter comments on the practice of skilled instrumentalists who work entirely without notation:

Do you not play the trombone by ear? Do you not create upon four notes of a cantus firmus, via fantasy, an endless sea of notes? Have you not heard four or six trumpeters [*Trombetti*] harmonise, operating without notes or keys [*tasti*], but via breath alone, with admirable sweetness and union, often varying their voices, now high, now low?

The passage constitutes a rare attestation to improvised music as practised by instrumental ensembles. The phrase 'un Mar di Note senza fondo' suggests progressive variation or division against the cantus firmus, appropriate to the civic *pifferi*, whose services were, on high occasions, requested to accompany dances.[41] In Siena, the *pifferi* in the mid-sixteenth century were much in demand at 'dinners, banquets, weddings, university ceremonies, and other kinds of festivities'.[42] The *Pasquinata* emphasises the role of fantasy in the performance of such music, a point also underscored in the creation of song. Heraldic trumpet ensembles, the *trombetti*, are likewise able to vary both harmony and texture by ear in the creation of a unified counterpoint.

Yet the most effective and revealing passage describes the problems that arise in the production and singing of written

[41] Timothy McGee, 'The Ademari Wedding Cassone', *Imago Musice*, 9–12 (1992–5), pp. 139–57, at pp. 148, 154. McGee describes the practice, however, only to the end of the fifteenth century. In his 'Giovanni Cellini, piffero di Firenze', *Rivista italiana di musicologia*, 32 (1997), pp. 201–21, at p. 217, McGee comments that 'I componimenti dei pifferi di Firenze erano musicisti molto abili ed esistono buoni motivi per credere che essi partecipassero all'esecuzione di un repertorio molto vasto per il piacere delle nobili famiglie fiorentine.'

[42] F. A. D'Accone, *The Civic Muse* (Chicago and London, 1997), 588.

polyphony. The *Pasquinata* takes dead-level aim at everything that can go wrong in a performance:

[Alfonso de' Pazzi] can, with the miracle of nature, with the gift of heaven and the influences of the planets, ascend to the level of perfection of music without notes; in which one does not spend so much coin, does not throw away so much time (to us so dear), nor do so much scoring [*spartimenti*] of notes. One does not spin like a top, when right after *B fa–B mi* comes *C sol fa ut*. You do not deny Christ in ruling so many books with rastrals, wasting the ink, and throwing away the varnish. You do not lose patience in copying *canzoni*, you do not knock yourself out going up and going down in *crome* and *semicrome*, you do not go crazy trying to find the key [*Chiave*] and the keyhole, keeping in mind whether or not *B molle* is entered from the natural, acute hexachord. Breathing does not give you trouble, torments do not suffocate you in keeping count during the rests. You do not beat with your hands, with your feet behind the beat; you do not rack your memory in the invention of airs and counterpoints. You do not sweat blood rehearsing a song ten times, and singing it badly eleven, you do not start again from the top at the request of those who get lost and blame it on you. You do not wear spectacles like Corteccia, but only with mastery, with the manner and the Brief Rules of Alfonso become a partaker of the beneficence of heaven.

The wealth of detail suggests that the author himself had undergone training in *canto figurato*.[43] He demonstrates how the copying of music books involves a great investment of time and money, besides requiring immensely painstaking work to do the job right, even down to the application of varnish to the finished pages. He implies that the clerical scribe neglects his Offices ('si rinnega Christo') in order to finish the work. In fact, since the entire letter is addressed to 'Reverendi, et Signori Musici con le note', the author emphasises the clerical status of polyphonic musicians. The composer himself has no easy time of it, trying to come up with new ideas while at the same time keeping in mind the precise relationship of one voice to another; the *Pasquinata* specifically cites the role of memory in the process of composition, an important consideration when composing in parts rather than in score.

Performance problems arise from the complexity of the music, which starts with the traditional bases of music theory: the

---

[43] The metaphoric usage of the word *chiave*, for example, is explained in Zarlino, *Le istitutioni harmoniche*, pt. 3, ch. 2, p. 148: 'Le quali Cifere si chiamarono sempre Chiavi; stando in questa similitudine, che si come per la Chiave si apre l'uscio, & si entra in casa, & ivi si vede quello, che si trova entro; Cosi per tali Cifere si apre la modulatione, & si conosce ciascuno delli nominati intervalli.' ('These signs were always called clefs after the key with which one opens a door and enters a house and then sees what is within. So by means of a clef one opens a melody and recognizes each of the designated intervals.') English version in G. Zarlino, *The Art of Counterpoint: Part Three of Le Istitutioni Harmoniche, 1558*, trans. G. A. Marco and C. V. Palisca (New Haven, 1968), p. 5.

application of both clefs (*chiavi*) and solmisation syllables (*voces*), hexachord mutation, and by extension, *musica ficta*. Rhythmic complexity of independent parts gives rise to a comical lag between the leader's hand and the singer's foot, not to mention intense worries over wrong entrances. The same inherent characteristics create purely vocal challenges as well, namely breath control and the strain to keep the eyes and voice moving fast in *crome* and *semicrome*. It gives us some comfort to discover that the difficulties of singing sixteenth-century polyphony have not changed much in four hundred years. Most tellingly, in the *Pasquinata* the musicians rehearse (*provare*) the music ten times through, without ever getting it right. The passage offers clear confirmation that written polyphony was by this time routinely performed with rehearsal. On the eleventh time, during performance, the singers get lost and have to start over again, making nonsense of the poem. We are left with the image of the composer Francesco Corteccia, member of the Accademia and *maestro di cappella* of Florence Cathedral, fumbling with his spectacles.

THE LETTER OF NICCOLÒ MARTELLI

A letter of 30 January 1546 (modern style), addressed to Alfonso de' Pazzi by Niccolò Martelli (Document 2), in large measure corroborates the *Pasquinata* in its defence of 'la dolce Musica senza note'. Martelli, as one of the founders and an early consul of the Accademia, commanded considerable respect. The letter was published by Antonfrancesco Doni in Martelli's *Il primo libro delle lettere* (1546), under the aegis of the Accademia Fiorentina. Although literary in intent, it lacks the extravagant language characteristic of the *Pasquinata*. Martelli begins by praising Pazzi's choice of academic name, Etrusco, for its brusqueness and grandeur:

all other names, Heroic, Greek or Latin, sound lesser by far and would have to yield completely, because – whether in antiquity or in Fiesole, whichever it may be – no others have ever known how to appropriate it, except you, with the workings of your mind; which found the way back to music without notes, leaving to Carpentras and Josquin and to the others who are in error their solfeggio. Whoever first took this name [Etrusco] never dreamed, however, that they would go fishing for voices in the air using [musical] scales. And in truth the harmony of song is nothing else than the delightful sweetness that expresses through the corporeal organs, with a certain grace and celestial air, the tempered unity of our soul; concerning which the great sages (who perhaps knew less) would want us to partake of that quality and manner, so that whoever today sings with the signs for *B quadro* and *B molle* is more foolish than he whom you cite in your great capricious Sonnets.[44]

As in the *Pasquinata*, the quality of writtenness, and the complexities it invites, remain at the centre of the distinction between two competing forces. Martelli specifically identifies the attributes of vocal polyphony, especially solfeggio, the overlapping system of hexachords and the attendant operation of *musica ficta*. The phrase 'e' pescon con le scale le voci in aria' employs puns on the words *voci* and *aria*. The first occurs in the technical, Latin usage of *voces*, the relative placement of a pitch within the hexachord, as well as in the implied, ordinary sense of 'voices'. As in the *Pasquinata*, the second word is meant in the physical sense, the air we breathe, besides its connotation of 'melody'. Martelli cites Josquin des Prez, together with Carpentras, the famous composer under the Medici pope Leo X, who earlier in his career had sung in the French Royal Chapel. The trope on the name 'Etrusco', Alfonso's academic sobriquet, makes the point that Alfonso has, in a sense, revived the ancient ideal of singing without notation. Reference to 'i gran Savi' reinforces the idea that the ancient Greeks and Latins would have approved of Alfonso's manner of song, and underscores the humanist qualities of his endeavours.

Later on, the letter strengthens its bias against the essentially foreign culture of written polyphony:[45]

However, gradually finding the door again, let us leave them their notes around their [clerical] collars (which in our language sound like mistakes) and let us adhere to song only if it is truly that of your lineage, and you will see that in relation to them, we will have a large following by mid-August [the feast of the Assumption]. And without telling you anything more for the moment, I will end. . . . And if such imaginative work did not produce a subsequent effect, it was nonetheless a fine honour to attempt it, if for no other reason than to make yourself known as being without equal; even the great Portio Napoletano, known beyond the skies, praises you, exalts you, and says that you are the rarest among the rare, because you tread upon a path with your imagination, no longer in the vicinity of any mortals, that you realise how to become more than a man; and between your fame and that of Mona Honesta da Campi, there will be no difference of any sort.

---

[44] Translated by Edita Nosowa, to whom I am also grateful for translations of several poems from the circle of the Accademia Fiorentina.
[45] Trans. Edita Nosowa.

Martelli expresses an anti-clerical stance, enjoining 'lasciamo lor le lor nuote intorno al collaretto (che in lingua nostra suonon macchie)'.[46] The passage reiterates the identification of polyphony with sacred music and musicians, already implicit in the *Pasquinata*. It suggests that Italian song, taking on the musical manners of the *oltremontani*, like a priestly collar, constricts the Tuscan tongue. For one hundred and fifty years, foreign singers in Italy overwhelmingly had been in holy orders. Martelli's argument thus bears on the question of language, in that he advocates musical means that are endemic to and congruous with Tuscan poetics.[47]

Martelli also takes an enthusiastic, directly expressed position with respect to Alfonso's abilities as a musician and poet. He reports the opinion of the philosopher Simone Portio (Porzio) Napoletano in support of his judgement, though it remains ambiguous whether the reference encompasses Alfonso's singing or his poetry. Portio was a fellow member of the Accademia and a lecturer at the Studio di Pisa, to whom Alfonso addressed two of his sonnets.[48] A clear sense of opposition or faction informs this portion of the letter. Martelli cites another name in conjunction with Alfonso, that of one Mona Honesta da Campi: 'et dalla fama nostra à quella di Mona Honesta da Campi, non ci sarà vantaggio alcuno'. No trace or explanation of the latter figure has yet appeared. To judge from the jocular context, she may been a fellow *improvvisatore*; if so, like many proponents of the unwritten tradition, her name and fame have been lost.

ALFONSO DE' PAZZI AND THE 'SONETTI CONTRO IL VARCHI'

Alfonso de' Pazzi, addressed in the *Pasquinata* as the master of 'il Grado perfetto della Musica senza Note', was a scion of the wealthy

[46] In this context, the word *collaretto* specifically refers to the clerical collar, as a diminutive of *collare*, or in the sense of *colletto*.

[47] A letter by Alfonso contained in Florence, Biblioteca Nazionale, Banco rari 71, fols. 62[r]–68[v], signed 'L'Etrusco', appears likewise to deal with the relationship of music and poetry, but the autograph hand is all but indecipherable.

[48] Sonetto XII, 'Mandovi, Porzio, certe melegrane', and Sonetto XIII, 'E' non sarà questa volta menzogna', in *Opere burlesche del Berni, del Casa, del Varchi, del Mauro, del Bino, del Dolce, del Firenzuola, Ricoretto*, 3 vols. ([Rome], 1771), iii, p. 312. Seven of Portio's books were published in Florence, all by Lorenzo Torrentino. The phrase 'davanti che e sia mezzo Agosto', may allude to Sonetto LXI, 'Tanci, se tu ordinavi a mezzo Agosto', in *Opere burlesche*, iii, p. 341, addressed to Leonardo Tanci.

Pazzi family of Florence (Figure 2).[49] He held only one official position in his life, as *podestà* ('chief magistrate') of nearby Fiesole, from May to September 1548. The *Pasquinata* also calls him *Governatore* of the Company of Sicilia, or Cicilia, an organisation for which Antonfrancesco Grazzini wrote the texts for seven masquerade songs, or *mascherate*.[50] Since at least one of these was intended for performance in Fiesole ('Cantato alla Cicilia a Fiesole'), and a character in Doni's *I marmi* mentions that 'on Friday evening I had a headache, because we spent the whole day in Fiesole at the Cicilia', the academy may have been situated there.[51] By the time Alfonso de' Pazzi was elected a member of the Accademia Fiorentina in September 1543, at age 34, he was known as one of the most eccentric men in all of Florence.

Antonfrancesco Doni, in his *Libraria*, describes Alfonso de' Pazzi as a formidable adversary:[52]

This is one of the most admirable intellects in all of Tuscany today, keen, quick of riposte, lively and, in short, he makes the most beautiful flowers and good fruits of the operations [of the intellect]. Moreover, he delights in writing, to pass the time, some sonnets, rather in the manner of Burchiello, and he calls these his most capricious fancies.

Doni's sketch helps explain the impact Alfonso made within the Accademia Fiorentina, as a debater quick on his feet and pointed in response. Alfonso also appears as an interlocutor in Doni's *I marmi*, in a startlingly modern discussion of the Tuscan language. The comparison to Burchiello, the fifteenth-century satiric poet,

---

[49] The source of the engraving is unknown. Although the execution dates more than two centuries later, its style raises the possibility that it derives from an original portrait.

[50] *Canti carnascialeschi, trionfi, carri e mascherate, secondo l'edizione del Bracci* (Milan, 1883), pp. 298–304. The edition is a reprint of *Tutti i trionfi, carri, mascherate, o canti carnescialeschi andati per Firenze dal tempo del Magnifico Lorenzo de Medici, fino all'Anno 1559*, 2nd edn., 2 vols., ed. R. M. Bracci ([Lucca], 1750). Grazzini, who edited the first edition, omitted the seven of his own poems published by Bracci.

[51] Doni, *I marmi*, i, p. 231: 'venerdì sera non mi sentivo troppo in cervello, perché eramo stati il giorno a Fiesole alla Cicilia . . .'. On a similar organisation in the early sixteenth century, see A. M. Cummings, 'The Company of the Cazzuola and the Early Madrigal', *Musica disciplina*, 50 (1996), pp. 203–38.

[52] Doni, *La libraria del Doni divisi in tre trattati*, ed. V. Bramanti (Milan, 1972), p. 342: 'HE-TRUSCO FIORENTINO: Questo è un dei mirabili intelletti che abbi oggi tutta la Toscana, arguto, presto nelle riposte, pronto e, brevemente, fa bellissimi fiori e buoni frutti d'operazione. Poi si diletta scrivere per passare il tempo alcuni sonetti più che alla burchiellesca, e chiama questi suoi ghiribizzosi capricci.' Doni avoids controversy by not mentioning either Alfonso's musicianship or the *Sonetti contro il Varchi*, using instead the title *Rime in ghiri*. A second title attributed to Alfonso, *Fanfalucole del Piloto*, is unknown and may be fictitious.

Figure 2   Engraved bust of Alfonso de' Pazzi, in Antonfrancesco Grazzini,
Tutti i trionfi, carri, mascherate, o canti carnescialeschi (1750), opposite p. 720.
Courtesy of Special Collections Library, Duke University

194

banished from Florence for his sharp tongue, is made in reference to the native burlesque tradition.[53] As a poet, Alfonso's best-known work was the two volumes of the *Sonetti contro il Varchi*, also called *Il Varcheida*. The first book of the *Sonetti contro il Varchi* runs to sixty-one sonnets and one *capitolo* with a series of shorter poems and epigrams, while the second has forty-four sonnets.[54] Poems from the first book, in particular, were copied into multitudinous poetry collections of the sixteenth and early seventeenth centuries. Although it is difficult to credit, these sonnets singlemindedly attack, in terms both personal and professional, Benedetto Varchi, official historian and pre-eminent man of letters to Duke Cosimo I de' Medici.

In consequence of his early association with the patrician Strozzi family, Varchi, a native Florentine, had lived in exile since 1537, first in Venice, then from 1540 in Padua, where he helped found the Accademia degli Infiammati.[55] In the Veneto, he became a friend and follower of Cardinal Pietro Bembo. Varchi eventually moved on to Bologna, whence Cosimo I and his emissaries convinced him to return to Florence to enhance the status of the ducal court. His acceptance into the Accademia Fiorentina in March 1543 aroused feelings of envy and resentment, however, and tended to polarise sentiment within an already contentious group of men. His wide learning and cosmopolitan ideas stood in contrast to figures such as Antonfrancesco Grazzini, the apprentice of an apothecary, who had received a limited classical education.[56]

---

[53] Domenico di Giovanni, called il Burchiello (1404–49), was the most famous fifteenth-century Italian satirist, renowned for his *sonetti caudati*, which inspired the adjective *burchiellesca*. A barber in Florence, and a thorn in the side of the Medici, he was exiled from the city for the last ten years of his life.

[54] The first book is published in *Opere burlesche*, iii, pp. 306–55. The second book is contained in Vatican City, Biblioteca Apostolica Vaticana, MS Capponi 85, titled 'La Varcheida D'ALFONSO DE' PAZZI (detto l'Etrusco), Accademico et gentilhuomo Fiorentino'. The manuscript contains forty-four sonnets from Book II, interspersed with forty sonnets from Book I, followed by twenty-five shorter poems and epigrams. For a manuscript inventory, see G. S. Cozzo, *I codici capponiani della Biblioteca Vaticana* (Rome, 1897), pp. 82–4.

[55] R. S. Samuels, 'Benedetto Varchi, the *Accademia degli Infiammati*, and the Origins of the Italian Academic Movement', *Renaissance Quarterly*, 29 (1976), pp. 599–633. Samuels demonstrates that Varchi took on many of the same roles in the Accademia degli Infiammati as he did later in the Accademia Fiorentina, and that their programmes had distinct similarities.

[56] See R. J. Rodini, *Antonfrancesco Grazzini: Poet, Dramatist, and Novelliere, 1503–1584* (Madison, Wis., 1970), pp. 4–5. Grazzini lamented on more than one occasion that he was a poor Latinist.

The forces aligned against Varchi scored a triumph when a young girl was raped nearby his country villa in February 1545, at a time when Varchi was in residence. The girl's father was encouraged to press charges, and Varchi was arrested and thrown in prison. There he wrote letters to several patrons, including Pietro Bembo, requesting them to intercede on his behalf. Although his gardener seems a more likely culprit, Varchi confessed to the crime, made a monetary restitution to the girl (as dowry for marriage or a convent) and obtained a pardon from Cosimo I on 25 March 1545.[57] Within weeks, on 12 April 1545, Varchi was inducted to a six-month term as consul of the Accademia Fiorentina. His standing within the Accademia was never threatened again.

When Alfonso de' Pazzi was elected to the Accademia Fiorentina in September 1543, six months after Benedetto Varchi, his entrance was greeted with outright derision. Grazzini, the most talented satirist and playwright in the group, addresses a *sonetto caudato*, 'Dell'Accademia or ben sperar si puote', to Giovanni Mazzuoli, known as 'Lo Stradino' or 'Il Consagrata' (lines 1–14):[58]

> Dell'Accademia or ben sperar si puote
>   Cose di fuoco, di ghiaccio e di vento,
>   Poi ch'Alfonso pazzissimo vi è drento
>   Che la musica vuol senza le note.
> Queste, padre Stradin, son le carote
>   Che vi son fitte dietro a tradimento:
>   L'Accademia basisce, e voi contento
>   Ne state a boca chiusa, ed a man vote.
> Gridate ad alta voce, o Consagrata,
>   Poi che gli Scribi iniqui, e' Farisei
>   L'hanno si stranamente profanata.
> Gridate e dite: o cari Umidi miei,
>   Or l'Accademia vostra è doventata
>   La burla, e 'l passatempo de' plebei!

> Now in the Accademia you can well hope for
>   Things of fire, or ice or wind,
>   Since Alfonso, the craziest [Pazzi] is here within,
>   Who wants music without notes.
> These, father Stradino, are the carrots
>   Stuck behind you in treachery;
>   The Accademia is astounded, and you remain content
>   With closed mouth and empty hand.

---

[57] The incident has been variously understood; see U. Pirotti, *Benedetto Varchi e la cultura del suo tempo* (Florence, 1971), pp. 25–7, and Manacorda, *Benedetto Varchi*, pp. 157–61.

[58] Grazzini, *Rime burlesche*, p. 9.

Cry aloud, O Consagrata,
  Because the iniquitous Scribes and Pharisees
  Have so strangely profaned it.
Cry out and speak: O Umidi, dear to me,
  Now your Accademia has become
  The joke and amusement of plebians.

Poetic satire, as employed here, or poetic burlesque, works by thrust and parry, the cut of the pen falling where it may. Although the language often contains a second, coded level of scurrilous or obscene import, it still operates principally on a localised basis, which allows us to compare texts in the search for specific subjects, attitudes or points of argument. For present purposes, the distortion or ironic inversion inherent in satire will be studied not so much with comical, or even aesthetic ends in mind, but with a view to tracing cultural associations.

Alfonso's eccentricities made him an easy target for such lampoons, especially since his surname, de' Pazzi, comes from the word *pazzo*, meaning 'crazy' or 'mad'. The inversion of social class that Grazzini introduces became a common point of ridicule, since Alfonso's clan ranked among the best-known and wealthiest in Florence. Grazzini's phrase, 'Il passatempo de' plebei', suggests an association between Alfonso's music and the improvised music of the *cantimbanco*, the poet-singer of the city piazzas.[59] The dual character of the unwritten tradition, as one that belonged to the common people, as well as one practised by courtly or humanist poet-singers, for want of a better term, comes into sharper definition. Indeed, it is Alfonso's advocacy of music *all'improvviso* that immediately attracts the attention of his opponents. On another occasion, Grazzini compares Alfonso to a swan:[60]

---

[59] On the history of the *cantimbanco* or *canta in panca* (literally, 'bench singer') see E. Levy, 'I cantari leggendari del popolo italiano nei secoli xiv e xv', *Giornale storico della letteratura italiana*, supplemento 16 (1914), pp. 1–22; B. Becherini, 'Un canto in panca fiorentino: Antonio di Guido', *Rivista musicale italiana*, 50 (1948), pp. 241–7; Haar, *Italian Poetry and Music*, pp. 77–85; and F. Luisi, 'Minima fiorentina: sonetti a mente, canzoni a ballo e cantimpanca nel Quattrocento', in I. Alm *et al.* (eds.), *Musica Franca: Essays in Honor of Frank A. D'Accone* (Stuyvesant, NY, 1996), pp. 79–95. Singers of epics (*cantastorie*) were active in Italy from the late medieval period through the early twentieth century.

[60] Grazzini, *Rime burlesche*, p. 222.

Chi cerca d'imitar l'altero stile
  O 'l dolce canto vostro,
  Gitta via 'l tempo, la carta e l'inchiostro,
  Rïuscendo snervato, basso e vile;
  Però che presso a cigno alto e gentile
  Par, cantando, ogni uccello
  Corbo, assiuolo, gufo, o pipistrello.

Whoever seeks to imitate the high style
  Or that sweet song of yours,
  Free yourself from measure, paper and ink,
  Becoming ennervated, base and mean;
  Because next to the swan, sublime and noble,
  All other birds, singing, appear
  As a crow, horned owl, small owl or bat.

Grazzini portrays the imitators of Alfonso as birds that try to sing, but only manage to squeak or croak. Grazzini's third line confirms that Alfonso viewed the quality of writtenness as a clear impediment to the *altero stile*. Such *ad hominem* attacks on Alfonso largely bypass or ignore larger points of engagement, as elaborated in the *Pasquinata*. This kind of discourse results from the elite, enclosed nature of the academy, in which there was little separation between professional opinion and personal character. At the same time, Grazzini's poem suggests that Alfonso was dictating the terms of debate.

Another poem, headed 'Capitolo del Gobbo da Pisa ad Alfonso de' Pazzi', by one Girolamo Amelonghi (using his academic name, 'The Hunchback of Pisa'), treats Alfonso in a rather gentler manner than Grazzini's typically hard-edged satire. The poem begins, 'One day, Etrusco, I want to set you down in a chronicle'.[61] It adds, in passing, a different voice to the debate, one that ironically acknowledges Alfonso's musical skill (lines 19–27):[62]

Voi avete più ghiri e più chimere,
  Più capricci, più stratte strafizzeche,
  Che non ha 'cetera, o contratti un sere.
Voi siete l'inventor delle bacheche,
  Poeta Etrusco, e per dir in progote
  Straccate giorno e notte le ribeche.
Musico raro e di quei senza note
  E ciurmador ne' cerchi a cicalare
  Ficcando a quest'e quel dreto carote.

---

[61] Edited in Pedrotti, *Alfonso de' Pazzi*, pp. 18–22; original in Florence, Biblioteca Riccardiana, MS 1199, fols. 90ᵛ–93ᵛ: 'Io voglio, Etrusco, un dì mettervi in cronaca'.

[62] I am indebted to the late Nino Pirrotta for his help with this translation.

> You have more fancies and more wild illusions,
>   More caprices, more banquet witticisms,
>   Than a notary has etceteras or contracts.
> You are the inventor of the Bacchic verses,
>   Etrusco, Poet, and to speak in *progote*
>   You wear out the rebecs night and day.
> Rare musician, and of those without notes,
>   And charlatan, to chatter in the circles,
>   Poking your carrot behind someone or another.

Amelonghi offers a portrait of the poet-musician at work, practising 'giorno e notte'. He comically associates Alfonso with the rebec, a peasant instrument by the mid-sixteenth century, though we might suppose the use of the traditional lira da braccio, as attested by the writings of Doni and Grazzini. Amelonghi mentions the composition of *Bacheche* or 'Bacchic verses', which may refer to a particular style or manner of poetic satire.[63] Details of the extravagant vocabulary (including the unknown word *progote*) help set the scene for Alfonso's performance. The adjective *strafizzeche* in the first tercet refers to the dinner banquets at which satires were pronounced, by means of *stratte*, or 'brusque jerks', hence the phrase, *stratte straffizeche*. The third tercet portrays Alfonso as a musical charlatan (*ciurmadore*) who hawks his wares in front of (or behind) his potential customers.[64] The verb *cicalare* ('to chatter') refers specifically to poetic satires. The word *carote*, besides its phallic connotation, carries the meaning of 'lies', as it does also in Grazzini's poem, 'Dell'Accademia or ben sperar si puote'. Amelonghi's association of music, banquets and satire helps solidify the conclusion that Alfonso sang his own sonnets before the Accademia Fiorentina.

Further amplification of the issues delineated in the *Pasquinata* comes from the preface to 'Gigantea', a long, mock-heroic poem also by Girolamo Amelonghi, under the name 'Il Forabosco'

---

[63] The word *bachecha* likewise appears in Grazzini's ballata 'Pianga ognuno a capo chino' (ll. 38–42) in *Rime burlesche*, pp. 159–61:
> Sendo morto quel cavallo,
> Che facea tanto onorallo
> Dalle gente folle e cieca:
> Gli è rimasto una bacheca
> Da comporre allo Stradino.

[64] Haar, *Italian Poetry and Music*, p. 78, notes that *ciarlatano* also could be used in reference to a poet-musician: the different terms available 'warn us that we are dealing not with a single category . . . but with a range of careers'.

('White-throat Warbler'). The preface is addressed 'Al Famoso et Etrusco de' pazzi' (Document 3):

If you recall, the sweet music without notes was the first thing you made me learn with such facility. You and none other taught me to mix at random and to compose in the manner that you see [below], swearing to me that a sonnet must be begun with the tercets and finished with the quatrains; demonstrating to me by philosophical arguments that to poetise via fantasy [à ghiri], beyond the pleasure it carries in itself, is desired by everyone, in not being subjected, like other styles, to gravity of judgement, to elegant language, to sophistic argument, and finally, to poisonous, muttered censure. You made me capable, like those whose job it is, to recite comedies and to adorn them, and you gave me the inventions of the carnival songs, with the masquerades *de le buffole*.

The passage offers an overview, via rhetorical sarcasm, of the issues Alfonso raised within the Accademia Fiorentina. First and foremost comes the idea of improvised music. Closely allied to this is the composition of poetry *à ghiri*. The comments concerning the pleasures of such poetry, according to Alfonso de' Pazzi, emphasise its immediate impact, in contrast to the sober criticism that values poetic elegance, sophistication, careful craftmanship and linguistic or psychological complexity. The preface evokes the academic qualities by which poetry was a subject for commentary as well as performance. Alfonso, in contrast, juxtaposes imagery and ideas with a brusqueness that can only be enhanced in performance as song.

Surprisingly, Amelonghi also refers to the recitation of comedies. Like other academies of the period, the Accademia Fiorentina produced plays, especially those written by its members. Comedies and ancient dramas, given in the vernacular, typically interposed intermedi between the acts, and these were the occasion for musical performance. The preface attributes to Alfonso the facetious suggestion that carnival songs, filled with sexual double meanings, and normally conceived without written music, would be appropriate for singing in the production of a comedy. On the other hand, only one sonnet by Alfonso, 'E ci hanno recitato letanie', addresses the subject of comedies, deploring the use of polyphony, emblematised once again by the music of Josquin (lines 12–14): 'Antique farces and modern tragedies, / For an intermedio the hymns of Josquin, / And in place of a proem, a lantern.'[65] The

---

[65] Sonetto XXXIII in *Opere burlesche*, iii, p. 324: 'Antica farsa, e tragedia moderna, / Per intermedij gl'inni di Josquino, / Et invece di proemio una lucerna.' One source, Florence, Biblioteca Nazionale Centrale, MS Magl. VII, 271, fol. 31ʳ, titles the poem 'Sopra la

lantern is needed, of course, to read sheet music, written in a style akin to sacred polyphony.

The fate of the carnival song is the subject of Grazzini's 'Sopra il compor canti moderni'.[66] Although Grazzini ridiculed Alfonso's views in a number of poems, directly or in passing, his opinions took a sharp reversal after the latter's death in November 1555. Grazzini decries how the high-flown and often incomprehensible madrigal has supplanted the traditional Florentine *mascherata* or *trionfo*. Carnival songs were worked out ahead of time, rather than improvised, then performed and transmitted by ear.[67] Grazzini's poem emphasises their popular character and ready availability to everyone in the city (ll. 33–40):

> Io mi ricordo già quando gli andava
>   Un canto, prima che fusse riposto
>   Che tutto quanto a mente s'imparava,
>   Tant'era bello e chiaro e ben composto;
>   Ma or non pure un vero se ne cava,
>   E non s'intende il nome che gli è posto,
>   Ché quei madrigaluzzi a i lor soggetti
>   Troppo stitiche sono e troppo gretti.

> I remember a time when, before a song
>   Was performed a second time,
>   Everyone had learnt the whole piece by heart,
>   Because it was so beautiful and clear and well composed;
>   But nowadays, not a single good one can be extracted from the lot,
>   And one cannot even understand the title placed upon it,
>   Because these lousy madrigals in their choice of subjects
>   Are too stingy and mean.

The ideal carnival song possesses an easy memorability, with an attendant clarity of text and music. Quoting a satirical sonnet by Alfonso de' Pazzi, Grazzini adds that current *mascherate* are even

---

comedia del lasca'. Consequently, the likely candidate for the play is the one by Grazzini performed at the Sala del Papa during carnival 1550. It was published in the following year together with six madrigal texts for the intermedi, but without music, as *La Gelosia. Comedia d'Antonfrancesco Grazzini fiorentino detto il Lasca* (Florence, 1551).

[66] Grazzini, *Rime burlesche*, pp. 407–9; A. Grazzini, *Opere*, ed. G. D. Bonino (Turin, 1974), pp. 399–400. Grazzini had a vital interest in the carnival song, not just as a poet, but as the first editor of the texts, in *Tutti i trionfi, carri, mascherate, o canti carnescialeschi andati per Firenze dal tempo del Magnifico Lorenzo de Medici, fino all'Anno 1559* (Florence, 1559). See also the later editions cited in n. 50.

[67] A number of composed songs survive from early in the century, however. A central source is Florence, Biblioteca Nazionale Centrale, MS Banco rari 230, published as Renaissance Music in Facsimile, 4, ed. F. A. D'Accone (New York, 1986). For a comprehensive discussion of two songs from the manuscript, see A. M. Cummings, *The Politicized Muse: Music for the Medici Festivals, 1512–1537* (Princeton, 1992), ch. 2, pp. 15–41.

harder to understand. He admits that 'Now I know, even though I am truly embarrassed to say so, / We could do with a thousand Alfonsos.'[68] Music 'with the notes' affects not just musical style, but the social position of the song and the poetic text itself. Like Alfonso de' Pazzi, Grazzini addresses the changes wrought by the adoption of written composition and finds it wanting.

In two of his *Sonetti contro il Varchi*, Alfonso de' Pazzi draws a sharp distinction between the tradition of written polyphony and the tradition of improvised song, a distinction that also touches upon larger cultural issues. The first of these, 'Tu canti con le note, et con gl'occhiale', portrays Benedetto Varchi as a singer of sheet music:[69]

> Tu canti con le note, et con gl'occhiale
>   Varchi, et vedi il riflesso, et non la luce;
>   Fai come quel, che con le nocche sdruce
>   Al lume della Luna gli Aiuali.
> Tu se' uno Strion da carnovali
>   Immitator di Castor, et Polluce;
>   Noi ti darem' un caval' con le muce
>   À te, et tutti gli altri manovali.
> Tu canti per B quadro, et per B molle,
>   Et usi di dì chiaro la lanterna
>   Come altre volte ho detto alla fraterna.
> La coltricie è tua vita; et la taverna
>   Et vorresti i responsi nell'ampolle
>   Et non credi, che Argo cio discerna.
>
> You sing with the notes and with eyeglasses,

[68] Lines 15–16: 'Or so, se ben di dirlo mi vergogno, / Di mille Alfonsi ci saria bisogno.' Alfonso de' Pazzi's sonnet most likely refers to a known text by Giovan Battista Strozzi, the 'Trionfo delle furie', edited in *Canti carnascialeschi* (Milan, 1883), p. 160. The sonnet appears in Vatican City, Biblioteca Apostolica Vaticana, MS Capponi 85, p. 65:

> *Per M. Gio. Batista Strozzi, quando fece la mascherata*
> E sarranno veduti et non intesi,
>   Batista, questi vostri mascherati,
>   Et per vostra cagion sien lacerati,
>   Et gittati e danari et non ispesi.
> Al primo lo diss' io, quando l'intesi
>   Che già sei volte al meno erano andati,
>   Diavoli, furie, et spiriti beati
>   Questa l'ottava sia co' loro arnesi.
> Un gran rumore el fine, un gran fracasso
>   Un guazzabuglio, una confusione
>   Un dar di se à tutto il mondo spasso.
> Un carro con le note, un drappellone
>   Che non l'harebbe fatto il Varchi o 'l Tasso
>   Senza fine, senza arte, o inventione.

[69] Florence, Biblioteca Nazionale Centrale, MS Magl. VII, 272, p. 47; trans. Edita Nosowa.

> Varchi, and you see the reflection, but not the light;
> You do as he, who with his knuckles
> Rips bird nets by the light of the moon.
> You are a carnival player,
> An imitator of Castor and Pollux;
> We will give you a horse among the cows,
> To you and to all the other manual labourers.
> You sing with the signs for *B quadro* and *B molle*,
> And use a lantern in broad daylight,
> As I have mentioned other times to the brotherhood.
> The mattress and the tavern are your life,
> And you would like to find the answers in the bottle;
> And you don't believe that Argos discerns all this distinctly.

'Tu canti con le note' ridicules the more practical aspects of singing from written music – the eyeglasses, the lantern, the thrashing about with the voice. It also calls attention to the use of *musica ficta*, which employs the signs for *B quadro* (♮) and *B molle* (♭). Varchi acts here as a figurehead, a stand-in for poets who favour song 'con le note'. Moreover, the sonnet advances a distinction concerning the practice of music by professionals – *manovali*, those who work with their hands – and its practice by the highly educated or sophisticated connoisseur.[70] On this view, the act of singing from writing reduces music to the status of a craft, rather than a liberal art, with attendant social overtones. In the relatively open social milieu of Florence, music *all'improvviso* was nonetheless practised by shopkeepers, such as Visino, as well as by patricians, treated with the same seriousness and enthusiasm as poetry.

A second sonnet by Alfonso de' Pazzi, 'In terra non potendo conseguire', mounts a lyrical defence of the tradition of orally conceived and performed song against its detractors, Varchi and Corteccia. It takes the form of an epitaph for Baccio Moschino (d. 1552), organist in Florence Cathedral and a singer under Francesco Corteccia.[71] Cosimo Bartoli, in his *Ragionamenti accademici*, set *c*.1552, writes of sometimes hearing Moschin improvise in syncopated counterpoint on the organ for an hour together, 'with

---

[70] I am obliged to Tim Carter for this reading of the poem. The line 'Noi ti darem' un caval' con le muce' alludes to Varchi's position as an aristocrat who, having run through his inheritance, worked of necessity as a tutor and court historian.

[71] J. Haar, 'Cosimo Bartoli on Music', in *The Science and Art of Renaissance Music*, pp. 58, 60, originally published in *Early Music History*, 8 (1988), pp. 37–79. The article quotes and discusses all those sections of Cosimo Bartoli, *Ragionamenti accademici sopra alcuni luoghi difficili di Dante* (Venice, 1567), that directly relate to music.

few listeners and solely for his own study'.[72] Yet as the modest composer of two madrigals, and a leading member of the choir of Santa Maria del Fiore and the Baptistery of San Giovanni, Moschin was involved in the production of part-music, hence the sonnet's attribution of imperfection:[73]

In terra non potendo conseguire
   Il Moschin con le note almo, e perfetto
   Quell'armonia che ciba l'intelletto,
   Constretto è suto di quaggiù partire.
Il Varchi presto il doverrà seguire
   P'el camin noto provo di diletto
   E sovra 'l cerchio ch'a volgari è tetto
   Oserà forse l'alma sua nodrire.
O felice colui ito nella spoglia
   Sedendo sopra se poggiando vola
   Ove 'l [d]iletto regna senza doglia
Qui il *Corteccia* non haverà scuola
   Und'il *Moschin* saria l'ardente voglia
   In tempo che la chiave eterna [invuola].

On earth, not being able to equal with the notes
   That divine and perfect harmony
   That feeds the intellect,
   Moschin was compelled to leave this world.
Varchi will no doubt be following him soon,
   Taking the well-known path, leading near to delight;
   And above the heavenly circle that serves the common
      folk as a roof,
   He will perhaps dare to nourish his soul.
O happy is he who has left his mortal remains
   And seated, resting upon his body, flies
   To where delight reigns without sorrow.
Here Corteccia will have no school,
   Which would be Moschin's ardent desire
   For all the time that flees the eternal key.

The association of the oral tradition with heavenly music on the one hand, propagated in the *Pasquinata*, and with the common people, *i volgari*, on the other, finds a subtle expression with 'In terra non potendo conseguire', one that depends more on imagery

---

[72] Cited in Haar, 'Cosimo Bartoli', p. 57: '[I]o lo ho sentito talvolta sonare per suo piacere senza molti uditori, solamente per suo studio, & durato una hora a pigliare un vaga di sonare in contrabattuta, che mi hà fatto deporre ogni fastidio, ogni dispiacere, & ogni amaritudine che io havessi qual si voglia maggiore nello animo.'

[73] Trans. Edita Nosowà; text from Florence, Biblioteca Nazionale Centrale, MS Palatino 245, fol. 20ʳ. The last line is emended by reference to Sonetto XXXII in *Opere burlesche*, iii, p. 323.

than logical argument. Yet the connection is an important one, for the aim of the Accademia in creating a Tuscan poetics that was both artistic and accessible demanded a style of song that was flexible, immediate and responsive to poetic form. As we have seen, formulaic *arie* were invented or fashioned to individual texts on the spot, balancing strophic repetition with ornamentation or variation. Solo song was able to project the words clearly at all times, unlike the polyphonic madrigal – an argument that resonated through the end of the sixteenth century.[74] The citation of Francesco Corteccia in the last tercet pulls the hook, since his name invokes the high status of the Florentine madrigal and Latin motet. As chief musician of Cosimo I, Corteccia represents an official policy weighted towards polyphonic music.

'In terra non potendo conseguire' attacks Varchi in large measure because of his particular position in the cultural politics of the age, as a leading voice and representative of the Medici state.

---

[74] See C. V. Palisca, *Humanism in Italian Renaissance Thought* (New Haven, 1985), ch. 13, pp. 369–407. In a remarkable passage, Zarlino, *Le istitutioni harmoniche*, pt. 1, ch. 9, p. 75, writes 'But when music is recited with judgement, and approaches more nearly the usage of the ancients, namely in a simple manner, singing to the sound of the lira, the lute or other similar instruments subjects that may treat of comedy or of tragedy, and other similar things with long narratives, then their effects may be seen: because truly those songs can little move the heart in which a brief subject is related in a few words, as is the custom nowadays in some *canzonette*, called madrigals, which, though they may delight greatly, do not, however, have the aforesaid power. And that it is true that music delights more universally when it is simple than when it is made with so much artifice and sung in many parts one can realise from this, that one hears with greater delectation someone sing solo to the sound of an organ, of the lira, or of the lute, or of other similar instruments, than one hears many [voices]. And yet if many singing together move the heart, there is no doubt that generally those songs whose words are pronounced together by the singers are heard with greater pleasure than those learned compositions in which the words are heard interrupted by many parts.' ('Ma quando la Musica è recitata con giudicio, & più si accosta all' vso de gli antichi, cioè ad vn semplice modo, cantando al suono della Lira, del Leuto, o di altri simili istrumenti alcune materie, che habbiano del Comico, ouer del Tragico, & altre cose simili con lunghe narrationi; allora si vedeno li suoi effetti: Percioche veramente possono muouer poco l'animo quelle canzoni, nelle quali si racconti con breue parole vna materia breue, come si costuma hoggidi in alcune canzonette, dette Madrigali; le quali benche molto dilettino, non hanno però la sopradetta forza. Et che sia il vero, che la Musica più diletti vniuersalmente quando è semplice, che quando è fatta con tanto artificio, & cantata con molte parti; si può comprender da questo, che con maggior dilettatione si ode cantare alcuno solo al suono di un' Organo, della Lira, del Leuto, o di altri simili istrumenti, che non si ode molti. Et se pur molti cantando insieme muoueno l'animo, non è dubbio, che vniuersalmente con maggior piacere si ascoltano quelle canzoni, le cui parole sono da i cantori insieme pronunciate, che le dotte compositioni, nelle quali si odono le parole interrotte da molte parti.') Zarlino focuses on the effects created in the listeners by musical style and the delivery of text, comparing them to the testimony of the ancient Greeks, rather than on the issue of notation.

His own poetic production consists primarily in scores of epistolary, pastoral and spiritual sonnets.[75] Earlier in his career, he had been commissioned by Ruberto Strozzi to write a madrigal text for one 'Pulisena', quite possibly the famous singer Polissena Pecorina who was a collaborator of Adrian Willaert in Venice.[76] Varchi was instrumental in the Accademia's programme to bring humanist knowledge and science – so long the province of an educated elite – to the population at large, and in the efforts to revitalise Tuscan literature. In so doing, he remained indelibly associated with the poetics of Pietro Bembo, as represented by the edition of Petrarch's *Canzoniere*, and especially the *Prose della volgar lingua*. Bembo, a Venetian, propagated a set of grammatical rules for Tuscan, based on and idealising the fourteenth-century usage of Petrarch and Boccaccio. To Alfonso, as to other members of the Accademia Fiorentina, including Antonfrancesco Grazzini and Giambattista Gelli, learning based on *lettere*, the written word, rather than on speech, falsified Tuscan, and presented the very real danger of manufacturing an artificial, literary language, severing the creation of literature from its roots in the life of Florence and Tuscany.[77] This is one reason that the performance of poetry, in declamation, recitative or song, takes on added importance, as the true projection and manifestation of the poetic voice.[78] With the ascendancy of the polyphonic madrigal, influenced by Bembo's theory of *piacevolezza* and *gravità* in the rhythm and sound of poetic lines, qualities of writtenness and artificiality threatened to destroy the normative processes of social and artistic endeavour.

In a dialogue from Doni's *I marmi*, the character of Alfonso de' Pazzi puts forth several sophisticated arguments in favour of

---

[75] The Italian poetry is edited in Varchi, *Opere*, ii.

[76] R. J. Agee, 'Ruberto Strozzi and the Early Madrigal', *Journal of the American Musicological Society*, 36 (1983), 1–17 at 1–3. I am indebted to Philippe Canguilhem for this reference.

[77] De Gaetano, *Giambattista Gelli*, p. 144, writes that Gelli 'believed that languages were not a stable phenomenon which should be kept in their original state, but that they evolved constantly according to the environment. Therefore, he was anti-archaistic and rejected forms used even by the best models of the *Trecento* period.' On Grazzini's views of language, see Rodini, *Antonfrancesco Grazzini*, pp. 12–13, 17–18, 89–91.

[78] Pirrotta and Povoledo, *Music and Theatre*, p. 22, observe that 'The humanist poets . . . regarded the musical performance of their verses as a natural extension of the process by which language becomes poetry.'

Tuscan as a living language.[79] Alfonso's interlocutor is Count Fortunato Martinengo of Brescia, a patron of Pietro Aaron's and the dedicatee of his *Lucidario in musica* of 1545.[80] Ironically, the dialogue does not concern music, at least not directly. If we can accept the arguments as representative – and they are more powerful than anything Doni is likely to have engendered on his own – they place Alfonso de' Pazzi in a position diametrically opposed to Bembo. Alfonso touches on the importance of idiomatic expressions and their aptness to different contexts; the necessity of learning the Florentine language by hearing it in the streets, not by piecing it together from books; the degree to which Florentine orthography follows pronunciation, rather than abstruse rules; the way Boccaccio places different vocabularies and even grammars in the mouths of his characters, high, middle and low, according to social significance; and how the purpose of different books requires differential use of language. Overall, Alfonso stresses the specificity of the spoken language in its various manifestations. In underscoring the importance of orality as the essential background for literature, he takes a stance parallel to his views on song: in both cases, art should be grounded in oral practice and the communal life of the city. As for grammatical rules such as Bembo's, he avers that 'It was enough that one wrote well and not too much.'[81]

Varchi did not respond directly in the face of Alfonso de' Pazzi's verbal onslaught, which apparently continued until the latter's death in November 1555. He complains in a 1548 letter to Pietro Aretino, 'Not being able to get me out [of the Accademia], or not wanting to, they leave me in the company of Alfonso de' Pazzi and Niccolò Martelli, and get rid of all my friends.'[82] Varchi's feelings can also be gauged indirectly from his remarks on the poets that

---

[79] Doni, *I marmi*, i, pp. 129–34.

[80] *Lucidario in musica* (Venice, 1545; facs. repr., Bologna, 1969). Aaron spent a month in Brescia in 1539 as the guest of the Martinengho and da Cavriolo families, whom he describes as 'all good singers'; see *A Correspondence of Renaissance Musicians*, ed. B. J. Blackburn, E. E. Lowinsky and C. A. Miller (Oxford, 1991), letter 64, pp. 715–25.

[81] Doni, *I marmi*, i, p. 130: 'Bastava uno che scrivesse bene e non tanto.'

[82] Pirotti, *Benedetto Varchi*, p. 114 n. 1: '[Gli Accademici Fiorentini], non potendo cavarne me [dall'Accademia], o non volendo, per lasciarmi in compagnia di Alfonso de' Pazzi e di Niccolò Martelli, ne cavarono tutti gli amici miei.' The comment probably refers to the expulsion of several members from the Accademia in 1547, most notably Antonfrancesco Grazzini.

he calls *maledici* in the lecture 'Della poetica in generale' of October 1553.[83] His commentary, invoking the authority of Aristotle, illustrates the underlying seriousness with which even jesting words were held within literary circles:[84]

> *Maledici* are all those who, not to reprove vices, as the satirists do, or for another worthy end, but either from their bad nature, or from hatred, or by request, or for money, or for amusement, malign others in writing; and those, Aristotle says, must be expelled from the well-ordered republic, because whoever becomes accustomed to speak evil, becomes accustomed also to do it, and whoever offends someone with words would also, if he could, offend him in deeds.

Neither did Varchi participate directly in the debate on song. He believed that the effect of mensural music could be extraordinary, as a remark in the lecture 'Della tragedia' of February 1554 demonstrates: 'What greater delight can one find, what more useful and laudable refreshment, what more honest and honoured solace to a well-composed soul, than a concordant consort [*concento*] of several diverse voices united, or else truly of several instruments, or of one and the other together?'[85] The word *concento*, or *concentus* in Latin, is a music-theoretical term used to denote counterpoint, while the combination of several voices with instruments alludes to the madrigal or motet. Varchi touches on one of the classic arguments in defence of music, namely that it creates or restores 'un animo ben composto'. He exposes his prejudices against the unwritten tradition, however, in the lecture 'Delle parti della poesia', during the course of an encomium on the dignity and powers of poetry. Varchi realises that, historically speaking, poetry

---

[83] In *Opere*, ii, pp. 681–94, the first in a series of six lectures that Varchi delivered before the Accademia Fiorentina between October 1553 and February 1554. 'Della poetica in generale' is a prefatory survey, followed by 'Lezione prima delle parti della poesia' (ii, pp. 694–701), 'Lezione seconda dei poeti eroici' (ii, pp. 701–9), 'Lezione terza del verso eroico toscano' (ii, pp. 709–20), 'Lezione quarta della tragedia' (ii, pp. 720–7) and 'Lezione quinta del giudizio e de' poeti tragici' (ii, pp. 727–35). Varchi, an expert on classical Greek, takes as his starting point Aristotle's *Poetics*, explicating both what Aristotle meant and how his analyses relate to the sixteenth century.

[84] *Ibid.*, p. 691: 'Maledici sono tutti quelli, i quali, non per riprendere i vizii, come fanno i satirici, o ad altro buon fine, ma o per loro cattiva natura, o per odio, o per preghi, o per danari, o per sollazzo, scrivono male d'altrui; e quelli, dice Aristotile, s'hanno a scacciare dalle repubbliche bene ordinate, perchè chi s'avvezza a dir male, s'avvezza anco a farlo, e chi offende uno colle parole, l'offenderebbe anco, se potesse, co' fatti.'

[85] Varchi, 'Lezione quarta della tragedia', *ibid.*, p. 720: 'Qual diletto può trovarsi maggiore, qual più utile e più lodevole ristoro, qual più onesto e onorato ricreamento a un animo ben composto, che un concordevole concento di più voci discordevoli unite, o veramente di più suoni, o dell'une e degli altri insieme?'

was sung, even though he disparages the itinerant poet-singers
who continue to practise music *all'improvviso*:[86]

> It is not, therefore ... that someone either should be able to judge poetry con-
> temptible, as I have heard that many do, because of its having had a mean and
> weak beginning, being born from those, who, drawn by the desire to imitate and
> by the sweetness of the harmony, used to proceed *ex tempore*, or, as we say, singing
> improvisatorily; or that someone should marvel, that poetry from such humble
> origin and ignoble commencement should rise to such great heights and to such
> manner of excellence, that no greater nor better prize can be bestowed upon the
> praiseworthy works of valorous men, than to be sung by some poet and made
> immortal.

Varchi turns the weapons and values of humanist discourse
decidedly against the practitioners of improvised song. Yet he is
hardly alone in his low estimation of the unwritten tradition. His
colleague Cosimo Bartoli, in the *Ragionamenti accademici*, discusses
a long series of composers, singers of polyphony and instrumentalists, while omitting all mention of singers *all'improvviso*.[87] Only
the instrumentalists, like the organist Baccio Moschini, who are
expected to work with or without musical notation, receive praise
for their skill at playing by ear. Among the composers, Verdelot
is singled out for special treatment, on the basis of personal friend-
ship, and as one whose madrigals achieve a great variety of effects
in their projection of the poetic text, rivalling even Josquin.[88]
Bartoli places direct and explicit emphasis on the practice of written polyphony. He praises, indeed, each of the composers mentioned in the letter of Niccolò Martelli and in the anonymous
Pasquinata. At the same time, he confirms the difficulty of that
music in performance, for a speaker in the *Ragionamenti accademici*,
Lorenzo Antinori, complains of 'voices out of tune, ungraceful and
most of the time not together'.[89]

---

[86] Varchi, 'Lezione prima delle parti della poesia', *ibid.*, p. 695: 'Non è dunque, non è, dis-
cretissimi ascoltatori, che alcuno o possa riputar vile la poesia, come ho sentito, che
molto fanno, per lo avere ella picciolo p[r]incipio e debile avuto, essendo da coloro nata,
i quali dal desiderio tratti dell'imitare e dalla dolcezza dell'armonia, andavano *ex tempore*, o, come noi diciamo, improvvisamente cantando: o debba maravigliarsi, che ella da
sì basso inizio e ignobile cominciamento a tanta altezza salisse e a così fatta eccellenza,
che niuno guiderdone può nè maggiore venire, nè migliore all'opere lodevoli degli uomini
valorosi, che l'essere da alcuno poeta cantate e fatte immortali.'

[87] Haar, 'Cosimo Bartoli', p. 58.

[88] *Ibid.*, pp. 49, 52.

[89] *Ibid.*, p. 53: 'A me piace piu il sonare, perche nello udir Cantare io sento talvolta certe
voci stonate, sgarbate, & il piu delle volte disunite che mi danno un fastidioso mara-
viglioso.'

It is difficult to estimate the effectiveness of Alfonso de' Pazzi's campaign against written polyphony. The relative dearth of madrigalian composition in Florence after 1540 might be taken as a sign of success, the result of a rear-guard action that, because of the Accademia's stature and influence, slowed down the pace of change. Only two composers of note, Francesco Corteccia and Giovanni Animuccia, practised the madrigal in Florence between 1540 and 1560. Corteccia was only 45 when he published his three books of madrigals in 1547, all dedicated to Duke Cosimo I de' Medici (the *Libro Primo de Madriali a quatro voci* of that year was a second, corrected edition), and he composed few madrigals thereafter. It appears that the patronage for madrigalian composition followed the lead of Cosimo I, whose interest in song extended only to celebratory or dramatic works:[90] of Corteccia's 108 published madrigals, as many as forty are theatrical in origin, one is a *mascherata* and six are political in nature.[91] In contrast, Animuccia's *Primo Libro de Madrigali a quatro a cinque et a sei voci*, published that same year, consists predominantly of settings of Petrarch. Only *Il Secondo Libro de i madrigali a cinque voci* of 1551 sets four poems by a member of the Accademia, the refined madrigalist Giovanni Battista Strozzi. Animuccia soon left Florence for Rome, probably in early 1550.[92] Even though the Accademia Fiorentina staged comedies such as Francesco D'Ambra's *Il furto* of 1544, for which Corteccia composed the intermedi, the academy

---

[90] I. Fenlon and J. Haar, *The Italian Madrigal in the Early Sixteenth Century: Sources and Interpretation* (Cambridge, 1988), pp. 85–6. The authors note that 'Cosimo I was interested in the arts as they might serve to glorify his rule and his family, hardly the kind of sympathetic concern that would keep alive the madrigal as we have described it.'

[91] H. M. Brown, 'A Typology of Francesco Corteccia's Madrigals: Notes towards a History of Theatrical Music in Sixteenth-Century Italy', in J. Caldwell *et al.* (eds.), *The Well Enchanting Skill: Music, Poetry, and Drama in the Culture of the Renaissance* (Oxford, 1990), pp. 3–39. I place one of the theatrical madrigals listed by Brown, *Di strani e vari luoghi d'ogn'intorno*, in the category of *mascherata*, following the edition in *Feste musicali della Firenze medicea (1480–1589)*, ed. F. Ghisi (Florence, 1939), pp. 39–43, headed 'Mascherata d'astrologi'. The work is also published in Corteccia, *The Second Book of Madrigals for Four Voices*, pp. 78–80.

[92] The time of Animuccia's departure from Florence can be determined from a *capitolo* by Antonfrancesco Grazzini, 'In lode degli Spinaci', addressed 'A M. Giovanni Animuccia Musico' (*Rime burlesche*, pp. 566–9). The poem, written during Lent (l. 2), contains a dinner invitation to Animuccia. Grazzini mentions the death of Giovanni Mazzuoli, 'il nostro Consagrata' (l. 40), which happened on 5 June 1549. Animuccia must therefore have left Florence after 19 February 1550, the start of Lent the following year. Two other allusions to the Accademia Fiorentina, including Benedetto Varchi (l. 85) and the group known as the Aramei (l. 94), suggest that Animuccia was well familiar with the academy.

probably contributed to the neglect of the polyphonic madrigal in Florence.[93] Two related sets of madrigal partbooks from the 1550s, of Florentine provenance, mitigate the situation, however: they were copied by Giovanpiero Masaconi, a known clerical music scribe, and contain fashionable *note nere* madrigals.[94]

THE DEBATE ON SONG

The particular historical moment of the debate on song results from the collision of two powerful traditions that had coexisted on the Italian peninsula for over a century. In Nino Pirrotta's thesis, the musical performance of serious poetry in the fifteenth century, both Italian and Latin, became the province of the educated humanist and courtier, as well as of the professional *improvvisatore*.[95] Yet throughout the fifteenth century and the first half of the sixteenth, northern-trained singers and composers, especially those from France and the Low Countries, practised the art of musical composition in Italy, largely in the form of Latin masses, motets and French chansons. It was the northern-trained masters – Verdelot, Arcadelt, Willaert, Rore – who were most responsible

---

[93] The texts of the intermedi were by the poet Ugolino Martelli, a long-time friend of Benedetto Varchi. On the three performances of *Il furto* by the Accademia Fiorentina, see De Gaetano, *Giambattista Gelli*, p. 120.

[94] The manuscripts are the subject of a study by Philippe Canguilhem, titled 'The "Libri di Lorenzo Corsini" and the Madrigal in Florence in the Middle of the Sixteenth Century'. The first set of four partbooks, Civitanova Marche, Biblioteca Comunale, Mus. MS 1, lacks only the Basso. As reassembled by Canguilhem, the second, related set includes the Tenor partbook at Civitanova Marche, Biblioteca Comunale, Mus. MS 2, two partbooks in the Bibliothèque Nationale de France (Soprano and Basso) and one at the Newberry Library in Chicago (Alto), lacking only the Quinto. I am most grateful to Dr Canguilhem for discussing his work in progress. On Masaconi, see Fenlon and Haar, *Sources and Interpretation*, pp. 123–6. See also J. Haar, 'The *Note nere* Madrigal', in *The Science and Art of Renaissance Music*, pp. 201–21; originally published in the *Journal of the American Musicological* Society, 18 (1965), pp. 22–41.

[95] See especially N. Pirrotta, 'Music and Cultural Tendencies in 15th-Century Italy' and 'The Oral and Written Traditions of Music', in *Music and Culture in Italy from the Middle Ages to the Baroque* (Cambridge, Mass., 1984), pp. 51–71, 72–9. Recent contributions include Haar, *Italian Poetry and Music*, ch. 4, pp. 76–99; F. A. Gallo, *Musica nel castello: trovatori, libri, oratori nelle corti italiane dal XIII al XV secolo* (Bologna, 1992), pt. 3, pp. 95–140, published in English as *Music in the Castle: Troubadours, Books, and Orators in Italian Courts of the Thirteenth, Fourteenth, and Fifteenth Centuries*, trans. A. Herklotz and K. Krug (Chicago, 1995); A. M. Cummings, 'The Sacred Academy of the Medici and Florentine Musical Life of the Early Cinquecento', in I. Alm *et al.* (eds.), *Musica Franca: Essays in Honor of Frank A. D'Accone* (Stuyvesant, NY, 1996), pp. 45–77; Brandolini, *On Music and Poetry*.

for the development of the polyphonic madrigal. The predominance of the madrigal, influenced in the course of its later development by the poetics of Pietro Bembo, derived in its turn from the study of Petrarch's *Canzoniere*, was apparent across Italy by 1540. Alfonso de' Pazzi raised the issue of 'la dolce Musica senza Note' within the Accademia Fiorentina because he wished to revive the older tradition of poetic performance, one that had been so strongly associated with Italian poetry and humanism at the turn of the century. As Martelli remarks, Alfonso 'ritrovò anchora insino alla Musica senza note'. And the *Pasquinata* calls him 'Primo inventore di quella Armonia', which may be translated as 'the foremost creator of that harmony'. In other words, the tradition was so weakened that extraordinary efforts were required to revive it. The controversy in the Accademia Fiorentina corroborates Pirrotta's view because it demonstrates not only that the two traditions were viewed as very different from one another, but that writers on either side saw them in the light of their cultural origins. More broadly, the mid-sixteenth century was a time in which literate culture of all kinds threatened to supplant ways and means of creation that depended on orality. One has only to think of the contemporaneous rise of instrumental notation to realise the profound significance of the changes.

Writing towards the end of his life, even Benedetto Varchi presented a different view of music *all'improvviso* in the unfinished dialogue *L'Hercolano*, c.1565:[96]

> I never heard anything that moved me more inside and seemed more wonderful (and I am old and have heard a few things) than the singing extemporaneously to the lira of M. Silvio Antoniano, when he came to Florence with the Most Illustrious and Excellent Prince of Ferrara, Don Alfonso d'Este, son-in-law of our Duke, by whom he was not only kindly recognised but most generously compensated.

The passage illustrates that the practice of performing poetry via the medium of improvised song did not die out in the second half of the sixteenth century, at least among professional singers. The tradition remained especially strong in Naples, among celebrated

---

[96] B. Varchi, *L'Hercolano, dialogo di Messer Benedetto Varchi, nel qual si ragiona generalmente delle lingue, & in particolare della toscana, e della fiorentina, composto da lui sulla occasione della disputa occorsa tra 'l commendator Caro, e M. Lodouico Casteluetro* (Florence, 1570), pp. 272–3; cited and trans. in Palisca, *Humanism in Italian Renaissance Thought*, pp. 375–6.

performers such as Luigi Dentice and the Sienese singer Scipione del Palla, teacher of Giulio Caccini.[97] But we need to ask why *improvvisatori* like Silvio Antoniano, Alfonso de' Pazzi and Scipione del Palla elicited such praise, and further, why the issue of music notation became the focus of debate.

Reinhard Strohm writes of the fifteenth century that 'The audience – patrons and humanists – were not interested in knowing whether the tune had been learned from a written copy or not, and to a musician this made no difference either.'[98] This hypothetical indifference to music notation certainly did not hold true in Florence of the 1540s. The *Pasquinata* focuses on the writing of music because it denotes a different process – musical, social and physical – than that employed by the *improvvisatori*. When the singer also functions as creator, even as he adapts common or standard musical materials to each performance of a poem, a direct, physical communication results between the performer and audience. In the formulation of literary theorist Paul Zumthor, orality enables 'the reciprocity of relationships that are set up between interpreter, text, and audience member during performance, and that provoke the interaction of each of these three elements with the other two in a common game'.[99] As a result, the performance embodies the poetic voice and generates social meaning. Even though the music Iacopo de' Servi sang before Pope Leo X is irrecoverable, any virtuoso would have developed his own manner and style of musical creation, relying perhaps as much on his virtuosity with the viola da gamba or other instrument as on the voice. The intensity of experience for the audience would only be increased when, as in the case of Iacopo, the performer-creator also acted as poet. In Italy, the figure of the poet-singer dates at least as far back as Francesco di Vannozzo in the late Trecento, who wrote several sonnets in colloquy among the poet, his lute and his harp.[100] The immediacy of creative power as much as their virtuosity helps explain the acclaim bestowed on such musicians.

[97] See D. G. Cardamone, 'The Prince of Salerno and the Dynamics of Oral Transmission in Songs of Political Exile', *Acta musicologica*, 67 (1995), pp. 77–108; Brown, 'Geography', pp. 147–68; Pirrotta and Povoledo, *Music and Theatre*, pp. 197–201.

[98] R. Strohm, *The Rise of European Music, 1350–1500* (Cambridge, 1993), p. 550.

[99] P. Zumthor, *Oral Poetry: An Introduction*, trans. K. Murphy-Judy (Minneapolis, 1990), p. 185.

[100] Edited in *Le rime di Francesco di Vannozzo*, ed. A. Medin (Bologna, 1928), nos. xxix, xxx, xxxiii–xxxvii.

Moreover, virtuosity itself can lead to marked differences of musical style, in the form of highly embellished melodic lines that, like the ornamentation of a Corelli violin sonata, change with each performance.

Musical notation, on the other hand, offers unsurpassed contrapuntal, harmonic, motivic and structural control, especially in four or more voices. Such characteristics lead the *Pasquinata* to call 'la Musica con le Note cosa artifitiosa' (fol. 177^v). It requires heavy investment of time and resources, and the end result oftentimes is poor. But the criticism goes further. The *Pasquinata* focuses on the matter of ink, rastrals and varnish, on the fact of notation itself, because it breaks the link between performer and audience. Notation erects a barrier between singers and listeners, for composition appropriates the act of creation to itself, confines it to another time and place. The singing of a notated work thereby acquires a different social and musical significance; hence the opposition to any form of song, even *arie*, dependent on notation.[101] The song becomes an object, symbolised by the spectacles of Varchi and Corteccia. It takes on the nature of hermetic display rather than communal experience. Moreover, according to Alfonso de' Pazzi and Niccolò Martelli, notation falsifies the Tuscan language, rendering poetry unintelligible in part because it engenders a complexity of musical relationships, at the expense of the poem. Criticisms of the artificiality of the madrigal find echoes in other writers, notably Gioseffo Zarlino, who defends the humanist values of accompanied song, and Vincenzo Galilei, who advocates simpler styles of song as models for a new art.[102]

Despite the survival of the art of the *improvvisatore* into the later sixteenth century, in one respect the debate on song marks the end of an epoch. After 1555, the figure of the poet-singer seems to have vanished from literary circles. Though his poetic output is almost

---

[101] Zumthor, *Oral Poetry*, p. 197, observes that 'The oral text, from the very fact of its modes of preservation, is less appropriable than the written text; it constitutes a common good within the social group wherein it is produced.' The process is illustrated by the widespread currency of stock bass harmonies such as that in Example 1, where the bass is combined with another stock element, the 'Aria di Sonetti'.

[102] On Zarlino, see the quotation in n. 74, above. On Galilei, see C. V. Palisca, 'Vincenzo Galilei and Some Links between "Pseudo-Monody" and Monody', in *Studies in the History of Italian Music and Theory* (Oxford, 1994), pp. 346–63, originally published in *Musical Quarterly*, 46 (1960), pp. 344–60; and I. Cavallini, 'Sugli improvvisatori del Cinque-Seicento: persistenze, nuovi repertori e qualche riconoscimento', *Recercare*, 1 (1989), pp. 23–40 at pp. 26–7.

entirely satirical in nature, Alfonso de' Pazzi counts as one of the last Italian poets to improvise settings of his own works, apart from such entertainers as in the commedia dell'arte.[103] The shift signals a broadening chasm between music and poetry: each was entrusted to specialists whose understanding of the corresponding art was potentially minimal, or at least significantly different. As a character remarks in Doni's *Dialogo della musica*, 'Perhaps singers who know as little of facts as they do of words (for them *sol mi fa re* would be words enough) are just satisfied with singing.'[104] The attribution of skill, rather than artistry, to singers of polyphony arises from the traditional distinction between *cantor* and *musicus*, a distinction based on different levels of priority and understanding in the relationship between the two arts. The known *arie di cantare* are formulaic, highlighting poetic structure and rhythmic flexibility rather than, as in the madrigal, the expressive and mimetic potential of individual lines, words, or word sounds. Even Corteccia's *Io dico et diss' et dirò* (Example 2), with an *aria* in the soprano, underscores the structural integrity of the poem. Again, the humanist ideal of the singer to the lute or lira da braccio was to create a unity of word and tone, which could be most fully realised (even in satire) by the performance of the poet himself.

The clash of ideals and values within the Accademia Fiorentina thus plays itself out in a number of different, primarily satirical ways. Only afterwards did the professionalization of roles help to sever the ties between two arts that, as Varchi remarks, 'have the greatest amity, or rather they are relatives, the one with the other'.[105] Still, the high regard in which song was held shows itself on both sides of the controversy. The conflicting views of that relationship bring us back to the point that far more and varied musicmaking went on than we have ever been aware of. In Florence, the seriousness, and the humour, of the debate demonstrate that the unwritten traditions did not fade quietly.

Cary, NC

---

[103] On the prominence of musical entertainers, including the *ciurmadori* and *cantimbanchi*, see Cavallini, 'Sugli improvvisatori del Cinque-Seicento', pp. 27–32.

[104] Doni, *Dialogo della musica*, p. 82; trans. Haar, 'Notes on the *Dialogo della musica*', p. 292: 'forse i Cantori che non sanno più di fatti, che di parole (a lor basta a raggiare sol mi fa re), restano sodisfatti a questo e non cercano più là.'

[105] Varchi, 'Delle poetica in genere', in *Opere*, ii, p. 690: 'Hanno la musica e la poetica grandissima amistà, anzi più tosto parentado l'una coll'altra.'

Robert Nosow

APPENDIX

Document 1. Anonymous, *Pasquinata*, in Florence, Biblioteca Nazionale Centrale, MS II.I.107 (Magl. VIII, 48), fols. 177ʳ–179ᵛ

Reverendi, et Magnifici Signori Musici con le Note

Acciò che voi siate consapevoli quanto me dolga, che le cose rare è perfette siano sottoposte al biasimo d'ogni folle giuditio come è il vostro, Non hò volsuto mancare scrivervi la presente, perche à quelli che la leggeranno sìa il paragone della Verità, à voi la stampa della Vergogna, et à mè solo la contentezza d'abbatere con le ragioni la caterva di voi tutti che, fuor' d'ogni buon costume, et creanza, lacerate il Nobilissimo Messer Alfonso, De Pazzj, Governatore à Bacchetta della Sicilia, et Primo inventore di quella Armonia, che vi fà ire Pazzi di Rabbia, crepare d'Invidia è morire di Gelosia: Al quale più si converriono tutte le lodi, tutte le dignità, et tutti gli honori, che à quel Babbuasso di Josquino, à quel Castrone di Gomberto, et à quella pecoraccia di verde lotto da voi tenuti in tanto pregio, et veneratione; Dipoi che dal Fonte del suo raro ingegno s'è versato la perfetione della dolce Musica senza Note, nella quale si sono in vano affaticati tanti elevati, et generosi spirti senza havere mai possuto penetrare quanto hà penetrato il suo continuo ghiribizzo. [C]osa certo meritevole di porgergli Sacrificcij, è incensi, et consecrarli mille, et mille statue d'oro, et d'Arcento per fare l'in immortale. [O]nde si puote ben gloriare la presente, et dolersi la passata etade; l'una d'essere alzata à tanto honore, l'altra d'essere stata priva di tanto bene; percioche in quella, senza dubbio, non gli mancavono le vere lodi; come in questa è falsi biasimi, poi che malevoli, et invidiosi che ci ne vadia altero, cercate lacerarlo, et affogarlo nella vera sciocca, et arrogante oppinione: Mà questo come saggio Nocchierj con la Nave della sua Musica, et con i remi de [177ᵛ] I rari concetti, s[']è ito schermendo talmente dalla tempesta delle vostre frenesie, che à mal grado di voi hà ritrovato il porto. Ne vi basta questo, Ne la dolcezza di quella, Ne le tante varie comparatione che lui in difesa del vero vi hà allegat[o]; che ancora star' volete ostinati nella Babbuaggine che vi mostra à dito, ne potete, ne dovete negarlo, mà come presaghi che cedendo cascherete nel centro del Vituperio, contrafatti coloro che vogliono più presto consumarsi à poco, à poco nella passione de Tormentj; che confessar[e] il furto che li torrebbe la Vita, tal che essendo di poi vinti dalle passionj confessando più de quello havevon fatto si muoiano disperatj. Tal avverra à voi, che doppo l'haver negato il fondamento et la dottrina della Musica Alfonsale, rinnegherete IDio cedendoli, domandandogli venia, et pregandolo vi faccia partecipi di tal dote. Onde egli che si vorrà giustamente, vendicare, vi terrà in sulla Cruccia di Compiacervi[;] ne potendo cantare la sua per non la sapere ne la vostra per Vergogna, vivendo in speranza vi morrete cacando, riportandone la fama, et l'honore che meritate: Mà sè con dritto Giuditio discoressi quanto, è, quale sia l'ingegno humano, non vi parria difficile che lui fusse stato, sia et possa essere in questa, et in maggiore cosa perfetta. Ne considerate che rare sono quelle cose della Natura che cedino all'Arte: Adunque essendo la Musica con le Note cosa artifitiosa, et trovata in questo Mondo da quel Filosofo, mercè di quei Fabbrj imbriachi, doverrà cedere alla naturale trovata Da Dio nell'altro, la quale senza Note, senza righi, et senza pause muove il cielo con tanto ordine, et così come essa si regge in Aria per essere cosa Celeste[.] [178^r] Così questa Alfonsale si regge con l'Aria del suo contrappunto, et Giuditio miracoloso, è quando tal Ragione non fussi bastante che è senza Dubbio, à empiervj l'orecchie, le quali turate per non udire il vero, Guardatene le migliaia che vi si parono innanzi le quali per fuggire la fatica; non allego, Voi non sentistj mai dir', ne sentirete che la Musica con le Note habbia contro all'loro natura le costume mosso è [i] montj, ne fermati i fiumi dal corso loro, come sentirete dire di quella che è in Cielo: la melodia che sparse il Trace mitigando le furie infernali, non hariano fatto il profitto, è la maraviglia che fecero se vi fussi stato una sol Nota: Nè erà la natura dei Sassi andare per l'Aria da loro stessi veloci; niente dimeno alle Thebane mure si raunorno al concento dell'Armonia Alfonsale: Non sapete voi che, i Greci anticamente usorno, et hoggi usono per più Brevità cantare in sulle dite? [E]t i Turchi nelle loro Mosche intuonono gli hinni di Macometto con certi segni che fanno nel Muro? Vegnjamo alli Animali Brutti. Non si vede egli tutto il giorno fare infinite, è nuove Musiche à quattro ò sei Ucceletti, solo con l'istinto naturale seguendosi l'un' l'altro? che direste voi se un' Pecoraio che non sentì mai ricordare la Musica, Rusticamente, come gli porse la Natura havessi imparato, à sonare un' zufolo tanto bene che per suo piacere insegnava ballare à una Pecora la quale, sentendo quella vera, et naturale Musica, movendosi à tempo faceva mille Giuochi? è lui hà insegnato cantare à Grilli? che alle Ranocchie che ne Pantani fanno si risonante Coro? chi alle Cicate, et Draganelle? chi alla serena che fà addormentare i Balordi che da lei si lassono sommergere? [C]hi Pubblicassi che uno Stornello dicessi l'Ave Maria, et una Ghiandaia [178^v] Cantassi la bella Franceschina, sarebbe lapidato[.] Mirate le zanzare che mai ti pugnerebbono prima se non ti facessino una serenata di Musica Alfonsale intorno à gli orechi, con tanta dolcezza che ti con[s]tringe à dormir' perche esse ti possino poi à l'hor' mondo mascherar' il Viso, et però quell'Arfasatto del Burchiello non senza Misterio, disse nel principio d'un' suo Sonetto le zanzare cantavono

Robert Nosow

il Teddeo, ò benedetta, et recolenda memoria di Grifone Tamburino, che congegnasti una Musica si bella d[i] Cani constringendoli à cantare Alfonsalmente, e portar le voci piu alte tal hora, che essi non harian voluto. Pigliamo hora l'Instrumenti. Non sonate voi con la pratica dell'orecchio il Trombone? Non fate voi in su quattro Note di Canto fermo, con la fantasia un Mar di Note senza fondo? Non havete sentito accordarsi Quattro, ò sei Trombetti senz' oprari Tasti o Note, ma col fiato solo con mirabil dolcezza, et Unione variando sovente le voci hor alto, hor basso? chj è quello che, per grosso che ci sia, n[on] sappia son[a]re il Cembolo, le Staffetti, la Zampogna, il Guscio di Tellina, le Nacchere[,] el Tamburo sopra qual si voglia suono, senza scordare una Dramma oprando solo il tempo, et l'Orecchio? chi narrassi havere veduto un' horiuolo in Avignone con Dodici Campane è Campanelli sonar[e] senza contrapesi in Musica di molte Canzone saria tenuto heretico. Non havete mai visto sonare senza Musica il Dabbuddà con le Cascagne? et chi sta in Dubbio che frà voi la Maggiore parte non lo suoni per Eccellentia? Non mi pervenne mai all'orecchie di quel Contadino che stridere faceva si dolcemente un' Cacapensieri? ò se queste, et infinite altre cose che io lasso in dietro Maggiori, vedete, sentite, è toccate perche non volete Credere [179^r] Che uno Alfonso, de Pazzi, che tiene nel Capo à livel di Chiesa, le Girandoli, i Ghiribbizzi, le Soffisticherie, i Capigiri, le Frenesie, i Bisquizzi, i Frinfri, i Castellui a i Capricci, e le Strafizzeche, possa col miracolo della Natura, con le doti del Ciel è con l[']influssi de['] pianeti ascendere al Grado perfetto della Musica senza Note[;] nella quale non si scombicchera tante piastre, Non si getta via tanto tempo à noi si caro, Non si fà tanti spartimenti di Note. Non s'aggira com' un Arcolaio dietro à Beffabemi, è Cessolfaut. Non si rinnega Christo à rigare con pettini tanti Libri, logorando l'inchiostro, è gettando via la Vernice: Non si perde la patienzia à copiari Canzoni[,] Non si spezza il Capo per salire, è scendere dietro alle Crome, è semiCrome, Non s'impazza per cercare dove sta la Chiave, et la Toppa; ponendo mente se[']l Bimmolle è entrato in corpo à Natura acuta: Non ti dan briga i Sospiri, non t'affogano i tormenti nel fare conto delle pose. Non ti dibatti con le Mani, è con piedi dietro alle Battute, Non si stilla la memoria nell'inventione dell'Arie et de contrappunti: Non si caca il Sangue à provare una Canzon' x volte, è cantarla male Undici[.] Non si ricomincia da Capo à peticione delle rimesse che ti son fatte addosso. Non s'adopera gli occhiali come il Corteccia, Mà solo con la Maestria, con la maniera è con la Breve Reg[o]la Alfonsale diventi partecipe del ben del Cielo: et che sia la stessa Verità sè la Cecilia, come Santa, et Donna dà bene, vorrà dire il vero non hebbe mai dopo la sua Edificatione maggiore honore, più gran pompa che il contento che gli hà fatto gustare la Musica: Alfonsale, et di qui

218

puote ogn'uno comprehendere che sia nato [179ᵛ] la Benivolentia di quei fratelli eleggendolo per le sue Virtuti et lodevoli costumi per governatore, sottomettendosi col freno de suoi discorsi à tutte le sue voglie, et voi stessi ne potreste fare fede, mà per usurparli quella grandezza che se li pervenne, et alla quale potrebbe, come si spera in breve, salire, fate S. Pietro, non volendo approvare la Verità, non volendo cederli alle sue ragioni, et non volendolo amare riverire, et adorare per vostro maggiore, privandolo di quelli honori, et di quelle debite reverentie che si li converrebbero, mà Vostro fia il danno con la Vergogna insieme, sue le glorie, et mia la fatica; et facendo fine aspetterò che questa habbia à fare in voi quel frutto che io desidero, non meno per suo honore; che per buon zelo del debito et benifitio che vi s'aspetta—Di Roma il di 30 di 7embre MDx[l]iiij

Pasquino Patritio Romano —

Document 2. Niccolò Martelli, letter to Alfonso de' Pazzi, 30 January 1545, in *Il primo libro delle lettere* (Florence, 1546), fols. 71ʳ–72ʳ

ALL'ETRUSCO

Io che non hò altre lettere che quelle ch'io m'arrecai dalla fossa del peccato, e insomma non sono altro che capricci, penna, e inchiostro. Scrivo à voi che componete à ghiri, etrusco galante; che vi havete saputo procacciare (oltr' al bel nome proprio d'Alfonso) un cognome, che non hà il triviale o 'l dappoco; perche quello Etrusco, hà un certo che di brusco, che apporta grandezza mirabile: tal ch'ogn'altro nome Heroico, Greco, ò Latino, suona meno assai; & gli doverrian ceder tutti di gran lunga; che per antico ò Fiesolano che e sia, non se l'è saputo mai appropriare altri che lo stratagemma del vostro cervello. Il quale ritrovò anchora insino alla Musica senza note; lassando à Carpentras & à Iosquino, & à gli altri erranti la lor zolfa; che chi prima tal no[71ᵛ]me gli pose, non sognava; però che e' pescon con le scale le voci in aria. Et nel vero l'harmonia del canto, non è altro che la soavità d'una dolcezza che proferisce per gli organi corporei, con una certa gratia & aria celeste la temperia unita dell'anime nostre, della quale vogliano i gran Savi (che forse manco seppono) che noi tegniamo parte di qualità, di modo, che chi canta hoggi per b quadro & per b molle, & più borgio che colui che voi citate ne i vostri gran Sonetti à ghiri. Dove vorreste saper Se le Cipolle, son dolci ò forti ò di mezzo sapore, E qual fu prima Abate ò ver Priore, Che chiamasse le Tonache Cocolle. Con quel che segue, & similmente in quell'altro mirabile, havendo un capo à ghiri, et considerando insino à gli An[i]mali che vanno co i suon grossi diceste: Che se 'l nome di colui

219

arrivi & suoni Dove le genti à noi volgan le piante Dica di gratia perche il Liofante Camina con le nacchere et co i suoni Et che anchor vi dica perche i tuoni Non son' un tempo in Ponente e 'n Levante Et che vi mostri il testo dove Dante Abborrisce le Prediche e i Perdoni. Et sic de singulis, dicono i Privilegi & gli stazzoni. Ma noi parlavamo della Musica et siamo entrati in un'altro Mondo. I hò paura che andando per questa via, il mio scrivere, non sia come il vostro comporre à ghiri. Pure ritrovando alquanto l'uscio, lasciamo lor le lor nuote intorno al collaretto (che in lingua nostra suonon macchie) et attegniamoci al canto, se e fosse ben quello del vostro casato, & vedrete gran seguito che noi haveremo à petto à loro, davanti che e sia mezzo Agosto. Et senza dirvi altro per hora, farò fine. Ma innanzi ch'io faccia cotal punto; non voleste voi gia riformare il Zodiaco? o mirabile Etrusco; chi è quello che insino à qui, habbia havuto mai tal'animo? Taccia lo impiumarse d'Icaro & di Dedalo, & forse ancho l'audacia di Phetonte? poi che 'l vostro molto piu bello humore, alzato da i ghiri ha voluto por mano insino à i Cieli, & non hà volsuto stare contento, come sono stati tanti Secoli, & pappatosi tanti età à quei primi che tai segni nel Zodiaco posero: parendovi che'l vostro AMBRAINO, col quale benche e fosse Cavallo, poetavi per eccellenza, vi stesse cosi bene come quella Pecora del Montone, o 'l Granchio ò lo Scarpione: trovando mille altre piu belle inventione, che non trovaron quelle genti grossi. Et se tal ghiri non hebbe dipoi effetto, vi è stato pur bello honore il tentarlo; se non per altro, per farvi conoscere senza pari: che insino al gran Portio Napoletano super ethera notus vi predica, vi loda, vi essalta, & dice che sete in tra i rari rarissimo; perche caminate per un sentiero co i vostro ghiri, non presso piu anchora da alcuno mortale; si che vedete in che modo si diventa piu c'huomo, & dalla fama nostra à quella di Mona Honesta da Campi, non ci sarà vantaggio alcuno; & io mi v'offero per terzo, col mio comporre ladramente, piu tosto che lambiccando le stitiche, superstitione della lingua nostra; sapendone il mal grado & la mala gratia à i Cacastecchi, se mai le leggerano. Di Fiorenza a di XXX di Gennaio MDXLV Nicolo Martelli.

Document 3. Girolamo Amelonghi, Il Forabosco, excerpt from letter 'Al Famoso et Etrusco de pazzi', 15 April 1547, in Florence, Biblioteca Nazionale Centrale, MS Magl. VII, 678, fols. 2^v–4^v

Dicano adunque quel vogliano perche a me basta solamente satisfar' a voi famossissimo et stravagantissimo Etrusco a cui non debbo meno che alla fortuna che mi vi fece esser' vicino percioche prima non cominciai a praticarvi che il mio cervello quasi a sembianza del vostro divento laberinto di girandole Umbicco di strattagemme, è guarda robba di chimere voi, se vi ricorda, foste il primo ch'apprendere mi feste con tanta facilità la dolce musica sanza note, voi et non altri m'insegnaste promis[cu]are à catafascio et comporre nel modo che vedete, giurandome che un sonetto haveva à essere cominciato con Interzetti et finito con i quadernali, mostrandomi per ragioni filosofiche che il poetare à ghiri, oltre al piacere che porta seco è bramato da ogn'uno, per non essere sottoposte come gl'altri stili a gravità di sentenze, à forbite lingue, à sofistichi argomenti et finalmente, à velenose, et masticate censure, voi me feste capace, come si havev[a]no affare le comedie recitarle, et ado[r]narle dandomi l'inventioni de i canti carnovaleschi con le mascherate de le buffole, voi mi persuadesti che a non volere perdere giamai gli speroni facessi, mettere due punte à miei si come voi à i vostri stivale voi mi deste ad intendere che a volere star' caldo il verno tenessi nel letto tutta notte i zoccoli à calcagnini et portassi il giorno per casa come voi sopra la camicia una certa guarnacciaccia de albagio che mettendola per il capo sino à i piedi agiugnessi, voi mi disegnaste ancora et mi faceste apparare à giucare con le nuove, et strogiloti pochitissime carte che volete se adoperino à primiera dove In vece di quadri, cuori, picche, Et fiori hanno à dipignersi Ranochi, Pappagalli, Ghiri et pipistrelli; et tante altre fantasie che io per brevita lasso à dietro di raccontare.

Early Music History (2002) Volume 21. © Cambridge University Press
DOI:10.1017/S0261127902002061 Printed in the United Kingdom

EMILIO ROS-FÁBREGAS

THE CARDONA AND FERNÁNDEZ DE CÓRDOBA COATS OF ARMS IN THE CHIGI CODEX

The Chigi Codex occupies a place of honour among music manuscripts of the Renaissance; thirteen masses by Ockeghem along with *L'homme armé* masses by Josquin, Busnoys, Brumel and Compère figure prominently among its contents. According to Herbert Kellman, it was copied between 1498 and 1503 for the Burgundian nobleman Philippe Bouton.[1] Several coats of arms of

An earlier version of this paper, concerning the Cardona coat of arms only, was read at the Annual Meeting of the American Musicological Society (Session of the International Hispanic Music Study Group) in Minneapolis (27–30 October 1994) and at the 23rd Conference on Medieval and Renaissance Music (University of Southampton, England; 5–9 July 1996). I should like to thank Flynn Warmington for sharing with me her knowledge about heraldry in the early stages of my research; her comments helped me enormously in the preparation of that version of this paper. I should also like to thank Professor Herbert Kellman for encouraging me in Minneapolis to extend my research to the Fernández de Córdoba shields in the manuscript. A later version of the paper with my findings about the Fernández de Córdoba coats of arms was first presented in Spanish at the Congreso Internacional Poder, Mecenazgo e Instituciones en la Música Mediterránea, 1400–1700 (Ávila, Fundación Santa Teresa, 18–20 April 1997) and then in English at the conference Burgundian-Habsburg Court Complex of Music Manuscripts (1500–1535) and the Workshop of Petrus Alamire (Leuven, 25–8 November 1999).

[1] H. Kellman, 'Introduction', *Vatican City, Biblioteca Apostolica Vaticana, MS Chigi C VIII 234* (Renaissance Music in Facsimile, 22; New York and London, 1987), p. vi: 'The coat of arms on f. 249v—the only one in the manuscript not overpainted—and the motto on ff. 281v–282 which originally read "Ung soeul Boutton" reveal that the Chigi Codex was prepared for Philippe Bouton (1418–1515), *Seigneur* of Corberon, a Burgundian nobleman and cousin of Olivier de la Marche, who served all the dukes of Burgundy from Philip the Good (his godfather) to Philip the Fair, and reached high rank and prestige under Charles the Bold.' See also H. Kellman (ed.), *The Treasury of Petrus Alamire: Music and Art in Flemish Court Manuscripts, 1500–1535* (Ghent and Amsterdam, 1999), pp. 125–7. Kellman announces that the full results of his research will appear together with a critical edition of the Chigi Codex by Edward F. Houghton in the series Monuments of Renaissance Music (University of Chicago Press). Earlier literature about the manuscript is cited in H. Kellman, 'The Origins of the Chigi Codex: The Date, Provenance, and Original Ownership of Rome, Biblioteca Vaticana, Chigiana, C.VIII.234', *Journal of the American Musicological Society*, 11 (1958), pp. 6–19; see also the *Census-Catalogue of Manuscript Sources of Polyphonic Music, 1400–1550*, 5 vols., compiled by the University of Illinois Musicological Archives for Renaissance Manuscript Studies (Renaissance Studies, 1; Stuttgart, 1979–88), iv, pp. 12–13.

the Spanish families Cardona and Fernández de Córdoba appear in different places in the manuscript and Kellman suggested that the transfer of the Chigi Codex to the Spaniards occurred after the death of its first owner in 1515.[2] Seven works, the foliation in the upper right margin of the recto folios and a table of contents with a heading that reads *Tabla de missas y motetes* were added by a Spanish scribe.[3] Since Mouton's motet *Quis dabit oculis*, written on the death of Anne of Brittany in 1514, is also among the added works, Kellman concluded that these additions to the Chigi Codex were made after that date. The assumption that the manuscript travelled to Spain is further supported by a seventeenth-century inscription written in Italian on the flyleaf of the manuscript, which affirms that the book was used in Spain.[4]

The new evidence presented here regarding the Cardona coat of arms suggests that the post-1514 additions to the manuscript were made, not, as traditionally assumed, in Spain, but rather in the Spanish milieu of the viceroyalty of Naples. Similarly, the identification of the three members of the Fernández de Córdoba family whose coats of arms, painted over those of the Bouton family, appear on folios 3^v and the beautifully illuminated 19^v–20^r further supports the Spanish-Neapolitan connection of the manu-

[2] Kellman, *The Treasury of Petrus Alamire*, p. 125: 'Fols. 3v, 19v–20, 56, 107, 143v, 249, and 281v–282, originally carried the arms of Philippe Bouton, Seigneur of Corberon, and one or another of his mottos, *Ung seul Bouton*, *Souvenir tue*, and *Au fort aille*. All these, except the arms on fol. 249v [Cardona], were later overpainted with the arms of the Spanish family Fernández de Córdova, and the mottos *Ung seul Dieu*, and *Infrangibile*.'

[3] The seven works added by the Spanish scribe are: *Regina celi letare* (anon., fols. 53^v–55); *Sancta trinitas unus deus* (Févin, fols. 87^v–88); *Quis dabit oculis nostris* (Mouton, fols. 136^v–139); *Ave Maria gratia plena* (Ockeghem, fols. 139^v–140); *Ave Maria gratia plena* (Compère, fols. 140^v–142); *Asperges me domine ysopo* (Madrid, fols. 284^v–286); and *Vidi aquam egredientem de templo* (anon., 286^v–287).

[4] The Italian inscription reads as follows: 'Libro di musiche di varie messe, e di mottetti di Autori francesi, scritto in Francia: usato in Spagna, che il foglio primo dell'Indice, che si trova dà principio è in lingua spagnola siccome ancora i tre ultimi fogli pare scritti in Spagna, circa il 1490. La musica è stimata molto buona, le miniature sono bizzarre, e di mostri, e di corpi ridicole per molte margini del d[ett]o libro. Quanto al nome Infrangibile, e le armi, che si trovano dipinte in esso . . . .' Kellman, 'Introduction', p. xi, translates this inscription as follows: 'Music book of diverse Masses, and of motets, by French composers, copied in France, used in Spain—since the first folio of the index, as is seen from its beginning, is in Spanish—and also the last three folios surely written in Spain, around 1490. The music is reputed to be very good, the miniatures are fanciful, with monsters and ludicrous bodies in many borders of the book. As to the word "Infrangibile," and the arms, which have been painted into it.' Fabio Chigi, who became Pope Alexander VII in 1655, acquired the manuscript, and Kellman suggests that his librarian might have added this inscription.

script and opens new vistas regarding the music patronage of the Spanish nobility. Although it is not known how the manuscript came into the possession of the Cardona/Fernández de Córdoba family, a possible history of transmission can be suggested, opening up still further lines of enquiry.

In the upper left margin of folio 284ᵛ, the Chigi Codex bears the coat of arms of an unidentified member of the Spanish Cardona family (see Figure 1a and the detail in Figure 1b). The Cardona family was one of the most illustrious of the Catalan nobility. A brief explanation of the different branches of the family will help to clarify the problem of identifying the coat of arms in the Chigi Codex. Figure 2 shows the family tree of the four branches of the Cardona family during the fifteenth and early sixteenth centuries.[5] They stem from Hug I, first Count of Cardona and Baron of Bellpuig. He passed these two titles on to two of his sons. Hug II and his descendants received the title of Baron of Bellpuig and constituted the Cardona-Anglesola branch of the family. Another son, Joan Ramon Folc, inherited the title of Count of Cardona and thus continued the main branch of the Counts and later Dukes of Cardona. From a third son, Antoni, descended the branch of the Cardona Counts of Collesano and Chiusa. Finally, from a son of the second count of Cardona descended the branch of the Marquises of Guadalest and Castellnou. At the time the additions were made to the Chigi Codex, many members of the branch of the Dukes of Cardona living in Barcelona held leading ecclesiastical and military positions in the Crown of Aragon (Figure 3). In the Catalan Parlament, known as the *corts*, the Duke of Cardona presided over the other delegates of the nobility. In 1515 a half-brother of the Duke, Pere Folc de Cardona, became Archbishop of Tarragona. This position was the highest ecclesiastical title in the Crown of Aragon, and it was accompanied by the honorary distinction of Chancellor of the king's entire administrative organisation in the territory. The archbishop's palace in Barcelona served as residence for royal visitors; his library and garden were praised in epigrams by Martí Ibarra, an influential Latin

---

[5] The information about the Cardona family tree has been taken from a much more detailed tree presented by the prestigious Catalan historian and heraldry specialist A. de Fluvià, 'Cardona', *Gran enciclopèdia catalana* (Barcelona, 1973), iv, pp. 404–5.

Figure 1a   Coat of arms of the Cardona family on folio 284ᵛ of the Chigi Codex.
© Biblioteca Apostolica Vaticana (Vatican)

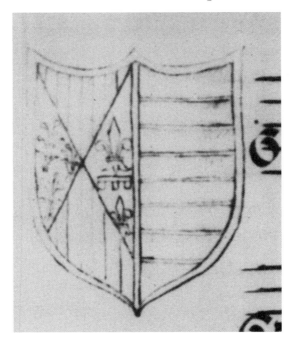

Figure 1b Detail of the Cardona coat of arms

teacher in Barcelona.[6] Close study of the manuscript Barcelona, Biblioteca de Catalunya, M.454, revealed that at least part of the manuscript may have been compiled for the Archbishop Pere Folc de Cardona before 1525.[7]

---

[6] Martí Ibarra contributed to the 1522 edition of the Catalan adaptation of the Latin dictionary by Antonio de Nebrija (1444?–1522). The first person to refer to Ibarra's epigrams was J. Villanueva, *Viaje literario a las iglesias de España* (Madrid, 1902), xi, pp. 141–2, who consulted this now-lost volume in the nineteenth century; according to him the epigrams were annotated by Juan Rollano Tamaritense and published in Barcelona by Carlos Amorós in 1512. Menéndez Pelayo, *Antología de poetas líricos castellanos*, 14 vols. (Madrid, 1916–24), x, p. 29, who did not see the volume, stated that it was stolen from the Biblioteca Colombina and sold in Paris in 1885 and later in Rome. He gives the title as follows: *Martini Iuarrae Cantabrici Orationes quae Crustula inscribuntur. Et ad reges Epigrammata at Saphica ad Marq . . . Impressum ex nouello prototypo Barcinone per Carolum Amorosium impressorem solertissimum tertio idus Augusti. Anno M. D. XI*. Since Villanueva stated that the exemplar he consulted had been published in 1512, he probably saw a different publication of Ibarra's works. He cited one of the epigrams in which Ibarra praises the archbishop Pere Folc de Cardona's library and garden above those of Numa and Caesar, mentioning Numa's *Sylva Capena* in Rome, dedicated to the Muses.

[7] E. Ros-Fábregas, 'The Manuscript Barcelona, Biblioteca de Catalunya, M.454: Study and Edition in the Context of the Iberian and Continental Manuscript Traditions' (Ph.D. diss., The City University of New York, 1992); a revised edition will be published by Reichenberger.

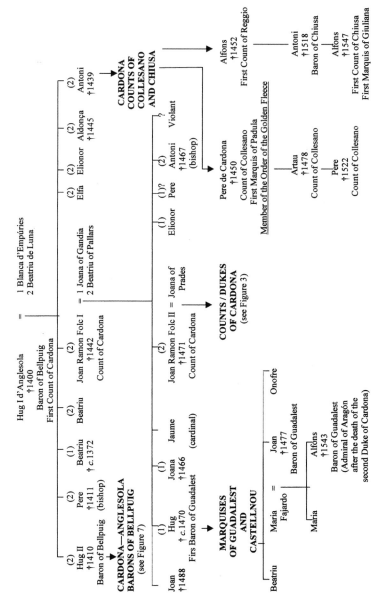

Figure 2   The four branches of the Cardona family tree during the fifteenth and early sixteenth centuries
After A. de Fluvià, 'Cardona', *Gran enciclopèdia catalana* (Barcelona, 1973), iv, pp. 404–5

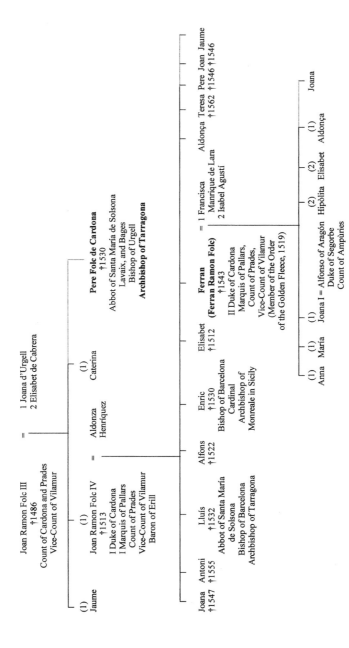

Figure 3   Family tree of the Dukes of Cardona in the early sixteenth century
After de Fluvià, 'Cardona', iv, pp. 406–7

229

The archbishop's elder brother, Joan Ramon Folc (d. 1513), was the first Duke of Cardona, a title he received, together with that of 'grandee' of Spain, from the Catholic Monarchs in 1491. His marriage to Aldonza Enríquez (an aunt of King Ferdinand) produced twelve offspring, some of whom were active as patrons of the arts and letters.[8] For instance, the *Libro de música práctica* by the Spanish theorist Francisco Tovar (d. 1522), published in Barcelona in 1510, was dedicated to the Duke's twenty-seven-year-old son, Enric Folc de Cardona, bishop of the city, who in 1522 left for Rome and later became a cardinal.[9] Ferran Ramon Folch, second Duke of Cardona, became a member of the Order of the Golden Fleece during the meeting that took place under Charles V in Barcelona in 1519, and, given the association of the Order with *L'homme armé* masses,[10] it might be posited that Chigi was brought to Barcelona for that occasion and was connected with the second Duke of Cardona.[11] It is striking that the only meeting of

[8] For a survey of the relationship between members of the Cardona family and humanists and Catalan literary figures, see J. Rubió y Balaguer, *Els Cardona i les Lletres, discurso leído el día 7 de abril de 1957 en la recepción pública de D. Jorge Rubió y Balaguer en la Real Academia de Buenas Letras de Barcelona* (Barcelona, 1957), pp. 15–42. A compilation of works in prose and verse by Pere Moner published in 1529 was dedicated to Ferran Folc, second Duke of Cardona. According to Rubió, 'Els Cardona', pp. 35–6, Moner, a Catalan from the now-French region of Rousillon, had already died when his 1529 publication appeared; the compiler, his cousin Miquel Berenguer, dedicated it to the second Duke of Cardona, but the poet himself had been in the circle of the first Duke, Joan Folc de Cardona. Another of his works (*La noche*), of dubious quality according to Rubió, was dedicated to Joana Cardona. Menéndez y Pelayo, *Antología de poetas líricos castellanos*, x, p. 383, refers to Moner as a prolific bilingual poet of the late fifteenth century, imitator of Juan del Encina but of a lesser category. See also J. Rubió i Balaguer, 'Humanisme i Renaixament', *VIII Congreso de Historia de la Corona de Aragón* (Valencia, 1–8 October 1967), III: *La Corona de Aragón en el Siglo XVI* (Valencia, 1973), ii, pp. 9–36.

[9] F. J. León Tello, 'Tovar, Francisco', *The New Grove Dictionary of Music and Musicians* [hereafter *New Grove II*], 2nd edn, 29 vols., ed. S. Sadie (London, 2001), xxv, p. 664, states that Tovar, an Andalusian theorist active in Catalonia, was attached to Barcelona Cathedral in 1510, and that he became *maestro de capilla* at Tarragona Cathedral, where he remained until 1516. Tovar also had appointments in Seville (1518) and Granada (1521). His book is influenced by Guillermo de Podio's *Ars musicorum* (1495), a work printed in Valencia but dedicated to the Bishop of Tortosa in the province of Tarragona; see H. Anglés, 'La notación musical española en la segunda mitad del siglo XV: un tratado desconocido de Guillermo de Podio', *Hygini Anglés Scripta Musicologica*, 3 vols., ed. J. López-Calo (Storia e letteratura, 131–3; Rome, 1975–6), iii, pp. 1143–70.

[10] L. Perkins, 'The L'homme armé Masses of Busnoys and Ockeghem: A Comparison', *Journal of Musicology*, 3 (1984), pp. 363–91; W. Prizer, 'Music and Ceremonial in the Low Countries: Philip the Fair and the Order of the Golden Fleece', *Early Music History*, 5 (1985), pp. 113–53; and R. Taruskin, 'Antoine Busnoys and the *L'homme armé* Tradition', *Journal of the American Musicological Society*, 39 (1986), pp. 255–93.

[11] Regarding the meeting of the Order in Barcelona, see E. Ros-Fábregas, 'Music and Ceremony during Charles V's 1519 Visit to Barcelona', *Early Music*, 23 (1995), pp. 375–91;

the Order of the Golden Fleece in Spanish territory took place in Barcelona, and that the manuscript Barcelona 454 is the only Iberian source for the *L'homme armé* Mass by Busnoys, a work that, according to Richard Taruskin, is very closely connected to the Order. Coincidentally, Barcelona 454 is the Iberian manuscript that shares the greatest number of concordances with the Chigi Codex and the reading of Busnoys's *L'homme armé* mass, despite its errors, is the only one that agrees with that in the Chigi manuscript in transmitting the correct mensuration signs for the Christe and the Benedictus; these signatures, as pointed out by Taruskin, play a crucial role in the overall structure of the mass and constitute the fundamental ground for preferring Chigi to all other sources.[12]

The coats of arms of the members of the Order of the Golden Fleece painted in 1519 above the back seats of the choir at Barcelona Cathedral are still extant. Even at a glance, the coat of arms in the Chigi Codex in Figure 1b and the coat of arms of the second Duke of Cardona (Figure 4) do not match.[13] A description of the shield of the second Duke of Cardona, however, serves to clarify some important points regarding the arms of the Cardona family in the Chigi Codex.

The shield of Ferran Ramón Folc, second Duke of Cardona, is divided per quarterly. In the first and fourth quarters the combined arms of Cardona and Urgell are repeated; the arms of Urgell (one of the oldest counties of Catalonia) came from his grandmother's family. On the second and third quarters the crowned double-headed eagle stands for his recently acquired possessions as Marquis of Pallars.[14] A separate shield on the upper left corner

---

see also W. F. Prizer, 'Charles V, Philip II, and the Order of the Golden Fleece', in B. Haggh (ed.), *Essays on Music and Culture in Honor of Herbert Kellman* (Paris, 2001), pp. 161–88, esp. pp. 180–5.

[12] For an edition and detailed discussion of the structure of Busnoys's mass and its connection with the Order, see A. Busnoys, *Collected Works. The Latin-Texted Works*, ed. R. Taruskin (Masters and Monuments of the Renaissance, 5; New York, 1990); see also Taruskin, 'Antoine Busnoys and the *L'homme armé* Tradition', pp. 255–93.

[13] To illustrate the coat of arms of the second Duke of Cardona I am using the one published in J.-B. Maurice, *Le blason des armoiries de tous les chevaliers de l'Ordre de la Toison d'Or* (The Hague, 1665), p. 178.

[14] According to V. Balaguer, *Historia de Cataluña* (Madrid, 1886), vi, pp. 267–8, the original counts of Pallars were declared traitors in 1491 and their title was taken away and given – elevated to that of Marquis of Pallars – to the Duke of Cardona.

Figure 4   Coat of arms of the second Duke of Cardona, member of the Order of
the Golden Fleece in 1519, published in J.-B. Maurice, *Le blason des armoiries de tous
les chevaliers de l'Ordre de la Toison d'Or*
(The Hague, 1665), p. 178. By permission of the Houghton Library,
Harvard University

in Figure 4 shows that, at the time, the arms of Cardona alone
consisted of a shield divided per saltire with the four bars of Aragon
in the first and fourth compartments, three thistles [in Spanish
'cardos', hence the name Cardona] in the second compartment,
and a field of fleurs-de-lis in the third compartment to indicate
that the Anjou were among their ancestors. This compartment
with the fleurs-de-lis bears a so-called label of cadency that looks
like a small bridge. These marks of cadency served either to dif-
ferentiate the shield of the head of a family from that of other
relatives or to distinguish one branch of the family from the senior
line. The Cardona connection with the Anjou dynasty, however,

goes back to the Middle Ages.[15] Thus, this particular label of cadency in the field of fleurs-de-lis had become an integral part of all Cardona shields very early in the history of the family, and by the sixteenth century had no specific meaning to identify a particular individual: all Cardona coats of arms should bear this mark of cadency in the field of fleurs-de-lis. Sometimes the mark is omitted, as can be seen in the same shield of the second Duke of Cardona in the choir stalls of Barcelona Cathedral (Figure 5); it is identical in all details to the printed version of 1665 (Figure 4) except for the mark of cadency, which is missing. Since the original coats of arms at Barcelona Cathedral were restored in the eighteenth century, it might well have been overpainted at that time.[16] This branch of the Dukes of Cardona can thus be discarded as possible owners of Chigi, since the coat of arms of the second Duke of Cardona, the head of the family around the time of the additions to the Chigi Codex, does not match the one in the manuscript. Furthermore, there is no ecclesiastical heraldry in the Chigi coat of arms to suggest that any of the Cardona bishops and/or archbishops in Barcelona were responsible for the additions.

Another coat of arms of a distinguished individual from a different branch of the Cardona family, namely that of the counts of Collesano and Chiusa, should be considered here. Pere de Cardona, Count of Collesano (d. 1450), was also a member of the Order of the Golden Fleece and thus his coat of arms appeared in Jean-Baptiste Maurice's book devoted to the heraldry of the members of the Order (Figure 6).[17] An important detail is the

---

[15] B. J. Llobet, in his *Genealogía de la nobilissima casa de Cardona* (Barcelona, 1665), fol. 1ᵛ, gives a summary of the early history of the family: 'aviendose conservado en esta de Cardona con tanta continuación el nombre de Fulcon (que es lo mismo que Folch en lengua catalana) mudandole de propio en patronimico, que era el que mas usaron los Condes de Anjou y aviendose siempre usado por armas y blason un campo azul sembrado de flores de lis de oro y un yugo rojo, que son las propias de aquellos Condes, como se ha visto después en otros de aquel titulo, que han sido Reyes de Nápoles y Condes en Provença . . . [fols. 5ᵛ–6] . . . De donde se saca con toda evidencia que el primero que dio principio a esta casa se llamo D. Ramon Folch y fue el primero de este nombre y hijo de Fulcon, Conde de Anjous, y que entro en Cataluña en tiempo del Emperador Carlomagno, y le dio principio en la Ciudad de Girona con el patronimico Folch antes del año del señor 792.'

[16] R. Piñol Andreu, *Heráldica de la Catedral de Barcelona* (Barcelona, 1948), copied the Duke of Cardona's coat of arms from the one in the choir stalls of Barcelona Cathedral, unaware of the missing label of cadency.

[17] Maurice, *Le blason des armoiries*, p. 52.

Emilio Ros-Fábregas

Escudo de Fernando Ramón Folch, duque de Cardona.
Véase la descripción en el índice.

273

Figure 5   Coat of arms of the second Duke of Cardona in the choir at Barcelona
Cathedral, as copied by R. Piñol Andreu,
Heráldica de la Catedral de Barcelona (Barcelona, 1948), p. 273

234

Figure 6   Coat of arms of Pere de Cardona (†1450),
Count of Collesano and Chiusa and a member of the Order of the Golden Fleece,
published in Maurice, *Le blason des armoiries*, p. 52. By permission of the
Houghton Library, Harvard University

presence of the same label of cadency in the field of fleurs-de-lis found in the shield of the other branch of the family. This confirms that the mark is an integral part of the Cardona field of fleurs-de-lis independent of both its location within the shield or the branch of the family to which a particular individual belonged. The mid-fifteenth-century coat of arms of this Cardona is also very different from the one in the Chigi Codex, and the other two Counts of Collesano who came after him (listed in Figure 2) could not have had, through family alliances, a coat of arms like the one in Chigi. Thus, this branch of the family should also be discarded.

The member of the Cardona family who owned the Chigi Codex in fact belonged to the branch of the Cardona-Anglesola, the

Barons of Bellpuig (Figure 7). The Cardona arms in the manuscript are those of Ramón Folc de Cardona (1467–1522), Viceroy
of Naples between 1509 and 1522. In 1503 he had joined forces
with Gonzalo Fernández de Córdoba in the siege of Gaeta (Naples)
and continued to help him in his Italian campaign. In 1505 he
commanded another successful expedition to conquer Mazalquivir

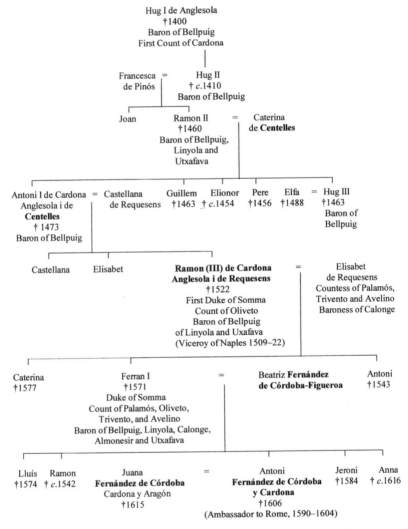

Figure 7   Family tree of the Cardona-Anglesola, Barons of Bellpuig
After de Fluvià, 'Cardona', pp. 396–7

in north Africa. He later distinguished himself as commander of the armies of the Holy League in the war against Venice, and then against France in 1511. Although his army was defeated at the famous battle of Ravenna in 1512, the death of the French commander Gaston de Foix in that conflict allowed him to rebuild his forces to lead the invasion of Tuscany, bringing the Medici back to power in Florence.[18] Though Ramón de Cardona died in Naples, he was buried in the town of Bellpuig – the family's ancestral home – in the Catalan province of Lleida.[19] His wife, Elisabet de Requesens,[20] commissioned his sepulchre in Carrara marble, built in Naples by Giovanni Merliano da Nola and then taken to Bellpuig (Figure 8a).[21] It is one of the most notable examples of Renaissance Italian art in the Iberian peninsula, and the coat of arms on this sepulchre matches the one in the Chigi Codex (Figure 8b).[22]

A comparison between the shield in the Chigi Codex and the one on Ramón de Cardona's tomb shows that both shields are

---

[18] One of the strophes in the *canción* 'França cuenta tu ganançia' by Juan Ponce in the Cancionero Musical de Palacio (Madrid, Biblioteca Real, II-1335) refers to that famous battle: 'En aquella de Revena, / do tanta sangre se vido, / tú te llevaste el sonido, / nosotros la dicha buena./ ¿Cómo no te quedó almena? /¡Par mon alma, je no sé! / Pues yo te lo contaré' (In that of Ravenna, where so much blood was seen, you took the sound, we, the good news. How come you were left without battlements? My soul, I don't know! Then I will tell you.)

[19] On Ramón de Cardona, see M. Ballesteros-Gaibros, *Ramón de Cardona, colaborador del rey católico en Italia* (Madrid, 1953). See also 'Libro donde se trata de los vireyes lugartenientes del Reino de Nápoles y de otras cosas tocantes a su grandeza, compilado por José Raneo (1634) e ilustrado con notas por D. Eustaquio Fernández de Navarrete', in *Colección de documentos inéditos para la historia de España*, xxiii, ed. D. Miguel Salvá (Madrid, 1853), pp. 42–64; and G. Coniglio, *I viceré spagnoli di Napoli* (Collana di Cultura Napoletana, 16; Naples, 1967), pp. 18–29.

[20] A portrait entitled *Juana de Aragón* (1518) attributed to Rafael in the Louvre seems to be in fact a portrait of Elisabet Requesens, and the artist is most likely Giulio Romano. I should like to thank professor Carmen Morte at the Universidad de Zaragoza for this information.

[21] R. Pane, *Il Rinascimento nell'Italia meridionale*, 2 vols. (Milan, 1977), ii, p. 181, suggests that the possible models for Merliano da Nola might have been the altar at the Santo Spirito in Florence and Cardinal Ascanio Sforza's tomb at Santa Maria del Popolo in Rome, both made by Andrea Sansovino between 1490 and 1505. See also V. Serra Boldú, *Lo Convent de Bellpuig* (Lleida, 1908) and E. Tormo, 'El sepulcro de Don Ramón Folch de Cardona en Bellpuig (Lérida)', *Boletín de la Real Academia de la Historia*, 87 (1925), pp. 288–91.

[22] Illustrations of Ramón de Cardona's tomb in art books are too small to see the coat of arms; it is also placed too high in order to see it *in situ*. I was fortunate enough to find a large poster of it published by the Department of Culture of the Generalitat [Government] of Catalonia as part of a series dedicated to Catalan monuments.

Figure 8a   Ramón de Cardona's tomb at the Convent of
Sant Bertomeu in Bellpuig (Lleida). By kind permission of the Generalitat
de Catalunya

Figure 8b   Detail of Ramón de Cardona's coat of arms on his tomb

divided per pale (that is in half), with the dexter side (left) also divided quarterly per saltire; the sinister side is barry of four horizontal bars. The identical shape of the shield and the bordure or border around it is sometimes borne as a mark of difference. On the dexter side of the shields can be found the now familiar Cardona arms: the bars of Aragon in the first and fourth compartments, the thistles in the second, and the field of fleurs-de-lis in the third. Although the compartment with the three thistles is partly damaged and difficult to see on the tomb, there is no doubt that the Cardona coat of arms must carry the thistles in that compartment. The only difference between the two shields is the label of cadency in the field of fleurs-de-lis in the fourth compartment. While the shield in the Chigi Codex carries the mark, the shield

239

on the tomb does not, or at least it is not visible. As stated before, however, for the purposes of identifying a particular individual within the family, the absence of this label of cadency in the shield of Ramón de Cardona is not important, since it is assumed that it pertains to all the members of the Cardona family. It is not possible to ascertain whether the sculptor Giovanni da Nola was incorrectly instructed about this detail in the coat of arms or whether he simply overlooked it. As was the case with the coat of arms of the second Duke of Cardona in the choir stalls of Barcelona Cathedral, this label of cadency is sometimes omitted.

The four horizontal bars on the sinister side of the shield (right) stand for the Centelles family of the Viceroy's grandmother. It should be pointed out that the most commonly found Centelles coat of arms differs from the example here, but there is a variant of the Centelles shield in which the sinister side of the arms also consists of four bars like those in the coat of arms in the tomb of the Viceroy.[23] Thus, in the same way that the coat of arms of the second Duke of Cardona contains the arms of Urgell from his grandmother, the shield of the Viceroy of Naples incorporates those of Centelles also from his grandmother.

As shown in Figure 1a, the scribe who added the Cardona coat of arms on folio 284^v of the Chigi Codex also drew the profile of a man's head with a helmet in the bottom margin. In the introduction to the facsimile edition of the manuscript, Kellman asked whether this drawing might have been 'a sketch of the owner'.[24] This sketch is not dissimilar to the profiles of Neapolitan viceroys as they appear on sixteenth-century coins.[25] The comparison of this sketch with an undated portrait of Ramón de Cardona (Figure 9) offers no definitive answer to Kellman's question.[26] At first the two figures seem to depict two different people, but the sketch portrays a mature man of arms, not a young man, and this fits

---

[23] See 'Centellas' in A. and A. García Carraffa, *Enciclopedia heráldica y genealógica hispano-americana*, 88 vols. (Madrid, 1919–63).

[24] Kellman, 'Introduction', p. ix.

[25] See the coin with Andrés Carafa's profile in 'Virreyes de Nápoles que figuran en las medallas del siglo XVI, conservadas en el Museo Arqueológico Nacional', *Numario hispánico*, 1 (1952), p. 199.

[26] Ramón de Cardona's portrait appears in D. A. Parrino, *Teatro eroico de' governi de' viceré del regno di Napoli dal tempo del re Ferdinando il Cattolico fino al presente* (Naples, 1692). The portraits of Neapolitan viceroys in this publication were made after those that were formerly in the Royal Palace in Naples, but later destroyed.

Figure 9   Anonymous portrait of Ramón de Cardona, Viceroy of Naples, in
D. A. Parrino, *Teatro eroico de Vicerè di Napoli* (1692)

very well with what is known about the Viceroy as commander of Ferdinand's army in Italy. Ramón de Cardona would have been approximately fifty years old at the time of the additions to the manuscript, and his age would also be consistent with that of the man in the drawing. At least the sketch does not in itself contradict the identification of the owner as the Viceroy Ramón de Cardona.

If the Cardona coat of arms in Chigi can be taken as that of the Viceroy of Naples, it can be concluded that the addition of seven works (as well as of the foliation and the table of contents) took place in the Spanish milieu of the Viceroyalty of Naples no later than 1522, the date of the Viceroy's death. How the Viceroy acquired the manuscript is difficult to ascertain. Since he had been fighting the French successfully for many years, possibly the Chigi Codex came to him as the booty of war, but it seems that the Bouton family was not involved in the Italian campaign. Ramón de Cardona maintained a lavish court in Naples, and an anonymous novel, *Question de amor*, first printed in 1513, affords a glimpse of the court life there. This mixture of novel and chronicle presents historical characters using fictitious names; Benedetto Croce was the first to disentangle who was who in the novel.[27] The work concludes with a description of Ramón de Cardona's impressive army going to the battle of Ravenna with a retinue that included a chapel of twelve singers with drums and Italian trumpets.[28] The

---

[27] B. Croce, *La Spagna nella vita italiana durante la Rinascenza* (Bari, 1968), pp. 127–53. The protagonist Belisena is in fact Bona Sforza, daughter of Gian Galeazzo and Isabella of Aragón. The narrator Vasquirán (Vazquez?) meets another Spaniard, Flamiano, in love with Belisena. The question presented is who suffers more, the one whose loved one is dead or the one whose love is unrequited. All sorts of games, letters and discussions are introduced; the narrative features, under fictitious names, the illustrious Spanish and Italian members of Neapolitan society, such as: Fabrizio e Prospero Colonna, don Carlo of Aragón, the Prince of Bisignano and of Melfi, the dukes of Ferrandina, Bisceglie, Atri, Termoli, Gravina and Traetto; the marquises of Pescara, Padula, Nocito, Bitonto, Atella; the counts of Monteleone, Avellino, Potenze, Popoli, Soriano, San Marco, Matera, Cariati, Trivento; Antonio de Leyva, Juan Alvarado, the prior of Messina Pedro de Acuña, Diego de Quiñones, Ettore and Guidone Ferramosca, Fernando Alarcón, Geronimo Lloriz, Geronimo Fenollet, Luigi Ixar and Gaspare Pomar. Among the ladies there are Giovanna of Aragón, widow of King Ferrante 'il vecchio', and her daughter of the same name, widow of King Ferrantino, the widowed Princess of Salerno, Marina of Aragón, the duchess of Francavilla Costanza d'Avalos, the duchesses of Gravina and Traetto; the marchionesses of Pescara, Vasto, Padula, Bitonto, Laino, and Nocito; the countesses of Venafro, San Marco, Capaccio, Matera, Soriano, Trivento and Terranova.

[28] A modern edition of *Questión de amor* was published by M. Menéndez y Pelayo, *Orígenes de la novela*, 4 vols. (Nueva Biblioteca de Autores Españoles, 7; Madrid, 1907), ii, p. 91:

Viceroy was also praised by Bartolomé Torres Naharro in his *Psalmo en la gloriosa victoria que los españoles ovieron contra venecianos* – presenting him as the hero at the battle of Motta in 1513 – and by the Catalan poet Romeu Llull in the collection of poems known as *Jardinet d'Orats*.[29]

Being able to document Ramón de Cardona's chapel of twelve singers, as mentioned in *Question de amor*, would certainly place the Chigi Codex in a musical context, but most of the Neapolitan archival material from the early sixteenth century has been destroyed.[30] Moreover, the identity and activities of the Spanish composer Madrid, whose *Asperges me* appears in the same folio as the Cardona coat of arms, are not known. At least three musicians with the name Madrid are active at this time: the rebec player Diego or Juan de Madrid who served Queen Isabella; Juan Fernández de Madrid, a singer in the royal Aragonese chapel between 1479 and 1482; and perhaps the most likely candidate, Juan Ruiz de Madrid, a singer in the same chapel between 1493 and 1501.[31] There are two complete rosters ('Libretti di salari

'Lleuaua su capilla con doze cantores muy complida. Lleuaua sus atauales e trompetas ytalianas, con todo los conplimentos de su casa e criados ordinarios como se requeria.' (His accomplished chapel of twelve singers accompanied him. He took with him his drums and Italian trumpets, with all that was necessary for his household and ordinary servants as was fitting.) For a discussion of *Questión de amor*, see also *Orígenes de la novela*, ibid., pp. 48–54. Regarding the contacts between Spain and Italy during this period, see M. Menéndez y Pelayo, 'Primeros contactos entre España e Italia', 'Historia Parthenopea. Las tristes reinas de Nápoles. Tratado de Educación de Galateo', and 'Cartas de Italia', in *Estudios y discursos de crítica histórica y literaria*, v, prepared by E. Sánchez Reyes, in *Edición nacional de las obras completas de Menéndez Pelayo*, x, ed. M. Artigas (Santander, 1942), pp. 275–353.

[29] On these two authors, see *Bartolomé Torres Naharro (ca. 1476–ca. 1524), Antología (teatro y poesía)*, ed. M. Á. Priego (Badajoz, 1995); and *Jardinet d'Orats* [microform], Barcelona, Biblioteca de Catalunya, Ms. 151, ed. S. Gascón (Barcelona, 1998).

[30] The basic reference work for music in fifteenth-century Naples is A. W. Atlas, *Music at the Aragonese Court of Naples* (Cambridge, 1985). D. Fabris, 'El nacimiento del mito musical de Nápoles en la época de Fernando el Católico', *Nassarre*, 9/2 (1993), pp. 53–93, presents among other things a table with Neapolitan events that took place between 1492 and 1522 for which there is mention of instruments or music making; he also comments upon the scarce extant documents regarding Naples in the early sixteenth century. See also J. Mateu Ibars, 'La documentación virreinal para el estudio del gobierno aragonés-austríaco en el reino de Nápoles', *Atti del Congreso internacionale di studi sull'età aragonese* (Bari, 15–18 Dec. 1968) (Bari, 1972), pp. 111–42; J. E. Martínez Ferrando, *Privilegios otorgados por el Emperador Carlos V en el reino de Nápoles* (Barcelona, 1943); and A. Calabria and J. A. Marino (ed. and trans.), *Good Government in Spanish Naples* (American University Studies, ser. 9, History, 71; New York, 1990), pp. 15–32.

[31] T. Knighton, 'Madrid, Juan Fernández de', *New Grove II*, xv, 544–5. Four villancicos, a Gloria and three motets are ascribed to 'Madrid' in various late fifteenth-century manuscripts.

243

ordinari') at Simancas Archive with payments to the entire viceroyal household and army in Naples for the years 1512 and 1514, but no one in the rosters is described as a singer; among the people who served regularly appear four 'trombetti bastardi' and four 'ministriles', as well as the 'cappellano maggiore', an administrative position more than a musical one. Perhaps some of the people paid there were also active as singers, but it is not possible to establish this.[32]

The coats of arms of the Fernández de Córdoba in the Chigi Codex must now be considered. The basic coat of arms of this family is barry of three horizontal red bars on a field of gold. This coat of arms appears several times throughout the manuscript, and was painted over the Bouton family coat of arms; Figure 10 shows the only Bouton coat of arms in the manuscript that was not over-painted. The three Fernández de Córdoba shields on folio 3[v] and in the opening of the illuminated folios 19[v]–20[r] are particularly important since they contain additional heraldic attributes that permit the identification of three different members of the family to whom they belong. The shield on folio 20[r] (see the opening of folios 19[v]–20[r] in Figure 11) has two heraldic elements that help to identify its owner. First, there is the rope or cord surrounding the shield. According to the *Enciclopedia heráldica* this rope indicates that the shield is that of a woman; moreover, the particular way in which this rope forms knots around the shield and the crown shows that the woman was a widow.[33] The second heraldic element is the crown itself surmounting the shield; this particular crown is that of a duchess. With this information, and after a detailed

---

[32] R. Magdaleno Redondo (*Papeles de Estado de la correspondencia y negociación de Nápoles. Catálogo XVI del Archivo General de Simancas* (Valladolid, 1942), p. 3) cited a 'Relación de salarios ordinarios que se dan en Italia'; indeed this 'Relación', dated 1514, is found in the legajo E 1004-50 and contains these payments. On p. 6, among the 'Officiali che servono ordinariamente', are found:
A quattro trombetti bastardi a d[uca]ti 60 per uno . . . 240
A quattro ministreri a d[uca]ti 69 uno di essi et li tre a d[uca]ti 52 per uno . . . 240 [*recte* 225]
In another similar payroll, 'Notamento deli salari et provisione se pagano in la tesoreria Regia del Reyno de Napole', also at the Archivo General de Simancas, Legajo E-1004-80, there is a payment to 'quatro trompete' and 'quatro ministrili'; this time each is paid 60 ducats. In both payrolls Joan Maria Poderico, Archbishop of Taranto, is paid 200 ducats as 'capellano maggiore'. The payrolls include payments to the additional one or two trumpeters accompanying other army captains (sixteen trumpeters altogether in the 1514 payroll), but there is no list of singers.
[33] García Carraffa, *Enciclopedia heráldica*, i, pp. 193–4.

Figure 10   Detail of the Bouton coat of arms on folio 149ᵛ of the Chigi Codex.
©Biblioteca Apostolica Vaticana (Vatican)

reading of the three volumes written by Francisco Fernández de Béthencourt devoted to this family, it is clear that the only woman of the different branches of the Fernández de Córdoba who had the title of duchess in the early sixteenth century was Doña María Manrique, Duchess of Terranova.[34] She was the wife of the famous Gonzalo Fernández de Córdoba, Duke of Sessa, better known as El Gran Capitán, and one of the most distinguished military figures of early sixteenth-century warfare. He participated in the wars leading to the conquest of Granada and especially in the Italian campaigns against the French in Naples between 1495 and 1504; appointed viceroy of Naples in March of 1504, he was recalled to Spain by King Ferdinand in 1507. His enforced retirement in Granada was only broken briefly in 1512, after the defeat of Ramón de Cardona at the battle of Ravenna.[35] Since he died in 1515, the shield of his widow must have been added after that date.

The coats of arms on folios 3ᵛ (Figure 12) and 19ᵛ (Figure 11) in the Chigi Codex share a heraldic attribute not found in the other shields in the manuscript: a small black figure surmounting the helmet with a pomegranate (symbol of Granada) in his hand. This figure represents the Moorish King Boabdil el Chico (or el Niño), a boy Moorish king captured at the battle of Lucena (province of Córdoba) in 1483. He was captured by two members of two different branches of the Fernández de Córdoba family (see the family tree in Figure 13a, the Line of Cabra, under number 2, and the Line of the Alcaides de los Donceles, under number 3); both had the same name, Diego Fernández de Córdoba: one was an elderly man, the other a young member of the family. As a

[34]   F. Fernández de Bethencourt, *Historia genealógica y heráldica de la monarquía española, casa real y grandes de España*, 10 vols. (Madrid, 1897–1920), vi, vii and ix.
[35]   *Ibid.*, vi, pp. 136–64.

Figure 11   Folios 19ᵛ–20 of the Chigi Codex with two different coats of arms of the Fernández de Córdoba family. ©Biblioteca Apostolica Vaticana (Vatican)

reward for the capture of the Moorish king, the Catholic Monarchs Isabella and Ferdinand allowed them to have, from then on, his figure depicted chained to the shield of their respective families. Only these two branches of the Fernández de Córdoba family carry

246

Figure 11 *Continued*

this distinction.[36] Thus the owners of Chigi should be among the descendants of those who captured the Moorish king. The only

[36] For a description of the battle of Lucena and the subsequent meeting of these two members of the Fernández de Córdoba family with the Catholic Monarchs, see *ibid.*, vii, pp. 44–50, and ix, pp. 39–45.

247

Figure 12   Folio 3ᵛ of the Chigi Codex with yet a different coat of arms of the Fernández de Córdoba family (compare with Figure 11). ©Biblioteca Apostolica Vaticana (Vatican)

difference between the coat of arms in folios 3ᵛ and 19ᵛ of the Chigi Codex is the rope surrounding the shield in the latter folio. As mentioned, this rope means that it is the shield of a woman.[37] She is most likely the wife of the man who has the same coat of arms without the rope on folio 3ᵛ (see Figure 12), since women often adopted the arms of their husbands. Who, then, is this Spanish couple who owned the Chigi Codex?

Taking into account the identification of the coat of arms on folio 20ʳ as that of María Manrique, it can be suggested that this couple is Elvira Fernández de Córdoba and Luis Fernández de Córdoba, daughter and son-in-law respectively of El Gran Capitán (see the family tree in Figure 13b, under family lines 1 and 2).

---

[37] Flynn Warmington pointed out in discussion at the Leuven conference that men could occasionally have similar attributes in their shields. However, it would seem inconsistent to have two coats of arms in the same manuscript referring to the same person but with only this difference.

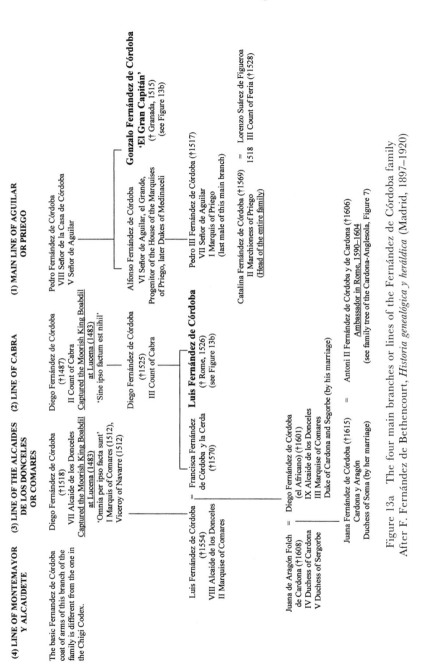

(4) LINE OF MONTEMAYOR Y ALCAUDETE

The basic Fernández de Córdoba coat of arms of this branch of the family is different from the one in the Chigi Codex.

(3) LINE OF THE ALCAIDES DE LOS DONCELES OR COMARES

Diego Fernández de Córdoba (†1518)
VII Alcaide de los Donceles
Captured the Moorish King Boabdil at Lucena (1483)
'Omnia per ipso facta sunt'
I Marquis of Comares (1512), Viceroy of Navarre (1512)

Luis Fernández de Córdoba (†1554)
VIII Alcaide de los Donceles
II Marquise of Comares

= Francisca Fernández de Córdoba y la Cerda (†1570)

Juana de Aragón Folch de Cardona (†1608)
IV Duchess of Cardona
V Duchess of Sergorbe

= Diego Fernández de Córdoba (el Africano) (†1601)
IX Alcaide de los Donceles
III Marquise of Comares
Duke of Cardona and Segorbe (by his marriage)

Juana Fernández de Córdoba (†1615)
Cardona y Aragón
Duchess of Soma (by her marriage)

(2) LINE OF CABRA

Diego Fernández de Córdoba (†1487)
II Count of Cabra
Captured the Moorish King Boabdil at Lucena (1483)
'Sine ipso factum est nihil'

Diego Fernández de Córdoba (†1525)
III Count of Cabra

Luis Fernández de Córdoba († Rome, 1526)
(see Figure 13b)

= Antoni II Fernández de Córdoba y de Cardona (†1606)
Ambassador in Rome, 1590–1604
(see family tree of the Cardona-Anglesola, Figure 7)

(1) MAIN LINE OF AGUILAR OR PRIEGO

Pedro Fernández de Córdoba
VIII Señor de la Casa de Córdoba
V Señor de Aguilar

Alfonso Fernández de Córdoba
VI Señor de Aguilar, el Grande,
Progenitor of the House of the Marquises
of Priego, later Dukes of Medinaceli

Pedro III Fernández de Córdoba (†1517)
VII Señor de Aguilar
I Marquis of Priego
(last male of this main branch)

Catalina Fernández de Córdoba (†1569)
II Marchioness of Priego
(Head of the entire family)

= Lorenzo Suárez de Figueroa (†1528)
1518   III Count of Feria

Gonzalo Fernández de Córdoba 'El Gran Capitán'
(† Granada, 1515)
(see Figure 13b)

Figure 13a   The four main branches or lines of the Fernández de Córdoba family
After F. Fernández de Bethencourt, *Historia genealógica y heráldica* (Madrid, 1897–1920)

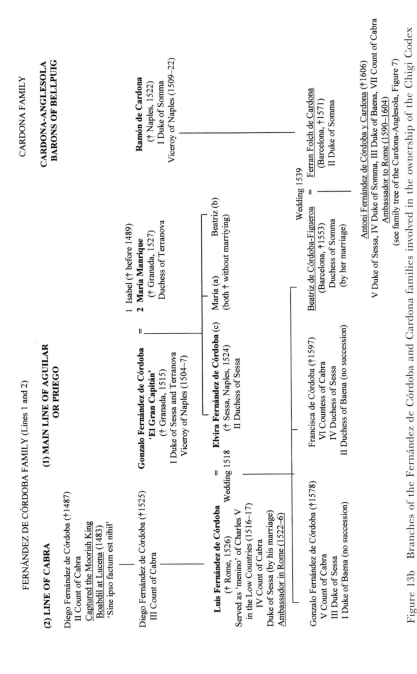

Figure 13b Branches of the Fernández de Córdoba and Cardona families involved in the ownership of the Chigi Codex. After Bethencourt, *Historia genealógica y heráldica*

Thus on folios 19ᵛ–20ʳ of the manuscript the shields of both mother and daughter can be found. Luis Fernández de Córdoba, fourth Count of Cabra, belongs to one of the branches of the family that uses the Moorish king in its shield. Through his marriage in 1518 he became Duke of Sessa and was heir to the properties and entitlements of El Gran Capitán in the Kingdom of Naples. He had served as a 'menino' of Charles V in the Low Countries in 1516–17 and was later named ambassador in Rome in 1522. He died there only four years later; Elvira, his wife, had died in 1524.[38]

The particular combination of these three different Fernández de Córdoba coats of arms in the Chigi Codex (two shields with the head of the Moorish king and one without it) can be explained only by an alliance between the main house of the family, namely the main line of Aguilar – which does not have the Moorish king chained to the shield – and one of the other two branches of the family with the Moorish king in the shield. This alliance only occurs with this particular marriage.[39] Moreover, as can be seen in the lower right corner of Figure 13b, a daughter of this couple married the son of the Viceroy Ramón de Cardona in 1539, and this alliance affords the closest possible association in place and time of the two families who placed their coats of arms in the manuscript.[40]

There is a hitherto unnoticed detail in the illumination on folio 20ʳ that is of particular importance (Figure 14). The kneeling figure, whose face has been painted over that of a previous donor figure, is wearing the collar of the French royal Order of St Michel,

---

[38] Bethencourt, *Historia genealógica*, vii, pp. 84–92.

[39] It should be mentioned that after 1517 the head of the entire Fernández de Córdoba family was Catalina Fernández de Córdoba (see her name in Figure 13a, under the main line 1 of the family). Since the illumination on folio 20ʳ includes the symbolic wheel of St Catherine of Alexandria it is tempting to think that the Fernández de Córdoba shield on that folio might be hers. However, this is not possible, since she married someone outside the Fernández de Córdoba family, and the shield would have combined her arms with those of her husband, who died in 1528. Curiously enough, both her cousins of the same name, Luis Fernández de Córdoba (from lines 2 and 3 of the family) did try to marry her. The Luis Fernández de Córdoba in question (from line 2) sent emissaries to her from the Low Countries to arrange the marriage, but these plans came to naught.

[40] The son of the Viceroy, Ferran Folc (d. 1571), and his wife Beatriz lived in Barcelona and sponsored the compilation of the works (copied in 1541–2 by Pere Vilasaló) of the illustrious Valencian poet Ausias March and their subsequent publication in Barcelona in 1543, 1545 and 1560. See A. Pagès, *Introducció a l'edició crítica de les obres de Auzias March, tesi per al doctorat de Lletres presentada a la 'Faculté des lettres de l'Université de Paris'* (Barcelona, 1912), pp. 55–83.

Figure 14   Detail of the kneeling figure on folio 20ʳ of the Chigi Codex.
©Biblioteca Apostolica Vaticana (Vatican)

also a later addition to the illumination.[41] It is possible that, since the coat of arms of Gonzalo Fernández de Córdoba's widow is included on this folio, the kneeling figure's face was modified to represent her husband, El Gran Capitán. In 1507, on their way back to Spain from Naples, King Ferdinand and Gonzalo Fernández de Córdoba stopped at Savona, where they were received by Louis XII. El Gran Capitán was especially treated with all honours as the invincible Spanish general who had defeated

[41]   See the illustration of this collar in García Carraffa, *Enciclopedia heráldica*, i.

the French on countless occasions.[42] According to Bethencourt, Gonzalo Fernández de Córdoba was invited to sit at the royal table, normally a royal prerogative, and at some point during the visit, Louis XII took his own collar – most likely that of the Order of St Michel – and gave it to El Gran Capitán.[43] Thus, it would seem plausible to identify the kneeling figure portrayed on folio 20[r] as Gonzalo Fernández de Córdoba. Although this meeting of El Gran Capitán with Louis XII would have provided the opportunity for the manuscript to be presented as a gift, there is a possible problem with this hypothesis. According to the statutes of the Order of St Michel, King Francis I, in his first meeting of the Order in 1516, changed the appearance of the collar: for the silk cord (probably used to connect the shell-like pieces of the collar) a double golden cord was substituted.[44] This was done in memory of St Francis and of Anne of Brittany, twice Queen of France and Francis I's mother-in-law, who had established the Order of the Cordelière.[45] The collar added to the kneeling figure on folio 20[r] of

---

[42] Perhaps the motto 'Infrangibile' (invincible) in the two coats of arms of Gonzalo Fernández de Córdoba's heirs refers to his victories.

[43] Bethencourt, *Historia genealógica y heráldica*, vi, p. 141. Other descriptions of the event indicate that Louis XII gave the collar first to King Ferdinand and he, in turn, gave it to Gonzalo Fernández de Córdoba. This does not seem very likely, since Ferdinand was apparently very jealous of the treatment El Gran Capitán was receiving from the French; in fact, Ferdinand was taking him back to Spain for fear that Gonzalo, owing to his popularity, might be proclaimed King of Naples. Ferdinand never fulfilled his promise of naming Gonzalo head of the Order of Santiago. 'El Gran Capitan' retired to Loja, near Granada, and died in the latter city; he is buried there with his wife at the church of San Jerónimo.

[44] R. Alleau, *Enigmes et symboles du Mont St.-Michel* (Paris, 1970), pp. 298–9: 'Les statuts de l'Ordre relatent, en effet, que "le Roi François Ier, au premier chapitre qu'il tint, après son sacre, en septembre 1516, changea les aiguillettes de soie du collier en doubles cordelières d'or, en mémoire de saint François, tant à cause qu'il s'appelait François, que pour conserver la mémoire de la reine Anne de Bretagne, mère de la reine Claude, sa femme, qui l'en avait prié".' (The statutes of the Order (of St Michel) say, in fact, that 'King Francis I, at the first meeting he held, after his coronation, in September 1516, changed the collar's silk cord for a double golden cord, in memory of St Francis, both because his name was Francis and to preserve the memory of Queen Anne of Brittany – mother of Queen Claude, his wife – who had asked him to do so'.) The statutes of the Order are found in the manuscript Paris, Bibliothèque Nationale de France, f. fr. 19819; the miniature on fol. 1 shows King Louis XI with fourteen members of the Order wearing the collar and four officers. See also below, n. 54.

[45] H. Sanborn, *Anne of Brittany: The Story of a Duchess and Twice-Crowned Queen* (Boston, 1917), p. 209: 'December 16, 1492, Robertet, secretary of Anne of Beaujeu, and one of the most polished and spirited men at court, received thirty-five *livres tournois* for chains to be distributed among ladies whom the queen deemed worthy to join the order of the Cordelière. The emblem of this order consisted of a plaque of gold hung around the neck, formed by a double letter interlaced and done in red and white enamel. Every let-

the Chigi Codex seems to reflect this post-1516 modification, and therefore it may not represent the actual collar that El Gran Capitán received in 1507.

Since, with the possible exception of El Gran Capitán, no members of the Bouton family or of the Cardona/Fernández de Córdoba families received the collar of the Order of St Michel, the question is who the kneeling figure on folio 20[r] wearing such a collar might be.[46] Was there another owner of the Chigi Codex besides those whose coats of arms have already been identified? According to Kellman, 'On fol. 20, it was Catherine [Philippe Bouton's wife] who was originally the donor, presented by St. Catherine, before her figure was overpainted with that of the nobleman we now see.'[47] While there is no doubt that the Bouton family at some point owned the manuscript,[48] the kneeling figure is wearing ermine, a royal attribute, over his/her shoulders, which perhaps was added together with the collar of the Order of St Michel.[49] Moreover, the illumination depicts no ordinary interior chamber or room, since it is open to the street on the left side. This setting would be more characteristic of a so-called 'lit de justice'; that is, the wooden scaffold, canopy, backdrop, and decorative draperies that cordoned off space for kings, symbolizing royal justice.[50] That this other owner,

---

ter was intwined with a cord in black enamel. The plaque for the queen was formed of thirty-two double Roman A's.'

[46] According to P. Vetter, *Der französische Ritterorder vom Heiligen Michael (1469–1830). Inaugural-Dissertation zur Erlangung der Doktorwürde der Philosophischen Fakultät der Rheinischen Friedrich-Wilhelms-Universität zu Bonn* (Bonn, 1979), p. 37, owing to the war between Ferdinand of Aragon and Louis XII, several unnamed Aragonese noblemen returned their collars of the Order of St Michel in 1511. For a list of members of the Order of St Michel, see J.-F.-L. d'Hozier, 'Recueil historique des Chevaliers de l'Ordre de Saint Michel', *Revue historique nobiliaire et biographique*, 3rd ser./4, 16 (1879), pp. 193–216, 344–55, 466–78, 505–21; 17 (1880), pp. 67–79, 257–70, 334–50; 19 (1882), pp. 88–94, 129–35, 271–4, 363–7, 443–52 and 547–53.

[47] Kellman, *The Treasury of Petrus Alamire*, p. 127. In a previous publication, Kellman, 'Introduction', p. ix, had stated that it was Philippe Bouton's face in the donor miniature that had been replaced.

[48] When I presented this paper in Leuven, I questioned the identification of the Bouton coat of arms in Chigi, owing to its similarity with the Fernández de Córdoba shield and the different description of the Bouton arms in De la Chenaye-Desbois et Badier, *Dictionnaire de la Noblesse*, 3rd edn (Paris, 1864), iii, p. 903, where it is described as 'de gueules, à la fasce d'or'. Herbert Kellman corrected my error, showing me a Bouton coat of arms like the one in Chigi in another manuscript. Both Kellman and Flynn Warmington pointed out that eighteenth- and nineteenth-century heraldic sources are often unreliable.

[49] Kellman, 'Introduction', p. ix.

[50] S. Hanley, *The Lit de Justice of the Kings of France* (Princeton, 1983), p. 28. Chronicles recounted Parisian entrées featuring tableaux set up at the Châtelet (the city tribunal of the provost of Paris) displaying a *lit de justice*.

a member of the Order of St Michel wearing ermine, probably was a French-speaking person is suggested by the fact that the word 'Bouton' or 'Boutton' in the motto 'Ung seul Bouton' was replaced by the word 'Dieu',[51] and, as we shall see, it is very unlikely that the Cardona or the Fernández de Córdoba owners would have made that change to produce the French motto 'Ung seul Dieu'.[52] These new pieces of evidence seem to point to a royal owner of the Chigi Codex and it is possible to speculate briefly about such a person.

Comparing the two coats of arms on folios 19^v and 20^r, it can be seen that the frames in which they are inserted are different; on folio 19^v the frame is square, while the frame on folio 20^r has a more irregular and artistic shape. The addition of the Moorish king on folio 19^v probably necessitated extensive changes in the space reserved for the illumination, and these changes may ultimately have affected the shape of the frame itself. On the other hand, the coat of arms on folio 20^r seems to have kept the original frame, which is more elaborate and even enters the decorated margin of the page. The letter B for the voice designation Bassus seems also to be original and as a whole everything is well proportioned. Perhaps the only modification in the original coat of arms of folio 20^r took place inside the shield, and therefore the heraldic attributes of the rope and ducal crown might be connected to a possible royal owner of the manuscript: a duchess and widow of the French royal family. If so, there are three possible candidates, but the one who seems the most likely is Anne, Duchess of Brittany and twice Queen of France;[53] it was she, as mentioned earlier, who established the heraldic fashion of the rope in her

---

[51] Kellman, 'Introduction', p. vii.

[52] Although mottoes in a foreign language (such as 'Mit Zait' for the Sforza dukes) are found, a French motto in sixteenth-century Spain is very rare. We do not know Luis Fernández de Córdoba's motto, but his grandfather used 'Sine ipso factum est nihil' (referring to the capture of the Moorish King Boabdil at Lucena in 1483). This same motto, often written within the border of the shield, was later used by other descendants of this line of the family. Mottoes should be distinguished from war cries such as 'Infrangibile'; the use of one does not necessarily exclude the other.

[53] The other possible candidates are Charles VIII's two sisters: Anne (1461–1522), Duchess of Bourbon, widow of Pierre de Beaujeu after 1503, and Jeanne (1464–1505), Duchess of Orléans and Berry, a severely crippled woman whose forced marriage to Louis d'Orléans (the future Louis XII) was nullified in 1498 to permit his marriage to Anne of Brittany. Jeanne founded the Order of the Annonciade. On these two women see, for example, M. Chombart de Lauwe, *Anne de Beaujeu ou la passion du pouvoir* (Paris, 1980) and R. de Maulde, *Jeanne de France, Duchesse d'Orléans et de Berry* (Paris, 1883).

coat of arms in memory of her first husband.[54] Anne's first marriage to Charles VIII ended with his death on 7 April 1498 and she married Louis XII on 8 January 1499; during those nine months she was a widow and therefore her coat of arms might have been inserted in the Chigi Codex at that time.[55] On the one hand, the presence of St Catherine in the illumination on folio 20[r] would seem to argue against Anne's connection with the manuscript,[56] but, on the other hand, the motto 'Ung seul Dieu' on folio 19[v] points directly to Anne's two husbands, Charles VIII and Louis XII. According to Robert Scheller, in a poem of consolation written shortly after Charles had left for Italy in 1494, 'France' urges 'Labeur', the fourth estate, 'to worship one God, honor one king and observe one law' ['. . . Ung seul Dieu adorer / Ung seul roy

---

[54] See above, n. 44. García Carraffa, *Enciclopedia heráldica*, p. 193: 'Las viudas, en lugar de esos adornos, usan cordones de seda blanca y negra anudados o entrelazados en cuatro partes, atados a los círculos de las coronas y rodeando el escudo enteramente. Este uso dimanó de Ana, Duquesa de Bretaña. A la muerte de su primer marido el rey Carlos VIII, de Francia, comenzó a llevar, como muestra del amor que le tuvo y que conservó toda su vida, unos cordones liados y atados a su cintura en la forma en que los llevan los religiosos de San Francisco, haciendo que la imitaran y que los pusiesen en sus escudos todas las damas de la corte y quedando así como ornamentos de las armas de las mujeres.' (Widows, instead of those ornaments, use cords of black and white silk, knotted or tied in four parts, attached to the crown and entirely surrounding the shield. This usage came from Anne, Duchess of Brittany. After the death of her first husband, King Charles VIII of France, she started to wear, as a sign of her love for him which lasted all her life, some cords tied around her waist, as Franciscans do, asking to be imitated and that the cords be placed in all the shields of women at the court, something that has remained as an ornament of women's coats of arms.)

[55] Kellman, *The Treasury of Petrus Alamire*, p. 127, pointed out the importance of certain calligraphic initials in the manuscript: 'A rose and a dragon, coupled with elements of the chain of the Order of the Golden Fleece, appear as part of an initial on fol. 191v, symbolizing, unmistakably, Philippe's [Bouton] ultimate allegiance to Burgundy and recognition of the patronage he had received from its dukes.' The description of the same initial in a previous publication by Kellman, 'Introduction', p. viii, adds other details that could be interpreted differently: 'The "K" on fol. 191v displays at the top of its stem a yellow fire steel surmounted by a yellow fleur-de-lis . . .'. If Anne of Brittany or a member of the French royal family had something to do with the compilation of the Chigi Codex, the initial 'K' with the fleur-de-lis, a French royal symbol, might refer to her first husband Charles VIII; according to Robert W. Scheller, 'Imperial Themes in Art and Literature of the Early French Renaissance: The Period of Charles VIII', *Simiolus: Netherlands Quarterly for the History of Art*, 12 (1981–2), pp. 56–7, a manuscript (Paris, Bibliothèque Nationale de France, f. fr. 2228) with two poems about Charles contains border decorations 'with highly stylized Ks (for Karolus), of the same type that adorn the king's tomb'.

[56] Anne of Brittany's book of hours contains, among others, an illumination devoted to St Catherine, but the three saints standing behind her in an illustration portraying Anne as a donor figure are St Anne, St Marguerite and St Ursula. See M. Abbé [Henri] Delaunay, *Le Livre d'heures de la Reine Anne de Bretagne, traduit du latin et accompagné des notices inédites* (Paris, 1841), p. 7.

honnorer / Une lois preferer . . .'.], pending the king's return.[57] As a motto, VNG DIEV. VNG ROI. VNE FOI also appears in a painting illustrating Louis XII's coronation, and this maxim was reproduced together with a prominent display of royal coats of arms in printer's marks of Jean Alexandre of Angers (active 1480–93), Philippe Pigouchet (from 1489), Antoine Caillaut of Paris (active 1482–1506) and Robinet Macé of Caen (active 1498–1506).[58] Thus, it seems plausible that during Anne's life the face of the kneeling figure, perhaps Charles VIII, would have been changed for that of another French monarch, possibly her second husband Louis XII, wearing ermine and the collar of the Order of St Michel modified according to her wishes.[59] This hypothesis must remain speculative, since it is not known how the manuscript came into the possession of its different owners. In the same way that the later additions to the Chigi Codex reflect the ownership of the

---

[57] R. W. Scheller, 'Ensigns of Authority: French Royal Symbolism in the Age of Louis XII', *Simiolus: Netherlands Quarterly for the History of Art*, 13 (1983), pp. 75–141, esp. pp. 122–3. He cites A. de Montaiglon, *Receuil de poésies françaises des XVe et XVIe siècles* (Paris, 1869), viii, p. 88: 'Pensez de labourer / Et de cueur savourer / Que devez reverer / Vostre prince et pleurer / Son ennuyeuse absence / Ung seul Dieu adorer / Ung seul roy honnorer / Une lois preferer / et loyaulx demourer / attendans sa présence.' For a detailed discussion and bibliography regarding the symbolism of this motto, see Scheller, 'Ensigns of Authority', pp. 120–3.

[58] The painting entitled *The Sacre of Louis XII* is one of the two wings of an altarpiece now at the Musée de Cluny in Paris; they come from the Chapelle du Puy in Amiens Cathedral, and can be dated to 1501. For illustrations of this painting and of the printer's device of Antoine Caillaut (before 1506), see Scheller, 'Ensigns of Authority', pp. 117 and 123. Caillaut's woodcut displays the royal crowned coat of arms with three fleurs-de-lis held by two angels above the arms of Paris, the motto in the border decoration. It should be pointed out that the Bouton coat of arms on fol. 249^v of the Chigi Codex appears between two angels, and that, according to García Carraffa, *Enciclopedia heráldica*, pp. 163–4, the presence of angels as so-called supporters of shields is exclusively reserved for kings and princes. He also states that the supporters are usually figures or animals already found in the shield; in Bouton's case this would be the eagle. A. C. Fox-Davies, *A Complete Guide to Heraldry*, revised and annotated by J. P. Brooke-Little (London, 1985), pp. 309 and 329, gives some examples of the presence of angels as supporters of shields.

[59] This modification would have not been unique in French royal manuscripts. Louis XII's face was painted over that of Charles VIII in a miniature in a book of hours (Madrid, Biblioteca Nacional, MS Vit. 24/1, fol. 3^r); see Scheller, 'Imperial Themes', pp. 24–5. In Leuven I pointed out that perhaps the original kneeling figure on fol. 20^r of the Chigi Codex was Charles VIII, and that the female figure of St Catherine – often associated with the gift of eloquence – might represent in a symbolic way the support Anne of Brittany provided to her husband's problems with speech. In fact, St Catherine's light brown dress in this illumination is similar to Anne's dress in her book of hours.

That Mouton's motet *Quis dabit oculis*, written for the death of Anne of Brittany in 1514, was added to the manuscript by a later owner may be more significant than previously thought.

Spaniards, perhaps the disposition of the three distinct sections of the main corpus of the manuscript reflects a change of intended recipient in the earliest stages of its compilation.[60]

The manuscript was probably kept by the Fernández de Córdoba family during the later part of the sixteenth century. A grandson of the Viceroy (see Figure 13b), who also married a member of the Fernández de Cordoba family, spent fourteen years as Ambassador to Rome between 1590 and 1604. This member of the Cardona Fernández de Córdoba family inherited all the nobility titles of both lines 1 and 2 of the Fernández de Córdoba family as well as those of the Cardona-Anglesola family (see Figure 13b), but subsequently had to sell part of his patrimony;[61] it was perhaps during this time that the manuscript passed to Italian hands before its acquisition by Fabio Chigi in the 1660s. The intriguing story of the Chigi Codex should certainly encourage further investigation of patronage by the Iberian nobility. Since traditional musicology has associated Spanish music of the late fifteenth and early sixteenth centuries almost exclusively with the royal chapels, it is now essential to pursue archival research in the records of families such as the Cardona and Fernández de Córdoba. The work ahead promises to be very fruitful and will enter uncharted territory.

Universidad de Granada

---

[60] According to F. Fitch, 'Vatican City, Biblioteca Apostolica Vaticana MS Chigi C VIII 234 ("Chigi Codex")', in *The Treasury of Petrus Alamire*, ed. Kellman, p. 127: 'The self-contained section devoted to Ockeghem's Mass-music (comprising the first eighteen gatherings of Chigi) may therefore have been a special project, assembled in rather a piecemeal fashion, in contrast to the clear ordering and gathering structure of the rest of the manuscript. The two subsequent sections devoted to the Mass music of other composers (settings by Barbireau, Agricola, Josquin, La Rue, Compère, Brumel, and Busnois), and to motets of various authorship (including several by Johannes Regis) may have been executed independently of each other. . . . The decision to bring these three discrete sections together may have been the last stage of the manuscript's elaboration at the scriptorium.'

[61] Bethencourt, *Historia genealógica y heráldica*, vii, p. 113.

Early Music History (2002) Volume 21. © *Cambridge University Press*
Printed in the United Kingdom

REVIEWS

RICHARD FREEDMAN, *The Chansons of Orlando di Lasso and their Protestant Listeners: Music, Piety, and Print in Sixteenth-Century France*. Eastman Studies in Music. Rochester, NY, University of Rochester Press. 2000. xxiv + 259 pp.
DOI:10.1017/S0261127902212073

JEANICE BROOKS, *Courtly Song in Late Sixteenth-Century France*. Chicago and London, University of Chicago Press. 2000. xvi + 560 pp. DOI:10.1017/S026112790222207X

Two recent books have filled in many of the gaps in musicologists' understanding of French song and its place in sixteenth-century society. Although they deal with different repertoires, both Jeanice Brooks's *Courtly Song in Late Sixteenth-Century France* and Richard Freedman's *The Chansons of Orlando di Lasso and their Protestant Listeners: Music, Piety, and Print in Sixteenth-Century France* address similar issues: what these songs meant to the people who sang them, what they signified to French society as a whole, and how our understanding of them is enhanced by a close examination of the cultures in which they flourished. The books also offer complementary views of the artistic creations of other prominent figures in the late Renaissance. Brooks's book provides detailed information that tells the reader more about the career of Lasso, for example, while Freedman's treatment of Protestant contrafacta gives a more complete picture of the reception of the poetry of Pierre de Ronsard, a pivotal figure in Brooks's monograph. Both works are the fruits of extensive research and provide transcriptions of primary sources, some of which were heretofore unavailable. They examine styles of music that have received relatively little musicological attention, either because they were considered corruptions of greater works (the Lasso contrafacta), or because they were less complex stylistically than a better known

genre (the *air de cour* as opposed to the polyphonic chanson repertoire). Both books have earned a spot on the shelves of those interested in music and society in the sixteenth century.

The reader who picks up a copy of Richard Freedman's book
might easily be misled about its contents, for the title on the book
jacket differs from that found on the title page of the book itself,
and suggests a different sort of study than what Freedman presents. Freedman's monograph is not intended to be a comprehensive study of *The Chansons of Orlando di Lasso*, as the title appears
on the jacket, but rather *The Chansons of Orlando di Lasso and their
Protestant Listeners*. This is an important distinction, since
Freedman's book deals primarily with the alterations Protestant
editors made to Lasso's chansons in order to render them appropriate for pious music lovers to enjoy without risk of exposure to
profane or lascivious texts. Freedman begins with an exploration
of the importance of the book in Calvinist thought. Many printers in French-speaking areas were Protestant, and the printed
word (or Word) was important in Huguenot communities as a way
to bring souls to Christ. Calvin subscribed to the Neoplatonic view
of music as reflecting the harmony of a smoothly functioning society, and while he limited its use within the liturgy to settings of
the Psalms, he approved of music-making in the home as a sign
of spiritual harmony.[1] Following Calvin, Protestant printers har-
nessed what he described as music's 'secret and almost incredible
power to move our hearts in one way or another'.[2]

Lasso in particular was known for his fine music, much of which
in the eyes of Protestant publishers was unfortunately soiled with
evil texts. In the opening chapter, Freedman introduces several
printers who managed to marry Calvin's acceptance of domestic
music-making with Lasso's splendid music by producing editions
of his chansons that were purged of all sensual or otherwise un-
Christian lyrics. These publishers included Thomas Vautrollier of
London (*Recueil du mélange d'Orlande*, 1570), Pierre Haultin's firm
in La Rochelle that published contrafacta with texts by Jean

---

[1] On Calvin and music in the Reformed church, see A. Dunning, 'Jean Calvin (Cauvin)',
in *The New Grove Dictionary of Music and Musicians*, 2nd edn [hereafter *New Grove II*]
(London, 2001).

[2] J. Calvin, preface to T. de Bèze and C. Marot, *Pseaumes octantetrois de David mis en rime
françoise* (Geneva, 1551), cited in Freedman, p. 9. Translation in O. Strunk, *Source Readings
in Music History*, rev. L. Treitler (London and New York, 1998), p. 366.

Pasquier (*Mellange d'Orlande de Lassus*, 1575) and Simon Goulart of Geneva (*Thrésor de musique d'Orlande*, 1576). The collections, which combined original Lasso chansons with contrafacted versions, were popular enough to prompt multiple editions. Freedman lists these works in his table of abbreviations that appears immediately before chapter 1, but I would have appreciated a more clear and detailed discussion of the prints, their contents and how they related to each other, perhaps with a diagram. Freedman does provide a list of the prints' contents in his seventh chapter, in which he discusses tonal types and modal organisation of the collections. A complete list, including such things as the authors of the original texts and publication information for both Lasso's original works and the contrafacta, would have been helpful.

Freedman makes an interesting and important point in his first chapter, comparing the making of Protestant contrafacta to the Calvinist's claiming of Catholic spaces. He cites Catharine Randall's recent work on how Calvinists transformed traditional Catholic sites like churches to serve a new religious aesthetic.[3] In addition, Reformed literature of the time emphasised interior spaces that were loci of prayer and contemplation. Freedman likens the hearing or performing of the Reformed chanson texts to the creation of such an internal space, allowing the soul a special place outside of daily life where it could meet the divine. He writes, 'Like the grottos, caves, and contained spaces that figure in the Calvinist view of buildings and cities, these songs make room for the expression of attitudes central to Huguenot piety. But we can also view the books of *contrafacta* themselves as "containers" that make room for the articulation of spiritual frames of mind.' Freedman could perhaps have made more of the similarities between Calvinists' appropriation of Catholic spaces and their revision of profane songs. Moreover, it is not entirely clear whether Lasso's own Catholicism was something the editors of his chansons wished to revise as well; I shall return to this issue below.

In his second chapter, 'The Chansons and their Listeners', Freedman begins to explore the processes by which chanson texts were made more fitting for Protestant ears. Most interesting here are his comments on the extent of editorial changes in the texts,

[3] C. Randall, *Building Codes: The Aesthetics of Calvinism in Early Modern Europe* (Philadelphia, 1999).

which varied even within single collections. Some lyrics appeared without change from the Parisian prints that were the models for the contrafacta collections, usually because their content was morally unobjectionable. In other cases, such as that of Lasso's setting of Clément Marot's 'Monsieur l'Abbé', the anticlericalism of the model text was acceptable to a community that was quite willing to see a Roman Catholic abbot as a drunkard. But Freedman cautions the reader against viewing the Lasso contrafacta as 'purified' chansons, noting that different editors had different ideas about what made a song text appropriate or inappropriate. Furthermore, rather than simply slapping together a new text, some, like Simon Goulart, took great pains to write revised lyrics that preserved the grace and beauty of Lasso's original marriage of music and text. He did this by retaining formal structure, including syntactic divisions and enjambments, and by carefully considering the musical motifs Lasso paired with phrases of text in order to find new words most fitting for the melodies.

Freedman's third to sixth chapters focus on the process of contrafaction as seen in individual songs. He centres each of these chapters on a particular category of song, those dealing with ideas of courtly love (chapter 3), those based on the poetry of Marot (chapter 4), songs dealing with personal contemplations of the divine (chapter 5), and those utilising the poetry of the most prominent of the Pléiade figures, Pierre de Ronsard (chapter 6). By providing scores, original texts with English translations and contrafacta texts with translations for each work discussed, Freedman makes his points about the relationship between Lasso's music and the various texts easy to comprehend.[4] One might occasionally disagree with certain details of interpretation, but on the whole, Freedman's analyses of Lasso's songs and the contrafacta texts are insightful, and they make apparent his deep and intimate knowledge of the body of Lasso's chansons. One quibble I have with the book is that the layout of the discussions of music can be confusing. Freedman is careful to include the texts of the songs under consideration in the body of his text, also providing very helpful English translations. The song texts, however, are

[4] Very few examples lack scores. These are generally chansons for which Freedman only wished to make a point about the textual changes, such as in Lasso's *Quand mon mari*, discussed on pp. 63–4.

generally not integrated with the prose, and might have been more clearly set as tables accompanying Freedman's text.

Having written a book, all authors find themselves dealing with the reviewer's complaint that 'it's not the book I would have written', and even reviewers with the best of intentions often cannot help but wish for a little more treatment of their own interests. In his review of *The Chansons of Orlando di Lasso and their Protestant Listeners*, for example, Peter Bergquist called for Freedman to put his extensive knowledge to work on a study of the chansons in their original forms.[5] I would echo that request, since a full study of the Lasso chansons is a lacuna in the literature on this towering figure. For my own part, however, I should like to read more of Freedman's views on the social and cultural contexts in which the contrafacta appear. The sixteenth century was a time of great turmoil in France, especially after the murder of seventy-four Protestants attending a sermon near Vassy opened the first of several Wars of Religion.[6] The St Bartholomew's Day massacre of 23–4 August 1572 resulted in the deaths of 4,000 Huguenots. Afterwards, political theorists began writing treatises defending the right to resist leaders who committed crimes against the people, making Henri III's inheritance of the French crown in 1574 a more unstable event than it would have been under more peaceful conditions. Indeed, Henri III would be murdered in 1589. These political events certainly would have had a profound effect on a Calvinist publisher in the 1570s and 1580s.

Freedman addresses these issues obliquely. For example, he speaks of the city of La Rochelle, whence the Haultin press hailed, as a 'Protestant stronghold' (p. 1) and as 'besieged' (p. 181), but does not explain why. From the late 1550s on, Geneva-trained ministers preached the Reformed faith in La Rochelle, and Calvinist works were published there in the 1560s.[7] A Reformed church was organised in 1557; the following year, the newly established consistory enforced church discipline. More significantly, iconoclastic

---

[5] P. Bergquist, review of R. Freedman, *The Chansons of Orlando di Lasso and their Protestant Listeners*, forthcoming in *MLA Notes*. I am grateful to Professor Bergquist for sharing his review with me before its publication.

[6] A concise account of the state of France in the sixteenth century appears in E. Cameron, *The European Reformation* (Oxford, 1991), pp. 372–6.

[7] See J. P. Meyer, 'La Rochelle', in the *Oxford Encyclopedia of the Reformation* (Oxford and New York, 1996).

riots raged there in May 1562, and the city increasingly became a symbol of Protestant resistance to royal authority. The king's forces besieged the city from December 1572 to June 1573, but the peace treaty was highly favourable to the Protestant residents. La Rochelle remained a sore point with the monarchy until it fell to a year-long siege orchestrated by Cardinal Richelieu in 1628.

Pasquier refers to this situation in his preface to the 1575 *Mellange d'Orlande de Lassus*, a statement to which Freedman draws attention on page 5 of his text: 'Madame, After retiring to this place, in order to save myself from the miseries and calamities of this most difficult and dangerous age, for fear that I not be found wasted or useless in the church of God, I decided to make music my calling . . .'.[8] Freedman does not elaborate on what made the times so 'difficult'. The very real physical dangers faced by the French Calvinists paralleled the spiritual dangers inherent in the worldly chansons. The first editions of each collection (Vautrollier's, Pasquier's and Goulart's) all appeared in the tumultuous 1570s; certainly this was a factor in their publication. A little more historical background would have made the position of an editor like Pasquier even more clear, and might have added to Freedman's already excellent analyses of the songs.

Likewise, I hoped for more detail in Freedman's chapter 4, in which he addresses a number of chanson settings of poems by Marot. In this instance he could have delved a bit more deeply into Marot's biography, which makes him a particularly interesting subject for a study of contrafacta. A prominent courtier under François I, Marot was famed for his elegant, witty poetry. His chanson texts are clever, suggestive, irreverent and even bawdy; witness the lyrics of the seductive and instructive 'Fleur de quinze ans':

> Fleur de quinze ans si Dieu vous sauve et gard'
> J'ay en amour trouvé cinq poins exprès:
> Premierement il y a le regard,
> Puis le devis et le baiser après,
> L'atouchement suit le baiser de pres,

[8] 'Madame, Apres m'estre retiré en ce lieu, pour me sauver des miseres et calamitez de ce tems tres difficile et dangereux, de peur que ne fusse trouvé oysif et inutile en L'eglise de Dieu, Je me deliberay y faire profession de la Musique . . .'. J. Pasquier, dedication to *Mellange d'Orlande de Lassus contenant plusieurs chansons, à quatre parties desquelles la lettre profane a este changée en spirituelle* (La Rochelle, 1575), cited in Freedman, pp. 5 and 190.

Et tous ceux le tendent au dernier point
Qui est—qui est?—Je ne le diray point,
Mais s'il vois plait en ma chambre vous rendre,
Je me mettray volontiers en pourpoint
Voire tout nud pour le vous faire apprendre.[9]

Reformation scholars know Marot better as the French translator and versifier of the Psalter. As Freedman notes, he lived for at time at the court of Renée de France, spouse of Duke Ercole II d'Este in Ferrara. Renée's Protestant associates and her views were a source of stress in her marriage, to say the least, and the presence of another Calvinist like Marot must have been a consolation to her.[10] Marot's personal service to the Reformed faith included his rhymed, metrical translations of thirty Psalms, published in Antwerp in 1541.[11] A far cry from his earlier poetry, these texts provided the Reformed church with appropriate musical material for worship, following Calvin's own dictates that only the Psalms be sung in the sacred service. The following year he took up residence in Geneva as a religious refugee, and translated additional psalms that were published with a preface by Calvin himself. Marot's 'lively person', as historian Owen Chadwick described it, was however 'not well suited to Geneva', and he left the city in 1543. Exiled in Turin, he died a year later.

Freedman comments that 'Marot's poem, with its explicit air of seduction, apparently offended a fair number of sixteenth-century readers and listeners, Calvinist and Catholic alike'. While it seems clear what it was about Marot's text that cried out for 'reformation', one must be careful not to suggest that it was beyond the pale of polite discourse in the sixteenth century. As we shall discover below, Jeanice Brooks describes many examples of eroticism in lyrics intended for the most elegant of courts, though of course these were more political than religious institutions. Still, late

---

[9] 'Flower of fifteen (may God preserve and keep you) I have found in love these five main points: First comes the glance. It is followed by talk and then by the kiss. Kissing yields to caressing without delay. And all the above brings us to the last point, which is—which is—I won't say exactly. But if you'd like to come to my chamber I'll be more than happy in my doublet or even better in the nude to teach you.' Translation by Freedman, p. 62.

[10] On Renée de France and her husband's efforts to use music to force her to conform to Catholic practice, see G. Nugent, 'Anti-Protestant Music for Sixteenth-Century Ferrara', *Journal of the American Musicological Society*, 43 (1990), pp. 228–91.

[11] See F. Dobbins, 'Clément Marot', in *New Grove II*. Marot also published thirteen psalm translations anonymously in Strasbourg in 1539.

medieval and early modern cultures did not shy away from discussions of sexuality, and I was curious about the evidence that this work was indeed seen as offensive. Marot's own personal history makes one wonder whether Pasquier, Vautrollier and Goulart saw his poetry as particularly appropriate for revision. He had himself turned from being a courtier, a part of an institution that was criticised in the sixteenth century for its licence and debauchery, to a follower of Calvin who devoted his manifold talents to the facilitation of the praise of God through music. What better tribute to his efforts than to 'rescue' his earlier sensual poems from the eroticism in which they wallowed?

And then we come to Lasso. The religious and political turmoil of late sixteenth-century France leads me to wonder what role, if any, Lasso's Catholicism played in his reception in Europe. While there is little evidence that Lasso was a zealous Catholic, he certainly spent most of his life at a court that practised some of the most visible Catholicism around, that of the Wittelsbach family in Bavaria.[12] Le Roy & Ballard prints from the 1570s prominently identify Lasso as a composer at the Bavarian court in Munich, and the 1571 Parisian print *Moduli quinis vocibus nunquam hactenus editi* is dedicated to Duke Wilhelm of Bavaria.[13] Did this affect how his French Huguenot audiences perceived his music? The popularity of these collections seems to show that his music transcended these confessional barriers, especially since, as Freedman hypothesises (p. 176), those who bought the contrafacta prints were in many cases already owners of the Le Roy & Ballard collections that contained the chansons in their original forms. But I wonder if any of the appeal of the contrafacta prints came from a satisfaction at correcting the wayward texts chosen by a Catholic. The prefaces, which Freedman provides with translations in his appendix A, sug-

---

[12] On the Wittelsbachs and their prominence as militantly Catholic rulers, see P. M. Soergel, *Wondrous in his Saints: Counter-Reformation Propaganda in Bavaria* (Berkeley and Los Angeles, 1993).

[13] The full title page reads: 'Superius. Moduli quinis vocibus nunquam hactenus editi Monachii Boioariæ composite, Orlando Lasso Auctore. Lutetiæ Parisiorum. Apud Adrianum le Roy, & Robertum Ballard, Regis Typographos. sub signo montis Parnassi. 1571. Cum privilegio Regis ad dece[n]nium.' *Moduli quinis vocibus nunquam hactenus editi (Paris 1571)*, ed. P. Bergquist (Orlando di Lasso: The Complete Motets, 8; Madison, Wis., 1999), plate 1. The dedicatory preface appears in plate 2, and is transcribed and translated on p. 3.

gest in a few cases that this might be so. Pasquier dedicated his 1575 collection to Catherine de Partenay, known for her family's protection of the Huguenot cause, writing:

Among all the musicians of our century Orlande de Lassus appears (and has good right) to deserve good standing, for the excellence and admirable sweetness of his music. Seeing this nevertheless employed in chansons so profane, so salacious and impudent that chaste and Christian ears must recoil in horror, I thought that I might do my Christian duty by purging these very graceful and pleasant chords of such evils and filth with which they have been soiled.[14]

If 'Christian ears' recoil in horror, then what of Lasso's ears? Simon Goulart used similar wording in his 'volume of the chansons of Orlande de Lassus, so altered that one may sing them or play them upon instruments without soiling the tongues or offending Christian ears'.[15] Goulart goes on to address those who might complain about changing the text ('inasmuch that Orlande designed it according to the words'), but he is satisfied that any who might disapprove of his contrafacta already have hearts soiled with 'filth and lewdness'. Did Goulart include Lasso himself among those who might disapprove of the new versions? Finally, Goulart called for Lasso to create new chansons with content acceptable to pious people: 'It would be good to wish that Orlande use his graces, which the Holy Spirit has adorned in him above all, to recall and magnify the one from whom they derive, as he has done in several Motets and Latin Psalms. I deeply wish that these chansons might provoke the urge in him, so that we have a chaste French Music.'[16] While other congregations like the Evangelical (or Lutheran) church retained the use of Latin, one wonders whether 'Motets

---

[14] 'Et pource qu'entre tous les Musiciens de notre siecle, Orlande de lassus semble (et a bon droit) devoir tenir quelque bon lieu, pour l'exellence et admirable douceur de sa Musique: Voyant icelle neantmoins employee à des chansons si profanes, si sales, et impudiques, que les oreilles chastes et chrestiennes en ont horreur: J'ay pensé que je ferois devoir de Chrestien, si repurgeant ces tresgracieux et plaisans accords de tant de villenies et ordures, dont ilz estoyent tous souillez . . .'. Pasquier, preface to *Mellange d'Orlande de Lassus* (1575), cited in Freedman, pp. 190–1.

[15] 'asavoir, Les chansons d'Orlande de Lassus, tellement changées, qu'on les peust chanter de la voix et sur les Instruments, sans souiller les langues ni offenser les oreilles Chrestiennes'. S. Goulart, preface to *Thrésor de musique d'Orlande contenant ses chansons à quatre, cinq et six parties* ([Geneva], 1576), cited in Freedman, pp. 193, 194–5.

[16] 'Il seroit bien à desirer qu'Orlande emploiast ces graces dont le S. Esprit l'a orné par dessus tous, à reconoistre et magnifier celui de qui il les tient, comme il l'a fait en quelques Motets et Pseaumes Latins: et je desire grandement que ces chansons lui en puissant donner la volonte: à fin que nous aions une chaste Musique Françoise.' Goulart, preface to *Thrésor de musique d'Orlande*, cited in Freedman, pp. 194, 195.

and Latin Psalms' suggested Catholicism to the late sixteenth-century reader. Goulart did not wish to keep his contrafacta from Lasso's eyes; rather, he hoped that in seeing them, Lasso might literally be *inspired* to create songs appropriate for Reformed use through the workings of the Holy Spirit.

One of the interesting side questions Freedman raises is that of Lasso's reaction to the contrafaction of his chansons. As he rightly comments, the impetus behind the Protestant rewordings of Lasso's work was the same as that which prompted Lasso to revise motets and chansons into the splendid imitation masses and Magnificats.[17] The recognition of something of value in another piece of music, even in a profane chanson, spurred many a composer to create a new and sometimes better version of the original work. While Lasso's techniques for producing words *ad imitationem* were much more sophisticated than those used by Goulart, Pasquier and Vautrollier, both types of music made use of the ideas of imitation, emulation and competition; both attempted to refine sacred gold from a secular or profane ore. Would Lasso have known of the contrafacta, and would he have recognised the likeness to his imitation works at their core?

I would be interested in reading Freedman's views on Lasso's reception of the contrafacta collections. In his final chapter, he discusses the legal implications of music publishing as they related specifically to Lasso in the late sixteenth century. In 1571, Charles IX granted Lasso a royal privilege for the printing of his own music, allowing him to control who printed his works and under what terms.[18] While such privileges were not unusual for authors by the end of the century, Lasso was one of the first musicians to receive the rights to control the distribution of his own work. As a rule, he continued to publish with the Parisian firm of Le Roy & Ballard; Adrian Le Roy was a personal friend of Lasso, as well as the royal printer. What might Lasso have thought about the contrafacta prints? Freedman writes, 'there is good reason to think that he would have objected to these publications as an infringement upon his right of intellectual property alone' (p. xvi). Well, did he? A surprising amount of Lasso's correspondence survives,

---

[17] Freedman, p. xv; on the imitation Magnificats see D. Crook, *Orlando di Lasso's Imitation Magnificats for Counter-Reformation Munich* (Princeton, 1994).

[18] Freedman discusses the privilege on pp. 177–80.

reproduced in Horst Leuchtmann's thorough *Orlando di Lasso: Briefe*, but he makes no mention of the contrafacted chansons.[19] Given the other actions he took with respect to the publication of his works, however, we might speculate on his views.

As Freedman points out, two of the three printers most involved in the publication of the contrafacta volumes were active in London and Geneva, beyond the reach of the French royal privilege and even the Imperial printing privilege that followed in 1581. While the La Rochelle firm of Haultin lay in French territory, it was also a besieged Huguenot stronghold that 'could hardly have cared at all whether they violated royal copyright or not' (p. 181). In other words, if he even knew of the contrafacta's existence, Lasso would have had little legal recourse if he wished to stop the publication of the volumes. But it is not clear that he would have wanted to. While it is true that Lasso was once entangled in a lawsuit over the rights to print his music, he was not the plaintiff and did not seek to limit publication of his works. In 1582, the Munich printer Adam Berg filed suit against Katharina Gerlach, a Nuremberg printer who had recently published a collection of Lasso motets, some of which were culled from volumes previously issued by Berg.[20] Though Berg and Lasso had a close working relationship comparable to that Lasso enjoyed with Le Roy, the composer rallied to the side of Gerlach, writing a letter on her behalf to the judges on the Nuremberg town council.[21] It is important to note that Lasso did not stop publishing with Berg after this incident; he did not choose Gerlach *or* Berg as a printer, but rather Gerlach *and* Berg, resulting in a wider web of distribution. Lasso was probably not dissatisfied with the quality of the original Munich publications, since the motets in question had in many instances been published under his direct supervision. Gerlach, too, had a long-standing business relationship with Lasso that dated back to the 1560s, when her press belonged to her first husband Johann vom Berg and Ulrich Neuber.[22] I suggest that in the Berg v. Gerlach

---

[19] H. Leuchtmann, *Orlando di Lasso: Briefe* (Wiesbaden, 1977).

[20] On the Gerlach case, see my introduction to *Sacrae cantiones quinque vocum (Munich, 1582)* (Orlando di Lasso: The Complete Motets, 12; Madison, Wis., 2001), pp. xi–xiii.

[21] H. Leuchtmann, *Orlando di Lasso: Sein Leben* (Wiesbaden, 1976), pp. 195–6.

[22] On the history of Gerlach's firm, see *Motets for Four to Eight Voices from Selectissimae cantiones (Nuremberg, 1568)*, ed. P. Bergquist (Orlando di Lasso: The Complete Motets, 6; Madison, 1997), pp. xii–xiv. Note that it was Johann vom Berg and Ulrich Neuber who

case, the composer was more interested in seeing his work distributed widely than he was concerned with defending his intellectual property. If this is the case, then Lasso may not have minded the contrafacta editions, which would have made his music acceptable to an even wider audience. Lasso was an astute businessman, one who would have recognised the opportunity to increase his fame. His own works *ad imitationem* display a willingness to see a musical creation as something flexible that can be altered in certain circumstances. Perhaps the reason we hear so little complaint about the contrafacta volumes from Lasso, or on his behalf from Le Roy & Ballard, is that he had no quarrel with those who changed the texts of his chansons in order to promote their further distribution. In Goulart's contrafacta publications, for example, the editor strove to retain as much as possible of the original poetry, using the same words whenever he could and even making efforts to preserve the original rhyme scheme.[23] It seems plausible that Lasso might not have minded the contrafacta, and might have seen them as a tribute to his skill and fame that only spread the latter farther across Europe, into the Calvinist homes where his typical Munich, Nuremberg or Parisian prints might not reach. It is impossible to say whether Lasso would have approved, but I should have liked to see Freedman tackle this issue in greater depth.

Of particular interest is Freedman's chapter 7, 'Lasso's Chansons in Printed Sets', in which he analyses the modal organisation of the contrafacta collections. Lasso and his publishers frequently arranged collections according to the tonal type of the composition, that is to say, according to presence or absence of a flat in the system, the set of clefs and the lowest pitch of the final sonority of the piece.[24] Freedman is especially concerned with the collections in which editors rearranged the order in which the chansons appeared in the model prints by Le Roy & Ballard, such

published Lasso's 1562 motet collection *Sacrae cantiones quinque vocum*, not Adam Berg of Munich, as Freedman states on p. 147.

[23] See, for example, Freedman's comparison of Goulart's text with Marot's for 'Qui dort ici?', pp. 72–3.

[24] On tonal types, see S. Hermelink, *Dispositiones modorum: Die Tonarten in der Musik Palestrinas und seiner Zeitgenossen* (Münchner Veröffentlichungen zur Musikgeschichte, 4; Tützing, 1960), and H. M. Brown, 'Tonal Types and Modal Categories in Renaissance Polyphony', *Journal of the American Musicological Society*, 34 (1981), pp. 428–70.

as Goulart's later editions of *Le Thrésor de musique d'Orlande*. In these (published in 1582 and 1594), Goulart superimposed his own organisation by tonal type in such a way as to represent the eight modes. He also managed to fit all Lasso's chansons into the modal system, including some anomalous ones that Le Roy & Ballard had left outside the organisational system they used (p. 164). Freedman's statement that the modal organisation, 'for Goulart, assumed a significance nearly as important as the chansons it framed' might be an exaggeration, but he makes a good argument for this point. Such an organisational system, encompassing all the chansons and not just those that fit tidily into a typical pattern of modal representation (for example, a flat system, high clefs and a G final indicating transposed mode 1), would have fit well with the dominant Neoplatonic philosophies of the power of music: every chanson had its ordained place in the musical order. But although editors like Goulart or Pasquier found places for the anomalous works, it is important to note that Lasso and the editors with which he worked the most closely intentionally left them outside the modal system; thus Freedman's statement (p. 149) that 'the modal identity of an individual chanson can change depending on the context in which it appears' is inaccurate.[25] The chanson, and its modal identity, remained the same; what differed was the editors' interpretations of it.

Freedman's book is a valuable study of music and religious culture in the sixteenth century. I should have liked more emphasis on how the song fitted into Reformed society, but his efforts to show that the contrafacta are valuable compositions in their own right are very important to Lasso studies. Freedman's book was interesting and enjoyable to read. I should mention that I was surprised at the number of typographical errors that slipped past the editors, all very minor but that nevertheless detract from an otherwise fine book. While there is little point in listing the mistakes, I found seven without really looking for them. Particularly when a book contains a section of transcriptions (such as Freedman's appendix A, with the prefaces to the contrafacta collections), an error-free text is important to give the reader confidence in the transcribed texts that would otherwise be unavailable. Freedman's

---

[25] I thank Peter Bergquist for drawing this comment to my attention.

knowledge of the secondary Lasso literature is superb, and his thoughtful analyses of the contrafacted chansons demonstrate a clear understanding of how Lasso used the music to express the text, and how others used Lasso's music to their own ends.

Jeanice Brooks's new book also addresses a repertoire little studied in its own right, that of the *air de cour*. General music textbooks on the Renaissance hardly mention its existence, preferring to concentrate on the polyphonic chanson as created by composers like Lasso or on *musique mesurée*, and even suggesting that the *air de cour* did not exist until the seventeenth century.[26] Brooks pulls the *air* from oblivion and places it at the centre of courtly society.

Courtly Song in Late Sixteenth-Century France is, as the title indicates, more concerned with the function of music within the peripatetic royal courts of the grandfather François I, the son Henri II, his spouse Catherine de Médicis, and their children François II, Charles IX and Henri III. In the first major section of her book, comprising chapters 1 to 3, Brooks provides an introduction to the Valois courts in the sixteenth century, followed by a discussion of professional and amateur music-making at those courts. The second section includes three chapters that could stand alone as individual studies, one of the role of women and their voice in the *air de cour*, one on Italian influences and echoes in the song repertoire, and one on the meaning of pastoral tropes in the courtly song. The book has already earned special praise from the Sixteenth-Century Studies Conference, which awarded it the 2001 Roland Bainton Prize for Art and Music History. The book itself is lovely to behold, with an attractive font and appealing 'illuminated' initials beginning each chapter. I prefer footnotes to endnotes, so Brooks's method of documentation was convenient. The decision to place all musical examples at the end of the chapter thus seems a bit paradoxical, as it results in the same sort of flipping around that one avoids with footnotes.

---

[26] Allan W. Atlas discusses the polyphonic chanson in detail and devotes two paragraphs (and one anthology example) to *musique mesurée* in *Renaissance Music: Music in Western Europe, 1400–1600* (New York, 1998), p. 624. In her revision of Howard Mayer Brown's *Music in the Renaissance* (2nd edn; Upper Saddle River, NJ, 1999), Louise Stein mentions that the influence of Jean de Baïf's Académie de poésie et de musique 'extended even to the strophic *airs de cour* of the early seventeenth century' (p. 335).

Brooks begins by orienting the reader to the French court of the sixteenth century, and what precisely was meant by an 'air de cour' and by 'court'. Those less familiar with this institution tend to imagine a fixed location, such as the Louvre palace in Paris, where courtiers visited to manage their affairs and press for benefits from the king or queen. The image of Louis XIV's late seventeenth-century court springs immediately to mind, but Brooks describes a court that was more a way of living than a specific place. The French royal court of the last Valois was peripatetic, making short visits to different chateaux and even travelling away from Paris and the Loire valley for years at a time (p. 3). Thus 'court' was defined not so much by its location, but by the activities that took place around the persons of the royal family and their entourage. Brooks provides a through introduction to the courts of François II, Charles IX, Henri III and Catherine de Médicis, the mother of three kings and a mighty figure in her own right. She describes the personal households such as the *hôtel du roi*, a group that included both nobles and servants and grew to almost 4,000 people in the 1580s, and provides helpful comparisons between the sizes of the French courts under different rulers. As France moved towards absolutism in the late sixteenth century, maintaining a presence at the court – wherever it may have been – became increasingly important for nobles, and the court continued to swell. This growth, along with changing philosophies about royalty and government, eventually lead to the type of court we more typically imagine, that of Louis XIV and the palace of Versailles.

Those seeking the favour or patronage of the royal family distinguished themselves in various manners, among them music. As Brooks comments, 'The Florentine Catherine de Médicis was well aware of the importance of the arts as a political tool. Her understanding of magnificence as an element of governance was expressed in an often-cited letter to her son Charles IX, advising him to ensure that his courtiers were continually occupied with *divertissements*' (p. 10). Just as the increasing size and importance of the Valois court led directly to the institution under Louis XIV, Catherine's views about music and the arts as techniques of rule seem to foreshadow the political uses to which the Sun King put music and dance. For him, the courtly diversions of Versailles were a method to keep French nobles so occupied with learning the latest elegant dance steps that they were unable to spend time in less agreeable pursuits such as plotting against the monarchy.[27] Music, then, was more than a simple pastime: it both shaped and reflected courtly society.

As expected, Brooks also spends part of her opening chapter discussing the genre of the *air de cour*. Although the term itself appeared only rarely before the 1590s, similar light works had circulated earlier as *voix de ville*, 'city voices' as opposed to 'court airs'. The pieces in question differ from the more often studied polyphonic chansons in a number of ways: they are strophic settings of secular French texts, with a prominent melody in the highest voice, and with lower voices that serve primarily as accompaniment. Standard bass patterns, many drawn from Italian vernacular song such as the romanesca or passamezzo, were common. The term *air de cour* emphasised the many connections this song repertoire had with the French court, including their publication by the royal printer, Le Roy & Ballard, the number of composers with close ties to the court and the popularity among them of texts by Pléiade poets, especially Pierre de Ronsard, Joachim Du Bellay, Jean de Baïf and Philippe Desportes.

Brooks was faced with a challenge in defining what, exactly, was courtly about these songs. Were they necessarily pieces performed at court, or in a certain style, or were they 'courtly' in that their poetry was that of court-sponsored poets like the Pléiades? Although Brooks does define a style for the *air*, she points out that the same song could exist in several versions. The first use of the term *air de cour* was in a 1571 print by Le Roy & Ballard, the title of which describes the *airs* as being 'set to the lute'.[28] Other prints present polyphonic versions of the same *airs*, but frequently there are variations between different settings of the same *air*, slight

---

[27] While Catherine saw music as a reflection of a harmonious society, under Louis XIV Neoplatonic imagery served more to emphasise the social order that supported an absolutist monarch. Cardinal Richelieu began to reshape Neoplatonic ideas of music to these ends under Louis XIII, and they were further developed by Jules Mazarin under Louis XIV. It was Mazarin who first had the idea to guard nobles (including the young Louis XIV) from mischief by keeping them busy with music and dancing. See M. Allain's entry for 'Jules Mazarin' and W. H. Cobb's entry for 'Cardinal Richelieu' in *Research Guide to European Historical Biography: 1450–Present*, ed. James A. Moncure (Washington, DC, 1992); further information from personal correspondence with Professor Georgia Cowart, 21 January 2002.

[28] A. Le Roy, *Livre d'airs de cour miz sur le luth* (Paris, 1571).

differences that suggest these, too, are arrangements (p. 30).
Brooks suggests that the format of the music was less important
than the cultural context of the *air*, and she spends the rest of the
book examining the role the *airs de cour* played in defining the court
itself and the relationships between noble members of the court,
the royal family and paid musicians.

Brooks's second chapter explores the positions of musicians
within the royal household and at court, and while she focuses
primarily on professional musicians, she also pays close attention
to the role of music in advancing the careers of nobles. The patronage system here extends to include the intricate relationships
between people of varying social levels and the bonds of loyalty
and protection, of service and payment that existed between them.
Brooks expands the definition of patronage provided by Sharon
Kettering to include musicians within the royal household.[29]
Musical talent became 'a commodity growing in value and . . .
musicians involved in song performance and publishing were
increasingly able to profit from the court's opportunities' (p. 74).
Thus not only did musicians gain benefits from their abilities, but
noble courtiers found that a knack for singing airs allowed them
to attract the attention of patrons and helped to secure a
favourable position at court. In this chapter, Brooks's exhaustive
archival work provides the most complete picture yet of the money
and other benefits that flowed towards those with musical talent.
Her examination of several sources allows her to see how musicians profited from appointments to multiple positions, religious
or secular, while only occupying one. French kings had gained the
right to distribute a number of prebends without papal interfer-
ence in the Concordat of 1516, and they used this right to reward
court musicians and help them to supplement their incomes.
Although the practice of holding multiple benefices was supposedly forbidden by the Council of Trent,[30] Brooks's research indicates that it continued in the 1580s. Surprisingly, she does not
mention the Tridentine ban or other religious-political issues that

---

[29] See S. Kettering, *Patrons, Brokers and Clients in Seventeenth-Century France* (New York, 1986),
p. 197.
[30] See W. M. Plöchl, 'Benefices', in the *New Catholic Encyclopedia* (New York, 1967–2001),
and G. Alberigo, 'Trent, Council of', in the *Oxford Encyclopedia of the Reformation* (Oxford
and New York, 1996). Alberigo describes the battle over benefices and bishops' rights
to fill them as 'the most serious crisis of the entire council'.

might have affected court musicians; I shall return to this issue below.

Companions to chapter 2 are the meaty appendices with which Brooks completes her book, pages containing transcriptions of documents relating to the payment of musicians and an amazing list of all musicians mentioned in court documents for a period of thirty years. Her 'Appendix 2' (the roll of musicians) alone is over one hundred pages, and provides a level of detail that bears witness to years of attentive archival work. The appendix contains the name of the musician, including alternative spellings, the archival source for the information, a brief description of the source, its date, the terminology it used to describe the musician, the amount of any payments recorded, and notes on the entry. This arrangement makes it easy to locate information on how and when a well-known composer like Jacques Arcadelt was paid (a total of 500 *livres tournois* over the course of two years, from the household and treasury accounts of François II). The structure of the appendix also facilitates assessment of the relative importance of particular composers and performing musicians for the French royal courts. The three entries for Arcadelt, for example, are easily compared with the far more extensive list of payments and appointments for the Italian-born Balthazar de Beaujoyeulx. *Valet de chambre* to Queen Catherine, Beaujoyeulx came to France in 1555 as a lowly violinist called Baltazarin, but by successfully learning the ways of the courtier, he became a man of substantial property and a member of the urban elite *bourgeoisie de Paris*.[31] His prominence at court is witnessed by the twenty-one appearances his name makes in the various court documents Brooks studied. Her 'Notes' column frequently contains interesting details: sons granted survivors' benefits to annual wages earned by their fathers, benefices requested and denied, a young boy whose pension was paid to another (a teacher, perhaps?) while he was learning a new instrument.[32] The appendix is fascinating to read, and is an

---

[31] Brooks, pp. 106–7; archival records on Beaujoyeulx are described on pp. 421–2.

[32] Brooks, appendix 2. Mathurin Dugué's yearly wages were to be assigned to his son as survivor (in Bibliothèque nationale de France [F-Pn], fr. 21451, fol. 367^r, as well as in other sources); Gilles Ferreau requested the first prebend to fall vacant at the church of Notre Dame de Loche but was denied the post (in F-Pn fr. 21480, fol. 72^r); François Bunel, 'one of the little singers of [Catherine de Médicis]', ceded his pension to Thomas Champion, called Mithou, for the first trimester of his training to play the epinette (in F-Pn fr. 26160, pièce 581).

extremely valuable source of information on the musicians serving the French courts of the late sixteenth century.

In chapter 3, Brooks addresses the changing image of nobility in the early modern era, and how music helped to define nobility in a time of uncertainty. Once based on military prowess, nobility in the sixteenth century faced challenges brought about by the changes in European society. The 'valorous knight on horseback' became less important in war as strategies that made use of infantry became more common; furthermore, as the bureaucracy of the court expanded and became more complex, many nobles who had inherited royal offices found that they were incapable of performing the duties required of them. Finally, saleable letters of patent called into question the very foundations of the noble class; if nobility could be purchased, what makes one noble? The answer, Brooks explains, was virtue and education, and the discourse of the day debated the relative merits of Arms and Letters. Arms, or valiant warfare, was dependent on Letters (including song) to preserve their glory for later generations, but Letters needed Arms to provide the subject matter. The *airs* performed at court reflected this symbiotic relationship while emphasising the close ties between virtue and military action. Strophic song approximated the bardic ballads that celebrated the deeds of Achilles and bestowed on the singers and listeners a small measure of the virtue of the warrior-heroes of old, while 'sonic images of battle' (like Janequin's famed *La guerre* or Clereau's strophic *Ores qu'on voit de toutes pars*) allowed the hearers to partake vicariously in the world of war (pp. 122–3).

Letters gradually became more important as the century progressed. Castiglione advocated noble participation in Letters, and '[a]fter Henri (II)'s accidental death in a tourney in 1559, actual tests of strength and military prowess such as jousting were increasingly replaced by *cartels* and staged combats, and balls and festivals multiplied at the expense of chivalric entertainments' (p. 124). Musical ability, then, was increasingly important to the successful courtier. Brooks details how the Neoplatonic ideals espoused by Catherine de Médicis helped to place music at the centre of court life, since courtiers, educated in both Arms and Letters, could use their knowledge of music to show their fitness for noble life. As the emphasis on actual physical combat lessened, solo song increasingly became a 'weapon in the warfare of love', as Brooks states. Here she begins to turn towards the role of women in the court, for the triumphant warrior in this sphere was the one who could please the ladies the most with his song (p. 155).

Women played a prominent role in courtly music-making. By singing songs that defended their honour in the wars of the heart, they earned a place in the world of Arms. This leads nicely into Brooks's fourth chapter, 'Women's Voices'. With such a strong feminine presence at court as Catherine de Médicis, it is not surprising that music would be accepted as an appropriate pastime for noblewomen. As Brooks writes, 'Musical skill became an attribute of the ideal female courtier, her song among the ornaments and graces that embellished her physical beauty' (p. 199). For women, however, music-making was fraught with dangers. Members of both sexes had to take care not to be *too* good at music, which would make them appear to be professional musicians, but women who displayed too much proficiency might also be seen as courtesans rather than 'courtiers'. Thus even females who were professional musicians, like Violante Doria, were described in payment records as 'ladies-in-waiting', or were paid in their husbands' names.[33] Most interesting to me in this chapter was the section on Catherine de Médicis and women's laments, drawn in part from Brooks's earlier work on the late Renaissance lament.[34] After the death of her husband Henri II, Catherine began to promote an image of herself as a new Artemisia, the ancient queen who constructed the Mausoleum at Halicarnassus in honour of her dead spouse, then drank a daily potion made up of her tears mixed with the ashes of her husband's cremated body in order to give him an even more worthy resting place. The sculptures Catherine commissioned for Henri's and her tomb portray her not as a *transi*, wasted by the ravages of death and time, but as a lovely woman who thus symbolically buried her sexuality. Catherine thus created a powerful image for the French people, who would see her reign

---

[33] Doria, for example, was married to one of the most successful musicians at court, Girard de Beaulieu. Of the thirteen entries her name has in Brooks's appendix 2, all but one mention Beaulieu. Frequently Doria is not even mentioned by name, but rather is included in payments to Beaulieu 'et sa femme' (pp. 463–4).

[34] 'Catherine de Médicis, *nouvelle Artémise*: Women's Laments and the Virtue of Grief', *Early Music*, 27 (1999), pp. 419–35.

as regent for her young sons, and the laments published in the female voice reinforced this image through their text and music. For example, the romanesca repeated bass pattern used in the lament *Mon coeur ma chere vie* reminds the listener of the faithfulness of the maiden Bradamante (from Ariosto's epic *Orlando furioso*), whose letter to Ruggiero was typically sung to the romanesca. Musically, the repetition of the bass line is a literal display of the constancy practised by the singer of *Mon coeur ma chere vie*, whose beloved asks her to bury love in the tomb with him.

Neoplatonism also figured in women's lives at court. Human love, as described by Castiglione or Marsilio Ficino, was a step towards divine love; thus the courtly love tropes enacted by the *air de cour* were not merely titillating, but were an appropriate part of courtly discourse (pp. 229–31). Even overtly sexual texts were acceptable, granting men and women the opportunity to practise human love in an innocent way (they were, after all, only singing the songs at court), and women then had the chance to prove their virtue by refusing the advances of amorous men. Brooks also describes how the Neoplatonic views of women and music often intertwined, conflating both into a 'component of a pure and transcendent ideal' (p. 230).

One of my few disappointments in Brooks's book was the lack of examination of the role of the court and the *air de cour* in sixteenth-century France as a whole. Although she generally does an exemplary job of placing the *airs de cour* in French courtly society, I would remind the reader again of the precarious and troubled state of the country, especially in the period *Courtly Song in Late Sixteenth-Century France* covers. The Neoplatonic ideas of Catherine de Médicis and her courtiers seem to make a good deal of sense at court, but much of French society was falling apart at this time, torn by religious disputes and wars. Brooks does mention anti-court literature, but I think that it is important to consider this repertoire in the light of the historical events traumatising France, lest one get the wrong impression of a country peacefully rolling along in harmony with the spheres and the songs of the court. Music and dance decidedly did not bring peace and order to the realm, as was dramatically proved in the St Bartholomew's Day massacre. Ironically, this occurred shortly after Catherine had sponsored a grand court *divertissement* entitled *Le Paradis d'amour* for the wedding of Henri of Navarre and Marguerite de Valois; the entertainment emphasised the Neoplatonic idea of music bringing harmony to society.[35] The court was not that insulated from daily life. For example, Brooks mentions a reference to the Huguenot city of La Rochelle in a book that likened Catherine to Artemisia; the city appears as Rhodes in an illustration depicting the ancient queen's capture of that city (p. 211).

Brooks's chapter 5, 'Dialogues with Italy', demonstrates how the French both emulated Italian models and attempted to surpass those models and prove themselves the true heirs of the culture of Antiquity. She pays close attention to Charles de Lorraine, Cardinal de Guise, whose frequent trips to Italy resulted in much Italian music coming to France (as well as many ancient Roman artefacts). Charles was also responsible for the arrival in France of Jacob (or Jacques) Arcadelt, whom he lured away from the papal choir. Brooks explores Arcadelt's relationship with Pierre Clereau, whose secular *airs* show a great deal of Italian influence (pp. 271–2). She pays particular attention to Arcadelt's settings of Horace's odes, homophonic chansons that link sixteenth-century France with the Antiquity they claimed to inherit. The Protestant polemicist Louis Régnier de La Planche attributed the fashion for singing Horace to Charles de Lorraine, and complained that from those lascivious odes the court moved to the silly love songs of Pierre de Ronsard and other Pléiade poets. Another connection with Italian practice is the poetry of Ronsard, who credited contemporary Italian musical practice with providing inspiration for his own odes (p. 280). Even the term *air* was borrowed from the Italian *aria*, and became the most common term for French strophic song in the 1550s. French writers of the time seemed frequently to conflate the Greece and Rome of Antiquity with Italy of the sixteenth century; Italian singers like the brothers Ferrabosco took on the musical guise of the ancient bards though they performed contemporary Italian music.

Brooks ends this chapter with a section exploring the relationships between *musique mesurée*, Jean de Baïf's Académie and the

---

[35] Henri de Navarre was a Huguenot leader, and Marguerite the sister of the king, thus their marriage might have given some hope for unity and stability. On *Le Paradis d'amour*, see J. R. Anthony, *French Baroque Music from Beaujoyeulx to Rameau*, 2nd edn (New York, 1978). I thank Georgia Cowart for drawing this performance to my attention.

Italian *villanella* genre. Poets at the time were particularly inspired by the works attributed to Anacreon; others, like Baïf, closely mimicked *villanella* poetry. How closely he followed Italian models came as a surprise to me.[36] Brooks compares nine of Baïf's poems to the works that inspired them, placing the French and Italian texts side by side and making the similarities unmistakable. Likewise, the *musique mesurée* settings of these poems bear likeness to the *villanella*, though the musical similarities are not as striking as the textual ones. In this way, composers looking to recreate the power of ancient music again used sixteenth-century Italy as the window through which to view Antiquity. Brooks makes a very interesting point that while prints of *musique mesurée* present polyphonic works, her research has shown that this did not preclude monophonic performance. A prominent melody in the top voice could just as easily have been performed by a soloist accompanied by a chordal instrument like a lute, as the *air de cour* repertoire was, and as Italian monody was (pp. 311–12). In other words, there is no clear distinction between the Italian monodic emulation of the ancients and the French 'polyphonic' style.

Brooks's final chapter, 'Pastoral Utopias', explores the recurrence of pastoral themes in the *air de cour* repertoire and how they reflected the court's ideas of its own identity. Pastoral romances allowed sexual themes into the court without posing a threat to courtly standards of behaviour: shepherds and shepherdesses participated in erotic adventures, and courtiers did so only in rustic settings, often with pastoral partners. Since country estates were the basis for the wealth of most of the nobility, the juxtaposition of rustic and courtly life was something they experienced regularly. Brooks shows how images of the pastoral in the *air de cour* helped the nobility to define who they were and to assert their authority over country life (and country folk). Though courtiers played at being shepherds in palace gardens, their pastoral games were a sign of 'newly opening gulfs' between high and low cultures (p. 376).

Courtly Song in Late Sixteenth-Century France overlaps Freedman's book slightly in the discussions of the music and career of Lasso.

---

[36] Brooks gives credit for the discovery of Baïf's use of Italian models to F. Dobbins, 'Les madrigalistes français et la Pléiade', in *La chanson à la Renaissance*, ed. J.-M. Vaccaro (Tours, 1981), p. 170.

Though he served at the Bavarian rather than the Parisian court, Lasso was a favourite of the French royalty, especially Charles IX. Brooks quotes Charles's court preacher Arnauld Sorbin, who stated that Lasso's 'music delighted [Charles] so much that he could hardly sample any other that pleased him in every regard' (p. 11).[37] The high esteem in which the French king held Lasso was evidenced by the granting of the 1571 privilege discussed above. Surprisingly, Brooks's appendix only lists two payments to Lasso, both made not by Charles IX but by his successor Henri III (p. 490). She notes the pension that Lasso was granted in 1574 by Charles; a record of this transaction apparently can be found in the *état des pensionnaires* in Paris, Bibliothè que Nationale de France, Dupuy 127. It was this pension that Adrian Le Roy announced to Lasso in a 1574 letter. The source for this payment had erroneously been dated at 1560, though Brooks shows this date to have been impossibly early (p. 98 n. 66).[38] I am not sure why the Dupuy 127 entry does not appear in her appendix table, however.

Lasso's music was also important as a stylistic foil to the *air de cour*. As mentioned, the term *air de cour* first appeared in print in 1571 in Adrian Le Roy's *Livres d'airs de cour miz sur le luth*. In the preface to this collection, Le Roy contrasts the 'difficult and arduous' chansons of Lasso with the 'very much lighter songs of the court' contained in his present volume.[39] Though Le Roy was referring specifically to an earlier volume of Lasso's chansons he had published, it seems that Lasso's work was seen as a general representative the more complicated polyphony of the late sixteenth-century chanson.

Jeanice Brooks has created a fine example of what musicology can be: interesting, culturally grounded and full of new information about the music itself. Thus my criticisms of *Courtly Song in Late Sixteenth-Century France* are few. Brooks assumes fluency in the French and Italian languages, and the texts in most of the musical examples are untranslated, as are the quotations with which she begins each chapter. Occasionally phrases within the

---

[37] Curiously, Brooks does not document her source for this quotation.

[38] She notes that the incorrect date, which has been repeated in later Lasso literature, first appeared in F. Lesure's 'Les premiers rapports de Roland de Lassus avec la France', *Revue belge de musicologie*, 3 (1949), p. 242.

[39] Adrian Le Roy, *Livres d'airs de cour miz sur le luth* (Paris: Le Roy & Ballard, 1571), cited in Brooks, p. 14.

body of the text are in French as well; while most of them are clear enough for one with a basic reading knowledge of the language, occasionally I needed to pull out my dictionary to follow her argument. It would be especially nice to have translations of the poetic headings to the chapters, even if only in a footnote, and translations would have been helpful for the *air de cour* lyrics found in the music examples.

I also wonder whether there might be more political content to the *airs de cour* than Brooks reveals. As mentioned above, French society was not particularly stable in the late sixteenth century; were the nobles all so satisfied at court? Did any expressions of discontent make their way into the *air de cour* repertory? Of course such types of lyrics would probably have not been printed by the likes of the royal printers Le Roy & Ballard, but perhaps other sources might reveal a less unified view of courtly life. Yet these are minor criticisms; both Brooks and Freedman have done fine work in examining little-studied repertoires and placing them in their cultural contexts. Both books are welcome additions to the literature on French music of the sixteenth century.

Rebecca Wagner Oettinger
University of South Carolina, Columbia

ERIC CHAFE, *Analyzing Bach Cantatas*. New York and Oxford, Oxford University Press, 2000. xviii + 286 pp.
DOI:10.1017/S0261127902232076

Eric Chafe's most extensive study on Bach appeared in 1991.[1] Since then he has published a shorter work on Bach, much of which is absorbed and revised in the present book, and – most significantly – an award-winning book on Monteverdi's tonal language.[2] This has clearly broadened his experience of the tortuous developments in tonal and modal thinking throughout the seventeenth century and thus brings a more developed historical perspective from which to view Bach's achievement. *Analyzing Bach Cantatas* focuses on a relatively small number of cantatas, which are generally

---

[1] *Tonal Allegory in the Vocal Music of J. S. Bach* (Berkeley and Los Angeles, 1991).
[2] *Monteverdi's Tonal Language* (New York, 1992).

treated as wholes. Thus the book comes a little closer to the form of a standard guidebook on Bach cantatas by first setting out the theoretical and theological background and then providing commentaries on complete works.

Chafe's use of the term 'analyzing' is immediately controversial. 'Analysis' can mean many things, of course, but as it developed in twentieth-century musical discourse, it came to refer to a range of approaches relating to how music works in and of itself; if analysis revealed ingenious aspects of musical construction, these were generally viewed at arm's length from the composer's wishes or from the meaning and sense conveyed by the music. More often than not, its aim was to confirm a greatness in the music that was already presumed rather than to rescue works that were undervalued (or to reveal the inadequacy of a cherished piece). This attitude often occasioned considerable censure from those who felt that analysis lacked a necessary critical edge.

Chafe's approach is something quite different: while there is considerable reference to aspects of tonal and modal theory and the way Bach might have exploited the various inconsistencies and ambiguities in the system he inherited, the primary aim is to show how the music articulates theological propositions and nuances within an orthodox Lutheran context. In proposing that analysis should be a process rather than a closed task, and one that 'involves the interaction of musical and extra-musical qualities' (p. ix), Chafe might seem to come close to self-proclaimed 'postmodern' forms of musical analysis. Moreover, he shuns the 'quasi-objective' approach of traditional analysis that assumes the pre-eminence of absolute music, and he claims to retain the term 'analysis' precisely to show that it should *not* be rigorously segregated from extra-musical factors (p. xiv), presumably because there is to him no such thing as a 'pure', unmediated musical experience. To use some other term for his discipline, such as 'interpretation', would thus leave the analysts unchecked in their erroneous ways. He clearly entertains the thought of Bach as an actual human being with real aesthetic and historical choices since he is so closely concerned with the composer's interaction with the musical-theological context of the age. Indeed, he believes that the very essence of Bach's genius lies in his complexity of thought that is manifested as much in allegorical procedures as it is in tone relationships; greater knowledge of the 'local' thus somehow feeds into the 'universal' value of Bach's music (pp. 239–40). In all, then, much of Chafe's terminology seems to resonate with the concerns of fashionable 'new musicology', yet the overriding intention is remarkably traditional (even reactionary in today's context): understanding the composer in his own context is to be the means of proving his enduring genius.

One problem with Chafe's 1991 book was that it presented a whole range of nested assumptions, many of them impossible to prove or disprove, and the reader felt somewhat trapped into either accepting the entire edifice or becoming sceptical of every stage in the argument. Chafe has developed a rather more critical tone in the present instance, asserting that 'the attempt to set up one-to-one correspondences between musical events and theoretical pronouncements is rightly viewed with suspicion' (p. 41). To him, it is likely that Bach would have indulged in a richly hermeneutic approach to composition because his musical thought is itself so self-evidently complex. Nevertheless, it is worth pointing out at this stage that Bach's credentials of complexity have almost always been gained within the outlook of autonomous, absolute music; a complexity of theological thought does not automatically follow from this. Chafe is obligingly open to a wide range of readership, intending that the book should bring more music lovers to appreciate Bach and his music (p. xvi); the book is designed so that most sections can be read independently – thus any parts proving intractable to any particular reader can be omitted. Certainly, Chafe's prose is considerably easier to tackle than in his earlier writings, although it is still comparatively opaque.

The new book improves on the older one with its rather broader frame of reference: the major–minor connotations of the *dur* and *moll* terminology are acknowledged rather more. Previously, Chafe tended to underplay these at the expense of the older system of hexachords, translated in Bach's time into comparative degrees of sharpness or flatness. Now, both conceptions, together with Chafe's consideration of modality, give a richer, multi-layered perspective from which to analyse both individual movements and complete works. Another development is Chafe's greater awareness of history, both viewing Bach's works in a richer historical context and tracing the development of historical thinking within

the Lutheran tradition. He intuits something of Bach's own awareness of historical texturing and is alert to historical change, even
within the relatively short Lutheran tradition. This is best demonstrated in a fascinating chronicle of the changing modal inflections
in the chorale *Dies sind die heil'gen zehn Gebot* (p. 166–70).

We learn more of the necessity of history in revealing God's
plan, particularly in the way the less complete revelation of the
Old Testament is furthered in the New and how the various forms
of interpretation in Bach's time imbue biblical history with new
levels of meaning (p. 4). This conception of history is, perhaps,
useful in helping us understand Bach's attitude to time and history as more a realisation of what is already there than as the
notion of 'progress' that would develop in the later eighteenth century and beyond. It also lays the foundation of the way Bach's cantatas themselves work in – and use – time, as Chafe himself shows
in his consideration of complete cantatas. He also links this issue
to the structure of the liturgical year, in which the coming of Christ
and his earthly ministry (Advent to Pentecost) is followed by the
time of the church (Trinity) and the anticipation of eternity (the
final weeks of Trinity; see p. 14). One direction in which this could
lead is the way in which Bach might subtly encompass the need
for temporal progress within God's necessary eternity, but this
would go beyond the brief of the present book. Chafe's most elegant formulation of Bach's conception of time and history is that
Bach's 'unique achievement was to mold rather than to defer to
tradition, to bring past and present together as if in a contrapuntal interaction whose ultimate outcome was to forecast a future
that very few in his time could foresee' (p. 95).

Central to Chafe's view of Bach's theological thinking is
Luther's analogy of faith, by which descent (man's failure in the
light of God's law) is followed by ascent (the promise of the Gospel;
see p. 5); faith thus works only once the transgression and hope-
lessness of the human condition have been recognised. This conception neatly accounts for virtually any dualism to be found in
Bach's music, whether in terms of its temporal progression (most
simply, by following the *katabasis–anabasis* model of flattening followed by sharpwards movement, as in the first movement of
Cantata 77) or stylistic contrasts. Sometimes, as in the case of the
chorale melody 'Dies sind die heil'gen zehn Gebot', a flattening

might occur right at the end (corresponding with the *Kyrieleis* that ends each verse), leaving us with a reminder that God's mercy is indispensable (pp. 173–4); Chafe shows that the whole of Cantata 77 displays a tonal weakening towards the final *cantus mollis*, as a way of demonstrating that humankind cannot love as God demands without his aid (summed up in the final plea, *Kyrieleis*, pp. 189, 218–19). Thus one model can provide an analogy of the hoped-for salvation, the other the incompleteness of our present condition and the need for God's support. The one drawback of this approach is that virtually any type of tonal shift in Bach's works can be interpreted as theologically meaningful even if there appear to be inconsistencies. As with the previous book, I develop the feeling that the more Chafe tries to explain, the less convincing the method becomes. For instance, he gives us a vir-tually literal description of the opening choral theme of Cantata 77 (rising fourth, followed by a descending sequential pattern), and, given that the opening ascent is constant throughout the sec-tion while the decorated descent is variable, this must 'mirror the manner in which love bridges the distance between God (the straightforward ascending fourth) and humankind (the decorated descent)' (p. 191). Such a process is so ubiquitous in Bach's compositional style that it is difficult to accept such a meaning in the absence of a much more sophisticated theory of musical signification.

Bach's modal chorales have been subject to detailed scrutiny before,[3] but Chafe considers the ways in which he may have exploited to theological ends what were already archaic elements of modality. This is particularly striking in the cases where there is a 'disparity between the "correct" modal final and our tendency to hear it as a dominant' (p. 54). Tonality, as represented in the quality of hearing, can thus be a metaphor for our inability to ful-fil God's demands (as represented by the 'correct' final; p. 88). This is especially evident in the case of Cantata 77, where our tonally oriented hearing of the end as 'wrong' reflects the inevitability of human weakness from the ideal modal standpoint (p. 217). The word 'our' is of course telling, and it might be impos-sible for us to imagine what this really sounded like in an age when

---

[3] Lori A. Burns, *Bach's Modal Chorales* (Stuyvesant, NY, 1995).

not only did the modal system sound 'old', but the tonal system was still 'new'. Moreover, it is difficult to be certain that Bach would have heard the 'correct' modal final as an unattainable ideal rather than as something productively archaic. Again, the more detail Chafe provides, the more difficult it is to believe him: the final cadence for the second chorale in Cantata 153 apparently shows the believer accepting his own weakness because the metrical placement somehow makes us hear the end correctly as a Phrygian final, 'despite its dominant sound'; the 'dualistic quality is subtly suggestive of the distinction between God's goal and the believer's tormented condition' (p. 121). Another odd assumption appears in Chafe's remark that around 1700 'key relationships and modulatory principles were often not well understood' (p. 30), as if the tonal system were something just waiting, fully formed, round the corner, rather than something that was still in the process of being invented through the countless, contingent interactions of music culture.

Chafe's basic claim is that modal qualities of chorales often reflect texts and, moreover, that Bach amplifies these qualities in relation to the cantata as a whole. This is exemplified, for instance, in Cantata 38 (based on the Phrygian chorale 'Aus tiefer Not'), where the melodic and tonal features of the melody influence the tonal descent by fifths in the first five movements and the return ascent for the final movement. The subdominant tendency thus reflects the believer's increasing despair (p. 88). There is certainly a point here, particularly if we take Chafe's view (developed from Dahlhaus and his own study of Monteverdi) that there was a 'dominant dynamic' in music after 1600, so that subdominant movement should really be heard 'against the grain'. Chafe sometimes considers the history of chorales that had been modally ambiguous: for instance, 'Es ist das Heil uns kommen hier' was originally a Mixolydian melody and various versions in the seventeenth and eighteenth centuries preserved this modality (at least in the key signature) while sharpening the leading notes at cadences. Bach, however, uses an Ionian signature in Cantata 9, while preserving the Mixolydian seventh only for the first line, where it coincides with the word 'uns'. Thus 'uns' acquires a quality of humility, while the next phrase, modulating to the dominant, presents the antithetical quality of God's strength. There is certainly a point here, even if it seems to contradict Chafe's other assertion that modality often represents a hidden, unattainable truth, and also if, in this melody, the flattened seventh is impossible to avoid (without allowing an ugly melodic tritone).

Chafe's attention to subdominant movement, in both small- and large-scale plans, sometimes causes him to develop a rather strange notion of tonality. For instance, in his examination of the final chorales of Cantatas 2 and 46, he notes the prominence given to the subdominant in the final phrase, as though this 'weakens' the ultimate cadence. However, it was quite commonplace, even in Bach's age, to use subdominant colouring towards the end, presumably to balance the initial tendency towards the dominant. Without this compensatory flattening, the tonic will perhaps sound dull in comparison to the dominant. Thus, some forms of subdominant colouring, far from weakening the tonic, actually helped to strengthen it. Elsewhere, Chafe sometimes seems to have an unorthodox understanding of tonality: the ritornello opening Cantata 77, which, to my understanding, begins in an unproblematic C major, with transitory modulations to D minor and A minor and a move back towards C, Chafe describes as a ritornello that 'does not clearly articulate a single key but, rather, remains basically in a diatonic white-note region' (p. 194).

Chafe may have good reason to turn his back on the mainstream of Bach scholarship, which over the last forty years has tended to eschew an overtly theological or interpretational approach. There is no doubt that his comparative isolation has brought benefits and forms of insight that might otherwise have been curbed. Nevertheless, some of his points could surely have been strengthened if he had engaged more with the existing literature: his view that the fourteen trumpet interjections relate to the idea of alpha and omega in the Greek alphabet (and how 14 can mean alpha as well as omega, the fourteenth letter, is unclear) needs to be placed in the context of Ruth Tatlow's work on number alphabets, in which she expresses caution about the ubiquity of 'natural-order' alphabets (where a = 1, b = 2, etc.).[4] Chafe's view that the *tromba da tirarsi* part for the aria 'Ach, es bleibt in meiner Liebe lauter Unvollkommenheit' is designed to capitalise on the 'imperfection'

---

[4] Ruth Tatlow, *Bach and the Riddle of the Number Alphabet* (Cambridge, 1991).

of certain notes for the natural trumpet could productively be substantiated by Michael Marissen's similar analysis of this movement.[5] More reference to established source studies would also refine certain points: Chafe observes that Bach did not include a text for the final chorale of Cantata 77 in his autograph score, as though he were searching for the perfect text or had a specific intention that we should try and discern (pp. 180–1). In fact, it was quite common for Bach not to write the final chorale text in his score (and often, neither text nor notes) and to specify these later in the performing parts. Presumably the chorale was chosen (by Bach or the preacher?) later in the compositional process in order to relate to specific readings or to the sermon.[6] Thus the only reason we do not have the text for this specific cantata is because the original parts are lost. Furthermore, the absence of figures in the choral cantus firmus in the bass line of the opening movement of the same cantata (p. 185) does not necessarily mean that Bach intended it to be played *tasto solo* since – again – we do not have the more specific directions that Bach would normally have included in the original continuo part.

In all, there is no doubt that Chafe alerts us to a side to the historical Bach that we might otherwise miss, and we do not necessarily have to accept his more far-fetched points. It would be difficult to argue that his insights are an absolutely crucial element in Bach appreciation, given that the composer has been more than adequately appreciated without them (and – generally – shorn of much of the religious context). If a theological approach along the lines that Chafe pursues *were* to contribute to the aesthetic appreciation of Bach (and one of Chafe's prime objectives is to unite the aesthetic and the historical; see p. 182), we would need a form of criticism that addressed more directly the quality and uniqueness of Bach's music. At the very least, we would want to come away from the study somehow thrilled. Theological analysis alone does not necessarily engender the most inspired form of musical analysis.

John Butt
University of Glasgow

[5] Michael Marissen, *The Social and Religious Designs of J. S. Bach's Brandenburg Concertos* (Princeton, 1995), pp. 3–4.
[6] See Robert L. Marshall, *The Compositional Process of J. S. Bach*, 2 vols (Princeton, 1972), i, pp. 66–8.

Early Music History (2002) Volume 21. © *Cambridge University Press*
Printed in the United Kingdom

INSTRUCTIONS FOR CONTRIBUTORS

EDITORIAL POLICY

Early Music History is devoted to the study of music from the early Middle Ages to the end of the seventeenth century. The journal demands the highest standards of scholarship from its contributors, all of whom are leading academics in their fields. *Early Music History* gives preference to studies pursuing interdisciplinary approaches and to those developing new methodological ideas. The scope is exceptionally broad and includes manuscript studies, textual criticism, iconography, studies of the relationship between words and music, and the relationship between music and society.

1. SUBMISSIONS

All contributions and editorial correspondence should be sent to: The Editor, Dr Iain Fenlon, *Early Music History*, King's College, Cambridge CB2 1ST, UK. The Editor can also be contacted via email at iaf1000@cus.cam.ac.uk.

Submission of an article is taken to imply that it has not previously been published, and has not been submitted for publication elsewhere. Upon acceptance of a paper, the author will be asked to assign copyright (on certain conditions) to Cambridge University Press.

Contributors are responsible for obtaining permission to reproduce any material in which they do not own copyright, to be used in both print and electronic media, and for ensuring that the appropriate acknowledgements are included in their manuscript.

2. MANUSCRIPT PREPARATION

All contributions should be in English and must be double spaced throughout, including footnotes, bibliographies, annotated lists of manuscripts, appendixes, tables and displayed quotations. In the event of the manuscript being accepted for publication the author will be asked to submit the text on computer disk (Apple Macintosh or IBM compatible PC) as well as in hard copy, giving details of the wordprocessing software used (Microsoft Word or WordPerfect). However, the publisher reserves the right to typeset material by conventional means if an author's disk proves unsatisfactory.

Typescripts submitted for consideration will not normally be returned unless specifically requested.

Artwork for graphs, diagrams and music examples should be, wherever possible, submitted in a form suitable for direct reproduction, bearing in mind the maximum dimensions of the printed version: 17.5 × 11 cm (7″ × 4.5″). Photographs should be in the form of glossy black and white prints, measuring about 20.3 × 15.2 cm (8″ × 6″).

All illustrations should be on separate sheets from the text of the article and should be clearly identified with the contributor's name and the figure/example number. Their approximate position in the text should be indicated by a marginal note in the typescript. Captions should be separately typed, double spaced.

Tables should also be supplied in separate sheets, with the title typed above the body of the table.

Spelling

English spelling, idiom and terminology should be used, e.g. bar (not measure), note (not tone), quaver (not eighth note). Where there is an option, '-ise' endings should be preferred to '-ize'.

Punctuation

English punctuation practice should be followed: (1) single quotation marks, except for 'a "quote" within a quote'; (2) punctuation outside quotation marks, unless a complete sentence is quoted; (3) no comma before 'and' in a series; (4) footnote indicators follow punctuation; (5) square brackets [ ] only for interpolation in quoted matter; (6) no stop after contractions that include the last letter of a word, e.g. Dr, St, edn (but vol. and vols.).

Bibliographical references

Authors' and editors' forenames should not be given, only initials: where possible, editors should be given for Festschriften, conference proceedings, symposia, etc. In titles, all important words in English should be capitalised; all other languages should follow prose-style capitalisation, except for journal and series titles which should follow English capitalisation. Titles of series should be included, in roman, where relevant. Journal and series volume numbers should be given in arabic, volumes of a set in roman ('vol.' will not be used). Places and dates of publication should be included. Dissertation titles should be given in roman and enclosed in quotation marks. Page numbers should be preceded by 'p.' or 'pp.' in all contexts. The first citation of bibliographical reference should include all details; subsequent citations may use the author's surname, short title and relevant page numbers only. *Ibid.* may be used, but not *op. cit.* or *loc. cit.*

Abbreviations

Abbreviations for manuscript citations, libraries, periodicals, series, etc. should not be used without explanation; after the first full citation an abbreviation may be used throughout text and notes. Standard abbreviations may be used without explanation. In the text, 'Example', 'Figure' and 'bars' should be used (not 'Ex.', 'Fig.', 'bb.'). In references to manuscripts, 'fols.' should be used (not 'ff.') and 'v' (verso) and 'r' (recto) should be typed superscript. The word for 'saint' should be spelled out or abbreviated according to language, e.g. San Andrea, S. Maria, SS. Pietro e Paolo, St Paul, St Agnes, St Denis, Ste Clothilde.

Note names

Flats, sharps and naturals should be indicated by the conventional signs, not words. Note names should be roman and capitalised where general, e.g. C major, but should be italic and follow the Helmholtz code where specific ($C_{\prime\prime}$ $C_{\prime}$ C c c' $c''c'''$; c' = middle C). A simpler system may be used in discussions of repertories (e.g. chant) where different conventions are followed.

Quotations

A quotation of no more than 60 words of prose or one line of verse should be continuous within the text and enclosed in single quotation marks. Longer quotations should be displayed and quotation marks should not be used. For quotations from foreign languages, an English translation must be given in addition to the foreign-language original.

Numbers

Numbers below 100 should be spelled out, except page, bar, folio numbers etc., sums of money and specific quantities, e.g. 20 ducats, 45 mm. Pairs of numbers should be elided as follows: 190–1, 198–9, 198–201, 212–13. Dates should be given in the following forms: 10 January 1983, the 1980s, sixteenth century (16th century in tables and lists), sixteenth-century polyphony.

Capitalisation

Incipits in all languages (motets, songs, etc.), and titles except in English, should be capitalised as in running prose; titles in English should have all important words capitalised, e.g. *The Pavin of Delight*. Most offices should have a lower-case initial except in official titles, e.g. 'the Lord Chancellor entered the cathedral', 'the Bishop of Salford entered the cathedral' (but 'the bishop entered the cathedral'). Names of institutions should have full (not prose-style) capitalisation, e.g. Liceo Musicale.

Italics

Titles and incipits of musical works in italic, but not genre titles or sections of the Mass/English Service, e.g. Kyrie, Magnificat. Italics for foreign words should be kept to a minimum; in general they should be used only for unusual words or if a word might be mistaken for English if not italicised. Titles of manuscripts should be roman in quotes, e.g. 'Rules How to Compose'. Names of institutions should be roman.

4. PROOFS

Typographical or factual errors only may be changed at proof stage. The publisher reserves the right to charge authors for correction of non-typographical errors.

5. OFFPRINTS

Contributors of articles and review essays receive 25 free offprints and one copy of the volume. Extra copies may be purchased from the publisher if ordered at proof stage.